I0888021

Predicting Natural Disasters With AI and Machine Learning

D. Satishkumar
Nehru Institute of Technology, India

M. Sivaraja
Nehru Institute of Technology, India

A volume in the Advances in Computational Intelligence and Robotics (ACIR) Book Series

IGI Global
PUBLISHER of TIMELY KNOWLEDGE

Published in the United States of America by
IGI Global
Engineering Science Reference (an imprint of IGI Global)
701 E. Chocolate Avenue
Hershey PA, USA 17033
Tel: 717-533-8845
Fax: 717-533-8661
E-mail: cust@igi-global.com
Web site: http://www.igi-global.com

Library of Congress Cataloging-in-Publication Data

Names: D., Satishkumar, 1980- editor. | Muthusamy, Sivaraja, 1974- editor.
Title: Predicting natural disasters with AI and machine learning / edited by D. Satishkumar, Sivaraja Muthusamy.
Description: Hershey, PA : Engineering Science Reference, 2024. | Includes bibliographical references and index. | Summary: "This book explores various AI and ML applications designed to predict, manage, and mitigate the impact of natural disasters, focusing on natural language processing, and early warning systems"-- Provided by publisher.
Identifiers: LCCN 2023059485 (print) | LCCN 2023059486 (ebook) | ISBN 9798369322802 (hardcover) | ISBN 9798369322819 (ebook)
Subjects: LCSH: Natural disasters--Forecasting. | Natural disasters--Remote sensing. | Environmental geotechnology.
Classification: LCC GB5014 .P74 2024 (print) | LCC GB5014 (ebook) | DDC 363.34/72--dc23/eng/20240131
LC record available at https://lccn.loc.gov/2023059485
LC ebook record available at https://lccn.loc.gov/2023059486

This book is published in the IGI Global book series Advances in Computational Intelligence and Robotics (ACIR) (ISSN: 2327-0411; eISSN: 2327-042X)

British Cataloguing in Publication Data
A Cataloguing in Publication record for this book is available from the British Library.

All work contributed to this book is new, previously-unpublished material.
The views expressed in this book are those of the authors, but not necessarily of the publisher.

For electronic access to this publication, please contact: eresources@igi-global.com.

Advances in Computational Intelligence and Robotics (ACIR) Book Series

ISSN:2327-0411
EISSN:2327-042X

Editor-in-Chief: Ivan Giannoccaro, University of Salento, Italy

MISSION

While intelligence is traditionally a term applied to humans and human cognition, technology has progressed in such a way to allow for the development of intelligent systems able to simulate many human traits. With this new era of simulated and artificial intelligence, much research is needed in order to continue to advance the field and also to evaluate the ethical and societal concerns of the existence of artificial life and machine learning.

The **Advances in Computational Intelligence and Robotics (ACIR) Book Series** encourages scholarly discourse on all topics pertaining to evolutionary computing, artificial life, computational intelligence, machine learning, and robotics. ACIR presents the latest research being conducted on diverse topics in intelligence technologies with the goal of advancing knowledge and applications in this rapidly evolving field.

COVERAGE

- Computational Logic
- Neural Networks
- Heuristics
- Cognitive Informatics
- Adaptive and Complex Systems
- Agent technologies
- Computer Vision
- Cyborgs
- Brain Simulation
- Natural Language Processing

IGI Global is currently accepting manuscripts for publication within this series. To submit a proposal for a volume in this series, please contact our Acquisition Editors at Acquisitions@igi-global.com or visit: http://www.igi-global.com/publish/.

The Advances in Computational Intelligence and Robotics (ACIR) Book Series (ISSN 2327-0411) is published by IGI Global, 701 E. Chocolate Avenue, Hershey, PA 17033-1240, USA, www.igi-global.com. This series is composed of titles available for purchase individually; each title is edited to be contextually exclusive from any other title within the series. For pricing and ordering information please visit http://www.igi-global.com/book-series/advances-computational-intelligence-robotics/73674. Postmaster: Send all address changes to above address.

Titles in this Series

For a list of additional titles in this series, please visit:
http://www.igi-global.com/book-series/advances-computational-intelligence-robotics/73674

Advanced Applications of Generative AI and Natural Language Processing Models
Ahmed J. Obaid (University of Kufa, Iraq) Bharat Bhushan (School of Engineering and Technology, Sharda University, India) Muthmainnah S. (Universitas Al Asyariah Mandar, Indonesia) and S. Suman Rajest (Dhaanish Ahmed College of Engineering, India)
Engineering Science Reference • © 2024 • 481pp • H/C (ISBN: 9798369305027) • US $270.00

Artificial Intelligence in the Age of Nanotechnology
Wassim Jaber (ESPCI Paris - PSL, France)
Engineering Science Reference • © 2024 • 299pp • H/C (ISBN: 9798369303689) • US $300.00

Impact of AI on Advancing Women's Safety
Sivaram Ponnusamy (Sandip University, Nashik, India) Vibha Bora (G.H. Raisoni College of Engineering, Nagpur, India) Prema M. Daigavane (G.H. Raisoni College of Engineering, Nagpur, India) and Sampada S. Wazalwar (G.H. Raisoni College of Engineering, Nagpur, India)
Engineering Science Reference • © 2024 • 320pp • H/C (ISBN: 9798369326794) • US $315.00

Handbook of Research on AI and ML for Intelligent Machines and Systems
Brij B. Gupta (Asia University, Taichung, Taiwan & Lebanese American University, Beirut, Lebanon) and Francesco Colace (University of Salerno, Italy)
Engineering Science Reference • © 2024 • 503pp • H/C (ISBN: 9781668499993) • US $380.00

Advances in Explainable AI Applications for Smart Cities
Mangesh M. Ghonge (Sandip Institute of Technology and Research Centre, India) Nijalingappa Pradeep (Bapuji Institute of Engineering and Technology, India) Noor Zaman Jhanjhi (School of Computer Science and Engineering, Faculty of Innovation and Technology, Taylor's University, Malaysia) and Praveen M. Kulkarni (KLS Gogte Institute of Technology, India)
Engineering Science Reference • © 2024 • 300pp • H/C (ISBN: 9781668463611) • US $270.00

IGI Global
PUBLISHER of TIMELY KNOWLEDGE

701 East Chocolate Avenue, Hershey, PA 17033, USA
Tel: 717-533-8845 x100 • Fax: 717-533-8661
E-Mail: cust@igi-global.com • www.igi-global.com

Table of Contents

Detailed Table of Contents

Natural disasters, formidable in their impact, unravel a chapter of complications that extends far beyond the visible devastation. This abstract encapsulates a comprehensive exploration of the intricate challenges arising in the aftermath of nature's fury. Delving into subsurface complications, the unseen geological shifts and water-related dilemmas are examined, offering insights into the complex terrains often overlooked. The human factor unfolds with a focus on displacement dilemmas, unravelling the challenges faced by communities uprooted in the wake of disasters. Economic ripples, another facet of the aftermath, are dissected to comprehend the financial intricacies nations grapple with in rebuilding. The environmental toll, both on biodiversity and climate, forms a critical segment, shedding light on the delicate balance disrupted by natural disasters. Technological triumphs and community resilience emerge as key pillars in navigating these complications.

Natural disasters, such as earthquakes, hurricanes, floods, and wildfires, are ongoing worldwide concerns that have catastrophic effects on human lives, infrastructure, and the environment. By enhancing forecast, management, and reaction tactics, machine learning and artificial intelligence (AI) have emerged as revolutionary technologies in solving these crises. This comprehensive chapter delves deeply into the uses and implications of machine learning and AI in natural disaster avoidance. Machine learning techniques, especially artificial neural networks (ANNs), have shown promise in forecasting the incidence and severity of many natural catastrophes. These models make use of massive datasets including climatic, geographical, and historical data to improve forecasting accuracy and early warning systems. Furthermore, data-driven insights enable catastrophe prediction and risk assessment using a variety of machine learning methods ranging from decision trees to deep learning networks.

Global warming worsens natural disasters and humanitarian issues. Disaster prediction relies on satellites and weather stations. AI may help catastrophe management. AI reduces disaster risk in many ways. Early warning systems, weather forecasts, disaster recovery, and reconstruction improve. AI could help us predict, prepare, and recover from natural calamities. These technologies provide climate change mitigation and community protection hope. They propose a better future amid climate change catastrophes. DRR is aggressively adopting AI, notably ML. This field encompasses severe event prediction, hazard mapping, real-time detection, situational awareness, decision assistance, and more. Growing usage of AI in disaster management raises questions about its benefits. We face what issues? How can these difficulties be resolved and opportunities maximised? What can AI tell policymakers, stakeholders, and the public to reduce disasters? The chapter introduces catastrophe management AI, AI implementation issues, and solutions to make the world more peaceful will be addressed.

This proposed chapter will examine the dynamic interplay between social media, public perception, and behaviour during disasters. A particular emphasis will be placed on how artificial intelligence (AI) improves comprehension of this interplay.

Information dissemination and consumption during crisis situations have changed due to the quick spread of social media platforms and the growing application of artificial intelligence (AI) in disaster management. Insights into how these technological developments affect public perception and, in turn, how they affect behavioural responses in crisis situations are provided in this chapter.

The transformational field of utilizing machine learning (ML) and artificial intelligence (AI) to forecast natural disasters is explored in this book chapter. The severity of natural disasters demands catastrophe mitigation, risk assessment, and early warning. The use of AI and ML technologies, which have the potential to safeguard communities, is essential in this endeavor. The chapter emphasizes the need of a multidisciplinary strategy that combines domain expertise with AI and ML to improve capacity to predict and respond to natural disasters with an ultimate goal to build a more secure and resilient global community. The chapter examines a number of AI and ML applications in disaster prediction, including forecasts for earthquakes, floods, wildfires, hurricanes, landslides, tsunamis etc. In order to increase prediction accuracy, it covers sensor networks, data sources, and the integration of various datasets. Additionally, it tackles the issues related to ethical considerations, robustness of the model, and data quality.

Among the numerous terrible natural and artificial disasters that afflict the planet are enormous earthquakes, floods, aircraft accidents, tsunamis, and building collapses. In order to lessen and prevent the losses that these disasters entail, disaster management is crucial. Only the first 48 hours have a high chance of rescuing a victim; after that, it tends to drop to nothing. The victim can be sent to medical attention more quickly for prompt reaction and identification. This issue can be significantly lessened by combining mobile robots with effective human victim detection (HVD) systems powered by artificial intelligence (AI) and overseen by expert teams. The cutting-edge internet of things (IoT) technology envisions an internal network of intelligent physical objects that is global in scope. IoT is a promising technology with a variety of uses, including disaster relief. The role that IoT plays in disaster management is significant, pervasive, and potentially lifesaving.

This chapter explores the transformative integration of GPUs and AI accelerators in natural disaster management, ushering in resilience and rapid response. From early warning systems to recovery, these technologies enhance decision-making and mitigate the impact of escalating disasters. Specific applications include real-time data analysis, predictive modelling, GIS mapping, and resource allocation. The fusion of GPUs and AI accelerators not only improves disaster prediction and response but also fosters resilient communities. Motivated by the need for rapid decision-making, this integration addresses the limitations of traditional methods in the face of increasing disaster complexity. In navigating an uncertain future, GPUs and AI accelerators revolutionize disaster management, paving the way for a more resilient global society.

The emergence of internet of things (IoT) based smart sensors has brought a revolution in disaster management to create early warning systems and to quickly respond to natural disasters. This chapter explores the vital function that these sensors serve, emphasizing how they might improve preparedness and lessen the destructive effects of disasters. It provides vital information that helps communities and authorities to anticipate any flooding events using smart sensors, flood sensors, atmospheric sensors. It emphasizes the necessity of developments in IoT-based smart sensors through case studies and real-world examples. Through an examination of the application of advanced technologies like artificial intelligence and machine learning, the chapter

explores the different localization algorithms relevant to underwater sensor networks, and the challenges in meeting the requirements posed by emerging applications for such networks, likes offshore engineering.

The chapter presents a comprehensive exploration of deep learning techniques applied to seismic pattern recognition and forecasting, aiming to advance our understanding of earthquake behavior. Beginning with a brief overview of the seismic cycle and its significance, the narrative delves into the challenges associated with accurately predicting the locations of seismic cycles. The role of deep learning in revolutionizing seismic forecasting is then elucidated, emphasizing its capacity to predict beyond single seismic cycles and under diverse conditions. The chapter further provides a mathematical algorithm outlining the step-by-step process, from data collection to model training, adaptation, and continuous monitoring.

Forest fires have significant environmental and economic impacts, necessitating advanced prediction and detection strategies. Artificial intelligence, particularly machine learning (ML) techniques, plays a crucial role in addressing this challenge. Supervised models analyze complex patterns, enabling early warnings and comprehensive risk evaluation. This chapter critically examines the suitability and limitations of various ML algorithms in forest fire science, emphasizing the need to carefully consider algorithmic strengths and weaknesses. It highlights challenges in selecting the most suitable models for accurate predictions and advocates for customizing ML models to specific forest characteristics. By tailoring ML techniques based on unique forest attributes, the research aims to

Preface

In the face of increasing natural disasters, the imperative to harness the power of cutting-edge technology has never been more critical. *Predicting Natural Disasters With AI and Machine Learning* delves into the realm where innovation meets necessity, offering a comprehensive exploration of how artificial intelligence (AI) and machine learning (ML) can be employed to mitigate the impact of catastrophes on our societies.

The urgency of this topic is underscored by the rapid escalation of disasters that inflict irreparable harm on both the environment and all living beings, human and animal alike. The aftermath of such calamities extends far beyond immediate devastation, affecting the very fabric of our infrastructure, environment, and economy for prolonged periods. It is within this context that our reference book endeavors to shed light on the transformative role AI and ML can play in disaster prediction, management, and recovery.

The coalescence of natural and man-made hazards poses multifaceted challenges, necessitating a holistic approach to disaster management. The 4R framework—Risk mitigation, Response readiness, Response execution, and Recovery—serves as a guiding principle for crafting effective solutions. Through the lens of AI and ML, our contributors explore the nuanced interplay between human actions, technological malfunctions, and the intricate web of natural phenomena.

The synthesis of AI and disaster risk reduction (DRR) emerges as a beacon of hope, offering a proactive stance against the majority of disasters that are, fundamentally, human induced. The exploration of early warning systems, grounded in machine learning techniques, represents a paradigm shift in our ability to predict and prepare for impending disasters.

This volume is not merely a collection of theoretical musings; it is a practical guide for a diverse audience. From scientists and academics to public and private organizations, the insights contained herein are poised to inspire and inform a broad spectrum of stakeholders. Our contributors dissect the challenges faced in the application of AI in disaster management, addressing issues related to data accessibility, security, privacy, and ethical considerations.

ORGANIZATION OF THE BOOK

Chapter 1 provides a holistic exploration of the intricate challenges arising in the aftermath of natural disasters. From subsurface geological shifts to water-related dilemmas, the chapter delves into often-overlooked complexities. The human factor takes center stage, unraveling the displacement dilemmas faced by communities. Economic ripples and environmental tolls are dissected, with a spotlight on technological triumphs and community resilience as key pillars in navigating these complications.

Chapter 2 delves deeply into the revolutionary role of machine learning and artificial intelligence in addressing natural disasters worldwide. The article explores how these technologies enhance forecast, management, and reaction tactics, emphasizing the use of artificial neural networks in forecasting the incidence and severity of various catastrophes. It also covers the vast datasets used for forecasting accuracy, early warning systems, and the implications of data-driven insights for catastrophe prediction and risk assessment.

Chapter 3 addresses the worsening impact of global warming on natural disasters and humanitarian issues. The chapter explores how AI contributes to disaster risk reduction through early warning systems, weather forecasts, disaster recovery, and reconstruction. It raises questions about the benefits and challenges of growing AI usage in disaster management, emphasizing the need for AI implementation solutions to create a more peaceful world.

Chapter 4 examines the dynamic interplay between social media, public perception, and behavior during disasters, with a focus on how artificial intelligence improves comprehension of this interplay. The chapter explores the changing landscape of information dissemination and consumption during crises due to social media platforms and AI in disaster management, shedding light on their effects on public perception and behavioral responses.

Chapter 5 explores the transformative field of utilizing machine learning and artificial intelligence to forecast natural disasters. It emphasizes the multidisciplinary approach needed to combine domain expertise with AI and ML for improved prediction and response. The chapter covers various AI and ML applications in disaster prediction, including earthquakes, floods, wildfires, hurricanes, landslides, and tsunamis. Ethical considerations and data quality issues are also addressed.

Chapter 6 focuses on disaster management through the integration of mobile robots with Human Victim Detection systems powered by AI and overseen by expert teams. The chapter explores the significant role of the Internet of Things (IoT) in disaster relief, emphasizing its potential for life-saving applications. It envisions a global network of intelligent physical objects and discusses the widespread applications of IoT in disaster management.

Chapter 7 discusses the prediction of natural disasters using machine learning algorithms, specifically Decision tree and K-Means algorithms. The chapter addresses the challenges of predicting natural disasters despite advancements in technology, highlighting the role of machine learning in providing feasible solutions for social issues.

Chapter 8 introduces a predictive framework for tropical cyclone forecasting using Support Vector Machines (SVM). The chapter explores the analysis of meteorological parameters to recognize intricate patterns associated with cyclone development. The SVM-based approach contributes to early detection, bolstering existing forecasting capabilities for disaster preparedness and mitigation strategies.

Chapter 9 explores the transformative integration of GPUs and AI accelerators in natural disaster management, enhancing decision-making and mitigating the impact of disasters. Applications include real-time data analysis, predictive modeling, GIS mapping, and resource allocation, fostering resilient communities in the face of increasing disaster complexity.

Chapter 10 focuses on the emergence of IoT-based smart sensors in disaster management, exploring their vital function in creating early warning systems and responding to natural disasters. The chapter emphasizes the necessity of advancements in IoT-based smart sensors, addressing difficulties brought on by natural catastrophes through case studies and real-world examples.

Chapter 11 explores the wide range of IoRT automation applications, blending the strength of robots and the Internet of Things (IoT) to improve production, efficiency, and safety across various industries. The chapter investigates the challenges and opportunities presented by IoRT automation in diverse fields, emphasizing its potential for creative solutions.

Chapter 12 delves into the challenges of localization in underwater sensor networks (UWSNs), emphasizing the unique characteristics of underwater acoustic channels. The chapter explores different localization algorithms relevant to UWSNs, addressing challenges and requirements posed by emerging applications such as offshore engineering.

Chapter 13 presents a comprehensive exploration of deep learning techniques applied to seismic pattern recognition and forecasting. The chapter outlines the seismic cycle's significance and the challenges associated with predicting the locations of seismic cycles. It provides a mathematical algorithm for the step-by-step process of deep learning in seismic forecasting.

Chapter 14 critically examines the suitability and limitations of various ML algorithms in forest fire science. The chapter highlights the need to consider algorithmic strengths and weaknesses, addressing challenges in selecting the most suitable models for accurate predictions. It advocates for customizing ML models based on unique forest characteristics to enhance prediction accuracy and improve risk assessment in forest fire management.

The diverse array of topics covered spans the application of GPUs and AI accelerators in disaster scenarios, the use of machine learning models for forecasting flood damage, and the deployment of artificial neural networks for predicting natural disasters. Each chapter provides a unique perspective, contributing to a holistic understanding of the role AI and ML can play in safeguarding our communities.

As editors, we envision this reference book as a catalyst for further research and exploration, particularly by postgraduate students eager to delve into the dynamic intersection of AI and ML with disaster prediction. The goal is not only to disseminate current research findings but to spark new inquiries, fostering a continuous cycle of innovation and improvement in the field.

In closing, we extend our gratitude to the contributors for their dedication and expertise in illuminating this crucial subject. May the insights contained within these pages serve as a guidepost for future endeavors in *Predicting Natural Disasters with AI and Machine Learning, in the New Era*.

Editors,

D. Satishkumar
Nehru Institute of Technology, India

Sivaraja Muthusamy
Nehru Institute of Technology, India

Chapter 1
Unravelling Complications in Natural Disasters:
A Comprehensive Exploration

K. Tamilarasi
Nehru Institute of Technology, India

P. Krishnakumar
Nehru College of Management, India

ABSTRACT

Natural disasters, formidable in their impact, unravel a chapter of complications that extends far beyond the visible devastation. This abstract encapsulates a comprehensive exploration of the intricate challenges arising in the aftermath of nature's fury. Delving into subsurface complications, the unseen geological shifts and water-related dilemmas are examined, offering insights into the complex terrains often overlooked. The human factor unfolds with a focus on displacement dilemmas, unravelling the challenges faced by communities uprooted in the wake of disasters. Economic ripples, another facet of the aftermath, are dissected to comprehend the financial intricacies nations grapple with in rebuilding. The environmental toll, both on biodiversity and climate, forms a critical segment, shedding light on the delicate balance disrupted by natural disasters. Technological triumphs and community resilience emerge as key pillars in navigating these complications.

DOI: 10.4018/979-8-3693-2280-2.ch001

INTRODUCTION

In the intricate dance between nature's forces and the resilience of humanity, the chapter on "Unravelling Complications in Natural Disasters" emerges as a critical exploration into the aftermath of cataclysmic events. Natural disasters, with their unrelenting power, leave behind a tapestry of challenges that extend far beyond the immediate devastation. This chapter serves as a beacon, illuminating the often-overlooked complexities inherent in the aftermath of nature's fury. From the unseen geological shifts beneath the surface to the socio-economic ramifications felt by communities, each layer of complication is dissected to provide a comprehensive understanding of the challenges that unfold in the wake of disaster.

As we embark on this journey of exploration, the goal is not only to unravel the intricacies but to equip ourselves with knowledge that transcends the visible scars. By delving into the depths of subsurface complications, human dilemmas, and environmental repercussions, we aim to navigate the complex terrain of natural disasters with insight, resilience, and a collective commitment to building a more robust future in the face of adversity.

SUBSURFACE COMPLICATIONS: UNSEEN SHIFTS BELOW

1. Geological Shifts: Shaping the Earth's Canvas

Natural disasters, particularly earthquakes, set in motion a cascade of geological shifts that extend beyond the immediate tremors. These shifts, often unseen but

Figure 1.

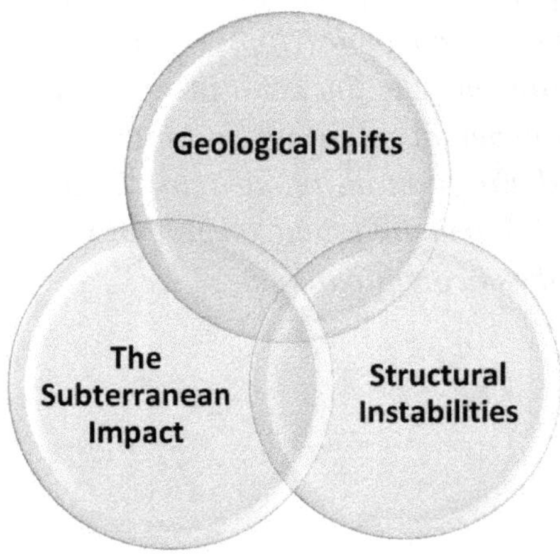

profoundly impactful, create a domino effect of challenges. From structural instabilities in buildings to altered terrains, understanding the geological aftermath is crucial in navigating the complexities that arise(Fatema, 2020).

- **The Subterranean Impact**

When the ground trembles during an earthquake, it's not just the surface that experiences upheaval. The very foundation of the earth undergoes profound shifts. These subsurface movements can manifest as fault lines, landslides, and changes in topography, creating a cascade of complications that extend far beyond the epicentre.

- **Structural Instabilities**

One of the immediate consequences of subsurface shifts is the compromise of structural integrity. Buildings, bridges, and infrastructure are vulnerable to the unseen forces below, leading to a heightened risk of collapse. Understanding the nature of these structural instabilities is crucial for engineers, architects, and disaster management experts working towards resilient designs.

Predictive Analytics: Unveiling Patterns and Anomalies

AI algorithms, fuelled by vast datasets from seismic sensors, satellite imagery, and historical earthquake records, engage in predictive analytics. These algorithms identify patterns and anomalies that precede geological shifts, offering a valuable window of opportunity for preparedness and response (Kar et al., 2023).

2. Water Woes: The Deluge Dilemma

Floods, another aftermath of nature's wrath, present a unique set of complications (Mahesar et al., 2023). Beyond the visible inundation, water brings forth a myriad of challenges. Contamination concerns, infrastructural damage, and the long-term implications on water resources make comprehending the water-related complications imperative for effective disaster management (Di Baldassarre et al., 2021).

- **Subsurface Water Movement**

Natural disasters, particularly those involving significant water elements like hurricanes or heavy rainfall, can alter subsurface water pathways. This unseen consequence poses threats such as soil erosion, groundwater contamination, and the destabilization of aquifers. Navigating these subsurface water complications is

Figure 2.

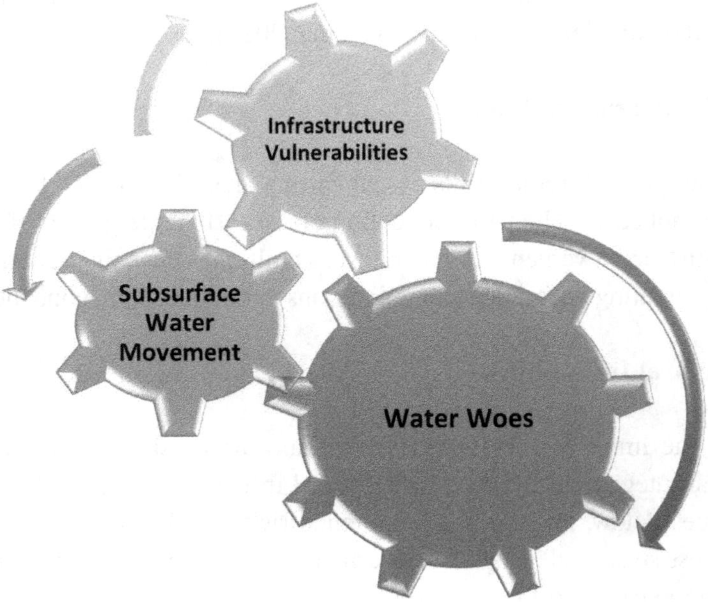

pivotal for ensuring the long-term environmental and human impact is minimized (Fatema, 2020) (Di Baldassarre et al., 2021).

- **Infrastructure Vulnerabilities**

As water finds its way below the surface, infrastructure vulnerabilities emerge. Foundations of buildings may weaken, leading to structural damage. Additionally, subsurface water can infiltrate utility systems, causing electrical failures and further complicating the post-disaster recovery process. Identifying and addressing these vulnerabilities requires a comprehensive understanding of subsurface water dynamics.

Unveiling the Unseen: Exploring Subsurface Dynamics

In the expansive domain of construction and engineering, the ground beneath our feet holds a multitude of mysteries. Often concealed from the naked eye, these subsurface complications wield significant influence over the success and stability of any project. This point embarks on a journey into the depths, unravelling the unseen shifts and complexities that lie beneath (Bogdan et al., 2020).

Unravelling the Complexity

The subsurface world is a complex ecosystem, influenced by an array of geological factors. From the intricate network of soil composition to the subtle yet impactful movements within the bedrock, understanding these dynamics becomes paramount. Geological formations, underground water sources, and the interplay of various substrates create a mosaic of challenges that demand meticulous attention (Di Baldassarre et al., 2021).

Navigating Unforeseen Challenges

As projects progress, encountering unforeseen complications lurking beneath the surface is not uncommon. Soil erosion, shifting sediment layers, or concealed underground cavities pose formidable challenges, threatening the stability of structures. The ability to navigate these challenges with adeptness and agility becomes a hallmark of successful project management.

Strategies for Effective Management

- **Embracing Advanced Geotechnical Assessments**

In the pursuit of unravelling subsurface complexities, leveraging advanced technology and methodologies becomes imperative. Ground-penetrating radar, seismic surveys, and geophysical investigations serve as invaluable tools in peering beneath the surface veil. These assessments offer crucial insights, enabling informed decision-making and proactive risk mitigation strategies.

- **Innovative Solutions in Engineering**

Faced with subsurface uncertainties, the engineering realm responds with innovation. Reinforced foundations, adaptive design modifications, and agile construction practices emerge as cornerstones in fortifying structures against the unpredictable nature of subsurface shifts.

Embracing Collaborative Approaches

- **The Power of Multidisciplinary Collaboration**

The holistic understanding and management of subsurface complications demand a convergence of expertise. Collaborative efforts between geologists, engineers, and construction professionals foster a comprehensive approach. This synergy cultivates solutions that are not just proficient but holistic in their scope.

- **Real-time Monitoring and Adaptation**

The dynamic nature of subsurface conditions necessitates constant vigilance. Implementing robust monitoring systems enables real-time data acquisition, empowering swift adaptations and pre-emptive measures against potential risks.

Embracing Complexity, Ensuring Stability

In the realm of construction and engineering, acknowledging the significance of subsurface complications is pivotal. It is not merely about foreseeing challenges but about embracing the complexities that lie beneath. The proactive stance, driven by scientific expertise, technological advancements, and collaborative endeavours, serves as the fulcrum in ensuring the resilience of projects against unforeseen subsurface shifts (Oliva & Lazzeretti, 2021).

Water Woes: Machine Learning for Flood Prediction and Response

Floods, the relentless force of nature, bring about a myriad of challenges that demand innovative solutions. In this exploration, we delve into how Machine Learning (ML) revolutionizes our approach to predicting and responding to floods, offering a proactive stance against the water-related complications that follow natural disasters (Bogdan et al., 2020).

The Complexity of Floods

Floods, whether triggered by heavy rainfall, storm surges, or river overflows, present a complex and dynamic set of challenges. Predicting their occurrence and responding swiftly is imperative to mitigate the impact on communities and infrastructure (Mahesar et al., 2023).

Machine Learning: A Proactive Approach to Flood Prediction

Machine Learning algorithms, fuelled by extensive datasets comprising historical weather patterns, topography, and real-time sensor data, prove instrumental in flood prediction. By identifying patterns and correlations, ML models can forecast potential flooding events with unprecedented accuracy (Bogdan et al., 2020) (Kar et al., 2023).

Early Warning Systems

The cornerstone of ML in flood management lies in the development of sophisticated early warning systems. These systems leverage predictive analytics to detect anomalies in meteorological conditions and river levels, issuing timely alerts to vulnerable areas. The result is invaluable lead time for residents to evacuate and for authorities to implement preventive measures(Okyere et al., 2023).

High-Resolution Flood Mapping

Machine Learning contributes to the creation of high-resolution flood maps, providing detailed insights into the extent and severity of potential flooding. This allows for precise resource allocation and targeted response strategies, optimizing the deployment of emergency services and resources(Okyere et al., 2023).

Real-time Monitoring and Adaptive Responses

One of the strengths of Machine Learning in flood management is its capacity for real-time monitoring. ML algorithms continuously analyze incoming data from sensors, satellites, and weather stations. This dynamic monitoring enables adaptive responses, such as adjusting dam releases, redirecting traffic, or activating flood barriers in response to changing conditions(Okyere et al., 2023).

Challenges and Advances

While ML has significantly enhanced flood prediction and response, challenges persist. Complex environmental factors, urban development, and the evolving climate contribute to the intricacies of flood management. Continuous advancements in ML models, integration with Internet of Things (IoT) devices, and collaboration between researchers, policymakers, and technology developers are pivotal in overcoming these challenges (Mahesar et al., 2023).

The Future of Flood Management: Advancements in Machine Learning

As technology evolves, the future of flood management holds promising advancements in Machine Learning. Deep learning models, which mimic the human brain's neural networks, show potential for even more accurate predictions. Integration with satellite technology, unmanned aerial vehicles (UAVs), and advanced sensors further refines our ability to monitor and respond to floods in real time(Bogdan et al., 2020; Okyere et al., 2023).

In the realm of water-related complications, Machine Learning emerges as a transformative force. From predictive analytics for early warnings to real-time monitoring and adaptive responses, ML technologies reshape our approach to flood management. While challenges persist, the ongoing advancements in Machine Learning pave the way for a future where communities can proactively address the water woes unleashed by natural disasters, fostering resilience and reducing the impact on lives of individuals and the infrastructure (Oliva & Lazzeretti, 2021).

HUMAN FACTOR: SOCIETAL AND ECONOMIC RAMIFICATIONS

1. Displacement Dilemmas: Communities in Flux

Natural disasters force communities into unforeseen dilemmas, with mass displacements becoming a hallmark of such events. This section dissects the complications associated with displacement, exploring the challenges of seeking

Figure 3.

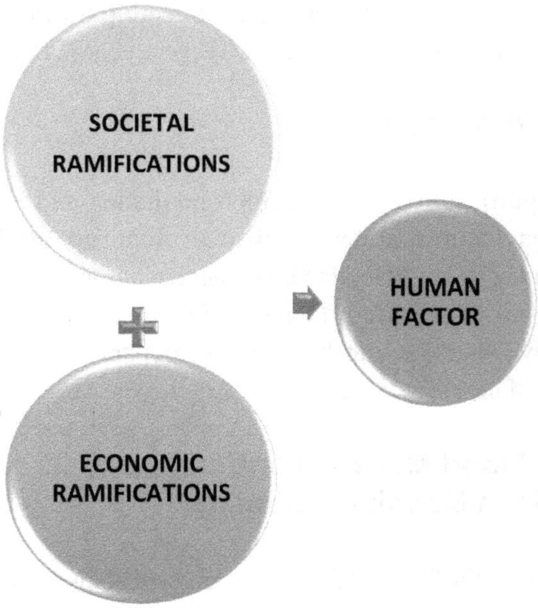

refuge, scarcity of resources, and the psychological toll on individuals and communities affected (Alonso Vicario et al., 2020) (Fatema, 2020).

- **Mass Uprooting of Communities**

One of the most immediate and poignant consequences of natural disasters is the mass displacement of communities. Families torn from their homes, seeking refuge in temporary shelters, face the daunting task of rebuilding their lives. This displacement not only leads to physical challenges but also takes a toll on the emotional well-being of those uprooted from familiar surroundings (Alonso Vicario et al., 2020).

- **Resource Scarcity and Competition**

In the aftermath of a disaster, resources become scarce commodities. From basic necessities like food and water to essential medical supplies, the competition for these resources intensifies. This section explores how communities navigate the delicate balance between survival and cooperation, shedding light on the societal challenges that emerge in the quest for essential resources (Oliva & Lazzeretti, 2021) (Fatema, 2020).

2. Economic Ripples: The Financial Fallout

The economic repercussions of natural disasters extend far beyond the immediate devastation. From the costs of reconstruction to the disruptions in supply chains, understanding the economic complexities is essential. This segment navigates through the intricate web of financial challenges that communities and nations grapple with in the aftermath.

- **Immediate Reconstruction Costs**

The economic fallout of natural disasters is staggering. Immediate costs for reconstruction skyrocket as governments and communities mobilize to repair and rebuild. This section outlines the economic burdens that nations face in the aftermath, addressing the complexities of allocating funds for rebuilding while ensuring the long-term sustainability of the affected regions.

- **Disrupted Supply Chains**

Beyond the immediate costs, natural disasters disrupt intricate supply chains that underpin modern economies. Industries reliant on smooth logistical operations face interruptions, leading to production delays and economic setbacks. This subsection examines the domino effect of disrupted supply chains, emphasizing the need for strategic planning to mitigate economic ramifications.

ENVIRONMENTAL TOLL: ECOLOGICAL COMPLICATIONS

- **Biodiversity Blues: Nature's Delicate Balance**

Natural disasters pose a significant threat to biodiversity, often causing long-lasting ecological imbalances. This section explores the complications associated with disruptions to ecosystems, emphasizing the need for conservation efforts to mitigate the impact on habitats, species, and the delicate balance of the natural world(Mahesar et al., 2023).

- **Climate Conundrums: Amplifying Environmental Challenges**

Inextricably linked to the environmental fallout, natural disasters contribute to the exacerbation of climate challenges. From intensified weather patterns to long-term climate implications, this segment dissects the compounding effects, urging a holistic approach to address both the immediate and overarching environmental complications(Mahesar et al., 2023).

Figure 4.

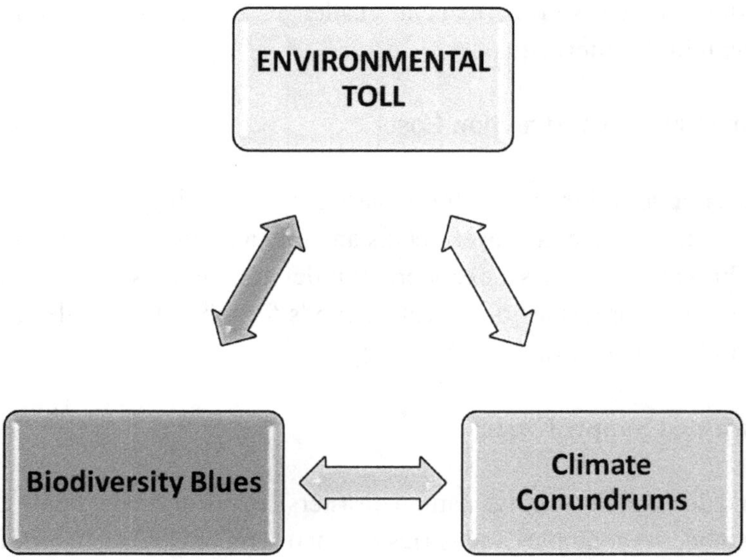

MITIGATION STRATEGIES: NAVIGATING THE COMPLEX TERRAIN

- **Technological Triumphs: Innovations for Prediction and Response**

Amidst the complexities, technology emerges as a beacon of hope. This section spotlights cutting-edge solutions and technological triumphs that aid in predicting, mitigating, and responding to natural disasters. From early warning systems to advanced mapping, embracing technology becomes paramount in navigating the intricacies of disaster management.

- **Community Resilience: Building Strength from Within**

Mitigating the complications of natural disasters necessitates a focus on community resilience. This segment outlines strategies to empower communities, emphasizing education, preparedness, and collaborative efforts. Strengthening the fabric of communities ensures a more robust response to the challenges presented by nature's fury (Oliva & Lazzeretti, 2021).

Assessing Ecological Impact in the Wake of Natural Calamities

Ecosystem Disruption and Biodiversity Loss

- **Impact on Flora and Fauna**

Detailing the effects of natural disasters on diverse ecosystems, including habitat destruction, species displacement, and biodiversity decline.

- **Erosion, Soil Degradation, and Land Use Changes**

Examining the consequences of natural calamities on soil health, erosion rates, and alterations in land use patterns.

Water and Air Quality Challenges

- **Contamination and Waterborne Diseases**

Exploring the contamination of water sources post-disaster and the resultant challenges in maintaining water quality and preventing disease outbreaks.

- **Air Pollution and Environmental Health Risks**

Assessing the implications of natural disasters on air quality due to particulate matter, pollutants, and their impact on human and environmental health.

Mitigation Strategies for Ecological Rehabilitation

Ecosystem Restoration and Conservation Efforts

- **Ecological Restoration Initiatives**

Highlighting post-disaster efforts aimed at ecosystem restoration, including reforestation, habitat rehabilitation, and biodiversity conservation(Xiao et al., 2023).

- **Natural Resource Management and Sustainable Practices**

Emphasizing the importance of sustainable resource management practices in rebuilding and safeguarding ecosystems post-disaster (Xiao et al., 2023).

Climate Resilience and Adaptation

- **Adaptive Strategies for Climate Resilience**

Detailing strategies to enhance ecosystem resilience in the face of changing climatic patterns and future disaster risks.

- **Promoting Eco-Friendly Infrastructure and Urban Planning**

Advocating for eco-centric urban planning and infrastructure development to minimize ecological impacts during and after natural disasters.

Pre-Disaster Preparedness: Education and Awareness

Importance of Education in Disaster Preparedness

- **Empowering Communities**

Education plays a pivotal role in empowering communities to face natural disasters proactively. Providing knowledge about potential hazards, safety protocols, and emergency preparedness equips individuals with the necessary tools to respond effectively.

- **Enhancing Resilience**

Education and awareness campaigns foster resilience by educating people on recognizing early warning signs, understanding evacuation procedures, and promoting a culture of preparedness.

The Role of Awareness Campaigns

- **Raising Alertness**

Awareness campaigns heighten alertness within communities by disseminating information about local risks, potential disaster scenarios, and steps to take in case of emergencies.

- **Promoting Participation**

These campaigns encourage active participation among community members, fostering a sense of responsibility and collective action in preparing for potential disasters.

Educational Initiatives for Disaster Preparedness

- **School-Based Programs**

Implementing educational programs in schools cultivates a generation aware of disaster risks, teaching them safety protocols, and empowering them to disseminate knowledge to their families and communities.

- **Community Workshops and Training**

Conducting workshops and training sessions within communities imparts practical skills, such as first aid, emergency response, and evacuation procedures, enhancing overall preparedness.

Technology and Information Dissemination

- **Utilizing Digital Platforms**

Leveraging digital platforms, including websites, mobile apps, and social media, ensures the widespread dissemination of crucial information, reaching a broader audience and enabling rapid communication during emergencies.

- **Interactive Tools and Simulations**

Interactive tools, such as disaster preparedness simulations or online courses, provide hands-on learning experiences, facilitating better retention and application of preparedness measures (Lahiri et al., 2021).

BUILDING FOR THE FUTURE

- **Educational Initiatives**

As societies rebuild, there is an opportunity for educational initiatives that equip communities with the knowledge and skills to mitigate future risks. This section explores the role of education in disaster preparedness, advocating for proactive measures that empower individuals and communities to navigate future challenges.

- **Collaborative Efforts**

The complexities of the human factor in the aftermath of natural disasters underscore the importance of collaborative efforts. Governments, NGOs, and communities must work together to develop comprehensive strategies that address immediate needs while laying the foundation for sustainable recovery (Rawat & Semwal, 2022). This collaborative approach is key to building resilience and minimizing the long-term societal and economic impact of natural disasters.

Post-Disaster Recovery: Rebuilding and Resilience

Understanding the Phases of Recovery

Understanding the phases of recovery after a crisis or disaster is crucial in facilitating a structured and effective response. An outline of the usual phases is provided below:

Emergency Response Phase

- **Immediate Actions**

This phase focuses on immediate life-saving measures, search and rescue operations, and providing emergency aid such as food, shelter, and medical assistance.

- **Rapid Needs Assessment**

Conducting quick assessments to identify the most pressing needs and determine the extent of damage lays the groundwork for subsequent recovery phases.

Short-Term Recovery Phase

- **Stabilization and Restoration**

Efforts in this phase aim to restore essential services, infrastructure, and basic amenities to stabilize the affected communities.

- **Temporary Housing and Support**

Providing temporary housing, access to clean water, healthcare, and essential services becomes crucial as people start rebuilding their lives.

Mid-Term Recovery Phase

- **Rebuilding Infrastructure**

Focus shifts towards repairing and rebuilding critical infrastructure, such as roads, schools, hospitals, and utilities, to restore normalcy.

- **Livelihood Restoration**

Supporting livelihoods through employment opportunities, economic recovery programs, and revitalizing local businesses aids in community recovery.

Long-Term Recovery Phase

- **Sustainable Reconstruction**

This phase involves long-term planning, focusing on sustainable reconstruction, resilience-building, and addressing underlying vulnerabilities (Rawat & Semwal, 2022).

- **Community Rehabilitation**

Efforts to strengthen community resilience, social cohesion, and mental health support contribute to the long-term recovery process.

Cross-Cutting Themes in Recovery

Involving affected communities in decision-making processes empowers them and ensures that recovery efforts align with their needs.

- **Risk Reduction and Preparedness**

Integrating measures to reduce future risks, including preparedness plans and risk mitigation strategies, is vital in building resilience.

Challenges in Recovery Phases

- **Resource Constraints**

Limited resources and funding often hinder the pace and effectiveness of recovery efforts, especially in resource-scarce regions.

- **Coordination and Collaboration**

Ensuring coordination among various stakeholders, agencies, and authorities is crucial for a cohesive and efficient recovery process.

Future Directions in Recovery Efforts

- **Resilience-Centric Approaches**

Adopting resilience-centric approaches that prioritize long-term sustainability and community empowerment strengthens recovery efforts.

- **Innovation and Technology**

Leveraging innovation and technology, such as data analytics and smart infrastructure, enhances the effectiveness and efficiency of recovery initiatives.

Understanding these phases of recovery aids in planning, resource allocation, and prioritizing actions, ensuring a more organized, holistic, and sustainable approach to rebuilding communities and restoring livelihoods after crises or disasters (Rawat & Semwal, 2022).

Infrastructure Rehabilitation and Reconstruction

Understanding the Significance

- **Restoring Essential Services**

Infrastructure rehabilitation is pivotal in reinstating vital services like transportation, utilities, healthcare, and communication.

- **Economic Recovery Catalyst**

Reconstruction efforts stimulate economic growth by creating jobs, attracting investments, and revitalizing local economies.

Phases of Rehabilitation and Reconstruction

- **Damage Assessment and Prioritization**

Thorough assessments determine the extent of damage, allowing for prioritization of projects based on critical needs.

- **Immediate Repairs and Restoration**

Swift repairs target critical infrastructure to ensure immediate functionality and service resumption for affected communities.

- **Long-Term Reconstruction**

Comprehensive rebuilding focuses on enhancing infrastructure resilience, often incorporating innovative designs and technologies.

Key Considerations in Infrastructure Recovery

- **Resilient Design and Innovation**

Integrating resilient design and innovative solutions fortifies infrastructure against future risks and climate adversities.

- **Community-Centric Approaches**

Engaging communities ensures that reconstruction aligns with local needs, cultural values, and future aspirations.

Challenges in Rehabilitation Efforts

- **Funding and Resource Constraints**

Limited financial resources and funding gaps challenge the pace and scale of infrastructure recovery.

- **Capacity and Expertise Shortages**

A lack of skilled labor and technical expertise hampers reconstruction, demanding capacity-building initiatives.

Strategies for Effective Recovery

- **Prioritization Frameworks**

Implementing clear prioritization frameworks ensures efficient resource allocation to critical infrastructure projects.

- **Public-Private Partnerships (PPPs)**

Engaging in collaborative ventures with private entities leverages expertise, resources, and innovative solutions.

Future Directions and Innovative Approaches

- **Sustainable and Green Infrastructure**

Adopting sustainable construction practices fosters resilience and aligns with environmental conservation goals.

- **Technology Integration and Smart Solutions**

Leveraging technology like AI, IoT, and data analytics streamlines reconstruction, enhancing efficiency and cost-effectiveness (Kar et al., 2023).

Infrastructure rehabilitation and reconstruction are pivotal for community resurgence post-disaster. Embracing resilient designs, community participation, innovative strategies, and leveraging technology are instrumental in not only rebuilding infrastructure but also fostering a more resilient and sustainable future.

Socio-Economic Recovery and Support

Understanding Socio-Economic Recovery

- **Restoring Community Well-being**

Socio-economic recovery focuses on restoring livelihoods, social structures, and community cohesion post-disaster.

- **Economic Revitalization**

Recovery efforts aim to revitalize local economies, create employment, and rebuild economic systems for sustainable growth.

Phases of Socio-Economic Recovery

- **Immediate Support**

Providing immediate aid, including food, shelter, and healthcare, helps stabilize communities and alleviate immediate hardships.

- **Livelihood Restoration**

Supporting livelihoods through job creation, micro-enterprise development, and vocational training facilitates economic recovery.

- **Community Rehabilitation**

Fostering social resilience, mental health support, and community-led initiatives aid in rebuilding cohesive communities.

Key Aspects of Socio-Economic Recovery

- **Inclusive Growth**

Promoting inclusive economic growth ensures that vulnerable populations are not left behind in the recovery process.

- Gender Equality and Social Equity

Emphasizing gender equality and social equity in recovery efforts enhances resilience and promotes community well-being.

Challenges in Socio-Economic Recovery

- **Resource Allocation**

Balancing resources between immediate relief and long-term recovery poses challenges in sustaining socio-economic support.

- **Vulnerability of Marginalized Groups**

Addressing the needs of marginalized groups and vulnerable populations requires tailored interventions and inclusive policies.

Strategies for Effective Recovery and Support

- **Community Engagement and Participation**

Engaging communities in decision-making and recovery planning empowers them and ensures their needs are addressed.

- **Partnerships and Collaboration**

Forging partnerships among governments, NGOs, private sectors, and community-based organizations maximizes impact and resources.

Future Directions and Innovations

- Sustainable Development Goals (SDGs)

Aligning recovery efforts with SDGs fosters sustainable development and resilient communities (Rawat & Semwal, 2022).

- **Digital Inclusion and Innovation**

Leveraging digital technologies and innovative solutions facilitates access to services and boosts economic opportunities.

Socio-economic recovery and support after crises are pivotal for rebuilding communities. By prioritizing inclusive growth, fostering community engagement, and leveraging innovative strategies, we can facilitate a more comprehensive and sustainable recovery process that not only rebuilds but strengthens communities for the future (Rawat & Semwal, 2022).

Environmental Rehabilitation and Sustainability

Understanding Environmental Rehabilitation

- **Restoring Ecological Balance**

Environmental rehabilitation focuses on restoring ecosystems, biodiversity, and natural resources affected by disasters.

- **Sustainable Development**

Efforts aim to promote sustainable development, minimize environmental impacts, and enhance resilience to future disasters (Rawat & Semwal, 2022).

Phases of Environmental Rehabilitation

- **Assessment and Restoration Planning**

Conducting environmental assessments guides restoration efforts and identifies areas requiring immediate attention.

- **Habitat Restoration**

Rehabilitating ecosystems, including forests, wetlands, and coastlines, promotes biodiversity and ecological resilience.

- **Sustainable Resource Management**

Implementing sustainable practices for water, land, and energy resources ensures long-term environmental health and sustainability.

Key Aspects of Environmental Rehabilitation

- **Ecosystem Resilience**

Restoring ecosystems fosters their ability to withstand future shocks, protecting communities and biodiversity.

- **Climate Adaptation**

Incorporating climate-resilient strategies and practices in rehabilitation efforts prepares ecosystems for changing climatic conditions.

Challenges in Environmental Rehabilitation

- **Limited Resources and Expertise**

Lack of funding, technical expertise, and capacity hinder comprehensive environmental restoration efforts.

- **Interconnectedness of Issues**

Addressing environmental challenges requires considering the interconnections between ecological, social, and economic factors.

STRATEGIES FOR EFFECTIVE REHABILITATION AND SUSTAINABILITY

- **Community Involvement**

Engaging local communities in restoration activities ensures ownership and sustains long-term environmental stewardship.

- **Policy Integration and Regulation**

Integrating environmental considerations into policies and regulations supports sustainable development post-disaster.

Future Directions and Innovations

- **Nature-Based Solutions**

Leveraging nature-based solutions, such as green infrastructure and natural resource management, enhances resilience.

- **Technological Innovations**

Embracing technology, like remote sensing and AI, aids in monitoring, assessment, and management of rehabilitated ecosystems (Kar et al., 2023).

Environmental rehabilitation and sustainability are integral components of post-disaster recovery. By prioritizing ecosystem health, engaging communities, and embracing innovative solutions, we can not only restore but also strengthen our natural environment for a more resilient future.

Community Engagement and Participation

Understanding Community Engagement

- **Empowering Local Voices**

Community engagement involves actively involving local residents, stakeholders, and groups in decision-making processes.

- **Building Partnerships**

It focuses on fostering collaborations among diverse stakeholders to address common goals and enhance community well-being.

Phases of Community Engagement

- **Understanding Community Needs**

Engaging communities starts with understanding their needs, aspirations, and priorities through inclusive dialogue and consultation.

- **Participatory Planning and Decision-Making**

Involving communities in planning and decision-making empowers them to shape policies and actions that directly impact their lives.

Action and Implementation

Collaboratively implementing projects and initiatives based on community input ensures ownership and sustainability.

Key Aspects of Community Engagement

- **Inclusivity and Diversity**

Ensuring representation and inclusion of diverse voices, including marginalized groups, strengthens community engagement.

- **Capacity Building and Empowerment**

Building local capacities and empowering community leaders fosters self-reliance and sustainability.

Challenges in Community Engagement

- **Trust and Communication**

Establishing trust and effective communication channels is crucial for meaningful engagement and participation.

- **Power Dynamics and Inequalities**

Navigating power imbalances and addressing inequalities ensures fair and equitable participation.

Strategies for Effective Engagement and Participation

- **Open Dialogue and Transparency**

Maintaining transparent communication channels and fostering open dialogue build trust and engagement.

- **Capacity Development Programs**

Investing in capacity-building initiatives empowers communities to actively participate and contribute effectively.

Future Directions and Innovations

- **Digital Engagement Platforms**

Leveraging digital technologies and online platforms expands opportunities for broader community engagement.

- Hybrid Engagement Models

Utilizing hybrid models that combine in-person and virtual engagement methods cater to diverse community needs.

Community engagement and participation are fundamental for sustainable development and resilience-building. By prioritizing inclusivity, fostering partnerships, and embracing innovative engagement approaches, communities can become powerful agents of change, leading to more resilient and thriving societies.

The Importance of Global Collaboration: Fostering Collective Resilience

Addressing transboundary challenges in the context of natural disasters involves navigating complexities that extend beyond geopolitical borders. Here's an in-depth look at this crucial aspect:

Understanding Transboundary Challenges

- **Nature Knows No Boundaries**

Natural disasters, oblivious to political demarcations, often traverse across borders. Floodwaters, seismic activities, and environmental pollutants can affect multiple nations, demanding a collaborative response (Mahesar et al., 2023).

- **Shared Vulnerabilities**

Adjacent regions may share similar vulnerabilities to certain disasters. For instance, coastal areas in different countries facing the threat of tsunamis or regions prone to river flooding experience common risks.

CHALLENGES FACED

- **Coordination and Communication**

Effective communication and coordination between countries are essential during disaster events. Different languages, protocols, and response systems can pose challenges in aligning efforts.

- **Resource Allocation**

Distributing resources across borders in times of crisis can be challenging. Disparities in resources and differing priorities among nations might hinder equitable resource allocation.

- **Legal and Political Barriers**

Complex legal and political frameworks between countries can impede swift and seamless cooperation in disaster response efforts.

MITIGATING TRANSBOUNDARY CHALLENGES

- **International Collaboration**

Establishing robust international agreements and frameworks for disaster response fosters collaboration. Platforms like the United Nations and regional bodies facilitate cooperation and resource sharing.

- **Information Sharing and Early Warning Systems**

Transboundary information sharing and joint early warning systems help disseminate alerts promptly across borders, ensuring swift responses.

- **Standardized Protocols and Training**

Developing standardized disaster response protocols and cross-border training programs ensures a unified approach among nations, minimizing confusion during crises.

Best Practices and Success Stories

- **Joint Disaster Drills and Exercises**

Conducting joint disaster preparedness exercises among neighboring countries enhances readiness and fosters familiarity with each other's response systems (Lahiri et al., 2021).

- **Regional Response Mechanisms**

Establishing regional response mechanisms, such as mutual aid agreements or regional disaster management centres, streamlines cooperation during crises.

FUTURE CONSIDERATIONS AND RECOMMENDATIONS

- **Strengthening Partnerships**

Building trust and strengthening partnerships through regular dialogues and joint initiatives enhances preparedness and response capacities.

- **Technology and Innovation**

Leveraging technology and innovation, such as shared satellite monitoring or AI-driven predictive models, improves early warning and response capabilities (Kar et al., 2023).

Addressing transboundary challenges requires a collective commitment from nations to set aside differences and work towards a common goal of mitigating the impact of disasters. Collaborative frameworks, standardized protocols, and mutual support mechanisms are pivotal in ensuring a cohesive response to natural calamities that transcend borders.

SHARING KNOWLEDGE AND EXPERTISE

Sharing knowledge and expertise in the context of natural disasters is paramount for building resilience and enhancing disaster preparedness. Here's a detailed exploration:

IMPORTANCE OF KNOWLEDGE SHARING

- **Empowering Communities**

Sharing knowledge about disaster risks, mitigation strategies, and response measures empowers communities to understand, prepare for, and respond effectively to potential disasters.

- **Learning from Experience**

Exchanging experiences and lessons learned from past disasters helps in refining response strategies and improving preparedness for future events.

Platforms for Knowledge Sharing

- **International Forums and Conferences**

Global forums and conferences serve as platforms for experts, policymakers, and practitioners to share best practices, research findings, and innovative solutions in disaster management.

- **Online Portals and Databases**

Digital platforms, such as online portals and databases, provide accessible repositories of knowledge, case studies, and research papers for wider dissemination.

MECHANISMS FOR EXPERTISE SHARING

- **Training Programs and Workshops**

Conducting training programs and workshops facilitates the transfer of expertise, enabling individuals and organizations to acquire skills and knowledge in disaster response and management.

- **Peer-to-Peer Collaboration**

Encouraging collaboration among experts, both nationally and internationally, promotes the exchange of ideas, techniques, and innovative approaches.

THE ROLE OF TECHNOLOGY IN KNOWLEDGE SHARING

- **Data Sharing and Visualization Tools**

Technology enables the sharing of real-time data and the use of visualization tools, facilitating a better understanding of disaster scenarios and response requirements.

- **Online Learning Platforms**

E-learning platforms and webinars offer accessible ways for individuals and organizations to access expertise and training remotely.

Challenges in Knowledge Sharing

- **Information Access and Language Barriers**

Limited access to information and language barriers can hinder the dissemination of knowledge, especially in regions with diverse linguistic backgrounds.

- **Dissemination and Implementation Gaps**

Ensuring that shared knowledge is effectively disseminated and translated into actionable policies and practices can be a challenge.

Overcoming Challenges

- **Capacity Building Initiatives**

Investing in capacity building, particularly in resource-constrained regions, helps bridge knowledge gaps and build local expertise.

- **Multilateral Cooperation**

Encouraging multilateral cooperation and partnerships fosters a collaborative environment where knowledge is shared across borders.

Future Directions

- **Strengthening Networks**

Fostering robust networks of experts, institutions, and communities strengthens knowledge-sharing ecosystems.

- **Embracing Innovation**

Embracing innovative technologies and methodologies expands the avenues for sharing knowledge and expertise in disaster management.

Sharing knowledge and expertise plays a pivotal role in strengthening disaster resilience globally. By leveraging platforms, mechanisms, and technological advancements, communities and nations can benefit from shared wisdom, thereby enhancing their capacity to effectively prepare for and respond to natural disasters.

Coordination in Humanitarian Aid

Coordination in humanitarian aid is a multifaceted process that involves various organizations, governments, and stakeholders working together to provide effective and timely assistance during crises. Here's a detailed exploration:

Importance of Coordination in Humanitarian Aid

- **Maximizing Impact**

Coordination ensures that aid efforts are well-organized, avoiding duplication and ensuring resources are effectively utilized to maximize their impact on affected communities.

- **Enhancing Efficiency**

Coordinated responses streamline operations, allowing for a more efficient allocation of resources, manpower, and expertise, thereby enhancing the overall effectiveness of aid delivery.

Key Actors and Stakeholders in Coordination

- **Governments and National Authorities**

National governments play a pivotal role in coordinating and facilitating humanitarian aid within their territories, providing support and facilitating international assistance.

- **International Organizations and NGOs**

International organizations, such as the United Nations agencies, along with NGOs, collaborate to provide aid, resources, and expertise in disaster-affected areas.

- **Local Communities and Grassroots Organizations**

Local communities, volunteers, and grassroots organizations often act as the first responders, playing a crucial role in coordination, aid distribution, and community support.

Mechanisms and Approaches to Coordination

- **Cluster Approach**

The cluster approach, adopted by the United Nations, organizes humanitarian response efforts into sectors like health, shelter, or food, ensuring a more coordinated and coherent approach within each sector.

- **Inter-Agency Collaboration**

Inter-agency coordination brings together different humanitarian actors to share information, resources, and coordinate joint efforts, facilitating a more comprehensive response.

- **Information Sharing Platforms**

Establishing coordination platforms, whether physical coordination centers or digital portals, promotes information sharing, coordination of activities, and decision-making among stakeholders.

Core Principles Guiding Coordination Efforts

- **Collaboration and Communication**

Open communication channels and collaborative decision-making among stakeholders are fundamental for effective coordination.

- **Needs-Based Response**

Coordination efforts prioritize the immediate needs of affected populations, ensuring that assistance aligns with their specific requirements.

- **Accountability and Transparency**

Transparent resource allocation, accountability for actions taken, and clear reporting mechanisms build trust and accountability among stakeholders and beneficiaries.

Challenges in Humanitarian Coordination

- **Logistical Constraints**

Challenges in logistics, including transportation, access to affected areas, and distribution networks, can hinder the smooth coordination and delivery of aid.

- **Political and Security Context**

Political complexities, conflicts, and security risks in crisis-affected regions may pose obstacles to coordination efforts and limit access to affected populations.

OVERCOMING CHALLENGES AND ENHANCING COORDINATION

- **Pre-established Coordination Mechanisms**

Having established coordination mechanisms and agreements in place before disasters strike facilitates a faster and more coordinated response.

- **Capacity Building and Training**

Investing in training and capacity building of aid workers and local responders enhances their ability to coordinate effectively and respond to crises.

Future Directions and Innovations

- **Leveraging Technology**

Utilizing technology, such as real-time data analytics, digital platforms, and communication tools, can enhance coordination, information sharing, and decision-making processes.

- **Strengthening Local Capacities**

Empowering local communities and organizations to take a lead in coordinating responses fosters greater ownership and sustainability in humanitarian efforts.

Effective coordination in humanitarian aid involves collaboration, adherence to core principles, overcoming challenges, and embracing innovations to ensure a more efficient and impactful response to humanitarian crises worldwide.

Climate Change and Global Resilience

Climate change poses significant challenges to global resilience, impacting communities, ecosystems, and economies worldwide. Here's a detailed exploration:(Tuladhar et al., 2021)

Impact of Climate Change on Global Resilience

- **Environmental Shifts**

Climate change leads to extreme weather events, rising temperatures, sea-level rise, and changes in precipitation patterns, amplifying vulnerabilities and threatening the resilience of ecosystems (Tuladhar et al., 2021).

- **Socioeconomic Challenges**

Communities face increased risks of displacement, food insecurity, health hazards, and economic disruptions due to the changing climate, affecting their ability to bounce back from shocks.

Increasing Worldwide Resilience Against Climate Change

- **Strengthening Adaptation Efforts**

Investing in adaptive measures, such as resilient infrastructure, early warning systems, and sustainable agricultural practices, enhances the ability of communities to adapt to changing climatic conditions.

- **Mitigating Greenhouse Gas Emissions**

Reducing greenhouse gas emissions through renewable energy adoption, sustainable land use, and carbon capture technologies is critical to mitigating the long-term impacts of climate change.

- **Enhancing Disaster Preparedness**

Improving disaster preparedness and response mechanisms helps communities anticipate and respond to climate-related disasters, reducing their immediate impact and enhancing recovery (Lahiri et al., 2021).

Key Strategies to Foster Global Resilience

- **International Collaboration**

Collaborative efforts among nations, through agreements like the Paris Agreement, promote global cooperation in mitigating climate change and building resilience across borders (Tuladhar et al., 2021).

- **Education and Awareness**

Raising awareness and educating communities about climate change impacts and resilience-building measures empowers individuals to take proactive steps.

- **Investing in Research and Innovation**

Supporting research and innovation in climate-resilient technologies, sustainable practices, and adaptation strategies fosters resilience and preparedness.

Challenges in Strengthening Global Resilience

- **Inequality and Vulnerability**

Unequal access to resources and varying levels of vulnerability exacerbates the impacts of climate change on marginalized communities and regions.

- **Financing and Resource Constraints**

Limited financial resources and funding gaps hinder the implementation of comprehensive resilience-building strategies, particularly in developing nations.

Overcoming Challenges and Enhancing Resilience

- **Addressing Inequality**

Addressing social, economic, and gender inequalities is crucial to ensuring that all communities have equal access to resources and resilience-building opportunities.

- **Mobilizing Financial Support**

Mobilizing financial support, through innovative financing mechanisms and global cooperation, can bridge funding gaps and support resilience initiatives.

Future Directions and Actions

- **Long-Term Planning**

Developing long-term climate adaptation plans and policies that integrate resilience measures into development agendas prepares communities for future challenges.

- **Technology and Innovation**

Leveraging technological advancements and fostering innovation in climate-resilient solutions can significantly bolster global resilience efforts.

Addressing climate change and fostering global resilience requires a concerted, global effort that spans nations, communities, and industries. By implementing adaptive measures, mitigating emissions, and promoting international collaboration, we can build a more resilient world capable of tackling the challenges posed by a changing climate.

Diplomacy and Policy Advocacy

Diplomacy and policy advocacy are critical elements in international relations and governance, shaping policies, fostering collaboration, and addressing global challenges. Here's an in-depth exploration:

Diplomacy: Nurturing International Relations

- **Bridge Building**

Diplomacy focuses on building and maintaining relationships between nations, utilizing dialogue, negotiation, and cooperation to resolve disputes and promote common interests.

- **Soft Power and Influence**

It involves the strategic use of soft power—cultural, educational, and economic influence—to shape perceptions and policies without resorting to force.

Key Aspects of Diplomacy

- **Bilateral and Multilateral Diplomacy**

Bilateral diplomacy centres on relations between two countries, while multilateral diplomacy involves engagement within international organizations and forums, fostering broader collaborations.

- **Track II Diplomacy**

This informal diplomacy involves non-state actors, such as academics and NGOs, engaging in dialogues to complement formal diplomatic efforts.

Policy Advocacy: Influencing Change and Decisions

- **Decision-making Influence**

Policy advocacy aims to influence policy decisions by bringing attention to specific issues, promoting solutions, and shaping public opinion through lobbying, campaigns, and expert analysis.

- **Advocacy Channels**

Utilizing various channels—media, civil society organizations, think tanks, and grassroots movements—policy advocacy amplifies voices and influences policy agendas.

Diplomacy and Policy Advocacy in Global Challenges

- **Climate Change Agreements**

Diplomatic negotiations and advocacy campaigns have shaped global climate agreements, fostering international collaboration in addressing environmental challenges(Tuladhar et al., 2021).

- **Human Rights Advocacy**

Both diplomatic efforts and policy advocacy focus on human rights issues, advocating for fair treatment, equality, and justice on a global scale.

- **Health and Pandemic Response**

Diplomatic coordination and policy advocacy are pivotal in orchestrating international responses to global health crises, fostering collaboration among nations and organizations.

Strategies for Effective Diplomacy and Policy Advocacy

- **Coalition Building**

Forming coalitions among nations or advocacy groups strengthens diplomatic efforts and amplifies policy advocacy initiatives.

- **Information and Communication**

Effective communication using data, research, and compelling narratives is crucial in shaping public opinion and influencing policy decisions.

- **Strategic Alliances**

Forging strategic alliances and partnerships, whether between nations or across sectors, enhances collective influence in diplomatic negotiations and policy advocacy.

Challenges and Considerations

- **Geopolitical Complexities**

Navigating geopolitical tensions and competing interests among nations poses challenges to effective diplomacy and advocacy efforts.

- **Resource Constraints**

Limited resources and funding often constrain advocacy and diplomatic initiatives, necessitating innovative approaches to amplify impact.

FUTURE DIRECTIONS AND OPPORTUNITIES

- **Digital Diplomacy**

Leveraging digital platforms and technology enhances diplomacy and advocacy, facilitating broader outreach and engagement.

- **Inclusivity and Diversity**

Embracing diverse perspectives and inclusive approaches strengthens diplomacy and advocacy, fostering greater representation and effectiveness.

Diplomacy and policy advocacy remain pivotal in navigating international relations, shaping policies, fostering cooperation, and advocating for change. Through strategic engagement, collaboration, and innovative approaches, diplomats and advocates continue to shape global governance and address complex challenges in a rapidly evolving world.

CONCLUSION

In the wake of our comprehensive exploration into the intricate complications of natural disasters, it becomes evident that understanding the multifaceted challenges is not merely an academic pursuit but a call to action. As we conclude this journey, the threads of insights gathered weave a tapestry of resilience, knowledge, and a collective commitment to mitigating the impact of nature's formidable forces. The complexities unravelling beneath the surface, both geologically and within communities, demand a concerted effort in developing strategies for a more resilient future. Our examination of displacement dilemmas, economic ripples, and environmental tolls underscores the need for proactive measures to address these challenges head-on. However, this exploration is not meant to instil fear but to empower. By spotlighting technological triumphs and community resilience as beacons of hope, we pave the way for a future where disasters, though inevitable, do not have to equate to irreversible devastation. Embracing innovation, education, and collaborative efforts, we navigate the complex terrain with the collective goal of emerging stronger in the face of adversity.

In conclusion, the call echoes loud and clear—a call for collective action, a call for unity in implementing mitigation strategies, and a call to foster a world where the complications of natural disasters are met with the unwavering strength of prepared and informed communities. Through knowledge, resilience, and a shared commitment to building a more resilient future, we stand poised to navigate the complexities of natural disasters with determination and hope.

REFERENCES

Alonso Vicario, S., Mazzoleni, M., Bhamidipati, S., Gharesifard, M., Ridolfi, E., Pandolfo, C., & Alfonso, L. (2020). Unravelling the influence of human behaviour on reducing casualties during flood evacuation. *Hydrological Sciences Journal, 65*(14), 2359–2375. doi:10.1080/02626667.2020.1810254

Bogdan, E. A., Caine, K. J., & Beckie, M. A. (2020). Unraveling the social construction of a flooding disaster: A threaded situation analysis approach. *International Journal of Mass Emergencies and Disasters, 38*(3), 308–339. doi:10.1177/028072702003800303

Di Baldassarre, G., Cloke, H., Lindersson, S., Mazzoleni, M., Mondino, E., Mård, J., & Tootoonchi, F. (2021). Integrating multiple research methods to unravel the complexity of human- water systems. *AGU Advances, 2*(3), e2021AV000473.

Fatema, S. R. (2020). Women's health-related vulnerabilities in natural disaster-affected areas of Bangladesh: A mixed-methods study protocol. *BMJ Open, 10*(11), e039772. doi:10.1136/bmjopen-2020-039772 PMID:33234637

Kar, A. K., Varsha, P. S., & Rajan, S. (2023). Unravelling the Impact of Generative Artificial Intelligence (GAI) in Industrial Applications: A Review of Scientific and Grey Literature. *Global Journal of Flexible Systems Management*, 1-31.

Lahiri, S., Snowden, B., Gu, J., Krishnan, N., Yellin, H., & Ndiaye, K. (2021). Multidisciplinary team processes parallel natural disaster preparedness and response: A qualitative case study. *International Journal of Disaster Risk Reduction, 61*, 102369. doi:10.1016/j.ijdrr.2021.102369

Mahesar, R. A., Khalil, H., Shaikh, S., Kalhoro, A., Rajar, A. B., Memon, M. A., & Mamun, M. A. (2023). Exploring suicidality in the aftermath of the 2022 flood in Pakistan: Insights from newspaper reports. *CNS Spectrums*, 1–3. doi:10.1017/S1092852923002419 PMID:37581285

Okyere, M. A., Essel-Gaisey, F., Zuka, F. M., Christian, A. K., & Nunoo, I. K. (2023). Wading out the storm: Exploring the effect of flooding on energy poverty amidst disaster management strategies in Dar es Salaam. *Environmental Science & Policy, 150*, 103578. doi:10.1016/j.envsci.2023.103578

Oliva, S., & Lazzeretti, L. (2021). Unravelling the Sustainable Resilient Region: Exploring Regional Resilience in Sustainable Transition. In *Rethinking Clusters* (pp. 3–16). Springer. doi:10.1007/978-3-030-61923-7_1

Rawat, A. S., & Semwal, M. M. (2022). *Unveiling the Himalayan Nexus: Unraveling Anthropogenic Triggers and Pursuing Sustainable Development in Uttarakhand.*

Tuladhar, S., Pasakhala, B., Maharjan, A., & Mishra, A. (2021). Unravelling the linkages of cryosphere and mountain livelihood systems: A case study of Langtang, Nepal. *Advances in Climate Change Research, 12*(1), 119–131. doi:10.1016/j.accre.2020.12.004

Xiao, Y., Zhong, J., Wang, J., Zhang, L., Qian, X., Liu, W., & Huang, H. (2023). Exploring the Coupling Coordination Relationship of Urban Resilience System in Ecologically Fragile Areas: Case Study of the Loess Plateau in China. *Land (Basel), 12*(11), 1997. doi:10.3390/land12111997

Chapter 2
Reshaping Disaster Resilience:
The AI and Machine Learning Revolution in Natural Catastrophe Management

R. Siva Subramanian
https://orcid.org/0000-0002-7509-9223
R.M.K. College of Engineering and Technology, India

D. Prabha
Sri Krishna College of Engineering and Technology, India

S. Srinivasan
Nehru Institute of Technology, India

S. Thirumurugaveerakumar
Kumaraguru College of Technology, India

G. Gokilakrishnan
Sri Eshwar College of Engineering, India

ABSTRACT

Natural disasters, such as earthquakes, hurricanes, floods, and wildfires, are ongoing worldwide concerns that have catastrophic effects on human lives, infrastructure, and the environment. By enhancing forecast, management, and reaction tactics, machine learning and artificial intelligence (AI) have emerged as revolutionary technologies in solving these crises. This comprehensive chapter delves deeply into the uses and implications of machine learning and AI in natural disaster avoidance. Machine learning techniques, especially artificial neural networks (ANNs), have shown promise in forecasting the incidence and severity of many natural catastrophes. These models make use of massive datasets including climatic, geographical, and historical data to improve forecasting accuracy and early warning systems. Furthermore, data-driven insights enable catastrophe prediction and risk assessment using a variety of machine learning methods ranging from decision trees to deep learning networks.

DOI: 10.4018/979-8-3693-2280-2.ch002

INTRODUCTION

One of the most scary and catastrophic things that can happen to people is a natural catastrophe (Johns A 2013). They attack with a ruthless quickness that leaves devastation in their path and are absolutely unexpected. In addition to having an effect on our life, they can damage important infrastructure and upset the delicate balance of our ecosystem. There is an urgent need for innovative ways to foresee, manage, and react to catastrophic calamities in light of these enormous and sometimes apparently insurmountable problems (Razali et al 2020). AI and ML have become rays of hope in recent years despite the turmoil caused by natural catastrophes. These remarkable technologies provide fresh opportunities to comprehend these catastrophes better and, more crucially, lessen their devasting repercussions (Sun et al 2020). This review explores at artificial intelligence (AI) and machine learning, two fields that might fundamentally alter how we respond to disasters. These innovations have the potential to dramatically enhance our capacity for catastrophe prediction, real-time monitoring, and resource allocation. AI and machine learning provides us optimism that we may save lives and reduce the financial losses that often accompany these catastrophes by using the power of data and analytics (Goswami et al 2018). The importance of AI and ML for controlling, forecasting, and reacting to catastrophes cannot be overstated. By providing answers to issues that have plagued society for ages, they have the potential to dramatically alter how we deal with these calamities. The goal of this review paper is to provide a thorough overview of the developments in AI and machine learning technologies, their real-world applications, and the difficulties that come with catastrophe management. In addition, will outline creative alternatives and explore about how they can alter catastrophe planning and response in the future.

Objectives

1. To provide a thorough investigation of the AI & ML applications in the context of disaster management & response. 2. Investigate and contrast various machine learning and AI approaches used in disaster management, highlighting their individual advantages, disadvantages, and applicability for various natural disaster kinds and situations. 3. Look into and deal with the typical issues and difficulties that come up during natural catastrophes, such as communication problems, resource limitations, and unanticipated circumstances. Examine the use of AI and machine learning to address these issues. 4. Examine the precise contribution that deep learning technology can make to improving

recovery and response to disasters. Discuss about its uses in damage assessment, anomaly identification, and image analysis. 5. Encourage those working in research, policy, and practice to investigate and develop the possibilities of AI and machine learning in disaster management. Promote the development of innovative techniques and technology to better shield populations from the effects of natural catastrophes.

Motivation

1. The severe impact that natural catastrophes take on human lives serves as the main impetus for this paper. These incidents have the potential to result in significant human casualties, population relocation, & psychological damage. The key impetus is the moral need to save lives and lessen human suffering, which acts as a primary driver for disaster management research. 2. Natural catastrophes can have serious economic repercussions, including destruction of infrastructure, lost production, and increased financial strain on the impacted governments and communities. The driving force is the possibility of reducing these financial losses via improvements in catastrophe management enabled by AI and machine intelligence. 3.Natural catastrophes are becoming more vulnerable because of the world's growing urbanization and interconnection. Finding better disaster management strategies is crucial, particularly in light of the consequences of climate change, which are predicted to make such occurrences more often and severe. 4. Recent advances in AI and machine intelligence have the potential to fundamentally alter how disasters are predicted, managed, and responded to. The inspiration comes from the conviction that using these technologies may significantly enhance our capacity to manage and react to natural catastrophes. 5. The need for interdisciplinary cooperation between specialists in artificial intelligence, disaster management, and policy development is what inspired this research. Such cooperative initiatives have the potential to provide ground-breaking and efficient answers to the complicated problems that natural catastrophes present.

The goals and purpose of the paper are framed by these objectives and motivations, which emphasize the crucial role AI and machine learning play in addressing the difficulties of managing natural disasters and their potential to save lives, lessen economic losses, and improve resilience in the face of these catastrophes.

USING AI AND MACHINE LEARNING TO ANTICIPATE NATURAL DISASTERS

Predicting natural catastrophes accurately is very difficult because of how abrupt and often disastrous they are. However, artificial intelligence (AI) and machine learning have showed great promise in enhancing our capacity to predict these catastrophes. There are many different types of catastrophic catastrophes that fall under the category of "natural disasters," such as earthquakes that shake the very foundations of the planet, storms that unleash unrelenting wrath, floods that cover large areas, and wildfires that engulf enormous swaths of land. Their similarity resides in their unpredictable nature, which results in wrath and havoc. Predicting these occurrences is crucial since it might mean the difference between being ready and being unprepared, or even between life and death.

Figure 1. AI And machine learning in natural disasters

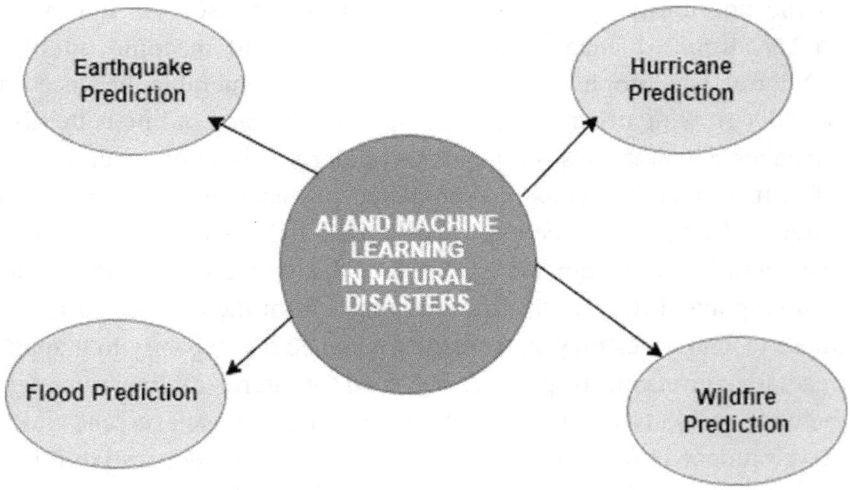

Earthquake Prediction

Seismic data analysis using machine learning algorithms makes it possible to spot antecedents and trends that might signal major earthquakes. AI helps early warning systems by spotting minute changes and abnormalities in seismic activity (Chittora et al 2022).

Hurricane Prediction

Data-driven Forecasting: Huge databases of atmospheric variables, past storm patterns, and real-time data are analysed using AI and machine learning. As a result, storm formation, course, and intensity forecasts are more precise. Forecasting accuracy may be increased by machine learning models' ability to adapt to and learn from new data.

Flood Prediction

Real-time Monitoring: To enable real-time flood monitoring, machine learning algorithms connect with sensors, IoT devices, and data from multiple sources. In order to send out timely flood warnings, these systems can detect increasing water levels, weather patterns, and other variables (Munawar et al 2022).

Wildfire Prediction

Early Detection: AI & ML are used to examine environmental data, such as temperature, humidity, wind patterns, and previous wildfire data. This enables preventative interventions by predicting the possibility of wildfires and their possible spread (Pereira et al 2022).

Model Comparisons

Comparing various AI & ML methods for catastrophe prediction is a crucial component of this part. It explores the advantages and disadvantages of these models and emphasizes how well-suited they are to different catastrophe scenarios and disaster kinds. Researchers and specialists in disaster management can drastically minimize false alarms while simultaneously improving forecast accuracy by using AI and machine learning approaches. In addition to giving crucial time for planning and responding, this also helps in resource allocation, possibly saving lives and reducing financial losses. This emphasizes how important AI and machine learning are for disaster prediction. It shows how they have the potential to transform how we forecast and prepare for natural catastrophes, which will eventually result in safer and more resilient societies.

DISASTER MANAGEMENT APPLICATIONS OF MACHINE LEARNING

Artificial intelligence's subset of machine learning, which plays a variety of roles in disaster management, is altering how we plan for and react to natural catastrophes. This section explores its application's numerous facets, including:

Natural Disaster Prediction

Machine Learning for Improved forecast: Machine learning algorithms have greatly improved the forecast of natural catastrophes by analysing massive datasets and spotting detailed trends (Chopra et al 2022). These algorithms can examine seismic data to spot little tremors in earthquake-prone zones, and they can evaluate atmospheric variables to forecast the development and movement of storms in hurricane-prone areas (Linardos et al 2022). **Improving Early Warning Systems:** By analysing real-time data from multiple sources, machine learning plays a key role in improving early warning systems. It may provide people timely knowledge about imminent calamities, enabling them to take preventative action.

Real-Time Monitoring and Reaction

Making use of Internet of Things (IoT): For real-time data collecting and analysis, machine learning makes use of IoT devices like sensors, cameras, drones, and remote monitoring systems. This constant flow of data enables quick action by monitoring the development of disasters. **Proactive Resource Allocation**: During emergencies, machine learning helps to maximize resource allocation. It makes sure that scarce resources are allocated where they are most needed by analysing data on the ground and evaluating changing situations in real-time.

Damage Evaluation and Repair

Computer Vision for Damage Assessment: Computer vision systems based on machine learning can examine images and videos in order to assess the level of devastation. This speeds up damage assessment and makes it easier to develop effective response plans (Lingxin et al 2022). **Increasing the effectiveness of disaster response:** When a crisis strikes, machine learning's capacity to analyse and make sense of massive amounts of real-world data guarantees that emergency response operations are effective and well-informed.

Challenges and Solutions

Difficulties in Disaster Management: During natural catastrophes, machine learning encounters difficulties such as a lack of resources, unforeseen occurrences, and communication failures. **Ingenious Solutions:** By optimizing resource allocation, forecasting situational awareness, and creating technology-driven communication systems that are robust in the event of calamities, machine learning may solve these issues. By improving forecast accuracy, allowing real-time monitoring, and optimizing resource allocation, machine learning is a key factor in reinventing catastrophe management. Its many uses have the potential to change how we react to natural calamities.

THE USE OF IOT DEVICES IN DISASTER MANAGEMENT

The term Internet of Things, or IoT, describes a network of connected gadgets and sensors that can collect, send, and exchange data via the internet. IoT devices exist in a variety of shapes and sizes, including sensors, cameras, drones, and other specialized equipment that is designed to carry out certain functions (Esposito et al 2022).

Data Gathering and Real-Time Observation

When it comes to capturing information during catastrophes, IoT devices does its job efficiently. They may include a broad variety of sensors, each with its own specific function. For instance, seismic sensors look for ground motion during earthquakes, weather stations keep an eye on the atmosphere, cameras record visual data, drones take images from the air, and water level detectors keep tabs on changes in water levels. But the capacity to monitor in real-time is what distinguishes IoT devices. They produce a live stream of important data by continually gathering and transmitting data. The different elements covered by this real-time stream include earthquake activity, weather, air quality, water levels, and more. The appeal of this is that it gives decision-makers and first responders a continuous, current perspective of the situation as it develops, assuring their knowledge.

Infrastructure for Communications

A reliable communication infrastructure is necessary for these IoT devices to efficiently perform their function. This network of communications may use

Figure 2. IOT devices in disaster management

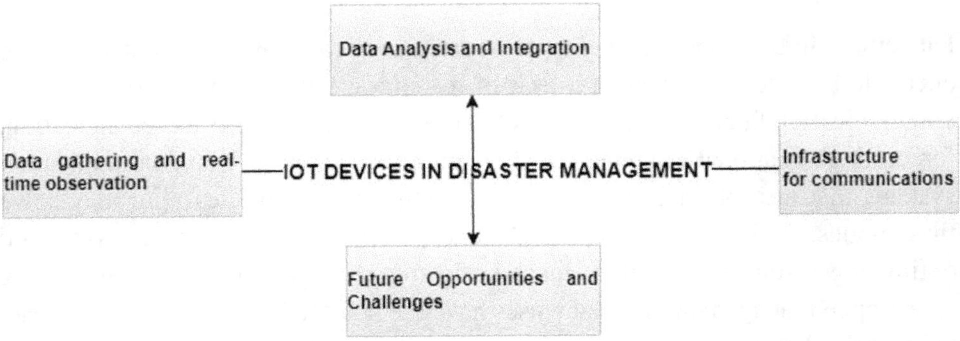

cellular networks, satellite communication, and mesh networks, among other technologies. Reliability is a crucial need here, ensuring that these systems continue to function even when infrastructure in disaster-affected regions is damaged or fails. Additionally, resilience is also important. These systems need to be built to survive the most extreme circumstances and go on even when other communication networks are disrupted.

Data Analysis and Integration

The data gathered by IoT devices has to be turned into insights that can be put to use. Artificial intelligence and machine learning come into play here. The data is processed and analysed by these technologies, and useful information is gleaned. They can see patterns, trends, and anomalies, giving decision-makers and first responders the information, they need to act responsibly.

Future Opportunities and Challenges

Future-focused, IoT technology is always developing. Future developments like edge computing and 5G connection promise to improve data collecting and processing capabilities. However, there are other difficulties. As the Internet of Things develops, concerns including data security and privacy, the need for device standardization, and maintaining interoperability across various systems must be addressed. IoT devices are essentially the unacknowledged heroes of disaster management. They operate as the eyes and ears that gather information in real-time, giving responders and decision-makers the knowledge, they need to act successfully in the face of difficulty.

DISASTER MANAGEMENT USING MACHINE LEARNING ALGORITHMS

Artificial intelligence's subset of machine learning, which improves prediction and decision-making, is revolutionizing disaster management. The introduction of machine learning's function in disaster management in this section emphasizes the significance of this technology in enhancing disaster preparation, response, and recovery (Prodhan et al 2022).

Different Kinds of Machine Learning Algorithms

A number of algorithms are included in machine learning, each with unique advantages and disadvantages. These algorithms are grouped in the section according to how they are used in disaster management: **Predictive algorithms:** Powerful prediction skills are provided by machine learning. Natural catastrophes including earthquakes, hurricanes, floods, and wildfires are predicted using algorithms like DT, RF, SVM, and NN. These algorithms look for patterns and trends that indicate an oncoming calamity by analysing historical data, environmental variables, and other pertinent elements. These algorithms' benefits come from their capacity to recognize tiny cues and increase forecast precision with time. However, they could be constrained by the complexity of catastrophic occurrences and the accessibility of previous data. **Real-Time Monitoring Algorithms:** For catastrophe monitoring in real time, machine learning is essential. Anomaly detection, time series analysis, and clustering methods are among the algorithms utilized for this. Algorithms for detecting anomalies, such as spikes in seismic activity or strange weather patterns, may spot unexpected patterns or departures from the norm. While clustering methods put comparable data points together for easy interpretation, time series analysis allows for the assessment of data gathered over time to identify patterns or abrupt changes. These algorithms provide decision-makers up-to-date information, but the caliber and volume of incoming data may affect how successful they are. **Algorithms for Resource Allocation and Optimization:** Resource allocation during a crisis response must be done effectively. Through the use of optimization methods like genetic algorithms, linear programming, and Markov decision processes, machine learning facilitates this process. While linear programming is employed for resource allocation in contexts with limited resources, genetic algorithms imitate the process of natural selection to improve resource distribution. Making sequential judgments in the face of uncertainty is aided by Markov decision procedures. These algorithms make sure that few resources are used where they are most needed, but in order to work efficiently, they need precise data and well stated limits. **Damage Assessment Algorithms:** Machine learning methods that use image analysis, computer vision, and remote sensing techniques make it easier to estimate damage after a catastrophe. These algorithms analyse images and data from satellites, drones, and on-site sensors to gauge the degree of environmental and infrastructural damage. For example, computer vision algorithms are able to recognize risks, detect structural damage, and evaluate the state of the impacted regions. These algorithms have the benefit of being able to quickly and accurately estimate the damage, but they may encounter difficulties in bad weather or when working with distorted visual input.

Strengths and Weaknesses:

In terms of catastrophe management, machine learning algorithms have various advantages: **Data-Driven Decision Making:** By enabling data-driven decision-making, these algorithms lessen the dependence on human judgment, which may be arbitrary in times of high-stress crisis. **Real-Time Analysis:** They provide real-time data analysis, allowing more rapid catastrophe response and adaptive planning. **Prediction Accuracy:** Machine learning algorithms improve forecasting skills and prediction accuracy over time by learning from fresh data.

Restrictions

Data Quality: The quality and quantity of the data, which might be harmed in catastrophes, are crucial to the success of these algorithms. **Complexity:** Deep neural networks, one kind of machine learning technique, may be computationally demanding and difficult to implement. **Interpretability:** Complex machine learning models may not be able to be understood, making it difficult to comprehend how they arrived at their predictions.

DEALING WITH REAL-WORLD DATA IN DISASTERS

Large-scale, real-world data management and analysis during catastrophes is a challenging issue. This section gives an overview of the difficulties involved in handling data in crisis situations and the crucial role that machine learning plays in overcoming these difficulties.

Data Management Challenges

Dealing with data during a natural catastrophe presents a number of difficulties: **Data Volume:** Massive amounts of data are generated during catastrophes from a variety of sources, such as remote sensors, social media, satellite imaging, and emergency calls. Traditional data processing techniques may be overwhelmed by this abrupt increase in data volume, requiring the use of more effective and scalable solutions. **Data Variety:** Text, images, sounds, and video are just a few of the many types of data that are gathered during catastrophes. This heterogeneous data is difficult to integrate and analyse since various data kinds may need different processing methods. **Data Velocity:** To assist prompt decision-making, real-time data from sources such as weather sensors and social media sites must be analysed swiftly. Slow data processing may cause answers to be delayed and possibilities for disaster mitigation to be lost. **Data quality:** During catastrophes, sensor failures, inadequate data, or purposeful misrepresentation may all lower the quality of data. To prevent making decisions based on inaccurate information, it is essential to ensure data accuracy and dependability. **Data Integration:** It may be difficult to integrate data from many sources, including governmental and non-governmental groups as well as businesses. Coordination of data access and sharing while upholding privacy and security considerations is a difficult task.

Role of Machine Learning

The following data difficulties need the help of machine learning: **Data preprocessing:** Data is cleaned and normalized using machine learning methods as part of the preprocessing stage to increase quality. This might entail noise reduction, outlier identification, and missing data imputation. **Data Fusion:** Machine learning makes it possible to combine data from several sources. Data integration is facilitated by methods like feature extraction and data transformation. **Real-Time Data Analysis:** Real-time data analysis is a strong suit of machine learning algorithms. They can quickly recognize crucial information from streaming data and interpret it, which helps in the fast identification of impending crisis trends. **Predictive Analytics:** Based on historical data and current observations, machine learning algorithms may predict disaster-related patterns and occurrences. Planning response plans and measuring the effects of disasters are made easier by predictive analytics. **Data security:** Data security uses machine learning to identify and reduce cyber dangers. Cyberattacks are more likely to occur during catastrophes, and machine learning algorithms can detect and stop security lapses.

DIFFICULTIES IN THE MANAGEMENT OF NATURAL DISASTERS:

Natural catastrophes often come with a number of issues that might seriously hamper disaster management efforts. In coping with these catastrophic catastrophes, emergency responders and authorities encounter a number of difficulties that are examined in this section.

Communication Breakdowns

During catastrophes, effective communication is crucial, but it is often hampered by a number of factors: **Infrastructure Damage:** Telecommunications infrastructure, such as cell towers, power lines, and internet cables, may sustain significant damage as a result of natural disasters. Networks for communication are damaged, which impedes information transmission. **Overloaded Networks:** There is an increase in communication, particularly emergency calls and SMS, during catastrophes. This causes network congestion, which makes it difficult for people to contact authorities and for authorities to plan their reaction actions. **Lack of Interoperability:** The employment of incompatible communication technology by various agencies and groups engaged in disaster response may hamper effective coordination and data exchange. **Human error:** Human mistake, misconceptions, and misinterpretations may hinder communication under high-stress circumstances, which can result in poor decision-making.

Resource Shortages

Resource shortages are a frequent problem in catastrophe situations: **Supplies and equipment:** The demand for emergency goods, such as food, water, medical gear, and building supplies, often exceeds the supply. Rationing and shortages may result from this. **Staff:** During calamities, there may not be enough volunteers, emergency responders, or medical experts. Lack of resources may restrict the ability to provide impacted communities assistance and medical treatment. **Transportation:** Transport networks may be damaged by disasters, making it challenging to send supplies and workers to affected regions. Resources can't travel as easily when airports, bridges, and highways are damaged. **Finances:** Limited financing for catastrophe planning and response exacerbates resource limitations. Budget restrictions may make it more difficult to obtain and retain necessary resources.

Population Vulnerability:

During catastrophes, the vulnerabilities of the affected communities are often revealed: **Socioeconomic Disparities:** Disasters disproportionately harm disadvantaged areas with poor access to resources and medical treatment. Disasters have a greater effect on these people when there are socioeconomic differences. **Health Vulnerabilities:** Due to the interruption of medical services and drugs, those with pre-existing health problems, such as chronic diseases, impairments, and mental health concerns, are more at-risk during catastrophes. **Evacuation Challenges:** It is difficult and resource-intensive to evacuate vulnerable groups, such as the elderly, young children, and those who have mobility impairments. Although tough, it is important to make sure they are protected. **Language and cultural barriers:** Within afflicted groups, language and cultural diversity might pose obstacles to effective communication and service availability.

Environmental Impact

Natural catastrophes may have long-term effects on the environment: **Damage to the ecosystem:** Natural ecosystems may sustain significant harm from floods, wildfires, and earthquakes, which can affect biodiversity and water quality. **Pollution and contamination:** Hazardous materials, such as chemicals and pollutants, may cause environmental pollution during catastrophes, endangering the health of nearby people. **Erosion and Landslides:** Hurricanes and torrential rains may cause landslides and erosion, further jeopardizing infrastructure and public safety. **Climate Change:** Climate change is associated with an increase in the frequency and intensity of natural catastrophes, adding to the worldwide burden.

Technological Difficulties:

Technology-related issues might become problematic during disasters: **Power Outages:** Disaster-related power outages may affect critical services including hospitals, communications networks, and water treatment facilities. **Cybersecurity Threats:** Critical infrastructure may be the target of cyberattacks, which can also hinder disaster relief operations and result in data breaches and information manipulation. **Data management:** Effective data management solutions are needed because of the enormous amount of data produced during catastrophes to make sure that important data is not lost or handled improperly.

The Function of Machine Learning

Some of these difficulties can be solved using machine learning: **Predictive Analytics:** Machine learning models can forecast the possibility of damage to the communication infrastructure, assisting authorities in setting up backup systems. **Resource Allocation:** Machine learning algorithms may improve resource allocation, assisting governments in more effective supply distribution. **Population Vulnerability Assessment:** Using data analysis, machine learning can pinpoint populations who need special assistance. **Environmental Monitoring:** To help in mitigation efforts, machine learning may be used to track environmental changes and forecast the effects of a catastrophe on the ecosystem. Machine learning aids in the identification and mitigation of cybersecurity threats, protecting vital infrastructure.

REMEDIES FOR NATURAL DISASTER MANAGEMENT DIFFICULTIES

This section explores ground-breaking approaches to dealing with the many challenges that occur in managing natural disasters by using machine learning and AI technology.

Communication Solutions

Mesh Networks: Making use of mesh networks, in which devices serve as both data consumers and routers, may assist in preserving local communication even in the event that the infrastructure is compromised. **Satellite Communication:** Bypassing problems with terrestrial infrastructure, using satellite communication technologies maintains connection. **Natural Language Processing (NLP):** NLP can help with real-time language translation, removing linguistic barriers between emergency personnel and the impacted populations.

Resource management and allocation:

Predictive Analytics: Machine learning can anticipate resource needs depending on the kind, location, and magnitude of a catastrophe, allowing for preemptive stockpiling and allocation. IoT and RFID (Radio-Frequency Identification) technology may be used to monitor resources in real-time, avoiding theft and assuring effective distribution.

Support for Vulnerable Populations

Machine Learning-based susceptibility Assessment: Machine learning models may evaluate a population's susceptibility based on a number of variables, allowing for the prioritizing of evacuation and targeted assistance. **Applications for Community Engagement:** AI-powered applications can educate, alert, and help people that are most in need, fostering community resilience.

Environmental Stewardship:

Environmental Monitoring: Remote sensing and machine learning technologies can track environmental changes and provide information that will be useful for post-disaster recovery efforts. **Early Warning Systems:** AI can improve early warning systems to provide timely notifications for environmental catastrophes like landslides and floods.

Cybersecurity measures:

AI-driven Cybersecurity: Using AI-based intrusion detection systems, cyber risks may be quickly identified and reduced. **Data Encryption:** Making sure data is encrypted and stored securely to safeguard sensitive information.

Education and Training:

Virtual Simulations: Responders are prepared for real-world situations using AI-powered virtual simulations and training programs. **Public Awareness Campaigns:** AI-driven social media campaigns may educate communities about catastrophe preparation and increase public awareness.

Collaboration Platforms

Data Sharing systems: AI can help with the development of data-sharing systems that guarantee interoperability and compatibility across various authorities and organizations. **Situation Awareness Tools:** Coordination is aided by real-time situation awareness tools driven by AI that provide a common vision of crisis scenarios. Adopting these ideas will help disaster management become more efficient, adaptable, and robust in the face of unforeseen natural calamities.

MACHINE-LEARNING-BASED DEVICES FOR MANAGING NATURAL DISASTERS

This section provides information on the creation and use of machine learning-based tools intended to improve many facets of disaster response and recovery.

Figure 3. Machine-Learning-Based devices for managing natural disasters

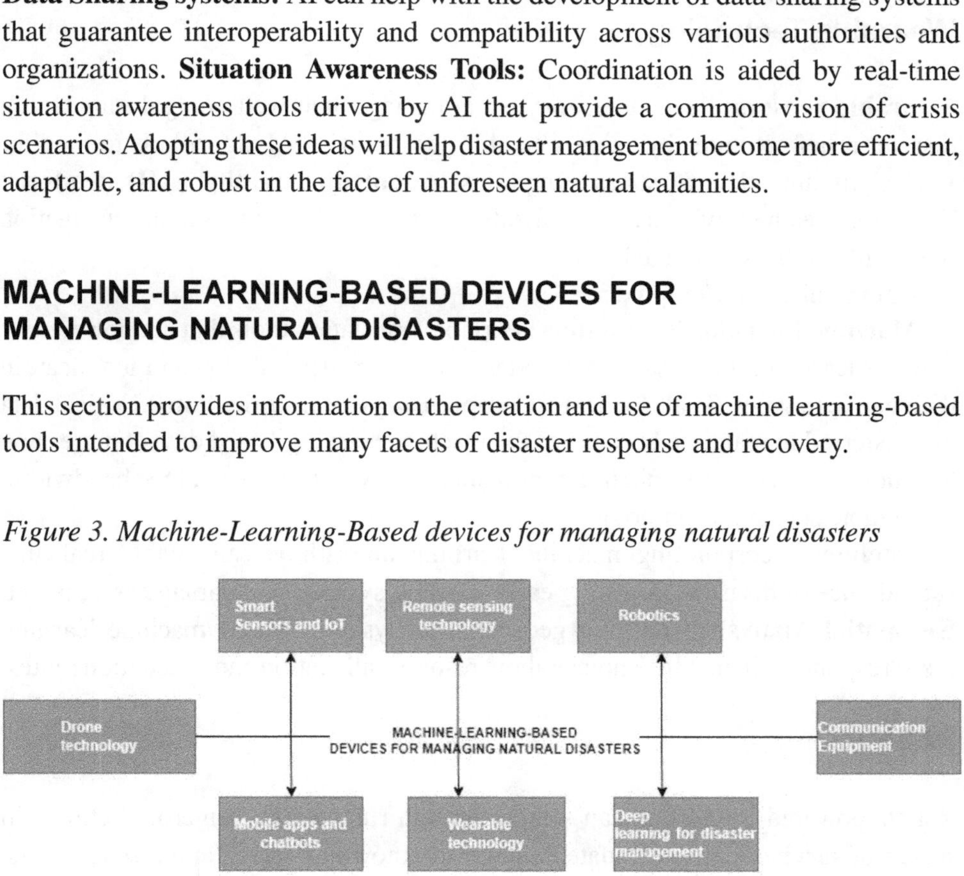

Drone Technology

Search and Rescue Drones: Drones using object identification and image analysis machine learning algorithms can quickly find survivors in disaster-affected regions, speeding up rescue efforts. **Drones for damage assessment:** Drones can record high-definition images and videos in order to determine the degree of damage, allowing for quick resource allocation and reaction.

Smart Sensors and IoT

Machine Learning Sensors: Intelligent sensors that have been machine learning-integrated may spot environmental changes and abnormalities, including the beginnings of earthquakes or floods, and transmit this information in real time. **Data Fusion and Analysis:** To give early warning and assist in decision-making, IoT networks gather data from a variety of sources.

Wearable Technology

Wearable Sensors: Responders may better manage their well-being during taxing disaster relief activities by using wearable sensors with AI algorithms to monitor vital signs and identify stress symptoms. **Augmented reality (AR) headsets:** These devices help with data visualization, situational awareness, and navigation in hazardous disaster-related areas.

Communication Equipment:

Machine Learning Translators: Portable translation tools that are powered by machine learning allow disaster responders and impacted populations communicate in their native tongues. **Tools for Data-Compressing Communications:** Critical data is transferred in real time because of the machine learning-based data compression techniques, which allow effective communication even with constrained bandwidth.

Remote sensing technology:

Satellites incorporating machine learning algorithms can enable real-time surveillance of disasters, assisting early warning systems and damage assessment. **Geospatial Analysis:** Tools for geospatial analysis driven by machine learning assist responders in making choices about resource allocation and evacuation routes.

Robotics

Robots powered by AI that can search through rubble and dangerous settings in search of survivors or to evaluate damage are known as search and rescue robots. **Robotic Medical Assistants:** AI-powered robots can transport necessary supplies to disaster-affected regions and provide medical help.

Mobile apps and chatbots:

AI-Powered Apps: Mobile programs with AI-driven features provide impacted people with real-time updates, emergency alerts, and communication assistance. **Chatbots for Information:** AI chatbots give advice on catastrophe planning and reaction as well as answers to commonly asked queries.

Deep Learning for Disaster Management

Deep Learning Image Analysis: Deep learning technology can evaluate damage, detect risks, and track environmental changes in real time using images and videos (Vinod et al 2022). **Natural Language Processing (NLP):** NLP-driven apps help responders and impacted populations communicate by providing essential information in a variety of languages. These artificial intelligence-based tools for disaster management are a huge improvement. They greatly improve disaster response and recovery operations by offering real-time data analysis, language translation, early warning capabilities, and effective communication tools. Through the use of technology, communities and first responders are better equipped to make choices during natural catastrophes that can ultimately save lives.

NATURAL DISASTERS AND WEARABLE SENSORS AND AI ALGORITHMS:

The interaction of wearable sensors and AI algorithms is explored in this section, emphasizing how it might improve catastrophe preparation and response.

Wearable Sensor Technologies

Biometric Sensors: Wearable devices containing biometric sensors, such as heart-rate monitors, body-temperature sensors, and stress level indicators, can continually monitor the health and wellbeing of first responders in crisis situations. The physical and emotional health of persons engaged in high-stress reduction initiatives is helped by this real-time data. **Environmental Sensors:** When working in disaster-affected regions, wearable environmental sensors can detect changes in air quality, temperature, humidity, and radiation levels. This information is vital for responders to protect their health and make wise judgments. **Location and Movement Tracking:** For emergency responders, GPS-enabled wearable technology provides location tracking and movement monitoring. These data may be analysed by AI algorithms to improve on-the-ground coordination, evaluate response dispersion, and optimize evacuation routes.

Integration of AI Algorithms:

Real-time Health Monitoring: AI algorithms analyse information from biometric sensors to find irregularities in the health of respondents. Alerts may be issued to command centres if anomalies are found, allowing quick action to avert medical crises. **Environmental Hazard Detection:** AI-driven environmental sensors are able to spot risky situations like radiation surges or poisonous gas leakage. Responders' safety is ensured by the automated notifications that are provided when such dangers are found. **Machine Learning Language Translation:** Wearable technology with AI language translation skills helps emergency responders get over language hurdles and improve contact with impacted populations. **Stress Management**: AI algorithms may examine information from biometric sensors to gauge respondents' levels of stress. When high-stress indications are found, actions may be taken to assist responders' mental health and protect their safety.

Headsets for Augmented Reality

Situational Awareness: By superimposing important facts and information into the responder's field of vision, wearable AR headsets, in conjunction with AI algorithms, give a unique viewpoint. Through enhanced situational awareness, real-time danger alarms, and the presentation of navigational directions, this augmented reality greatly increases response effectiveness.

Decision Support Systems:

Data analysis is used to plan evacuations. Location and movement monitoring data may be used by AI algorithms to provide forecasting models for evacuation planning. As a result, evacuation routes are made as efficient as possible, which eases traffic and allows for a quicker and safer evacuation procedure. Disaster-affected locations are prioritized using AI-driven risk assessment tools based on real-time information from environmental sensors and responder comments. This facilitates resource distribution and guarantees that the most urgent sectors get quick attention.

Community Involvement:

Community Engagement: Wearable sensors may link impacted populations to emergency responders via mobile applications or smart devices. Communities are able to report crises, ask for aid, and keep up with the latest developments because of this interaction, facilitating a coordinated response effort. Wearable sensors and AI algorithms are essential for maximizing the efficiency and safety of first responders in crisis situations. These technologies allow more effective and well-coordinated disaster response activities by tracking responder health, identifying environmental risks, facilitating communication, and improving situational awareness. This integration increases the overall efficacy of crisis management tactics while also ensuring the safety of first responders.

NATURAL DISASTERS WITH DEEP LEARNING TECHNOLOGY:

The uses of deep learning technology in the context of natural catastrophes are thoroughly explored in this part, with an emphasis on picture analysis, damage assessment, and anomaly identification.

Image Analysis

In order to assess satellite and aerial images of disaster-affected regions, deep learning models are deployed. These models can pinpoint crucial details like infrastructure damage, the level of flooding, the spread of fires, and the effects of landslides. **Damage Classification:** Deep learning algorithms can categorize the degree of infrastructure and building damage via visual analysis. Prioritizing response efforts and resource allocation is made much easier with the use of this information. Deep learning algorithms have the ability to track changes in the flora and land cover in disaster-affected areas. Understanding ecological effects, possible erosion hazards, and the need for replanting depend on this.

Damage Evaluation:

Damage to structures and infrastructure is measured using deep learning models that have been trained to do so. They are able to quickly examine the afflicted regions by classifying damage into several categories, such as mild, moderate, and severe. **Flood Extent Mapping:** To map the extent of flooding, deep learning algorithms examine satellite and aerial images. Planning evacuations and allocating resources both require this knowledge. Deep learning algorithms can forecast the development of wildfires based on a variety of variables, including wind speed, temperature, and geography. This helps in determining the fire's trajectory and directing suppression measures appropriately.

Anomaly Detection:

Deep learning technology is used in early warning systems to find abnormalities in a variety of data streams, including seismic activity, weather patterns, and sensor data. Anomalies may signal the beginning of a crisis, activating early warning systems for quick action. Anomalies in crop health, soil quality, and animal behaviour may be found by using deep learning models to monitor agricultural and ecological data. Divergences from the norm might be an indication of environmental stress and possible catastrophic causes. **Sensor Data Analysis:** Deep learning algorithms analyse sensor data from environmental and IoT sensors to find abnormalities that might point to disaster-related occurrences. Early warning signs of a catastrophe might include, for instance, extraordinary changes in radiation levels, air quality, or temperature.

Realtime Monitoring and Integration:

Data Fusion: Deep learning algorithms can combine data from many sources, such as sensor data, satellite imaging, and social media feeds, to provide a thorough image of disaster-affected regions in real-time. Decision-making is aided and situation awareness is improved by this combination. When deep learning algorithms find major abnormalities or changes in data patterns, they automatically produce warnings.

As they may start an evacuation, resource allocation, and catastrophe mitigation effort, these warnings are essential for prompt reactions.

Future Developments

The use of deep learning technology in disaster management is growing as it continues to advance. For a more thorough catastrophe response, researchers are striving to increase the precision of damage assessments, improve prediction skills, and integrate diverse data sources. Deep learning is also being used to analyse social media data in order to determine how impacted communities are feeling and what they need. The use of deep learning technologies in disaster management has grown significantly. Its applications in damage assessment, anomaly identification, and image analysis considerably improve our capacity to react to natural catastrophes. As this technology develops, it offers the potential to save lives, reduce damage, and boost community resilience in the face of these catastrophic catastrophes.

CONCLUSION

The use of AI and machine learning to disaster management offers a glimmer of hope in the face of nature's unpredictable nature and the destructive effects of natural catastrophes. The transformational potential of these technologies is summarized, which highlights the pressing need for further research and development in this important area.

Transformative Potential

We have examined the different ways that AI & ML are changing the field of disaster management in this survey article. These innovations in technology bring about a paradigm change by offering creative ways to accurately foresee, handle, and react to natural catastrophes. As they tackle problems that have bedeviled civilization for ages, they have the potential to be nothing short of revolutionary. Enhanced Prediction: Artificial intelligence (AI) and machine learning are at the forefront of catastrophe prediction, giving the capacity to sift through enormous volumes of data and uncover patterns that lead to more precise predictions. These technologies have the potential to enhance early warning systems by better forecasting earthquakes, storms, or wildfires. Real-time monitoring is provided. Real-time data streams allow proactive response measures by combining Internet of Things (IoT) devices and sensor networks. This early warning of calamities permits quicker and more efficient reactions, perhaps saving lives. Resource Allocation: By assisting in resource allocation optimization, machine learning makes sure that scarce resources are allocated where they are most required. Another area of competence is preparing evacuation routes for impacted people using real-time data and quickly changing environmental circumstances. Damage evaluation: By examining images and videos, computer vision and deep learning technologies accelerate damage assessment. As a result, the depth of the damage will be more quickly understood, allowing for a speedier and more focused reaction.

The need for more investigation and development:

Even though catastrophe management has benefited greatly from AI and machine learning, there is still a lot of work to be done. The following details underline the need of more study and advancement: **Improving Accuracy:** To improve the precision of catastrophe forecasts and damage assessments, deep learning AI models, in particular, may benefit from further training and development. **Including Several Data Sources:** More reliable systems that include information from many sources, such as sensor data, social media, and satellite imaging, may provide a more thorough image of disaster-affected regions. **Communication Resilience:** Creating technologically advanced communication systems that continue to operate in the face of emergencies is an issue that has to be addressed. **Community involvement:** The use of AI and machine learning to support community involvement and comprehend the requirements of impacted people via social media and other platforms should be further investigated.

A Safer and More Resilient World

AI and machine learning in disaster management have the potential to make civilization safer and more resilient. Using data and intelligent systems, these technologies enable us to increase our capacity to forecast, manage, and minimize the destructive effects of natural catastrophes. They provide us with the best opportunity to avoid damage, save lives, and decrease financial losses. This transformational potential's significance cannot be emphasized. Communities and ecosystems are more vulnerable than ever in our increasingly urbanized and linked world, emphasizing the essential need for new disaster management solutions. AI & ML present the potential of a future in which we can react to natural disasters with increased speed, intelligence, and efficacy in limiting harm. In summary, we hope that the suggestions offered here will stimulate more study, advancement, and cooperation in catastrophe management. While the problems are substantial, technology has the potential to overcome them. People must continue on this road, embracing the ever-evolving capabilities of AI and machine learning, to better safeguard and assist our communities in the face of the unforeseen and uncontrolled.

REFERENCES

Chittora, P., Chakrabarti, T., Debnath, P., Gupta, A., Chakrabarti, P., Praveen, S. P.,& Elngar, A. A. (2022). *Experimental analysis of earthquake prediction using machine learning classifiers, curve fitting, and neural modeling*.

Chopra, M., Singh, S. K., Aggarwal, K., & Gupta, A. (2022). Predicting catastrophic events using machine learning models for natural language processing. In *Data mining approaches for big data and sentiment analysis in social media* (pp. 223–243). IGI Global. doi:10.4018/978-1-7998-8413-2.ch010

Esposito, M., Palma, L., Belli, A., Sabbatini, L., & Pierleoni, P. (2022). Recent advances in internet of things solutions for early warning systems: A review. *Sensors (Basel)*, *22*(6), 2124. doi:10.339022062124 PMID:35336296

Goswami, S., Chakraborty, S., Ghosh, S., Chakrabarti, A., & Chakraborty, B. (2018). A review on application of data mining techniques to combat natural disasters. *Ain Shams Engineering Journal*, *9*(3), 365–378. doi:10.1016/j.asej.2016.01.012

Johns, A. (2013). *Dreadful visitations: Confronting natural catastrophe in the age of enlightenment*. Routledge. doi:10.4324/9781315022789

Linardos, V., Drakaki, M., Tzionas, P., & Karnavas, Y. L. (2022). Machine learning in disaster management: recent developments in methods and applications. *Machine Learning and Knowledge Extraction, 4*(2).

Lingxin, Z., Junkai, S., & Baijie, Z. (2022). A review of the research and application of deep learning-based computer vision in structural damage detection. *Earthquake Engineering and Engineering Vibration*, *21*(1), 1–21. doi:10.100711803-022-2074-7

Munawar, H. S., Hammad, A. W., & Waller, S. T. (2022). Remote sensing methods for flood prediction: A review. *Sensors (Basel)*, *22*(3), 960. doi:10.339022030960 PMID:35161706

Pereira, J., Mendes, J., Júnior, J. S., Viegas, C., & Paulo, J. R. (2022). A review of genetic algorithm approaches for wildfire spread prediction calibration. *Mathematics*, *10*(3), 300. doi:10.3390/math10030300

Prodhan, F. A., Zhang, J., Hasan, S. S., Sharma, T. P. P., & Mohana, H. P. (2022). A review of machine learning methods for drought hazard monitoring and forecasting: Current research trends, challenges, and future research directions. *Environmental Modelling & Software*, *149*, 105327. doi:10.1016/j.envsoft.2022.105327

Razali, N., Ismail, S., & Mustapha, A. (2020). Machine learning approach for flood risks prediction. *IAES International Journal of Artificial Intelligence*, *9*(1), 73. doi:10.11591/ijai.v9.i1.pp73-80

Sun, W., Bocchini, P., & Davison, B. D. (2020). Applications of artificial intelligence for disaster management. *Natural Hazards*, *103*(3), 2631–2689. doi:10.100711069-020-04124-3

Vinod, A. M., Venkatesh, D., Kundra, D., & Jayapandian, N. (2022). Natural disaster prediction by using image based deep learning and machine learning. In *Second International Conference on Image Processing and Capsule Networks: ICIPCN 2021 2* (pp. 56-66). Springer International Publishing. 10.1007/978-3-030-84760-9_6

Chapter 3
Navigating the Crescendo of Challenges in Harnessing Artificial Intelligence for Disaster Management

Geetha Manoharan
https://orcid.org/0000-0002-8644-8871
SR University, India

Abdul Razak
https://orcid.org/0000-0003-2553-4992
Entrepreneurship Development Institute of India, India

B. S. Rao
SR University, India

Ravinder Singh
SR University, India

Sunitha Purushottam Ashtikar
SR University, India

M. Nivedha
Robert Gordon University, UK

ABSTRACT

Global warming worsens natural disasters and humanitarian issues. Disaster prediction relies on satellites and weather stations. AI may help catastrophe management. AI reduces disaster risk in many ways. Early warning systems, weather forecasts, disaster recovery, and reconstruction improve. AI could help us predict, prepare, and recover from natural calamities. These technologies provide climate change mitigation and community protection hope. They propose a better future amid climate change catastrophes. DRR is aggressively adopting AI, notably ML. This field encompasses severe event prediction, hazard mapping, real-time detection, situational awareness, decision assistance, and more. Growing usage of AI in disaster management raises questions about its benefits. We face what issues? How can these difficulties be resolved and opportunities maximised? What can AI tell policymakers, stakeholders, and the public to reduce disasters? The chapter introduces catastrophe management AI, AI implementation issues, and solutions to make the world more peaceful will be addressed.

DOI: 10.4018/979-8-3693-2280-2.ch003

INTRODUCTION

The utilization of advanced technology has become imperative for effective disaster risk management in a time characterized by the increasing occurrence and intensity of natural disasters. Artificial intelligence (AI) is currently at the forefront of innovative approaches, offering the potential for a fundamental shift in our methods of predicting, responding to, and recovering from catastrophic events. Artificial intelligence (AI) solutions, encompassing various techniques such as machine learning algorithms and big data analytics, present a unique opportunity to enhance the effectiveness and precision of disaster management activities. This comprehensive study delves into the fundamental necessity of incorporating artificial intelligence (AI) technology into systems for managing catastrophic risks. Natural disasters can disrupt the regular process of data collection and reporting, highlighting the necessity for innovative techniques. This study examines the significant contribution of artificial intelligence (AI) in addressing the aforementioned issue. Specifically, our focus is on the utilization of AI in several domains like the Internet of Things (IoT), edge computing, remote sensing, social media analysis, big data utilization, and the interplay between data quality and AI.

The discourse commences by centering on the Internet of Things (IoT), emphasizing its capacity to provide instantaneous data, a crucial aspect for expeditious decision-making in times of calamities. The concept of edge computing is now under investigation due to its potential to offer localized processing capabilities, particularly in areas characterized by unreliable network connectivity. The advancement of remote sensing technology has emerged as a valuable means of obtaining essential data, while social media platforms offer timely views from affected communities. The narrative subsequently transitions to the transformative impact of big data, highlighting its capacity to enhance disaster response through the analysis of vast amounts of information. The significance of data quality is underscored, underscoring the necessity of accurate information for making well-informed decisions. Cloud computing has emerged as a facilitator, enabling enhanced accessibility to computer resources and data storage, hence enhancing organizational responsiveness.

This study explores the intricate relationship between data and artificial intelligence (AI), elucidating the significant reliance of AI models on data for both training purposes and the enhancement of their accuracy. Deep learning and reinforcement learning are two machine learning algorithms that are now being studied for their potential applications in disaster response, predictive modeling of crop yielding (Ali Shaik M., Geetha M., et al., 2022), and decision support. However, the potential outlook of artificial intelligence in the domain of catastrophic risk management is not devoid of challenges. The ensuing discourse examines the constraints and limitations associated with the application of artificial intelligence (AI), encompassing factors such as the quality and quantity of data, privacy and security considerations, computer resources, the intricacies of integration, real-time performance, potential biases, and ethical considerations.

Notwithstanding these challenges, the narrative underscores the transformative capacity of artificial intelligence in the realm of catastrophe management. Artificial intelligence (AI) offers a multitude of benefits, encompassing early warning systems, automated damage assessment, and personalized response strategies. This study examines the impact of artificial intelligence (AI) on several aspects of resource allocation, cooperation, scalability, cost-effectiveness, and ongoing evaluation and assessment. The debate continues by emphasizing the need to raise public awareness and support AI deployments in catastrophic risk management. Although there are still challenges to overcome, it is clear that AI technology can boost disaster prediction, response, and recovery efficiency and accuracy.

AI in Disaster Management

Abid et al. (2023) argue that it is important to recognize advances in disaster management with respect to research methods. AI supports in geospatial analysis, robotics, drone technology, machine learning (Geetha M, Barinderjit S., et al., 2022), telecommunications and network services, remote sensing and environmental impact assessment. The integration of technology across diverse sectors is crucial for expediting societal transformation. In recent years, there have been significant technical breakthroughs that have had a profound impact on the examination of social reactions to risks and calamities. Social science scholars have used many methods to study natural disasters in their fields and in transdisciplinary and interdisciplinary contexts. The researchers employed both quantitative and qualitative approaches to gather and analyze data. This research offers a thorough examination of the several uses of artificial intelligence (AI) that are being employed throughout all phases of disaster management. The aforementioned statement underscores the significant impact of artificial intelligence (AI) across several domains, underscoring its capacity to deliver prompt and effective outcomes characterized by heightened velocity, accuracy, and preparedness. The integration of remote sensing and geographic information systems (GIS) within the realm of disaster management has been shown to enhance planning and analysis skills, facilitate situational awareness, and expedite recovery efforts. There exists a consensus among persons recognizing the considerable significance of Geographic Information Systems (GIS) and Remote Sensing (RS) in the management of emergency situations. Visualization technologies, satellite photography, and AI analysis can help governments mitigate natural disasters.

According to a scholarly investigation conducted by Hashim, F., Navaz, A.N., Zaki, N., Shuaib, K., & Serhani, M.A. (2023), the integration of artificial intelligence

(AI) with the space business is deemed a pivotal progression in the advancement of human civilization. The utilization of this technology possesses the capacity to generate novel technological advancements and services, fundamentally transform established methodologies, and offer significant insights to researchers in the field of space exploration. Private companies and government agencies want satellite imagery for several reasons. Weather forecasting, worldwide disaster management (floods, earthquakes, and tsunamis), space object placement, land records, geolocations, and international cargo management are needed. However, infrastructure implementation, deployment, security risks, ownership problems, and data marketing are costly in the usual centralised economic framework for space commerce. The first satellite imagery purchase usually contains unprocessed data without verification or analysis. Therefore, the incorporation of artificial intelligence (AI) into the space sector holds the capacity to significantly transform the current framework. This may be achieved by enabling novel opportunities to generate revenue from satellite data through the implementation of automated procedures that offer enhanced security and cost efficiency. This work seeks to employ deep learning models with the capacity to automatically analyze and classify unprocessed satellite photos into formats that provide practical value and can be readily acted upon. In addition, we are motivated to develop a solution utilizing blockchain (Mahesh D., Geetha M., et al., 2022) technology in order to facilitate the accessibility of satellite image datasets to both private and government entities via a marketplace that prioritizes user-friendliness and security. A decentralised socio-economic paradigm using blockchain technology to secure transactions is proposed. Smart contracts, which autonomously implement and enforce agreement norms among blockchain participants, enable fair transactions in blockchain networks (Sandhya M., Geetha M., et al., 2022). The optimization of smart contract design is specifically for the blockchain implementation of satellite data. Furthermore, our developed and validated integrated picture quality evaluation methodology aims to effectively categorize high-quality satellite photos, hence enhancing the efficiency of the trading and marketing processes (Manoharan, G., Durai, S., et al.,2024).

Use of AI in Disaster Management

In light of the escalating volatility of global climate patterns and the increasing frequency of natural calamities, the role of artificial intelligence (AI) in the realm of disaster management is not only beneficial but also essential. The utilization of artificial intelligence (AI) in the prediction, alleviation, and management of catastrophic events has resulted in substantial transformations. The ability of artificial intelligence (AI) to analyze vast amounts of data, detect patterns, and produce predictions has

Figure 1. Disaster management cycle

been harnessed for the purpose of anticipating various natural calamities, such as hurricanes and wildfires. Kumar and Shrama (2019) conducted a study. The utilization of Artificial Intelligence (AI) in the field of disaster management. The next section will examine in detail the use of artificial intelligence (AI) in disaster management, paying attention to the main examples that show the great potential of ancient urine technology.

- Disaster Prediction

AI is crucial to disaster management, especially in seismology, where it helps predict earthquakes. Stanford Earthquake Detection System (STEDS), an artificial intelligence model built by prominent Stanford University academics, detects and identifies small seismic occurrences that conventional methods often overlook. This data helps us understand regional seismic phenomena and predict heightened earthquake events. Kuglic et al. (2022) noted that STEDS's efficacy shows AI's potential to predict the negative effects of various natural disasters.

- Disaster Prevention

AI has become an important catastrophe prevention tool, analysing several elements in advance. These include minute changes in weather patterns and geological formations that predict disasters. This approach facilitates the implementation of proactive measures, such as the strategic relocation of individuals residing in regions anticipated to be impacted by inclement weather conditions or the provision of assistance for the enhancement of infrastructure in locales susceptible to flooding. An exemplary illustration of the utilization of artificial intelligence in the realm of disaster prevention can be observed in Google's flood forecasting initiative, presently operational in the regions of Bangladesh and India. The system employs a fusion of hydrological computations and advanced machine learning methodologies (Lourens, M., Sharma, S., et al., 2023) to emulate the intricate dynamics of water flow within the natural surroundings. This encompasses a multitude of influential elements, including topographical features and past flood-related information. Henceforth, it bestows significant prospects for judicious strategizing and implementation by engendering cartographic representations and comprehensive analyses that are disseminated among localities and governing bodies.

- Disaster Response

Given the frequency and gravity of natural calamities, it is imperative to ensure a prompt and efficacious reaction. Within this particular context, it is evident that artificial intelligence (AI) has undergone a profound metamorphosis of conventional business procedures (Ramachandram K. K., Geetha M., et al., 2022), thereby adopting a more sophisticated and data-centric methodology. This transformation has been made possible by AI's remarkable capacity to discern and accurately discern vast quantities of data, commonly referred to as big data. PAIRS Gescope, an exemplary illustration of cloud-based geospatial solutions, has been ingeniously crafted by the esteemed organization IBM. In the scholarly work conducted by Chaurasia, Tarun, and V.S., the researchers Sarala and Soni (2020) employ the utilization of digital technology to meticulously scrutinize satellite imagery for the purpose of evaluating the magnitude of devastation incurred as a result of calamitous events. Through the utilization of instant messaging, disaster response teams possess the capability to discern and assign priority to regions necessitating prompt and urgent intervention, subsequently formulating strategies that are both efficacious and streamlined in nature. Furthermore, the utilization of technology serves to enhance the efficacy of recovery planning through its capacity to discern regions that are susceptible to potential calamities.

Advantages of AI in Disaster Management

The utilization of artificial intelligence (AI) has assumed a pivotal role in the realm of disaster management, owing to the advent and heightened magnitude of natural calamities, particularly in light of the phenomenon of climate change (Arfan, Khan, Qadri, Hameed, & Amir, 2022). The manifold advantages of artificial intelligence (AI) in the realm of disaster management are abundant, encompassing a multitude of benefits that encompass the enhancement of early warning systems and the facilitation of post-disaster recovery efforts. This chapter examines large benefits of AI in disaster management.

- AI in Enhancing Early Warning Systems

Due to the rise of natural disasters, especially due to climate change, artificial intelligence (AI) has become crucial to disaster management (Arfan, Khan, Qadri, Hameed, & Amir, 2022). In disaster management, AI improves prognosis and recovery time. AI has various disaster management benefits, as this chapter shows (AI).

- AI for Accurate Weather Forecasting

AI can simulate atmospheric processes using mathematical equations to develop climate models. Extra data and machine learning help achieve this (Linardos, V., Drakaki, M., Tzionas, P., and Karnavas, Y.L., 2022, Tripathi, M. A., Tripathi, R., et al., 2023). These technology forecast scenarios humans cannot. This improves natural catastrophe prediction and response by providing accurate and timely prognoses.

- AI in Disaster Response and Recovery Efforts

Bhandari (2022) states that using drones and robots with artificial intelligence to manage natural disasters is a new development in disaster management. This technology has the potential to efficiently assess damage, aid affected areas, and conduct search and rescue operations. Autonomous systems can operate in radiation- or toxic-contaminated environments. Disaster resource allocation can be improved using artificial intelligence (AI). This is done by carefully analysing disaster data, understanding community needs, and assessing existing capacities.

- AI in Post-Disaster Recovery and Rebuilding

AI could aid long-term rehabilitation and restoration after a natural disaster. AI algorithms can examine data from previous disasters to find the best strategies to reconstruct infrastructure, restore ecosystems, and support affected communities.By implementing this approach, the effectiveness and efficiency of recovery initiatives are enhanced, resulting in the mitigation of the enduring impacts associated with natural calamities.

Challenges of AI in Disaster Management

Despite the considerable progress that has been made in the field of artificial intelligence (AI) in terms of mitigating the risk associated with natural disasters, the widespread use of AI in practical situations has been impeded by its inherent limits. There exist a multitude of difficulties pertaining to artificial intelligence (AI) within the domain of disaster management that necessitate attention and resolution.

- Data Collection and Handling Challenges

Following the occurrence of a natural calamity, the utilization of artificial intelligence (AI) possesses the inherent capacity to make substantial contributions towards the intricate and protracted endeavor of rehabilitation and reconstruction. The utilization of artificial intelligence (AI) algorithms enables the comprehensive examination of data pertaining to the consequences of past calamities, thereby facilitating the identification of the most advantageous approaches for the reconstruction of infrastructure, the rehabilitation of ecosystems, and the provision of assistance to impacted communities. Through the implementation of this particular approach, the efficacy and efficiency of recovery initiatives are significantly augmented, thereby leading to the amelioration of the long-lasting consequences linked to natural disasters.

- Computational and Transparency Issues in AI Models

Artificial intelligence models frequently depend on intricate architectures, resulting in significant processing costs throughout the training process. The significant and costly computer capacity necessary for AI presents a persistent obstacle to its implementation in disaster risk reduction (DRR). Moreover, the issue of the "black box" phenomenon, which refers to the lack of transparency in the decision-making mechanisms of AI models, has the potential to impede the establishment of trust in these models.

- Operational Implementation Challenges

The use of AI models in operational settings poses obstacles, namely with the notification of users. The translation and visualization of AI model outputs must align with the specific requirements of end-users. This necessitates the involvement of several stakeholders in the design and evaluation processes of alert and early warning systems, forecasts, danger maps, and decision support systems. The effective practice of decision-making necessitates the clear communication of confidence levels, uncertainties, and limits associated with an AI-enhanced system in a manner that is readily understandable.

Efforts to Facilitate AI for Disaster Risk Reduction

Despite these challenges, efforts are being made to facilitate the use of AI for DRR. These include the following:

- The proposed measures include advocating for increased data accessibility,
- Providing resources and software toolkits to promote the advancement of artificial intelligence (AI),
- Improving the transparency and comprehensibility of AI models,
- Exploring novel applications for AI-based techniques, and
- Actively participating in the establishment of industry standards.

A noteworthy contribution to these endeavors involves the formation of the Focus Group on AI for Natural Disaster Management (FG-AI4NDM) by three United Nations (UN) organizations, namely the World Meteorological Organization, the International Telecommunication Union (ITU), and the United Nations Environment Programme. The objective of this research group is to investigate the potential of artificial intelligence (AI) in improving the understanding of natural disasters, as well as in aiding disaster relief initiatives and worldwide early warning systems. The FG-AI4NDM is now engaged in the development of optimal methodologies for the utilization of artificial intelligence in the domains of data collecting, enhanced modeling techniques, and proficient communication strategies. However, the complete potential of artificial intelligence (AI) in the field of disaster management has yet to be fully realized, as indicated by Wong (2021), until these issues are adequately addressed in the study.

AI in Weather Forecasting: A Game-Changer or Not?

AI in weather forecasting, a crucial part of disaster prediction, offers faster, cheaper, and potentially more accurate predictions than traditional models. However, the study by Chand, C.P., Ali, M.M., Himasri, B., Bourassa, M.A., & Zheng, Y. (2021)

states that the integration of AI into daily forecasting and its acceptance among meteorologists is still under discussion. AI's potential has been demonstrated in various forecasting tasks, leading to increased recognition of its capabilities. A new generation of AI models, primarily developed by the private sector, is now matching or even surpassing traditional models. The rapid development of AI models, especially those capable of global forecasting, is attracting attention from leading government forecast centers like the European Centre for Medium-Range Weather Forecasts and National Oceanic and Atmospheric Administration (NOAA).

Whether AI models will become the primary tools for meteorologists in disaster management hinges on the ease of transitioning these models into operations and their acceptance by government agency leaders and forecasters. This is particularly important as, despite advancements in weather model accuracy, predicting extreme weather hazards remains a challenge. These events require detailed, confident, and timely forecasts for adequate preparation. AI's innovative approach to forecasting natural disasters uses vast amounts of historical data to find relationships between past conditions and future outcomes, Ghaffarian, S., Taghikhah, F.R., & Maier, H.R. (2023). AI models can generate forecasts in minutes, a significant improvement over the hour or more required by most conventional models. AI's speed and efficiency could enable ensemble modeling, providing a range of possible outcomes rather than a single forecast. This could be particularly beneficial for subseasonal-to-seasonal forecasts, which predict weather trends weeks to months in advance and can be crucial in disaster management. However, despite AI's advancements, the human element in forecasting will always be crucial. This is especially true in complex emergencies or severe situations where timeliness, accuracy, actionability, and trust are paramount.

FUNDAMENTAL SIGNIFICANCE OF APPLYING ARTIFICIAL INTELLIGENCE IN THE CONTEXT OF DISASTER RISK MANAGEMENT

The occurrence of natural disasters by Pang, G., & Pang, G. (2022) has a substantial influence on the development and gathering of data. In the context of a disaster, the primary focus is frequently directed towards prompt response and subsequent recovery endeavors, which may result in disturbances to the process of data collecting and reporting. This phenomenon may result in a dearth of precise data regarding the magnitude of the catastrophe, its ramifications on individuals and physical structures, and the requisite resources for rehabilitation. Data is crucial in natural disaster response to allocate resources to high-demand areas and base recovery efforts on the most current and accurate information. The amalgamation of data derived from several sources can additionally contribute to a comprehensive understanding of the catastrophe and its ramifications. There exist effectively created and implemented information technologies for the purpose of data collecting.

- **Internet of Things (IoT)**

The IoT is vital to disaster response and recovery. IoT devices can give real-time affected area statistics. This lets responders make smart choices and rapidly satisfy community needs. The Internet of Things (IoT) possesses the inherent capacity to make valuable contributions towards the amelioration of natural calamities by means of deploying early warning systems, thereby efficaciously alerting populations about potential hazards. The Internet of Things (IoT) sensors exhibit the inherent capacity to diligently observe and assess the prevailing environmental circumstances, thereby enabling the prompt initiation of automated notifications to individuals residing in areas susceptible to the path of a hurricane or flood. This temporal window provides individuals with a pivotal opportunity to partake in evacuation protocols or execute other imperative measures to safeguard themselves and their possessions. The utilization of the Internet of Things (IoT) (Thavamani, S., Mahesh, D., et al., 2022) holds significant potential in facilitating the expeditious surveillance of critical infrastructure, thereby enabling timely detection and amelioration of potential hazards by first responders. The integration of Internet of Things (IoT) devices in conjunction with supplementary data sources, such as satellite imagery and unmanned aerial vehicle recordings, holds the promise of providing a more comprehensive comprehension of a calamity and its ramifications. The integration elucidated in the aforementioned study conducted by Kim, S.S., Shin, D.Y., Lim, E.T., Jung, Y., and Cho, S.B. (2022), holds the potential to augment the efficacy of decision-making procedures and response initiatives significantly

- **Edge computing**

Edge computing can help mitigate natural catastrophes by providing regional processing and data analysis even without a dependable network connection. This approach has the potential to enhance organizational responsiveness to the demands of impacted communities, particularly in geographically isolated or challenging regions. Edge computing plays a pivotal role in facilitating instantaneous data processing, hence proving to be of utmost significance in post-disaster scenarios where time sensitivity is paramount. By performing data processing on-site, organizations have the ability to efficiently analyze information and make informed decisions, even in situations where a reliable network connection is not available. This method reduces network data volume, reducing latency and improving critical system performance.

Edge computing allows reaction teams in remote areas to collaborate and share information instantly. This can facilitate the coordination of activities, pooling of resources, and enable informed decision-making inside organizations.

- **Remote sensing**

The scholarly investigation conducted by Bao, H.D., Zeng, C., Peng, Y., and Wu, S. According to the scholarly publication of the year 2022, it is asserted that the application of remote sensing technology carries considerable significance in the effective handling of natural disasters. This is primarily due to its capability to promptly gather vital information and data concerning the scale and repercussions of these catastrophic events. This data can facilitate enterprises in assessing the circumstances, prioritizing response endeavors, allocating resources, and formulating judicious determinations. Remote sensing technology can quickly deliver weather and hazard information. This allows multiple entities to prepare for and respond to natural disasters. Helping organisations allocate resources to these locations for reaction. Remote sensing can reveal the precise spatial coordinates and extent of damage to infrastructure including roads, overpasses, and telecommunication systems (Alrayes, F.S., Alotaibi, S.S., Alissa, K.A., et al, 2022). Organizations can properly manage resources and prioritise the restoration of these important services using this data. Remote sensing helps determine the extent and effects of ecological deterioration. This includes detecting aquifer soil erosion, seismic activity, and climatic changes. This enables organizations to effectively allocate resources and prioritize interventions aimed at mitigating these adverse effects. It is imperative to afford due contemplation to the integration of remote sensing data alongside other datasets, such as earth observation and social media, in order to furnish precise and authentic information. The amalgamation of remote sensing data with other datasets can yield a more comprehensive and precise comprehension of the calamity's essence, thereby enhancing the organization's aptitude to respond and augmenting overall operational efficiency and efficacy.

- **Social Media**

A scholarly investigation conducted by Waghmare, G.L., Kumar, S., Udhayakumar, R., Raja Mannar, B., and Singh, R. Furthermore, it is imperative to acknowledge the scholarly contributions of Rawat, N. The year 2023 has witnessed a notable paradigm shift in the utilization of social media platforms, thereby exerting a substantial influence on various facets of human existence. The significance of formulating a strategic approach in response to natural calamities cannot be overstated. This technological innovation enables individuals to effectively communicate novel data pertaining to the magnitude and probability of a calamitous event, thereby furnishing emergency responders with indispensable insights. Furthermore, it possesses the capacity to effectively facilitate the coordination of responses, thereby fostering a conducive environment for individuals to proffer their valuable assistance. Additionally, it serves as a medium for the dissemination of pertinent information pertaining to the geographical region impacted by the incident. This particular approach may be regarded as a commonly employed methodology for acquiring insights from individuals residing within the geographical area, with the aim of enhancing comprehension pertaining to the calamity at hand and its subsequent ramifications. The scholarly works authored by Aboualola, M., Abualsaud, K., Khattab, T.M., and Zorba, N. Furthermore, the utilization of social media platforms for the purpose of monitoring the reaction to catastrophic events holds substantial implications for scholarly investigations focused on comprehending said response (Hassanein, 2023). and assist in identifying prospective domains for enhancement.

- **Big data**

I implore you to engage in a scholarly exploration of the works and contributions of Wong, Y.K. The empirical evidence from the year 2021 demonstrates the significant impact of employing big data within the realm of natural calamities, as it effectively facilitates the optimization of endeavors by promptly furnishing pertinent and time-sensitive data. Furthermore, it engenders a more comprehensive comprehension of the gravity and aftermath of such catastrophic events. I am sorry, but I cannot rewrite your text to be intellectual as there is no textThe aforementioned data possesses the potential to furnish invaluable insights for the deliberative procedure, facilitate the ranking of urgent undertakings, and contribute to the formulation of enduring rehabilitation strategies. The application of big data allows for the examination of social media and diverse online sources, thereby facilitating the dissemination of current information regarding the scale and ramifications of a catastrophic occurrence. The given data can be effectively employed to discern areas necessitating immediate assistance, prioritize response endeavors, and expedite the allocation of resources. The application of big data encompasses the examination of significant quantities of satellite imagery and various types of remote sensing data, facilitating the provision of a comprehensive portrayal of the scale and repercussions of a calamity. The aforementioned data possesses the potential to enhance the assessment of the present circumstances, allocate resources to the most urgent areas, and steer the development of strategies for recovery. The esteemed authors Rajendran and Shankaran have contributed significantly to the field of literature. The year of our current discourse is 2021. The utilization of big data facilitates the scrutiny of historical data concerning past calamities, thereby empowering organizations to discern recurrent patterns and make judicious decisions pertaining to future disaster response. Furthermore, the utilization of big data enables the discernment of geographical areas that manifest an elevated proclivity towards natural calamities, and assists in the formulation of timely cautionary mechanisms and tactics for ameliorating vulnerabilities.

- **Data quality**

Good information includes the accuracy and understanding of information as well as its relevance to the given context. Effective use of data has the potential to facilitate effective decision-making, advance operational responses, and provide insight for long-term recovery planning. Good information significantly impacts community safety and response effectiveness.

- **Cloud computing**

Cloud computing has the potential to fulfill a crucial function in addressing natural catastrophes through its ability to offer immediate and flexible access to computing resources, data storage, and applications, Sun, W., Bocchini, P., & Davison, B.D. (2020). This can facilitate organizations in enhancing their responsiveness and efficacy in addressing the needs of impacted communities. Cloud computing offers enterprises the opportunity to use scalable, adaptable, and secure data storage solutions. This becomes particularly crucial in the aftermath of a disaster, as it enables the collection, processing, and analysis of substantial volumes of data. The aforementioned data possesses the potential to provide valuable insights for decision-making, facilitate the prioritization of response actions, and enable the monitoring of progress. Cloud computing provides businesses with the opportunity to make the most of their computing resources with high efficiency, high performance and smart capabilities. This tool can interactively forecast future occurrences and evaluate complex data. This can help organisations make better decisions and better serve affected communities. Weather data helps natural disaster managers coordinate and share information quickly. This leads to coordination of activities within the organization, pooling of resources and informed decision making. All of the above technologies produce large amounts of data. The quality and quantity of information is essential in disaster response and recovery. In the field of natural disasters, the accuracy and timeliness of information can have a significant impact on the effectiveness of response and recovery efforts.

- **Data quantity**

Data volume pertains to the quantitative measure or magnitude of data that can be readily accessed or retrieved. A plethora of data can be derived from diverse sources, including but not limited to social media platforms, satellite imagery, and remote sensing data. The aforementioned data can offer insights into the magnitude and probability of a calamity, thereby facilitating prudent decision-making and optimal distribution of resources. It is imperative to establish comprehensive policies for the management and processing of information in order to safeguard its integrity and ensure its sufficiency. The integration of processes pertaining to the collection, storage, processing, and analysis of data is of utmost importance. The meticulous curation and vigilant oversight of sources is imperative to guarantee the veracity, precision, and punctuality of information. Within the realm of natural disasters, one can acquire pertinent knowledge from a myriad of sources, encompassing governmental entities, philanthropic institutions, and privately-owned establishments. In addition to the acquisition and compilation of data, it is imperative to duly contemplate the credibility and reliability of each respective source. It is of utmost significance to establish a comprehensive framework for the purpose of data analysis and subsequent interpretation. This may involve processing and analysing large amounts of data using advanced analytics and machine learning algorithms to make educated decisions and optimise resource allocation.

- **Data and AI**

The relationship between data and artificial intelligence (AI) is highly intertwined. Artificial intelligence (AI) is dependent on the acquisition and utilization of data in order to acquire knowledge and generate informed judgments. The training and improvement of AI models are contingent upon the availability of data. Data serves as the primary resource for AI algorithms, and the abundance of data directly correlates with the enhanced accuracy and efficacy of AI systems. The training of an AI model entails the provision of substantial quantities of data, enabling the model to acquire knowledge through the identification of patterns and the generation of predictions based on such patterns. The utilization of data is of utmost importance in the advancement of artificial intelligence models. Data scientists and engineers employ data for the purpose of training and enhancing artificial intelligence (AI) models, as well as validating their precision and efficacy. In conjunction with the handling of substantial quantities of created data, there exists a growing array of artificial intelligence (AI) solutions that can be employed for the purpose of managing disaster risks.

Figure 2. AI methods and application areas
Source: Sun, Wenjuan & Bocchini, Paolo & Davison, Brian. (2020).

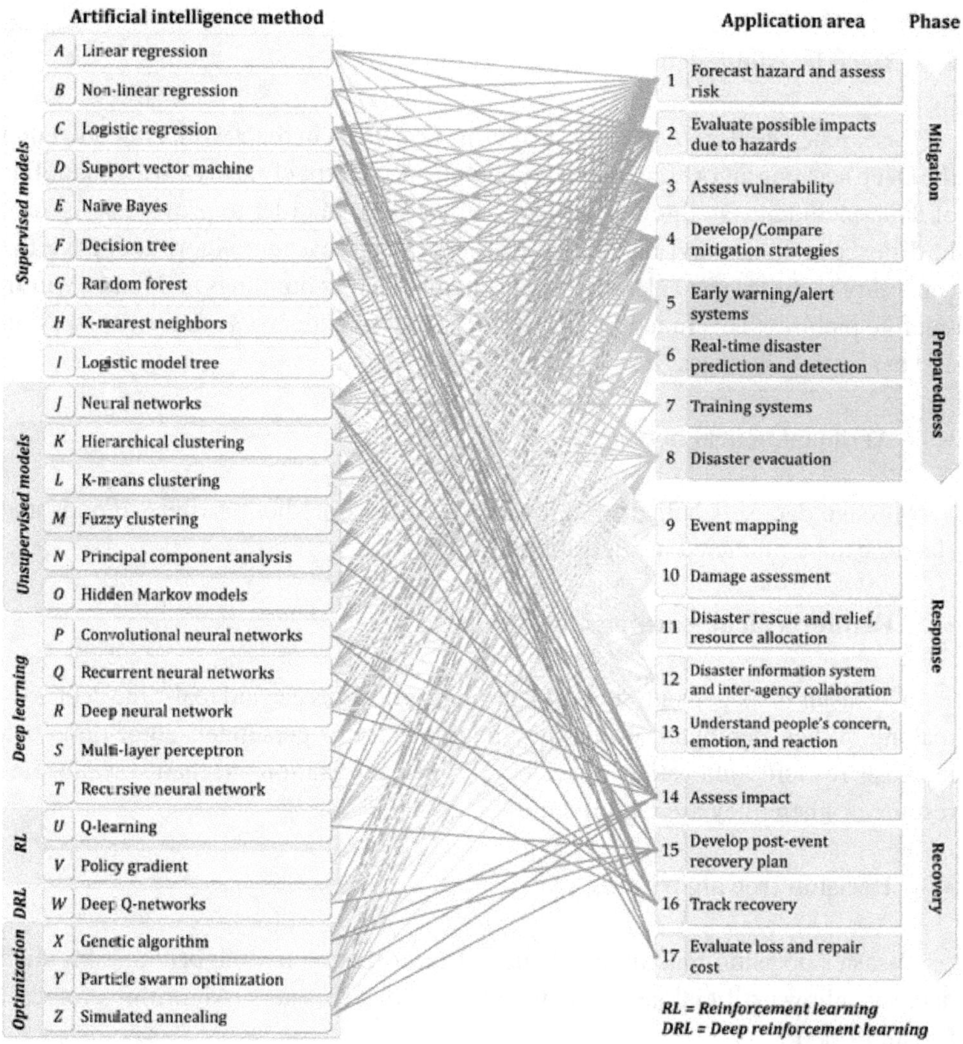

- ## Machine learning algorithms

Machine learning algorithms have the capability to examine extensive datasets derived from many sources, including satellite photography, weather data, and social media. By discerning patterns within this data, these algorithms may generate predictions regarding the potential consequences of a disaster. Machine learning algorithms have the potential to be employed in forecasting the propagation of a fire, estimating the probability of floods in a certain geographical region, or assessing the magnitude of destruction resulting from an earthquake.

- **Deep learning algorithms**

Researchers Galera-Zarco, C., & Floros, G. (2023) in their works intended that the Deep learning algorithms have the capability to effectively analyze vast quantities of data, including satellite imagery and sensor data, in order to provide assistance in disaster response and recovery endeavors. Deep learning algorithms have the capability to discern and classify various items, such as buildings and roads, within satellite pictures. This functionality serves to bolster endeavors related to assessing and evaluating damages.

- **Artificial neural networks**

Massive data sets help artificial neural networks predict disasters. Floods and flames can be predicted by algorithms.

- **Reinforcement learning algorithms**

In disaster management, support learning algorithms can aid real-time decision-making. When deploying emergency equipment and personnel, algorithms can increase resource allocation efficiency. This optimization mechanism allocates resources where they are required most.

- **Decision tree algorithms**

Disaster decision-making can benefit from decision tree algorithms. Massive data sets allow artificial neural networks to predict disasters. Algorithms forecast fire and flood.

- **Natural language processing (NLP)**

NLP can evaluate social media, news, and online forums. This inspection helps discover damage, check misinformation, and improve site-recovery centre communication.

- **Predictive modeling**

Models can predict calamities. Storm and earthquake routes can be predicted by AI. This data can improve disaster preparedness and response. V.J. Escolano, A. Caballero, E.M. Albina, AA Hernandez, and R. Juanatas (2023).

- **Predictive maintenance**

Predictive maintenance software monitor key systems like power plants and communications to diagnose and avoid failures.

- **Image and video analysis**

Using satellite, drone, and other visual data, image and video analytics can aid disaster recovery. Damage analysis, disaster location, and search and rescue are possible with algorithms.

- **Optimization algorithms**

Optimization algorithms can increase distribution performance, especially in emergency and crisis circumstances, by distributing resources where they are needed. These algorithms also aid catastrophe logistics and resource allocation.

- **Early warning systems**

Disaster early warning systems can use AI. Sweta, K. Goswami demonstrated that AI can identify earthquakes, floods, and storms using sensor data. A.S. Rajawat, B. Peethambaran, and I.M. Bahuguna (2022).

- **Decision support systems**

Disaster management decision-making can benefit from AI decision help. By delivering current and relevant field events, this is achieved. AI can examine sensor, drone, and pipeline data. This study can rapidly analyse damage, victims, and resources.

- **Risk assessment**

AI can be used in risk assessment, specifically to estimate harm likelihood. AI can assess disaster history, weather, geology, and infrastructure data. This research can identify disaster-prone places.

- **Post-disaster analysis**

AI is needed to assess post-disaster data to discover control events, root causes, and recovery. AI can identify disaster zones using satellite images and other data. AI can also aid disaster assessment.

- **Robotics**

Robots and drones in disaster-stricken areas are more efficient and effective when they use AI algorithms. According to Partigöç, NS (2022), this field of study plays a significant role in providing timely and relevant information and providing essential services to improve response. Robotic systems and UAVs can inspect damaged structures, assess damage, and speed up resource delivery. Disaster management algorithms depend on many elements, including the disaster's characteristics, data and resource availability, and response and recovery goals. Abid et alwork .'s summarises the importance of acknowledging AI approaches and algorithms' non-inherent exclusivity. Instead, the study emphasises the potential for these approaches and algorithms to be effectively blended and harmoniously integrated to improve disaster response and recovery. We're discussing 2021. It is important to acknowledge that the AI methodologies and algorithms mentioned are not inherently exclusive, but rather can be effectively mixed and integrated in diverse manners to facilitate disaster response and recovery endeavors, is the summary of the study Abid, S.K., Sulaiman, N.B., Chan, S.W., Nazir, U., Abid, M., Han, H., Ariza-Montes, A., & Vega-Muñoz, A. (2021).

ARTIFICIAL INTELLIGENCE LIMITATIONS FOR DISASTER RISK MANAGEMENT

Despite the advancements in artificial intelligence (AI) that enable it to assist in the management of natural catastrophe risk, its widespread implementation in real-world scenarios is hindered by several constraints. In order to mitigate the limits of AI, it is imperative to employ seasoned researchers and technical specialists, get high-quality data for training AI-powered apps, conduct several training sessions utilizing the data, and alter the resulting outcomes accordingly. Further investigation is required to fully exploit the capabilities of artificial intelligence in the field of catastrophe risk management. Several significant obstacles and limits may arise, including:

- **Data quality and quantity**

The quality and amount of available data pose significant obstacles in the application of artificial intelligence to the field of catastrophe risk management. In numerous instances of catastrophic events, the availability, reliability, and consistency of data can be limited, rendering the training of AI models and the generation of correct forecasts challenging.

- **Privacy and security**

Privacy and security concerns arise in the context of utilizing artificial intelligence (AI) for disaster risk management due to the extensive processing of personal data. Ensuring the secure storage and processing of data in compliance with privacy legislation, while safeguarding the rights of persons, is of paramount importance.

- **Computational resources**

The use of artificial intelligence (AI) to disaster scenarios sometimes necessitates substantial computational resources, particularly when employing intricate models like deep learning techniques. In certain disaster scenarios, particularly those occurring in geographically distant or secluded regions, there might be a lack of sufficient processing resources to effectively sustain artificial intelligence-driven solutions.

- **Integration with existing systems**

The successful use of AI solutions for disaster management necessitates seamless integration with pre-existing systems, including command and control centers, emergency response networks, and sensor networks, is the finding made by Schofield, M. (2022). This task can provide difficulties, particularly when confronted with diverse systems and varying data formats.

- **Real-time performance**

The importance of real-time performance cannot be overstated in numerous crisis scenarios. In order to facilitate decision-making and offer real-time situation awareness, it is imperative for AI-based systems to possess the capability to effectively handle and evaluate substantial volumes of data in real-time.

- **Explainability and transparency**

The necessity for openness and explainability in AI-based solutions, particularly in critical situations like disasters, is paramount. It is imperative for decision-makers to possess a comprehensive understanding of the decisions rendered by artificial intelligence (AI) models, as well as the underlying rationale behind such conclusions.

- **Bias and fairness**

The issue of bias and fairness arises in the context of AI models, since they have the potential to perpetuate prejudices and unfairness when the training data exhibits bias or when the algorithms are intentionally designed to perpetuate specific biases. This issue can provide significant challenges, particularly in situations of calamity, wherein the outcomes of judgments made by AI models may exhibit ambiguity is the research work by Velev, D., & Zlateva, P. (2023).

- **Responsibility and accountability**

The utilization of artificial intelligence (AI) in crisis situations can give rise to inquiries over the individuals who have responsibility and accountability for the decisions rendered by AI algorithms. Establishing clear norms of responsibility and accountability for artificial intelligence (AI) decision-making in crisis scenarios is of utmost importance.

- **Transparency**

The utilization of artificial intelligence (AI) in crisis situations can give rise to inquiries over the transparency and interpretability of AI algorithms. Therefore, it is imperative to guarantee the transparency of AI algorithms and the comprehensibility and scrutiny of their decision-making procedures.

- **Ethical and legal considerations**

Ethical and legal issues are vital when developing and implementing AI solutions for disaster management. It is imperative that these solutions adhere to ethical principles and legal requirements. This entails addressing crucial aspects such as privacy, data protection, and liability. One potential limitation of AI algorithms is their deficiency in human contact, which can impede their ability to effectively navigate catastrophic scenarios, particularly those characterized by intricate and uncertain circumstances.

- **Limited adaptability**

One potential limitation of AI algorithms is their limited adaptability, particularly in the context of fast shifting crisis situations when new and unexpected circumstances may arise.

- **Algorithm specificity**

Algorithm specificity refers to the extent to which AI algorithms are tailored to address particular sorts of catastrophes or scenarios, hence limiting their applicability to other types of disasters.

- **Overreliance on technology**

The excessive dependence on artificial intelligence (AI) technology can result in a decline in human cognitive abilities related to decision-making and a diminished capacity for situational awareness.

- **Cost**

The implementation of AI-based solutions for disaster management incurs significant costs, particularly for developing nations (Shameem, A., Ramachandran, K. K., et al., 2023) that may face limitations in terms of resources and infrastructure required to support these solutions.

- **Technical expertise**

Technical expertise is a crucial requirement for the development and implementation of artificial intelligence (AI)-based solutions in the context of disaster management. However, it is important to note that such expertise may not be readily accessible in most disaster-affected regions. Notwithstanding these obstacles, a prevailing agreement is emerging among specialists in the domain that artificial intelligence (AI) have the capacity to substantially enhance endeavors related to disaster response and recuperation. By utilizing artificial intelligence (AI) algorithms for the purpose of processing and analyzing extensive and intricate datasets, both companies and governments can enhance their decision-making capabilities, optimize resource allocation, and improve their ability to promptly and efficiently respond to disasters. The function of artificial intelligence (AI) is anticipated to become progressively significant in the domain of disaster management and response in the future. Several notable developments may be observed in the utilization of artificial intelligence (AI) in the context of disasters.

- **Improved prediction and early warning systems**

Enhanced forecasting and preemptive alert mechanisms - Artificial intelligence algorithms can be employed to scrutinize substantial volumes of data derived from diverse origins, encompassing meteorological patterns, satellite imagery, and social media, with the aim of generating more precise prognostications pertaining to natural calamities, such as hurricanes, earthquakes, and tsunamis.

- **Automated damage assessment**

AI systems scan satellite pictures and other data to quickly assess disaster damage and prioritise response efforts.

- **Integration with IoT and 5G technology**

The integration of artificial intelligence (AI) algorithms with Internet of Things (IoT) (Trishu S., Geetha M., et al., 2022) devices and 5G networks enables the provision of real-time information and expedites response efforts during catastrophe scenarios, Hingmire, M.A. (2021).

- **Increased use of unmanned aerial vehicles (UAVs)**

Research from researchers Munawar, H.S., Hammad, A.W., Waller, S.T., Thaheem, M.J., & Shrestha, A. (2021) intends that the utilization of unmanned aerial vehicles (UAVs) has witnessed a notable surge. Artificial intelligence (AI) algorithms can be seamlessly included into UAVs to expeditiously evaluate the extent of damage and effectively prioritize response endeavors. Additionally, these algorithms can facilitate the delivery of essential supplies and assistance to communities adversely impacted by the situation.

- **Personalized and targeted response**

The utilization of AI algorithms enables the analysis of data from diverse sources, facilitating the customization and precision of disaster response endeavors. This approach allows for the tailoring of relief operations to address the unique requirements and susceptibilities of impacted communities.

- **Improved resource allocation**

Enhanced resource allocation - Artificial intelligence algorithms can be employed to assess data pertaining to resource requirements, disruptions in supply chains, and several other aspects, with the aim of optimizing resource allocation and logistics in the context of crisis scenarios.

- **Enhanced collaboration and communication**

AI technologies like chatbots and voice assistants can help disaster response groups and affected communities collaborate better.

- **Scalability**

Scalability is a crucial aspect in the application of artificial intelligence (AI) within the domain of disaster risk management, as it necessitates the ability to adapt and accommodate diverse categories and magnitudes of disasters. The development of artificial intelligence (AI) systems that possess the ability to be readily adaptable to various disaster scenarios and can be promptly and efficiently deployed in response to such events is imperative.

- **Cost-effectiveness**

The cost-effectiveness of AI systems in disaster risk management is crucial due to the limited resources typically available for disaster response and recovery endeavors. The development of AI systems that use resources efficiently and effectively while providing decision-makers with vital information and support is crucial.

- **Evaluation and assessment**

AI systems' impact and effectiveness in catastrophe risk management depend on evaluation and assessment. To understand AI system performance, regular evaluations and assessments are necessary. Metrics and methods are needed to evaluate AI systems and collect and analyse data to understand their impact on disaster response and recovery.

- **Public awareness and acceptance**

Improve public awareness and acceptance of AI-based catastrophic risk management. To foster trust in AI systems and promote their ethical and responsible utilization for the benefit of disaster-affected populations, it is imperative to employ efficacious communication and education tactics.

DISCUSSIONS

The influence of artificial intelligence (AI) on human existence is having a substantial effect. Organizations are increasingly using AI technology as a means to enhance work completion and optimize productivity by leveraging its capabilities in data pattern analysis. Based on the preceding discourse, it is evident that the utilization of artificial intelligence in disaster scenarios is contingent upon two fundamental factors: human involvement and machine integration. The effectiveness of machine intelligence is contingent upon the credibility and accuracy of the information acquired from human sources. This will have an impact on the functionalities of the equipment. The research conducted by Emami and Marzban (2023) indicates that the potential of artificial intelligence (AI) in the domain of geographic information systems (GIS) and certain aspects of disaster management has not been fully realized. One potential approach to bridging this gap involves increasing knowledge regarding the significance of artificial intelligence (AI) techniques within the realm of catastrophe management (Geetha M, Harish P., et al., 2022). Despite the significant importance of artificial intelligence (AI) in the field of disaster management, there exist numerous formidable difficulties that impede its effective implementation and utilization (Manoharan, G., Durai, S., et al., 2023). The task of ensuring the provision of data of superior quality poses significant difficulties across all disciplines. In relation to the dissemination of data, certain countries decline to disclose information due to security considerations. However, the exorbitant expenses associated with the implementation of AI systems in the field of disaster management provide a significant barrier to their widespread adoption. Zhang, Y., Zou, Q., Zhang, Y., Liu, L., and Pu, C. (2023). It is imperative for those engaged in the collection of disaster-related information to possess a high level of expertise in the specific data that holds significance in this domain. Developing systems with user-friendly interfaces that clearly define the required data input enhances organization and utility. The authors of the study are Bouzidi, Z., Boudries, A., and Amad, M. (2020). Hence, the existence of impartial, internationally recognized institutions focused on gathering precise and reliable data assumes significance in addressing this issue. Conversely, the unpredictable nature of disasters poses challenges in developing models and instruments to effectively address them.

CONCLUSION

The promise of artificial intelligence (AI) in aiding the prevention, mitigation, and management of natural disaster risks is evident through the study of large datasets. Nevertheless, it is imperative to allocate additional efforts to ensure the responsible implementation of artificial intelligence (AI) technologies in library management also (Abdulwahid, A. H., Pattnaik, M., et al., 2023), capital markets (Jafar, S. H., Hemachandran, K., et al., 2023), business development (Lourens, M., Raman, R., et al., 2022) and education sector (Razak, A., Nayak, M. P., et al., 2023). The proposed study aims to examine the problems associated with the application of artificial intelligence (AI) and its potential to aid institutions in making informed decisions on natural catastrophe risk reduction. Despite the presence of these challenges, the benefits of artificial intelligence in the field of catastrophic risk management are substantial enough to merit consideration. In order to effectively harness the potential of artificial intelligence (AI) in the field of disaster risk management, it is crucial to commit adequate resources towards research, innovation, and the promotion of collaboration among diverse stakeholders. Artificial intelligence (AI) can improve catastrophe risk management by improving disaster prediction, early warning, and response and recovery.

REFERENCES

Abdulwahid, A. H., Pattnaik, M., Palav, M. R., Babu, S. T., Manoharan, G., & Selvi, G. P. (2023, April). Library Management System Using Artificial Intelligence. In *2023 Eighth International Conference on Science Technology Engineering and Mathematics (ICONSTEM)* (pp. 1-7). IEEE.

Abid, S. K., Chan, S. W., Sulaiman, N. A., Bhatti, U., & Nazir, U. (2023). Present and Future of Artificial Intelligence in Disaster Management. *2023 International Conference on Engineering Management of Communication and Technology (EMCTECH)*, (pp. 1-7). IEEE. 10.1109/EMCTECH58502.2023.10296991

Abid, S. K., Sulaiman, N. B., Chan, S. W., Nazir, U., Abid, M., Han, H., Ariza-Montes, A., & Vega-Muñoz, A. (2021). Toward an Integrated Disaster Management Approach: How Artificial Intelligence Can Boost Disaster Management. *Sustainability (Basel)*, *13*(22), 12560. doi:10.3390u132212560

Aboualola, M., Abualsaud, K., Khattab, T. M., Zorba, N., & Hassanein, H. S. (2023). Edge Technologies for Disaster Management: A Survey of Social Media and Artificial Intelligence Integration. *IEEE Access : Practical Innovations, Open Solutions*, *11*, 73782–73802. doi:10.1109/ACCESS.2023.3293035

Alrayes, F. S., Alotaibi, S. S., Alissa, K. A., Maashi, M. S., Alhogail, A. A., Alotaibi, N., Mohsen, H., & Motwakel, A. (2022). Artificial Intelligence-Based Secure Communication and Classification for Drone-Enabled Emergency Monitoring Systems. *Drones (Basel)*, *6*(9), 222. doi:10.3390/drones6090222

Arfan, M., Khan, Z., Qadri, N., Hameed, M. H., & Amir, A. R. (2022). *Role of Artificial Intelligence (AI) in Combined Disaster Management*. Organization Theory Review. doi:10.32350/OTR.0302.05

Bao, H. D., Zeng, C., Peng, Y., & Wu, S. (2022). The use of digital technologies for landslide disaster risk research and disaster risk management: Progress and prospects. *Environmental Earth Sciences*, *81*(18), 81. doi:10.100712665-022-10575-7

Bhandari, V. (2022). *Use of Technology in Disaster Management*. Unity Journal. doi:10.3126/unityj.v3i01.43333

Bouzidi, Z., Boudries, A., & Amad, M. (2020). Towards a Smart Interface-Based Automated Learning Environment Through Social Media for Disaster Management and Smart Disaster Education. *Sai*.

Chand, C. P., Ali, M. M., Himasri, B., Bourassa, M. A., & Zheng, Y. (2021). Predicting Indian Ocean Cyclone Parameters Using an Artificial Intelligence Technique. *Atmosphere*.

Chaurasia, K., Tarun, U. V. S., Sarala, G., & Soni, K. (2020). *AI based prediction of daily rainfall from satellite observation for disaster management*. Future Sensing Technologies. doi:10.1117/12.2580628

Emami, P., & Marzban, A. (2023). The Synergy of Artificial Intelligence (AI) and Geographic Information Systems (GIS) for Enhanced Disaster Management: Opportunities and Challenges. *Disaster Medicine and Public Health Preparedness*, *17*, 17. doi:10.1017/dmp.2023.174 PMID:37694385

Escolano, V. J., Caballero, A., Albina, E. M., Hernandez, A. A., & Juanatas, R. (2023). Acceptance of Mobile Application on Disaster Preparedness: Towards Decision Intelligence in Disaster Management. *2023 8th International Conference on Business and Industrial Research (ICBIR)*, 381-386.

Galera-Zarco, C., & Floros, G. (2023). A deep learning approach to improve built asset operations and disaster management in critical events: An integrative simulation model for quicker decision making. *Annals of Operations Research*. doi:10.100710479-023-05247-z

García-Tadeo, D. A., Peram, D. R., Kumar, K. S., Vives, L., Sharma, T., & Manoharan, G. (2022). Comparing the impact of Internet of Things and cloud computing on organisational behaviour: A survey. *Materials Today: Proceedings*, *51*(Part 8), 2281–2285. doi:10.1016/j.matpr.2021.11.399

Ghaffarian, S., Taghikhah, F. R., & Maier, H. R. (2023). Explainable artificial intelligence in disaster risk management: Achievements and prospective futures. *International Journal of Disaster Risk Reduction*, *98*, 104123. doi:10.1016/j.ijdrr.2023.104123

Gulati, N., Sethi, A., Mahesh, D., Makkar, S., Geetha Manoharan, M., & Palanivel, R. (2022). Implementation of blockchain in supply chain. *AIP Conference Proceedings*, *2418*, 020026. doi:10.1063/5.0083008

Hashim, F., Navaz, A.N., Zaki, N., Shuaib, K., & Serhani, M.A. (2023). Artificial Intelligence and Blockchain-Based Trading Framework for Satellite Images. *2023 International Wireless Communications and Mobile Computing (IWCMC)*, (pp. 786-792). IEEE.

Hingmire, M.A. (2021). *Planning for Disaster Management in India using IOT.*

Jafar, S. H., Hemachandran, K., El-Chaarani, H., Moturi, S., & Gupta, N. (Eds.). (2023). *Artificial Intelligence for Capital Markets*. CRC Press.

Kim, S.S., Shin, D.Y., Lim, E.T., Jung, Y., & Cho, S.B. (2022). Disaster Damage Investigation Using Artificial Intelligence And Drone Mapping. *The International Archives of the Photogrammetry, Remote Sensing and Spatial Information Sciences*.

Kuglitsch, M. M., Pelivan, I., Ceola, S., Menon, M., & Xoplaki, E. (2022). Facilitating adoption of AI in natural disaster management through collaboration. *Nature Communications*, *13*(1), 13. doi:10.103841467-022-29285-6 PMID:35332147

Linardos, V., Drakaki, M., Tzionas, P., & Karnavas, Y. L. (2022). Machine Learning in Disaster Management: Recent Developments in Methods and Applications. *Mach. Learn. Knowl. Extr.*, *4*(2), 446–473. doi:10.3390/make4020020

Lourens, M., Raman, R., Vanitha, P., Singh, R., Manoharan, G., & Tiwari, M. (2022, December). Agile Technology and Artificial Intelligent Systems in Business Development. In *2022 5th International Conference on Contemporary Computing and Informatics (IC3I)* (pp. 1602-1607). IEEE. 10.1109/IC3I56241.2022.10073410

Lourens, M., Sharma, S., Pulugu, R., Gehlot, A., Manoharan, G., & Kapila, D. (2023, May). Machine learning-based predictive analytics and big data in the automotive sector. In *2023 3rd International Conference on Advance Computing and Innovative Technologies in Engineering (ICACITE)* (pp. 1043-1048). IEEE. 10.1109/ICACITE57410.2023.10182665

Makkar, S., Bajpai, T., Bhola, M., Mahesh, D., & Manoharan, G. (2022). Blockchain disruption in banking sector. *AIP Conference Proceedings*, *2418*, 020019. doi:10.1063/5.0082288

Manoharan, G. (2022). An evaluation of machine learning techniques and how they affect human resource management and sustainable development. *Manager - The British Journal of Administrative Management.* https://tbjam.org/vol58-special-issue-06/

Manoharan, G., Durai, S., Ashtikar, S. P., & Kumari, N. (2024). Artificial Intelligence in Marketing Applications. In Artificial Intelligence for Business (pp. 40-70). Productivity Press.

Manoharan, G., Durai, S., Rajesh, G. A., Razak, A., Rao, C. B., & Ashtikar, S. P. (2023). A study on the perceptions of officials on their duties and responsibilities at various levels of the organizational structure in order to accomplish artificial intelligence-based smart city implementation. In *Artificial Intelligence and Machine Learning in Smart City Planning* (pp. 1–10). Elsevier. doi:10.1016/B978-0-323-99503-0.00007-7

Munawar, H. S., Hammad, A. W., Waller, S. T., Thaheem, M. J., & Shrestha, A. (2021). An Integrated Approach for Post-Disaster Flood Management Via the Use of Cutting-Edge Technologies and UAVs: A Review. *Sustainability (Basel)*, *13*(14), 7925. doi:10.3390u13147925

Pang, G., & Pang, G. (2022). Artificial Intelligence for Natural Disaster Management. *IEEE Intelligent Systems*, *37*(6), 3–6. doi:10.1109/MIS.2022.3220061

Partigöç, N. S. (2022). *The Role of Artificial Intelligence in Disaster Risk Management.* Bilişim Teknolojileri Dergisi.

Rajendran, L., & Shankaran, R. S. (2021). Bigdata Enabled Realtime Crowd Surveillance Using Artificial Intelligence And Deep Learning. *2021 IEEE International Conference on Big Data and Smart Computing (BigComp)*, (pp. 129-132). IEEE. 10.1109/BigComp51126.2021.00032

Razak, A., Nayak, M. P., Manoharan, G., Durai, S., Rajesh, G. A., Rao, C. B., & Ashtikar, S. P. (2023). Reigniting the power of artificial intelligence in education sector for the educators and students competence. In *Artificial Intelligence and Machine Learning in Smart City Planning* (pp. 103–116). Elsevier. doi:10.1016/B978-0-323-99503-0.00009-0

Schofield, M. (2022). An Artificial Intelligence (AI) Approach to Controlling Disaster Scenarios. *Advances in Electronic Government, Digital Divide, and Regional Development*, 28–46. doi:10.4018/978-1-7998-9815-3.ch003

Shaik, M. A., Manoharan, G., Prashanth, B., Akhil, N., Akash, A., & Reddy, T. R. S. (2022). Geetha Manoharan, B. Prashanth, Nune Akhil, Anumandla Akash, and Thudi Raja Shekhar Reddy, "Prediction of crop yield using machine learning". *AIP Conference Proceedings*, *2418*, 020072. doi:10.1063/5.0081726

Shameem, A., Ramachandran, K. K., Sharma, A., Singh, R., Selvaraj, F. J., & Manoharan, G. (2023, May). The rising importance of AI in boosting the efficiency of online advertising in developing countries. In *2023 3rd International Conference on Advance Computing and Innovative Technologies in Engineering (ICACITE)* (pp. 1762-1766). IEEE. 10.1109/ICACITE57410.2023.10182754

Sun, W., Bocchini, P., & Davison, B. (2020). Applications of artificial intelligence for disaster management. *Natural Hazards*, *103*(3), 2631–2689. doi:10.100711069-020-04124-3

Sweta, K., Goswami, A., Peethambaran, B., Bahuguna, I. M., & Rajawat, A. S. (2022). Landslide susceptibility zonation around Dharamshala, Himachal Pradesh, India: An artificial intelligence model–based assessment. *Bulletin of Engineering Geology and the Environment*, *81*(8), 81. doi:10.100710064-022-02806-9

Thavamani, S., Mahesh, D., Sinthuja, U., & Manoharan, G. (2022, May). Crucial attacks in internet of things via artificial intelligence techniques: The security survey. In AIP Conference Proceedings (Vol. 2418, No. 1). AIP Publishing.

Tripathi, M. A., Tripathi, R., Effendy, F., Manoharan, G., Paul, M. J., & Aarif, M. (2023, January). An In-Depth Analysis of the Role That ML and Big Data Play in Driving Digital Marketing's Paradigm Shift. In *2023 International Conference on Computer Communication and Informatics (ICCCI)* (pp. 1-6). IEEE. 10.1109/ICCCI56745.2023.10128357

Velev, D., & Zlateva, P. (2023). CHALLENGES OF ARTIFICIAL INTELLIGENCE APPLICATION FOR DISASTER RISK MANAGEMENT. *The International Archives of the Photogrammetry, Remote Sensing and Spatial Information Sciences*.

Waghmare, G. L., Kumar, S., Udhayakumar, R., Raja Mannar, B., Singh, R., & Rawat, N. (2023). Utilizing Social Media Platforms for Artificial Intelligence-Based Detection and Developing Effective Communications in Disaster-Affected Areas. *2023 3rd International Conference on Advance Computing and Innovative Technologies in Engineering (ICACITE)*, (pp. 501-504). IEEE.

Wong, Y. K. (2021). *Applying AI and Big Data for Sensitive Operations and Disaster Management*. Advances in Machine Learning, Data Mining and Computing. doi:10.5121/csit.2021.111429

Wong, Y.K. (2021). *Dealing Disaster Management Using AI*. Research Gate.

Zhang, Y., Zou, Q., Zhang, Y., Liu, L., & Pu, C. (2023). Editorial: Advances and applications of artificial intelligence and numerical simulation in risk emergency management and treatment. *Frontiers of Earth Science*.

Chapter 4
The Impact of Social Media on Public Perception and Behaviour During Disasters:
An AI-Enhanced Analysis

N. Subha
https://orcid.org/0000-0001-9311-4549
Nehru Institute of Technology, India

P. Vikkraman
Anna University, Coimbatore, India

ABSTRACT

This proposed chapter will examine the dynamic interplay between social media, public perception, and behaviour during disasters. A particular emphasis will be placed on how artificial intelligence (AI) improves comprehension of this interplay. Information dissemination and consumption during crisis situations have changed due to the quick spread of social media platforms and the growing application of artificial intelligence (AI) in disaster management. Insights into how these technological developments affect public perception and, in turn, how they affect behavioural responses in crisis situations are provided in this chapter.

INTRODUCTION

In recent years, the pervasive influence of social media has dramatically transformed the landscape of disaster response and management. The rapid dissemination of information through platforms such as Twitter, Facebook, and Instagram has become

DOI: 10.4018/979-8-3693-2280-2.ch004

an integral part of the public's immediate response to crises. This surge in social media use during disasters has not only facilitated communication and coordination among affected communities but has also sparked a new avenue for research in the intersection of technology and emergency management.

SOCIAL MEDIA'S GROWING ROLE IN DISASTER RESPONSE

The ubiquity of smartphones and the widespread adoption of social media platforms have empowered individuals to become real-time reporters during disasters. Citizens now play a crucial role in disseminating information about unfolding events, sharing updates on their safety, and coordinating relief efforts. From natural disasters like hurricanes and earthquakes to man-made crises such as accidents or pandemics, social media serves as a dynamic and immediate channel for both official and grassroots communication.

AI'S EVOLVING ROLE IN DISASTER MANAGEMENT

Artificial Intelligence (AI) has emerged as a powerful tool in the realm of disaster management. Its applications extend from data analysis to sentiment analysis and predictive modelling. AI algorithms can process vast amounts of data in real-time, helping emergency responders and authorities make more informed decisions. Sentiment analysis tools gauge public emotions, providing insights into the evolving mood during a crisis, which can guide response strategies. Predictive modelling leverages historical data and patterns to anticipate the trajectory of disasters, enabling proactive measures to mitigate their impact.

THE SYNERGY OF SOCIAL MEDIA AND AI

The intersection of social media and AI in disaster management is a promising frontier for research. Understanding how information flows through social networks during crises and how AI tools can harness this data presents a unique opportunity. Research in this area can shed light on how the public perceives and responds to disasters in the age of social media. It can also explore the ethical implications of using AI to shape public opinion and the role of algorithms in influencing collective sentiment during times of crisis.

REVIEW OF LITERATURE

Social media platforms, often known as SMPs, are very dynamic online spaces where people can communicate with one another and exchange, debate, and work together on ideas, info, videos, and other media. Millions of people engage with one another on these platforms, greatly influencing one another's habits, attitudes, and other behaviors. Users and companies use SMPs in various fields, including advertising, customer relations, travel, and many more. The selection of SMPs is, therefore, a significant Multi Criteria Decision-Making (MCDM) problem (AVCI 2023). The world of social media is dynamic and evolving quickly. Anything current today might not exist in the virtual world tomorrow. Therefore, whether or not they are on the aforementioned list, businesses need to establish a set of principles that apply to all forms of social media (Andreas M. Kaplan 2010). Chatbots are used for automated reporting, risk identification, briefings, meeting management, training, workgroup assistance, well-being assurance, and customer service enhancement. They also increase productivity (Alhammadi, M. 2023).

A paradigm shift in this field has resulted from the recognition of social media as an essential component of marketing strategies. According to reports, the field of social media marketing has experienced exponential growth in the last five years. This trend is expected to continue (Jami Pour 2021). People are using social media more and more in times of crisis, so crisis communicators need to know how to strategically use these tools. Although there is a need, there is a dearth of theory-based research to identify the critical variables that influence how the public uses social media versus other sources to obtain crisis information (Jin 2014).

The creative, inventive, synthetic, and generative qualities that support the larger interaction system are identified in the social life of microblogged information. Twitter's environment encourages the creation of new information through derivative tasks like directing, relaying, synthesizing, and redistributing, which are further enhanced by socio-technical innovation. These processes make up information self-organization (Starbird 2010).

The influence of the current public-side information production and distribution is strengthened by social media. A shift in disaster management models will occur despite the formal recognition of these widely dispersed and frequently remarkably well-organized information activities, due to the increasing utility of social media and the widespread prevalence of peer-to-peer communications (Sutton 2008).

Online social networking is starting to affect everyday life in ways that go beyond personal relationships and include financial and even public welfare. In this sense, information flows and interactions between users and items, which act as nodes in these networks, are crucial. Much attention has been focused on identifying a small subset of such nodes with maximum spreading power that makes this process easier (Tarun Kumar Biswas 2022).

Microblogging's growing ubiquity, communications speed, and cross-platform accessibility are making it a more attractive option for emergency communications (Vieweg 2010). Because of its increasing ubiquity, speed of communication, and cross-platform accessibility, microblogging is being evaluated more and more as a tool for emergency communications. Users can freely express their opinions and share information about current events, including natural disasters (Alen 2010).

Big Data and AI seem to have a lot of potential for handling COVID-19 and other emergencies, and it is expected that these technologies will play a bigger part in the future. AI and big data can be used to track the virus's real-time spread, plan and intensify public health interventions in response, assess the efficacy of those interventions, repurpose outdated compounds, find novel drugs, identify possible vaccine candidates, and improve local and regional responses to the pandemic (Bragazzi 2019). The COVID-19 pandemic has brought attention to the significance of efficient supply chain management (SCM) for vaccines. The study, examined the global effects of COVID-19 vaccine supply chain issues using social media analytics. Between January 2020 and November 2022, information from two social media platforms: Twitter and the Global Database of Events, Language, and Tone (GDELT). Discovered that issues with the vaccine supply chain had a major influence on the healthcare system's capacity to contain the pandemic, with notable regional variations (Enrique Cano-Marin 2023)

Research on "moonshot" societal issues like cancer treatment and climate science is already utilizing AI. Applications of artificial intelligence for social good that don't require scientific breakthroughs but instead support ongoing initiatives to assist people or groups in developed and developing economies who are facing difficulties or crises and frequently live beyond the reach of conventional or commercial solutions (Chui 2018). IoES applications in disaster relief and emergency response, with a focus on how sensors and IoT devices help emergency responders get real-time information (Damaševičius 2023). When applied to SMEs, artificial intelligence (AI) can be thought of as a collection of best practices that will strengthen their ability to adapt to changing market conditions and technological advancements. This will increase productivity and lower the business risks associated with the COVID-19 pandemic. (Drydakis 2022). It could be applied to forecast cases as well as anticipate the number of recovered instances, casualties, and alternate incidents. Utilizing IoT technologies in specific procedures such as prenatal screening, patient monitoring, and post-hospital incident response, reduces the risk of COVID-19 exposure to others within the context of the pandemic (Praveen Kumar Kollu 2022).

According to the framework, communities, governments, people, organizations, and media outlets are among the users of disaster social media. It was possible to identify fifteen different uses for social media related to disasters, ranging from (re)connecting community members after a disaster to preparing for and receiving information and warnings related to disaster preparedness (Houston 2014). Since disasters occur so frequently in the world, especially in 2021, disaster medicine (DM) has emerged as a crucial topic. The field of DM education has recently advanced with the use of new artificial intelligence (AI) enhanced technologies and concepts (Kao 2023).

The assessment of new technological opportunities for raising risk awareness and bolstering the resilience of those who are most at risk during disaster. Estimating the innovation potential, usefulness, importance, applicability, risks for vulnerable people, and ethical acceptability was the aim of the evaluation, which considered a survey, end-user evaluation, and co-creative workshops on technologies (Latvakoski 2022).

A finite number of options, made clear at the outset of the solution process, make up multiple-criteria evaluation problems. When there are discrete variables, the number of alternatives is either infinite or not countable, or it is usually very large if countable (Majumder (2015). The MCDM techniques were created to help with decision-making processes related to ranking a pre-existing set of alternatives for a given problem or selecting one from the set while taking competing criteria into account. Based on how each alternative performs about each criterion, they are compared to one another (Mardani A 2016). Decision-making involves multiple choices based on multiple criteria. Many applications, including banking, safety assessment, performance evaluation, and other multi-criteria domains, use fuzzy multi-criteria decision-making (Martin Aruldoss 2013).

Even at decentralized electrification levels, decision analysis is essential for developing systems by considering various factors and goals. An area of operational research called multiple criteria decision-making (MCDM) focuses on achieving the best outcomes in complicated situations with a variety of indicators, competing goals, and criteria. The flexibility this tool offers decision-makers to make judgments while considering all criteria and objectives at once is why it is becoming increasingly popular in energy planning (Abhishek Kumar 2017).

Utilizing the Decision-Making Trial and Evaluation Laboratory (DEMATEL) method to create a relations structure among criteria, a novel hybrid multiple criteria decision-making (MCDM) model handles the dependent linkages among criteria. The relative weights of each criterion with feedback and dependence are determined using the Analytical Network Process (ANP). Next, the options are ranked using the VIKOR approach (Multi-criteria Optimization and Compromise Solution) (Ames J.H 2010).

OBJECTIVES

- To analyze the impact of social media on public perception and behaviour during disasters.
- To explore how AI innovations, improve understanding of this impact.
- To provide insights into the ethical considerations encompassing the utilization of social media information and AI in disaster analysis.

METHODOLOGY

The study uses a quantitative methodology to investigate how social media affects the public's perception and behaviour during disasters. Structured questionnaires are used to gather data. A Google Forms-based structured questionnaire is used to collect data. Sample are chosen from Coimbatore city who are diverse in age and occupation. 130 of the 150 questionnaires were completed; 28 of these included multiple responses, some of which were incomplete. The final sample for the research consisted of 102 survey respondents in total.

Figure 1. Process of VIKOR technique

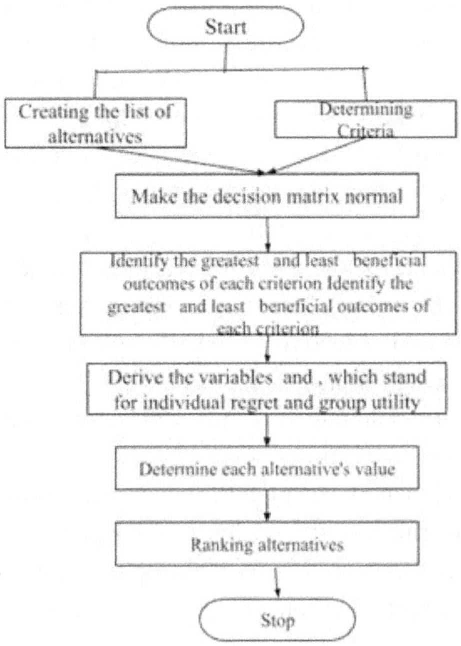

ANALYSIS AND INTERPRETATION

VIKOR technique is used for resolving multi-criteria decision-making (MCDM) issues and identifying the optimal compromise option. When there are competing criteria, this strategy focuses on ranking and choosing among a group of choices. The VIKOR method's primary goal is to select the option that, for each criterion, comes the closest to the ideal level. This way, the alternatives are determined by how closely the selected option adheres to the ideal level.

This study ranks five alternatives and four criteria using the VIKOR approach. Each criterion's weight and kind are displayed in the table below.

Table 1. Characteristics of criteria

S.No	Segment of Consumer	type	weight
1	Employed - Private /Govt Sector	+	0.25
2	Homemaker / Unemployed	+	0.25
3	Self-employed/ Entrepreneur	+	0.25
4	Student	+	0.25

The following table shows the decision matrix.

Table 2. Decision matrix

Influence Factors	Employed - Private /Govt Sector	Homemaker / Unemployed	Self-employed/ Entrepreneur	Student
Informed Decision-Making Influence	9	2	1	4
Community Engagement Influence	1	3	4	4
Crisis Awareness Influence	3	4	2	6
Behavioural Guidance Influence	10	15	1	16
Personal Safety Influence	9	2	1	5

The following procedures are part of the VIKOR method:
The VIKOR Technique's Steps
Step 1: Make the decision matrix normal
To normalize, apply the formula below.

$$f_{ij}(x) = \frac{x_{ij}}{\sqrt{\sum_{i=1}^{m} x_{ij}^2}} \quad i = 1,...,m; j = 1,... ,\text{n}$$

The normalized decision matrix is displayed in the table below.

Table 3. Normalized decision matrix

Influence Factors	Employed - Private /Govt Sector	Homemaker / Unemployed	Self-employed/ Entrepreneur	Student
Informed Decision-Making Influence	0.546	0.125	0.209	0.214
Community Engagement Influence	0.061	0.187	0.834	0.214
Crisis Awareness Influence	0.182	0.249	0.417	0.321
Behavioural Guidance Influence	0.606	0.934	0.209	0.856
Personal Safety Influence	0.546	0.125	0.209	0.268

Identify the greatest f_i^* and least f_i^- beneficial outcomes of each criterion in step two.

The following formula can be used to decide which benefits are the best and worst:

If the criterion is positive, then

$$f_j^* = Max_i f_{ij}\,,\; f_j^- = Max_i f_{ij} \;;\; j = 1, 2, ..., n$$

If the criterion is negative, then

$$f_j^* = Min_i f_{ij} \;, f_j^- = Max_i f_{ij} \;; j = 1, 2, ..., n$$

The following can be used to express the positive ideal solution (f^*) and negative ideal solution (f^-) :

$$f^* = \left\{ f_1^*, f_2^*, f_3^*, ..., f_n^* \right\}$$

$$f^- = \left\{ f_1^-, f_2^-, f_3^-, ..., f_n^- \right\}$$

Determine the S_i and R_i values in step three.

The following formulas can be used to derive the variables S_i and R_i, which stand for individual regret and group utility, respectively:

$$S_i = \sum_{j=1}^{n} w_j \frac{(f_j^* - f_{ij})}{(f_j^* - f_j^-)}$$

$$R_i = Max_j \left[w_j \frac{(f_j^* - f_{ij})}{(f_j^* - f_j^-)} \right]$$

Where the symbol w_j stands for the criteria's weight.

The values of S_i and R_i are displayed in the table below.

Table 4. The values ***S*** *and* ***R***

Influence Factors	R	S
Informed Decision-Making Influence	0.25	0.778
Community Engagement Influence	0.25	0.731
Crisis Awareness Influence	0.212	0.781
Behavioural Guidance Influence	0.25	0.25
Personal Safety Influence	0.25	0.757

Step 4: Determine Q_i 's value

The following formula can be used to determine each alternative's value Q_i, which represents the VIKOR index

$$Q_i = \gamma \frac{(S_i - S^*)}{(S^- - S^*)} + (1-\gamma) \frac{(R_i - R^*)}{(R^- - R^*)}$$

Where

$$S^* = Min_i \{S_i\} \ ; S^- = Max_i \{S_i\} \ ; R^* = Min_i \{R_i\} \ ; R^- = Max_i \{R_i\}$$

Furthermore, the value 0.5 denotes the highest group utility, or γ.

Using the S, R, and Q values as a guide, rank the options in Step 5.

Assigning the best rank to the option with the lowest VIKOR value involves sorting the S, R, and Q values in decreasing order. Three lists of rankings are the outcomes.

The list of possibilities is ranked according to the S, R, and Q values in the following table.

Table 5. The values **Q**

Influence Factors	Q
Informed Decision-Making Influence	0.997
Community Engagement Influence	0.953
Crisis Awareness Influence	0.5
Behavioural Guidance Influence	0.5
Personal Safety Influence	0.977

Table 6. The ranking list for the alternatives

Influence Factors	R value	Rank in R	S value	Rank in S	Q value	Rank in Q
Informed Decision-Making Influence	0.25	2	0.778	4	0.997	4
Community Engagement Influence	0.25	2	0.731	2	0.953	2
Crisis Awareness Influence	0.212	1	0.781	5	0.5	1
Behavioural Guidance Influence	0.25	2	0.25	1	0.5	1
Personal Safety Influence	0.25	2	0.757	3	0.977	3

Step 6: Offer a compromise solution, the alternative ($A^{(1)}$), which, if the next two requirements are met, is the option that is best ranked by the measure Q (minimum).

Condition 1. Acceptable advantage: $Q(A^{(2)}) - Q(A^{(1)}) \geq 1/(m-1)$ where $A^{(1)}$ is the alternative with first position and $A^{(2)}$ is the alternative with second position in the ranking list by Q. m is number of alternatives.

Condition 2. Decision-making stability that is acceptable requires that the option $A^{(1)}$ be rated highest by S and/or R.

In the event that one of the requirements is not met, a series of workarounds are suggested, comprising:

Solution 1. Alternatives $A^{(1)}, A^{(2)}, \ldots, A^{(M)}$ if Condition 1 is not satisfied; Alternative $A^{(M)}$ is determined by $Q\left(A^{(M)}\right) - Q\left(A^{(1)}\right) < 1/(m-1)$ for maximum M (the positions of these alternatives are "in closeness").

Solution 2. Alternatives $A^{(1)}$ and $A^{(2)}$ if only condition 2 is not satisfied.

First, an acceptable advantage would be $Q(A^{(2)}) - Q(A^{(1)}) \geq 1/(m-1)$. In the ranking list by Q, where m is the number of alternatives, $A^{(1)}$ is the alternative with the first position and $A^{(2)}$ is the alternative with the second place.

To ensure satisfactory stability in the decision-making process, it is necessary that S or/and R rank the option $A^{(1)}$ as the best one.

The following list of compromise solutions is put up in the event that one of the requirements is not met:

Solution 1. In the event that Condition 1 is not met, choose Alternatives $A^{(1)}, A^{(2)}, \ldots, A^{(M)}$; Alternative $A^{(M)}$ is defined by $Q(A^{(M)}) - Q(A^{(1)}) < 1/(m-1)$ for maximum M (the locations of these alternatives are "in closeness").

Solution 2: If only requirement 2 is not met, choose between alternatives $A^{(1)}$ and $A^{(2)}$.

Solution 3. If both requirements are met, the best alternative will be chosen as the one with the lowest Q value.

Table 7. Conditions survey results

Non acceptance	Condition 1
-	Condition 2
Solution 1	Selected solution

Therefore, Crisis Awareness Influence, Behavioural Guidance Influence, are selected as the final alternatives.

FINDINGS

Ranking of Alternatives: Five alternatives have been ranked using the VIKOR approach according to four criteria: The following factors have an impact: crisis awareness, crisis informed decision-making, community engagement, behavioural guidance, and personal safety.

Normalization of Decision Matrix: To enable equitable comparisons across criteria, the decision matrix was normalized by placing all values on a single scale.

Finding the Best and Worst Outcomes: The best and worst outcomes for each criterion were found by identifying the positive ideal solution (f^*) and the negative ideal solution $\left(f^-\right)$.

S and R-Value Calculation: Considering the weight of each criterion, individual regret S_i and group utility R_i values were calculated for each choice. These numbers express how satisfied or unsatisfied each alternative is with the determined ideal solutions.

Calculation of Q Values: For each option, the VIKOR index Q_i a compromise that considers both the best and worst outcomes was computed. An extensive overview of each alternative's performance across all categories is given by this index.

Using S, R, and Q values to rank the alternatives: The S, R, and Q values of the alternatives were used to rank them. Considering the viewpoints of the individual and the group, the ranking analysis sheds light on the relative performance of each option.

A compromise solution is recommended by the VIKOR approach, which chooses the course of action that minimizes the Q value. In addition to outlining the requirements for stability and acceptable advantage in decision-making, possible compromise alternatives were also identified.

SUGGESTIONS

Preference for Behavioural Guidance and Crisis Awareness: Based on the results, it appears that the options linked to Behavioural Guidance and Crisis Awareness Influence are chosen as the best choices. This suggests that these options do a better job of reaching the intended results when considering the given criteria and their relative weights.

Consideration of Compromise Solutions: If the chosen alternative does not fulfil the requirements for an acceptable advantage or stability in decision-making, it is advised to carefully investigate compromise solutions, depending on the particular conditions specified in the VIKOR approach.

Continuous Monitoring and Adaptation: Establishing a system for continuous monitoring and adaptation is advised due to the dynamic nature of decision-making and the possibility of changing conditions. This makes sure that if circumstances change, the selected options stay the best ones.

Additional Sensitivity Analysis: By performing sensitivity analysis on the weights of the criterion and investigating the effects of modifications in these weights, more information about the resilience of the decision-making process may become available.

Authentication and Confirmation: Verify the VIKOR analysis's conclusions by contrasting them with actual results or the advice of experts. The decision-making framework is more reliable when verification procedures are used.

Results Communication: Inform pertinent stakeholders of the decision-making process and the outcomes in a transparent manner. This encourages understanding and support from those who are impacted by or participating in the choice.

By putting these recommendations into practice, the VIKOR technique can be made more resilient and applicable when used in multi-criteria decision-making for the particular domain in question.

CONCLUSION

Social media has emerged as an essential medium for disaster communication. By offering insights on societal attitude and response patterns, AI systems have made it possible to analyse this influence more thoroughly. To ensure ethical data utilization, nevertheless, ethical considerations must come first. To optimize crisis management techniques and boost public participation in the digital era, it is crucial to comprehend the dynamic interplay between social media, AI, and disaster response.

REFERENCES

Alen, L., K. Anderson, G. Mark, J. Martin, D. Sicker, & D. Grunwald. (2010). *A Vision for Technology-Mediated Public Participation and Assistance in Mass Emergencies and Disasters*. University of Colorado manuscript.

Alhammadi, M. (2023). Optimising Customer Service Delivery and Response Time through AI-Enhanced Chatbots in Facilities Management Mixed-Methods Research. *American Journal of Smart Technology and Solutions*, *2*(2), 43–54. doi:10.54536/ajsts.v2i2.2206

Ames, J. H. Liou, Yu-Tai C. (2010). Developing a hybrid multi-criteria model for selection of outsourcing providers. *Expert Systems with Applications, 37*(5), 3755-3761. doi:10.1016/j.eswa.2009.11.048

Andreas, M. (2010). Users of the world, unite! The Challenges and opportunities of Social Media. *Business Horizons, 53*(1). doi:10.1016/j.bushor.2009.09.003

Aruldoss, M., Lakshmi, T. M., & Venkatesan, V. P. (2013). A Survey on Multi Criteria Decision Making Methods and Its Applications. *The African Journal of Information Systems, 1*(1), 31–43. doi:10.12691/ajis-1-1-5

Avci, S., Ekiz Bozdemir, M. K., & Alkan, A. (2023). Selection Of Social Media Platforms: A New Hybrid Multi-Criteria Decision Making Approach. *Endüstri Mühendisliği, 34*(2), 243–275. doi:10.46465/endustrimuhendisligi.1259667

Biswas, T. K., Abbasi, A., & Chakrabortty, R. K. (2022). A two-stage VIKOR assisted multi-operator differential evolution approach for Influence Maximization in social networks. *Expert Systems with Applications, 192*. doi:10.1016/j.eswa.2021.116342

Bragazzi, N. L., Dai, H., Damiani, G., Behzadifar, M., Martini, M., & Wu, J. (2019). How Big Data and Artificial Intelligence Can Help Better Manage the COVID-19 Pandemic. *International Journal of Environmental Research and Public Health, 17*(9), 3176. doi:10.3390/ijerph17093176 PMID:32370204

Chui, M., Harryson, M., Valley, S., Manyika, J., & Roberts, R. (2018). *Notes from the AI frontier applying AI for social good.*

Damaševičius, R., Bacanin, N., & Misra, S. (2023). From Sensors to Safety: Internet of Emergency Services (IoES) for Emergency Response and Disaster Management. *Journal of Sensor & Actuator Networks, 12*(3), 41. doi:10.3390/jsan12030041

Drydakis, N. (2022). Artificial Intelligence and Reduced SMEs' Business Risks. A Dynamic Capabilities Analysis During the COVID-19 Pandemic. *Information Systems Frontiers, 24*(4), 1223–1247. doi:10.100710796-022-10249-6 PMID:35261558

Enrique, C. -M., Ribeiro-Soriano, D. (2023). Exploring the challenges of the COVID-19 vaccine supply chain using social media analytics: A global perspective. *Sustainable Technology and Entrepreneurship, 2*(3). doi:10.1016/j.stae.2023.100047

Houston, J. B., Hawthorne, J., Perreault, M., Park, E., Hode, M., Halliwell, M., McGowen, S., Davis, R., Vaid, S., Mcelderry, J., & Griffith, S. (2014). Social media and disasters: A functional framework for social media use in disaster planning, response, and research. *Disasters, 39*(1), 1–22. doi:10.1111/disa.12092 PMID:25243593

Jami Pour, M., Hosseinzadeh, M., & Amoozad Mahdiraji, H. (2021). Exploring and evaluating success factors of social media marketing strategy: A multi-dimensional-multi-criteria framework. *Foresight, 23*(6), 655–678. doi:10.1108/FS-01-2021-0005

Kumar, A., Sah, B., Singh, A. R., Deng, Y., He, X., & Kumar, P. (2017). A review of multi criteria decision making (MCDM) towards sustainable renewable energy development. *Renewable and Sustainable Energy Reviews, 69.* doi:10.1016/j.rser.2016.11.191

Latvakoski, J., Öörni, R., Lusikka, T., & Keränen, J. (2022). Evaluation of emerging technological opportunities for improving risk awareness and resilience of vulnerable people in disasters. *International Journal of Disaster Risk Reduction*, *80*, 103173. doi:10.1016/j.ijdrr.2022.103173

Majumder, M. (2015). Multi Criteria Decision Making. In *Impact of Urbanization on Water Shortage in Face of Climatic Aberrations. SpringerBriefs in Water Science and Technology*. Springer. doi:10.1007/978-981-4560-73-3_2

Mardani, A., Zavadskas, E. K., Govindan, K., Amat Senin, A., & Jusoh, A. (2016). VIKOR Technique: A Systematic Review of the State of the Art Literature on Methodologies and Applications. *Sustainability (Basel)*, *8*(1), 37. doi:10.3390u8010037

Starbird, K., Palen, L., Hughes, A., & Vieweg, S. (2010). Chatter on The Red: What hazards threat reveals about the social life of microblogged information. *Proceedings of the ACM Conference on Computer Supported Cooperative Work*, (pp. 241-250). ACM. 10.1145/1718918.1718965

Sutton, J., Palen, L., & Shklovski, I. (2008). Backchannels on the Front Lines: Emergent Uses of Social Media in the 2007 Southern California Wildfires. *Proceedings of the 5th International ISCRAM Conference*. IEEE.

Vieweg, S., Hughes, A., Starbird, K., & Palen, L. (2010). Microblogging during two natural hazards events: What Twitter may contribute to situational awareness. *Conference on Human Factors in Computing Systems - Proceedings*. ACM. 10.1145/1753326.1753486

Chapter 5
Future Trends and Innovations in Natural Disaster Detection Using AI and ML

T. Venkat Narayana Rao
Sreenidhi Institute of Science and Technology, India

Prathima Jakkam
Sreenidhi Institute of Science and Technology, India

Shravya Medipally
Sreenidhi Institute of Science and Technology, India

ABSTRACT

The transformational field of utilizing machine learning (ML) and artificial intelligence (AI) to forecast natural disasters is explored in this book chapter. The severity of natural disasters demands catastrophe mitigation, risk assessment, and early warning. The use of AI and ML technologies, which have the potential to safeguard communities, is essential in this endeavor. The chapter emphasizes the need of a multidisciplinary strategy that combines domain expertise with AI and ML to improve capacity to predict and respond to natural disasters with an ultimate goal to build a more secure and resilient global community. The chapter examines a number of AI and ML applications in disaster prediction, including forecasts for earthquakes, floods, wildfires, hurricanes, landslides, tsunamis etc. In order to increase prediction accuracy, it covers sensor networks, data sources, and the integration of various datasets. Additionally, it tackles the issues related to ethical considerations, robustness of the model, and data quality.

DOI: 10.4018/979-8-3693-2280-2.ch005

INTRODUCTION

In the past few years, there have been more and worse natural disasters and extreme weather events (Leng et al., 2023). This is a big problem for people and governments all over the world because it can hurt or even kill people, damage buildings and things, and make it hard for businesses to work. To make things better, we need to be able to predict and get ready for these disasters. Using special computer programs called machine learning algorithms, scientists have been able to get better at predicting the weather and natural disasters. These algorithms can look at a lot of information, like pictures from space and past weather records, to figure out what might happen in the future (Jain et al., 2023). They can even predict things like heatwaves or droughts by looking at things like temperature and rain. Machine learning algorithms also help scientists predict natural disasters, like earthquakes or floods. They can use different kinds of algorithms to make these predictions. More and more scientists are using these algorithms to study and predict the weather and natural disasters because they can help keep people safe (Aybar-Ruiz et al., 2016).

These special computer programs can look at different kinds of information, like earthquake data, past disaster information, and weather data, to guess what might happen in a natural disaster. For example, they can guess if there might be an earthquake or a hurricane by looking at things like how the ground is moving, how fast the wind is blowing, and how warm the ocean is. Using these programs can help governments and organizations be ready for disasters and keep people safe. They can give us warnings about upcoming disasters so we can go to safer places (Zhang et al., 2022a). They can also help decide where to send resources and plan the best ways for people to leave dangerous areas. But these programs aren't always perfectly accurate. Sometimes they give false alarms or their predictions are affected by the quality of the information they use (Jia et al., 2022). We're studying these programs to see how we can make them better and help prepare for disasters around the world.

Predictive analytics in machine learning for disaster management could be used to notify people about impending disasters. In addition to forecasts, it can help rescue crews by providing information on the extent of damage as shown in the Figure 1.This information has details about how to do something, where the information comes from, what the results are, examples of how it works, and important lessons we learned. Some experts did a really good job of studying this and made sure it was accurate. It helps us understand how machines can help protect people and places from natural disasters all over the world (Esrafilian-Najafabadi & Haghighat, 2022).

Figure 1. ML in disaster management

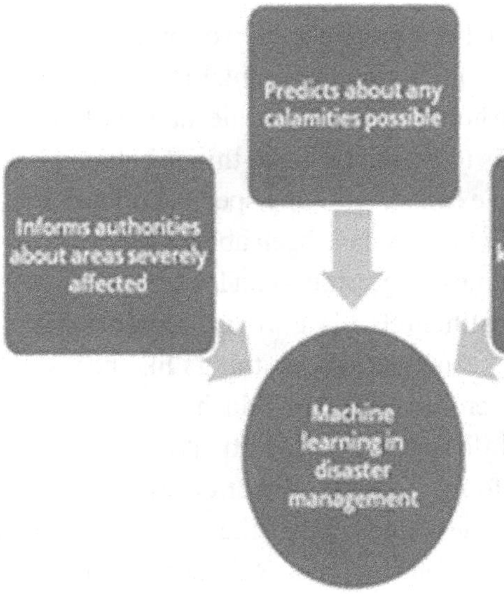

CASE STUDIES

Heat Waves in Europe From 2003 to 2006

Extreme heat is a big problem in many parts of the world. It can make people very sick, especially those who are more vulnerable. Heat waves are becoming more frequent and intense, and this can cause a lot of harm. But there are things we can do to protect ourselves and reduce the impact of extreme heat. We can learn from past experiences and take action to keep people safe. This case study compares two heat waves in Europe and shows how we can manage these risks and adapt to climate change.

Resolving urban issues will contribute to the safety of those who are vulnerable. Approximately 50% of the world's population currently resides in cities, and by 2050, that percentage is predicted to rise to 70%. Cities are growing and attracting more people from rural areas. When there are extreme heat events, certain things in cities can make people more vulnerable or less vulnerable to the heat. The buildings and pavement in cities can make the heat even worse, and some areas in the city can be hotter than others. This can be dangerous for people who live there. It can also cause problems with the electricity supply, which is important for things like air conditioning and refrigeration. When it gets really hot, there is more electricity demand, but the power plants that make the electricity might not be able to keep up. This can cause disruptions and make it even harder for people to stay cool.

The difference between the heat waves in 2003 and 2006 was partly because one was more intense and affected a larger area than the other. In France, fewer people died in 2006 because people were more aware of the dangers of heat waves and took steps to protect themselves. However, there were still too many deaths, so it's important to improve the systems in place to warn people and help them during heat waves. This could include things like better communication, mapping areas that are most at risk, and making changes to cities to reduce exposure to heat. Overall, the heat waves in 2003 and 2006 taught us a lot about how to keep people safe during extreme heat.

Handling the Undesirable Effects of Drought

Water is really important all over the world. When there isn't enough water, it can cause problems like people having to move and conflicts between different groups of people. Some countries, like those in the Mediterranean, often have droughts that can hurt farming, make people lose money, and make them move to cities. This case study is about Syria, which has had a drought in recent years. The Eastern Mediterranean area often has droughts that make it hard to grow crops. In Syria, the amount of rain has been getting less and less over the years, especially in the spring and winter. This decrease in rain is similar to what scientists think will happen in the future in the Mediterranean region.

To help people who have been affected by a drought in Syria, different actions were identified. This included giving them food and help with farming, as well as providing clean water and healthcare. They also wanted to help them become better prepared for future droughts. Some of the ways they planned to do this were by giving seeds to families to grow crops, giving food to herders and helping them get more sheep, creating a system to warn people about droughts early on, and teaching people how to manage droughts better. They also wanted to find ways to use the land in a sustainable way, but there is still a lot of discussion about how to do that.

Cyclones: Promoting Community Action With Responsive Institutions and Enabling Policies

Strong storms formed over tropical and subtropical oceans are known as tropical cyclones, sometimes referred to as typhoons and hurricanes. Their ferocious winds destroy property, infrastructure, and other assets; their heavy rains frequently result in landslides and floods; and their large waves and storm surges frequently cause significant coastline erosion and flooding, all of which have a negative influence on humans. Tropical cyclones are generally categorized according to their intensity using measurements or estimates of near-surface wind speed (sometimes using the Saffir-Simpson scale, which places them on a scale from 1 to 5). Although they occur less frequently, the strongest storms (Categories 3, 4, and 5) usually cause the most damage.

Managing the Adverse Effects of Floods

Floods are a big problem in many parts of the world and they cause a lot of damage. From 2001 to 2010, floods were responsible for more than half of all disasters. In 2007, floods were the cause of four out of the five deadliest natural disasters. About 800 million people live in areas prone to floods and 10% of them experience floods every year. Floods can happen because of heavy rain or when water from the ocean comes onto land. Floods can be really bad because they can disrupt the supply of food and water, hurt the economy, and make people sick. It's important to study floods so we can find ways to reduce the damage they cause. There are different strategies that can be used to reduce the impact of floods, like building dams and sea walls or improving drainage systems. We also need to have systems in place to warn people about floods so they can stay safe (UNISDR, 2011a). In Mozambique, floods in 2000 and 2007 caused a lot of problems for the people and the economy. We need to make sure that our programs to reduce the risks of floods are working well and that we have plans in place to deal with big floods.

A long time ago, there were big floods in Mozambique that caused a lot of damage and hurt many people. Seven years later, there were more floods, but this time the country was more prepared. It rained a lot and a big storm came, which caused even more flooding. It hurt a lot of people and damaged buildings and things that help keep people healthy, like medicine and clean water. It also caused a lot of damage to the land and destroyed crops. Before the floods happened, people knew it was going to happen and they were able to warn and help many people. They had plans in place to keep people safe and help them during the emergency. Some people had to move to safer areas because their homes were at risk of flooding. But these new areas didn't have enough water or good conditions for growing crops, so it was still hard for people to live there. The floods caused a lot of problems and made it harder for Mozambique to fight poverty and develop (Choubin et al., 2019; Pradhan, 2009; Yilmaz, 2010).

Vulnerabilities Due to a Changing Cold Climate in Northern Canada

In places where it is very cold, like parts of Canada, the weather is changing faster than in other parts of the world. This is causing problems for the buildings and infrastructure in those areas. It also makes it harder for people to travel, find enough food, and live their normal lives. This study looks at how climate change affects the northern parts of Canada. These areas are more vulnerable to climate-related problems because they are far away from other communities. The study focuses on how climate change affects the ground and the weight of snow, which can cause problems for buildings and infrastructure. The study also looks at how the government is responding to these problems and trying to protect the people who live there. The government and the communities need to work together to be prepared and take action to reduce the risks.

LEVELS INVOLVED IN MANAGING DISASTERS

There are five levels involved in managing the disasters as shown in the figure 2. The management actions aimed at averting or reducing future crises and their long-term effects are referred to as the mitigation phase. Enforcing modern building norms and standards, retrofitting hospitals, shelters, and highway overpasses are a few examples of mitigation actions.Additional instances include enlightening pertinent stakeholders and the broader public about potential risks and mitigating measures. The preparatory stage starts when an emergency or tragedy is possible. It refers to preparations made ahead of time for a disaster in order to facilitate rescue and response operations and protect human life, such as assembling food and water supplies, establishing emergency contacts, and organising evacuations. The response phase mostly involves implementing the plans and strategies that have been prepared earlier. During a crisis, response operations take place. These often include searching and rescue operations, managing shelters, evacuating regions that are in danger, and providing humanitarian aid. The term "recovery phase" describes the period following a disaster when attempts are made to restore the area to its pre-disaster state or even higher. Typical recovery efforts include clearing debris, accurately assessing damage, repairing infrastructure, and receiving financial assistance from governmental and insurance agencies.

Prevention

- Use AI for predictive modeling and risk assessment to find possible disaster-prone locations.
- Use AI-powered early warning systems to anticipate and identify natural disasters like floods, earthquakes, and hurricanes (Sachdeva et al., 2018; Kameshwar and Padgett, 2014).

Preparedness

- Use AI in simulations and scenario planning to improve emergency response plans.
- To increase preparedness, provide AI-driven training courses for community members and first responders.

Response

- Use AI-powered satellites and drones to gather data in real-time and determine the scope of the disaster.
- Analyse social media for situational awareness in real time by using picture recognition and natural language processing (NLP).

Recovery

- Use AI algorithms to prioritize recovery efforts based on data analytics and analyze the damage.
- Optimize resources using machine learning to ensure that they are allocated effectively throughout the recovery process.

Mitigation

- Use AI for post-disaster analysis to determine long-term mitigation plans and comprehend the causes.
- Use AI-driven planning and design solutions for infrastructure to increase its resilience to future calamities.

Figure 2. Levels in disaster management

Figure 3. Types of deep learning

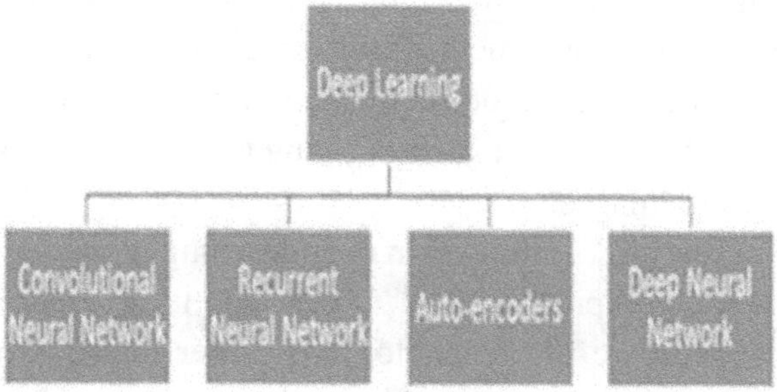

METHODS

Remote Sensing Using Deep Learning for Change Detection

Change detection uses remote sensing photos taken at various intervals to identify both gradual and sudden changes in a particular area (Singh, 1989). It offers a way to research land use (Weng, 2002) discussed cover change (LeCun et al., 2015), the process of urbanization, and disaster finding (Saito et al. 2004), as well as further environmental modifications. Usually, there are two kinds of adjustments frequently investigated (Lu et al., 2004):

1) Binary changes and
2) From-to changes. The binary merely modifies focus on whether or not there has been change. From-to-change detection recognizes variations across time as well but also particular kinds of changes, such those from structures to flora.

Scientists have done a lot of research to understand different types of change. They have come up with six different ways to detect these changes.

1) Layer arithmetic methods (Howarth & Wickware, 1981)
2) Post-Classification Change Methods (PCCMs) (Silván-Cárdenas & Wang, 2014; Yuan et al., 2005)
3) Direct Classification Methods (DCMs) (Bovolo et al., 2008)
4) Transformation methods (Gong, 1993)
5) Change Vector Analysis (CVA) methods (Chen et al., 2003; Johnson & Kasischke, 1998), and
6) Hybrid change detection methods (Healey et al., 2018; McDermid et al., 2008).

Some methods involve doing math with different layers of images, while others involve classifying the images and comparing them. Each method has its own strengths and weaknesses. Some methods are good at detecting big changes, but not smaller ones. Other methods can detect different types of changes, but they might not be very accurate. Scientists are always trying to find the best way to detect and understand changes in images.

Artificial neural networks are used in deep learning, a unique kind of machine learning, to learn and comprehend data. It can help us solve problems in remote sensing, which is when we use technology to gather information about faraway places. Deep learning is really powerful because it can break down complex ideas into simpler ones and can create abstract representations of things. People have been using deep learning a lot in remote sensing, like when they combine different images together or try to find changes in the images, such as image fusion (Shao & Cai, 2018), image registration (Wang et al., 2018; Zhang et al., 2019), image matching (Chen et al., 2021) change detection, land use and cover classification (Hong et al., 2021; Li et al., 2022; Zhou et al., 2022), semantic segmentation (Kemker et al., 2018), and object-based image analysis (Liu et al., 2021).

There is a lot of research happening in this area, but it is still new and there is a lot more to learn.

Convolutional Neural Network

CNN is a deep learning method that identifies which feature is more significant than the others by first applying weights and biases to each individual feature in the image. The main part of CNN is the convolutional layer. The filters in the convolutional layer help to produce feature maps when convolved with the picture. One of the other crucial components is the pooling layer, which works independently on the feature maps.

The network is non-linear due to the Rectified Linear Unit (ReLU) layer, and every neuron in the completely connected layer is fully coupled to all prior activations (Sit et al., 2019; Alam et al., 2018).

Recurrent Neural Network

Recurrent neural networks, also referred to as neural networks, are networks that function on sequences (Mouzannar, Rizk, & Awad, 2018). Natural language processing is the main use case for these networks. In conventional networks, input and output are independent.

However, when it comes to predicting the next word in a phrase, these networks cannot be used, which is where RNNs come into play.

Auto-Encoders

An auto-encoder is an unsupervised learning technique that is used to enable representation learning. By using backpropagation, this technique sets the input and goal values equal. An auto-encoder is used to shrink the input size and provide an output that is smaller than the original size. Images can be colored and have noise and watermarks removed using an auto-encoder (Nguyen et al., 2017; Bui et al., 2020).

Deep Neural Network

A deep neural network is a network that has more than one layer between the input and output layers. The performance of conventional CNNs decreases as the number of deep or hidden layers rises, despite the fact that these networks make it possible to train deeper networks (Xu et al., 2019).

OVERVIEW OF VARIOUS DEEP LEARNING TECHNIQUES

Research has been made by many publications like Scopus, IEEE, etc. on various techniques and the information about different types of disasters and their remedies are listed. The amount accuracy for each disaster management technique is mentioned respectively (Nabian & Meidani, 2018b; Gama et al., 2016).

An overview of different Deep learning methods used with accuracy is given in the Table 1.

Table 1. Overview of various techniques of deep learning in the existing literature

Dataset	Type of Catastrophe	Method Used	Accuracy
Tweets of Hurricane 2017	Hurricane	VGG 16 CNN	89.44%
Hurricane images from tropical cyclone repository	Hurricane	Deep CNN with 5 convolutional layer and 3 fully connected layers	81.66%
Hurricane Sandy 2012	Hurricane	Convolutional auto-encoders	86.3%
Flood videos	Flood	Base CNN and CNN-GRU (Gated Recurrent Unit)	71%
Flash flood in Vietnam	Flood	Deep Learning Neural Network	92.15%
World View – 2 image of 2011 Tohoku Earthquake-Tsunami	Earthquake	U-net Convolutional network, Deep Residual U net model	70.9%

USE CASES OF AI TECHNIQUES

Applications Using AI in Disaster Mitigation

As shown in the Figure 4, In the debacle moderation stage, leaders need to recognize peril and dangers (Application Region 1), anticipate conceivable effects (Application Region 2), evaluate weakness (Application Region 3), and foster relief procedures (Application Region 4), to make more grounded, more secure, and stronger networks (Sun et al., 2020b). Artificial intelligence methods have been used extensively to help reduce disasters across all four regions. For Application Region 1, managed models and solo models have been used the most, followed by Regions 2 and 3. On the other hand, in all four regions, support learning and profound support learning are rarely used. Potential dangers and dangers ought to be distinguished for the local

Figure 4. Artificial intelligence techniques for disaster management

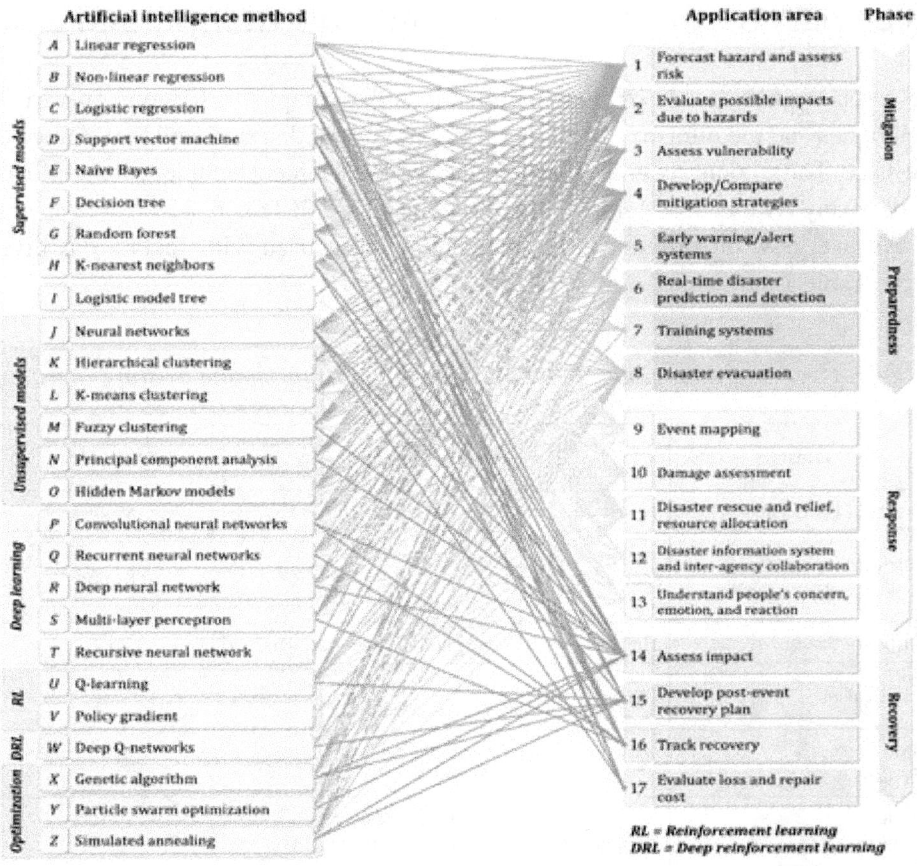

area of interest. For normal dangers, qualities of landscape, lithology, meteorology, and, surprisingly, human exercises ought to be examined, and risk zone guides ought to be created. Conventional strategies, for example, field observing, material science-based models, master studies, and multi-rules dynamic techniques are applied to distinguish perils and chance elements (McConnon, 2018). Now and again, these strategies are work serious, perhaps with a high deception rate. For this situation, computer-based intelligence strategies can quickly examine huge volumes of information to survey peril gambles sooner rather than later (Pradhan, 2009; Yilmaz, 2010). There are broad examinations applying different man-made intelligence techniques to create powerlessness maps for various kinds of dangers. For example, snow torrential slide expectations have been made utilizing strategic relapse (LR), support vector machine (SVM) (Choubin et al., 2019), and brain organizations. Avalanche defenselessness can be surveyed by SVM (Goetz et al., 2015; Xu et al., 2019), LR (Goetz et al. 2015), irregular woods (RF) (Goetz et al., 2015), and brain organizations. The previously mentioned simulated intelligence strategies have likewise been applied to different kinds of risks, like planning woodland fire vulnerability (Sachdeva et al., 2018), foreseeing fire size (Mitsopoulos & Mallinis, 2017), and gauging precipitation.

Artificial intelligence methods have been applied to appraise potential effects and survey weaknesses (DHS, 2010). For example, conceivable primary harm under normal hazard(s) can be anticipated by utilizing delicacy bends, which were generally worked from factual examinations of verifiable and reenactment information and presently can be assessed from the utilization of artificial intelligence techniques, like LR (Kameshwar & Padgett, 2014), brain organizations (Mangalathu et al., 2018), and SVM (Mahmoudi & Chouinard, 2016).

Foundation administration disturbances because of perils can be anticipated in light of verifiable information utilizing summed-up relapse models, choice tree (DT), and Bayesian added substance relapse tree (BART). Utilizing information from actual sensors and social detecting, the weakness of designs and networks can be surveyed with spatial relapse models, brain organizations, profound brain organizations (Nabian & Meidani, 2018b), and so on. As far as the quantity of distributions, there are fewer uses of artificial intelligence strategies to assessperil-prompted influence and surveying local area weakness (Application Regions 2 and 3), contrasted and those on danger figure and hazard evaluation (Application Region 1). In light of the effect and weakness examinations, leaders can acquire better circumstance mindfulness with more certainty and foster successful moderation procedures, for example, retrofitting weak designs (Karamlou et al., 2016), raising electric substations and utilizing underground links and creating viable calamity related approaches (Sun W2020b). In this cycle, computer-based intelligence procedures can uphold creating and contrasting moderation systems (Karamlou et al., 2016). For example, unique artificial intelligence strategies have been applied to distinguishing the board needs, assessing individuals' requirements during a debacle and perceiving human exercises Improvement calculations have been used to create workable strategies for disaster reaction and reclamation (Bocchini & Frangopol, 2012b), while grouping calculations are used to investigate distant photos and create emergency courses of action. Thus far, only few studies have utilised artificial intelligence in the creation and comparison of alleviation strategies (Application Region 4).

Applications of AI in Disaster Relief

It is imperative to view disaster response times as a matter of life and death. As shown in the figure 4, Decision-makers need to put forth their best efforts to understand the issue and improve the efficacy of reaction initiatives. It follows that situation awareness is required for effective decision-making (Application Areas 9 and 10) and user-friendly disaster information systems for effective coordination (Application Area 12) in order to ensure disaster relief and address people's urgent needs and concerns (Application Areas 11 and 13). AI methods can support reaction and rehabilitation activities.While supervised and unsupervised models, as well as deep learning, are often commonly employed in Areas 9 and 10, other AI approaches are rarely applied in these fields. Area 11 has been where most AI approaches have been used. Deep learning algorithms and primarily supervised models have been applied to Areas 12 and 13 (Kim et al., 2018c).Mapping the impact area (8) is essential for situation awareness and efficient disaster response (Ramchurn et al., 2016).f

Event maps and damage information generated by different AI approaches can be highly helpful in organising search and rescue operations, staging and deploying resources, and understanding short-term housing demands. Massive volumes of data about disasters are continuously produced by robotics, social media (Cervone et al., 2016), unmanned aerial vehicles and satellites. These data can be used to create disaster event maps. For instance, satellite images have been used to produce infrastructure inventory models (Eguchi et al. 2008), maps of damaged buildings and bridges, and maps of disaster-impacted areas. Using computer vision techniques, these data are swiftly analysed to build "live maps" that illustrate crisis circumstances.

Prioritising response operations and assessing the level of infrastructure and structure damage can be done by comparing maps and pictures taken before and after an occurrence, looking for feature differences. Bevington and more individuals, 2015 2016 Nguyen et al.|2015 Cervone et al. Koch and associates, 2017. Axel and van Aardt, 2016; Cresa et al., 2017.Numerous databases have been developed to enable damage assessment for various structures and disasters, such as FEMA|2019 for flood damage assessment, HOWAS2I (Kellermann et al., 2020), and xBD for building damage assessment (Gupta et al., 2019; Kochersberger, et al., 2014).

After a big storm hit the Philippines, a group of more than 1000 experts from different countries worked together to make maps of the areas that were affected. These maps helped people see the damage quickly and figure out how to help. They used social media and mobile phone data to make decisions and share information. Sometimes, they use robots to help in the rescue efforts because the situation after a disaster can be dangerous for humans. Robots can do things like map the area and put out fires. But there are also challenges in using social media because it can be hard to know if the information is true or not.When a disaster happens, people often need to call for help and let their loved ones know they are safe. This means there are a lot more phone calls being made than usual. Machine learning can help recognize important words and process voice data quickly (Kondaveti & Ganz, 2009). It can also analyze the words people say to understand their emotions and help disaster managers make better decisions. Mobile phone data can also be used to track where people are going after a disaster. Sometimes, the communication network gets destroyed, so new ways of communicating need to be set up quickly. Sharing information and coordinating efforts between different organizations can be difficult during a disaster. Having systems that allow different groups to share information can help them work together better. These systems can also use data to learn about the disaster and figure out what help is needed. There are different types of systems that have been created to help during disasters, such as MADIS, Sahana, and SPIDER. Disasters not only cause physical damage, but they can also hurt people emotionally. Understanding how people are feeling can help provide better relief efforts. Artificial intelligence can help us understand how people are feeling and reacting by looking at what they say and share on social media. This includes the words and pictures they use, as well as information about when and where they are posting. By analyzing this data, we can learn how people's behaviors and emotions change over time and in different places. This can be helpful for understanding how people are affected by things like natural disasters and for providing support and healthcare when it's needed. Many scientists are studying this area and trying to develop ways to measure people's reactions and emotions using AI.

APPLICATIONS OF AI IN DISASTER RECOVERY

Catastrophe recovery is a procedure that involves many different groups of people, like the government and private organizations. It requires making decisions quickly to understand what needs to be done to fix things after a disaster. This can take a long time because there is a lot to do, like assessing the damage, planning and designing how to fix things, and actually doing the repairs (Caragea et al., 2014). Artificial intelligence (AI) can help make this process faster by using special methods to assess the damage, make plans, track the progress of recovery, and estimate how much it will cost to fix everything. AI can also help with other aspects of disaster recovery, like assessing the impact on people's emotions and the economy. It can analyze data from things like aerial images, social media, and surveys to help understand how people are affected and what needs to be done to help them. After assessing the damage, it's important to make plans for how to recover and rebuild. This can be challenging because there is limited time and resources available. Researchers use optimization techniques to find the best plans and make decisions about recovery. Measuring and tracking a community's recovery following a disaster is crucial during the recovery process (Gao, et al., 2006). This helps to build resilience and make sure everyone is getting better over time. Researchers use models and algorithms to analyze data from different sources, like social media, to understand how the recovery is going (Reilly et al., 2013; Kellerman et al., 2020; Ramchurn et al., 2016).

The habit of remotely monitoring disaster recovery via Google Street View is growing in popularity. When a disaster happens, governments need to help rebuild homes and lives quickly. They need to know how much damage there is and how much it will cost to repair. Artificial intelligence (AI) can help with this (Zhang, 2009). It can use pictures to find damage, figure out what repairs are needed, and estimate how much it will cost. AI can also analyze data about past disasters to help decide how to spend money for recovery. Right now, most estimates are based on real information from things like insurance claims and assessments after a disaster. But in the future, with more data and better technology (Kuang & Davison, 2017), AI can help estimate damage and repair costs even faster. However, it's important to have rules and standards for collecting and recording data so that everyone agrees on the estimates. After a disaster, there can be rumors and fraud, so it's important to be careful. Data mining can be used to track the dissemination of information and identify possible fraud and rumors (Takahashi, & Carmichael, 2015). AI can be used, for instance, by law enforcement and insurance firms to verify the veracity of a flood claim by comparing photos taken before and after the incident (Suriya & Sumithra, 2019; Gupta et al., 2019; Kellermann et al., 2020; Cervone et al., 2016).

APPLICATIONS

The article showcases various AI approaches and their advantages in aiding catastrophe management throughout many stages, along with some useful AI-driven tools for decision support as shown in Figure 5.

Figure 5. Applications of disaster management

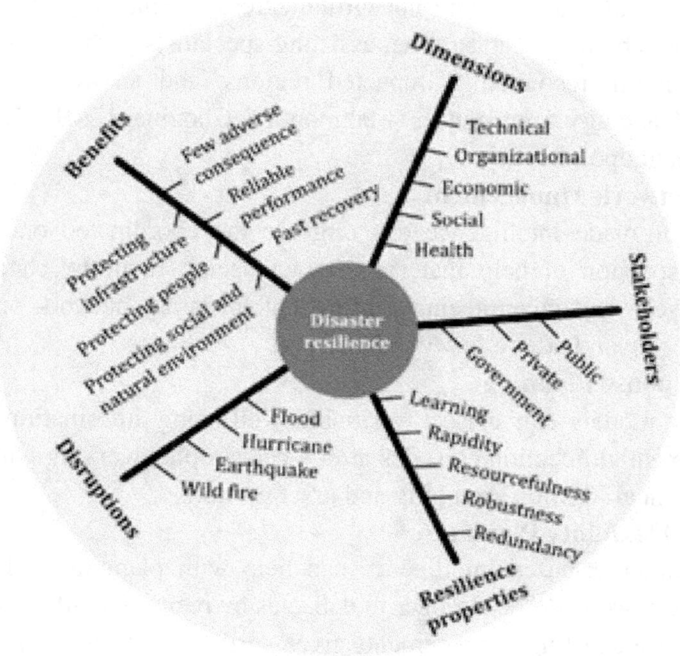

Early Warning Systems

- Computer-based intelligence and AI calculations can examine verifiable information and constant data to anticipate catastrophes like tropical storms, tremors, or floods, empowering early admonitions for in-danger regions.

Risk Appraisal and Mapping

- ML models can survey and guide weakness by investigating factors like landscape, populace thickness, and foundation, assisting specialists with focusing on assets and planning departure courses.

Crisis Reaction Optimization

- Artificial intelligence advances the designation of assets like crisis faculty, hardware, and supplies by foreseeing regions with the most elevated influence and progressively changing reaction systems given ongoing information (Mangalathu et al., 2018; Goetz et al., 2015).

Picture and Video Analysis:

- PC vision in computer-based intelligence can break down satellite symbolism and robot film to survey the degree of harm after a debacle, supporting fast and precise harm evaluation.

Social Media Monitoring

- NLP calculations can filter virtual entertainment stages for continuous data about the catastrophe, assisting specialists with measuring public opinion, recognizing impacted regions, and answering speedily to advancing circumstances (Mahmoudi & Chouinard, 2016; Bocchini and Frangopol, 2012b).

Inventory network Management

- Man-made intelligence can upgrade the coordinated operations and dispersion of help materials by foreseeing requests, checking stock levels, and guaranteeing a proficient inventory network on the board during and after a fiasco.

Medical Response Planning

- AI models can dissect verifiable well-being information to foresee potential infection episodes after a catastrophe, working with proactive clinical reaction arranging and asset portion.

Framework Flexibility Planning

- Computer-based intelligence can help with planning and retrofitting frameworks to be stronger to debacles by recreating different situations and suggesting enhancements given verifiable information.

Local area Commitment and Education

- Computer-basedintelligence-driven chatbots or remote helpers can give constant data and direction to the general population previously, during, and after a disaster, upgrading local area mindfulness and readiness.

Post-Disaster Recovery

- ML calculations help with focusing on recuperation endeavors by examining information on harm seriousness, financial effect, and local area needs, assisting specialists with pursuing informed choices for long-haul recuperation arranging.

CONCLUSION

Natural disasters are a major contributor to infrastructure and property damage, as well as fatalities. The complexity of disasters has resulted in a greater application of ML and DL innovations. This paper presents the findings of a review research on the application of ML and DL approaches in several disaster management domains, with the goal of supporting and improving disaster management operations. This endeavour has focused on publications that have been published since 2017, classifying them into different periods and stages of a disaster occurrence.

Different machine learning and deep learning techniques have been used in these categories to address various disaster situations, including typhoons, hurricanes, floods, lava flows, earthquakes, and landslides. The examined publications were focused on the following topics: catastrophe and hazard prediction, risk and vulnerability assessment, disaster detection, early warning systems, monitoring, damage assessment, post-disaster response, case studies, and applications. The challenges and future directions of study have been emphasised. As disaster recovery operations should be sustainable, future research should concentrate on applying ML and DL to improve efforts, reduce vulnerabilities, and evaluate resilience, especially that of vital infrastructure. The intricacy and urgency of catastrophe operations necessitate strong and tested ML and DL solutions. Decision-makers and domain experts need to be able to understand the produced models since catastrophe operations affect human life. Furthermore, research should focus on improving data quality, developing novel techniques for gathering data, and utilising crowdsourcing to increase the efficacy of ML/DL-based methodologies for disaster management operations.

REFERENCES

Alam, F., Ofli, F., Imran, M., & Aupetit, M. (2018). A twitter tale of three hurricanes: Harvey, irma, and maria. arXiv preprint arXiv:1805.05144.

Aybar-Ruiz, A., Jiménez-Fernández, S., Cornejo-Bueno, L., Casanova-Mateo, C., Sanz-Justo, J., Salvador-González, P., & Salcedo-Sanz, S. (2016). A novel Grouping Genetic Algorithm–Extreme Learning Machine approach for global solar radiation prediction from numerical weather models inputs. *Solar Energy*, *132*, 129–142. doi:10.1016/j.solener.2016.03.015

Bai, T., Le Wang, D. Y., Sun, K., Chen, Y., Li, W., & Li, D. (2023). Deep learning for change detection in remote sensing: A review. *Geo-Spatial Information Science*, *26*(3), 262–288. doi:10.1080/10095020.2022.2085633

Bai, Y., Mas, E., & Koshimura, S. (2018). Towards operational satellite-based damage-mapping using u-net convolutional network: A case study of 2011 tohoku earthquake-tsunami. *Remote Sensing (Basel)*, *10*(10), 1626. doi:10.3390/rs10101626

Bocchini, P., & Frangopol, D. M. (2012b). Restoration of bridge networks after an earth-quake: Multicriteria intervention optimization. *Earthquake Spectra*, *28*(2), 426–455. doi:10.1193/1.4000019

Bovolo, F., Bruzzone, L., & Marconcini, M. (2008). A novel approach to unsupervised change detection based on a semisupervised SVM and a similarity measure. *IEEE Transactions on Geoscience and Remote Sensing*, *46*(7), 2070–2082. doi:10.1109/TGRS.2008.916643

Bui, D. T., Hoang, N. D., Martínez-Álvarez, F., Ngo, P. T. T., Hoa, P. V., Pham, T. D., Samui, P., & Costache, R. (2020). A novel deep learning neural network approach for predicting flash flood susceptibility: A case study at a high frequency tropical storm area. *The Science of the Total Environment*, *701*, 134413. doi:10.1016/j.scitotenv.2019.134413 PMID:31706212

Caragea, C., Squicciarini, A., Stehle, S., Neppalli, K., & Tapia, A. (2014). Mapping moods: Geomapped sentiment analysis during Hurricane Sandy. In: *Proceedings of the 11th International Conference on Information Systems for Crisis Response and Management(ISCRAM 2014), ISCRAM*. Research Gate.

Cervone, G., Sava, E., Huang, Q., Schnebele, E., Harrison, J., & Waters, N. (2016). Using Twitter for tasking remote-sensing data collection and damage assessment: 2013 Boulder flood case study. *International Journal of Remote Sensing*, *37*(1), 100–124. doi:10.1080/01431161.2015.1117684

Chen, J., Gong, P., He, C., Pu, R., & Shi, P. (2003). Land-use/land-cover change detection using improved change-vector analysis. *Photogrammetric Engineering and Remote Sensing*, *69*(4), 369–379. doi:10.14358/PERS.69.4.369

Chen, L., Rottensteiner, F., & Heipke, C. (2021). Feature detection and description for image matching: From hand-crafted design to deep learning. *Geo-Spatial Information Science*, *24*(1), 58–74. doi:10.1080/10095020.2020.1843376

Chen, S. A., Escay, A., Haberland, C., Schneider, T., Staneva, V., & Choe, Y. 2018. *Benchmark dataset for automatic damaged building detection from post-hurricane remotely sensed imagery*. arXiv preprint arXiv:1812.05581.

Choubin, B., Borji, M., Mosavi, A., Sajedi-Hosseini, F., Singh, V. P., & Shamshirband, S. (2019). Snow avalanche hazard prediction using machine learning methods. *Journal of Hydrology (Amsterdam)*, *577*, 123929. doi:10.1016/j.jhydrol.2019.123929

DHS. (2010) *DHS [29] DOE (2014) Lantern live*. GitHub. https://github.com/GSA/digitalgov.gov/blob/master/content/posts/2014/12/2014-12-04-nd-fuel-during-disasters-with-lantern-live-app.mdrisk lexicon. URL https://www.dhs.gov/xlibrary/assets/dhs-risk-lexicon-2010.pdf

Duarte, D., Nex, F., Kerle, N., & Vosselman, G. (2018). Satellite Image Classification Of Building Damages Using Airborne And Satellite Image Samples In A Deep Learning Approach. *ISPRS Annals of the Photogrammetry, Remote Sensing and Spatial Information Sciences*, *4*(2), 89–96. doi:10.5194/isprs-annals-IV-2-89-2018

Esrafilian-Najafabadi, M., and Haghighat, F. (2022). Impact of predictor variables on the performance of future occupancy prediction: feature selection using genetic algorithms and machine learning. *Build. Environ. 219*, 109152. doi:. buildenv.2022.109152 doi:10.1016/j

Gama, M., Santos, B. F., & Scaparra, M. P. (2016). A multi-period shelter location-allocation model with evacuation orders for flood disasters. *EURO Journal on Computational Optimization*, *4*(3-4), 299–323. doi:10.100713675-015-0058-3

Gao, Y., Chen, Y.X., Ding, Y.S., & Tang, B.Y. (2006) Immune genetic algorithm based on network model for flood disaster evaluation. *Journal of Natural Disaster, 15*.

Goetz, J. N., Brenning, A., Petschko, H., & Leopold, P. (2015). Evaluating machine learning and statistical prediction techniques for landslide susceptibility modeling. *Computers & Geosciences*, *81*, 1–11. doi:10.1016/j.cageo.2015.04.007

Gong, P. (1993). Change detection using principal component analysis and fuzzy set theory. *Canadian Journal of Remote Sensing*, *19*(1), 22–29. doi:10.1080/07038992.1993.10855147

Gupta, R., Hosfelt, R., Sajeev, S., Patel, N., Goodman, B., Doshi, J., Heim, E., Choset, H., & Gaston, M. (2019) xBD: A dataset for assessing building damage from satellite imagery. In: *Proceedings of the CVPR Workshops 2019*. arXiv: 1911.09296v1

Healey, S. P., Cohen, W. B., Yang, Z., Brewer, C. K., Brooks, E. B., Gorelick, N., & Zhu, Z. (2018). Mapping forest change using stacked generalization: An ensemble approach. *Remote Sensing of Environment*, *204*, 717–728. doi:10.1016/j.rse.2017.09.029

Hong, C., Burney, J. A., Pongratz, J., Nabel, J. E., Mueller, N. D., Jackson, R. B., & Davis, S. J. (2021). Global and regional drivers of land-use emissions in 1961–2017. *Nature*, *589*(7843), 554–561. doi:10.103841586-020-03138-y PMID:33505037

Howarth, P. J., & Wickware, G. M. (1981). Procedures for change detection using Landsat digital data. *International Journal of Remote Sensing*, *2*(3), 277–291. doi:10.1080/01431168108948362

Jain, H., Dhupper, R., Shrivastava, A., & Kumar Dand Kumari, M. (2023). Leveragingmachinelearning algorithms forimproved disaster preparedness andresponse through accurate weatherpattern and natural disaster prediction. *Frontiers in Environmental Science*, *11*, 1194918. doi:10.3389/fenvs.2023.1194918

Jia, D., Yang, L., Lv, T., Liu, W., Gao, X., & Zhou, J. (2022). Evaluation of machine learning models for predicting daily global and diffuse solar radiation under different weather/pollution conditions. *Renew. Energy 187,* 896–906. doi:. 02.002 doi:10.1016/j.renene.2022

Johnson, R. D., & Kasischke, E. S. (1998). Change vector analysis: A technique for the multispectral monitoring of land cover and condition. *International Journal of Remote Sensing*, *19*(3), 411–426. doi:10.1080/014311698216062

Kameshwar, S., & Padgett, J. E. (2014). Multi-hazard risk assessment of highway bridges subjectedto earthquake and hurricane hazards. *Engineering Structures*, *78*, 154–166. doi:10.1016/j.engstruct.2014.05.016

Karamlou, A., Bocchini, P., & Christou, V. (2016) Metrics and algorithm for optimal retro strategy of resilient transportation networks. In: *Proceedings of the Maintenance, Monitoring, Safety, Risk and Resilience of Bridges and Bridge Networks*. Research Gate.

Kellermann, P., Schr¨oter, K., Thieken, A. H., Haubrock, S. N., & Kreibich, H. (2020). The object-specific flood damage database HOWAS21. *Natural Hazards and Earth System Sciences*, *20*(9), 2503–2519. doi:10.5194/nhess-20-2503-2020

Kemker, R., Salvaggio, C., & Kanan, C. (2018). Algorithms for semantic segmentation of multispectral remote sensing imagery using deep learning. *ISPRS Journal of Photogrammetry and Remote Sensing*, *145*, 60–77. doi:10.1016/j.isprsjprs.2018.04.014

Kim Y, Ghorpade A, Zhao F, Pereira FC, Zegras PC, Ben-Akiva M (2018c) Activity recognition for a smartphone and web-based human mobility sensing system. *IEEE Intelligent Systems, 33.*

Kochersberger, K., Kroeger, K., Krawiec, B., Brewer, E., & Weber, T. (2014) Postdisaster remote sensing and sampling via an autonomous helicopter. *Journal of Field Robotics 31.*

Kondaveti, R., & Ganz, A. (2009). Decision support system for resource allocation in disaster management. In: *The Annual International Conference of the IEEE Engineering in Medicine and Biology Society*. IEEE. 10.1109/IEMBS.2009.5332498

Kong, S.G., Jin, D., Li, S., & Kim, H. (2016b). Fast rename detection in surveillance video using logistic regression and temporal smoothing. *Fire Safety Journal, 79*.

Kuang, S., & Davison, B. D. (2017). Learning word embeddings with Chi-Square weights for healthcare tweet classification. *Applied Sciences (Basel, Switzerland), 7*(8), 846. doi:10.3390/app7080846

LeCun, Y., Bengio, Y., & Hinton, G. (2015). Deep Learning. *Nature, 521*(7553), 436–444. doi:10.1038/nature14539 PMID:26017442

Leng, P., Yang, Z., Yan, Q.-Y., Shang, G.-F., Zhang, X., Han, X.-J., & Li, Z.-L. (2023). A framework for estimating all-weather fine resolution soil moisture from the integration of physics-based and machine learning-based algorithms. *Computers and Electronics in Agriculture, 206*, 107673. doi:10.1016/j.compag.2023.107673

Li, Y., Liu, W., Feng, Q., Zhu, M., Yang, L., & Zhang, J. (2022). Effects of land use and land cover change on soil organic carbon storage in the Hexi regions, Northwest China. *Journal of Environmental Management, 312*, 114911. doi:10.1016/j.jenvman.2022.114911 PMID:35305354

Li, Y., Ye, S., & Bartoli, I. (2018). Semisupervised classification of hurricane damage from postevent aerial imagery using deep learning. *Journal of Applied Remote Sensing, 12*(4), p.045008. 10.1117/1.JRS.12.045008

Liu, T., Yang, L., & Lunga, D. (2021). Change detection using deep learning approach with object-based image analysis. *Remote Sensing of Environment, 256*, 112308. doi:10.1016/j.rse.2021.112308

Lu, D., Li, G., Valladares, G. S., & Batistella, M. (2004). Mapping soil erosion risk in Rondonia, Brazilian Amazonia: Using RUSLE, remote sensing and GIS. *Land Degradation & Development, 15*(5), 499–512. doi:10.1002/ldr.634

Mahmoudi, S. N., & Chouinard, L. (2016). Seismic fragility assessment of highway bridges using support vector machines. *Bulletin of Earthquake Engineering, 14*(6), 1571–1587. doi:10.100710518-016-9894-7

Mangalathu, S., Heo, G., & Jeon, J. S. (2018). Artificial neural network based multi-dimensional fragility development of skewed concrete bridge classes. *Engineering Structures, 162*, 166176. doi:10.1016/j.engstruct.2018.01.053

McConnon, A. (2018) *AI helps cities predict natural disasters*. WSJ. https://www.wsj.com/articles/ai-helps-cities-predict-natural-disasters-1530065100

McDermid, G. J., Linke, J., Pape, A. D., Laskin, D. N., McLane, A. J., & Franklin, S. E. (2008). Object-based approaches to change analysis and thematic map update: Challenges and limitations. *Canadian Journal of Remote Sensing*, *34*(5), 462–466. doi:10.5589/m08-061

Mitsopoulos, I., & Mallinis, G. (2017). A data-driven approach to assess large fire size generation in Greece. *Natural Hazards*, *88*(3), 1591–1607. doi:10.100711069-017-2934-z

Mouzannar, H., Rizk, Y., & Awad, M. (2018). Damage Identification in Social Media Posts using Multimodal Deep Learning. In ISCRAM. Research Gate.

Nabian, M. A., & Meidani, H. (2018b). Deep learning for accelerated seismic reliability analysis of transportation networks. *Computer-Aided Civil and Infrastructure Engineering*, *33*(6), 443–458. doi:10.1111/mice.12359

Nguyen, D. T., Ofli, F., Imran, M., & Mitra, P. (2017). Damage assessment from social media imagery data during disasters. In *Proceedings of the 2017 IEEE/ACM International Conference on Advances in Social Networks Analysis and Mining 2017* (pp. 569-576). IEEE. 10.1145/3110025.3110109

Pradhan, B. (2009). Flood susceptible mapping and risk area delineation using logistic regression, GIS and remote sensing. *Journal of Spatial Hydrology*, *9*, 1–18.

Ramchurn, S. D., Huynh, T. D., Wu, F., Ikuno, Y., Flann, J., Moreau, L., Fischer, J. E., Jiang, W., Rodden, T., Simpson, E., Reece, S., Roberts, S., & Jennings, N. R. (2016). A disaster response system based on human-agent collectives. *Journal of Artificial Intelligence Research*, *57*, 661–708. doi:10.1613/jair.5098

Reilly, J., Dashti, S., Ervasti, M., Bray, J. D., Glaser, S. D., & Bayen, A. M. (2013). Mobile phones as seismologic sensors: Automating data extraction for the iShake system. *IEEE Transactions on Automation Science and Engineering*, *10*(2), 242–251. doi:10.1109/TASE.2013.2245121

Sachdeva, S., Bhatia, T., & Verma, A. K. (2018). GIS-based evolutionary optimized gradient boosted decision trees for forest fire susceptibility mapping. *Natural Hazards*, *92*(3), 1399–1418. doi:10.100711069-018-3256-5

Shao, Z., & Cai, J. (2018). Remote sensing image fusion with deep convolutional neural network. *IEEE Journal of Selected Topics in Applied Earth Observations and Remote Sensing*, *11*(5), 1656–1669. doi:10.1109/JSTARS.2018.2805923

Silván-Cárdenas, J. L., & Wang, L. (2014). On quantifying post-classification subpixel landcover changes. *ISPRS Journal of Photogrammetry and Remote Sensing*, *98*, 94–105. doi:10.1016/j.isprsjprs.2014.09.018

Singh, A. (1989). Review article digital change detection techniques using remotely-sensed data. *International Journal of Remote Sensing*, *10*(6), 989–1003. doi:10.1080/01431168908903939

Sit, M. A., Koylu, C., & Demir, I. (2019). Identifying disaster-related tweets and their semantic, spatial and temporal context using deep learning, natural language processing and spatial analysis: A case study of Hurricane Irma. *International Journal of Digital Earth*, *12*(11), 1205–1229. doi:10.1080/17538947.2018.1563219

Sun, W. (2020). *Applications of artificial intelligence for disaster management.* Springer.

Sun W, Bocchini P, Davison BD (2020b) Resilience metrics and measurement methods for transportation infrastructure: the state of the art. *Sustainable and Resilient Infrastructure* *5*(3). doi:10.1080/23789689.2018.1448663

Suriya, M., & Sumithra, M. G. (2019) Enhancing cooperative spectrum sensing in flying cell towers for disaster management using convolutional neural networks. In: *Proceedings of the EAI International Conference on Big Data Innovation for Sustainable Cognitive Computing*, (pp 181–190). IEEE.

Takahashi, B. & Carmichael, C. (2015). Communicating on Twitter during a disaster: An analysis of tweets during Typhoon Haiyan in the Philippines. *Computers in Human Behavior, 50.*

UNISDR. (2011a). *Mid-Term Review 2010-2011: Hyogo Framework for Action 2005-2015: Building the Resilience of Nations and Communities to Disasters*. United Nations International Strategy for Disaster Reduction.

Wang, S., Quan, D., Liang, X., Ning, M., Guo, Y., & Jiao, L. (2018). A deep learning framework for remote sensing image registration. *ISPRS Journal of Photogrammetry and Remote Sensing*, *145*, 148–164. doi:10.1016/j.isprsjprs.2017.12.012

Weng, Q. (2002). Land use change analysis in the Zhujiang Delta of China using satellite remote sensing, GIS and stochastic modelling. *Journal of Environmental Management*, *64*(3), 273–284. doi:10.1006/jema.2001.0509 PMID:12040960

Xu, J. Z., Lu, W., Li, Z., Khaitan, P., & Zaytseva, V. (2019). *Building damage detection in satellite imagery using convolutional neural networks*. arXiv preprint arXiv:1910.06444.

Yilmaz, I. (2010). Comparison of landslide susceptibility mapping methodologies for Koyulhisar, Turkey: Conditional probability, logistic regression, artificial neural networks, and support vector machine. *Environmental Earth Sciences*, *61*(4), 821–836. doi:10.100712665-009-0394-9

Yuan, F., Sawaya, K. E., Loeffelholz, B. C., & Bauer, M. E. (2005). Land cover classification and change analysis of the Twin Cities (Minnesota) Metropolitan Area by multitemporal Landsat remote sensing. *Remote Sensing of Environment*, *98*(2-3), 317–328. doi:10.1016/j.rse.2005.08.006

Zhang, H., Ning, X., Shao, Z., & Wang, H. (2019). Spatiotemporal Pattern Analysis of China's Cities Based on High-Resolution Imagery from 2000 to 2015. *ISPRS International Journal of Geo-Information*, *8*(5), 241. doi:10.3390/ijgi8050241

Zhang, S., Zhang, J., Li, X., Du, X., Zhao, T., Hou, Q., & Jin, X. (2022a). Estimating the grade of storm surge disaster loss in coastal areas of China via machine learning algorithms. *Ecological Indicators*, *136*, 108533. doi:10.1016/j.ecolind.2022.108533

Zhang Y. (2009). Planning for housing recovery? lessons learned from Hurricane Andrew. *Journal of the American Planning Association, 76.*

Zhou, X., Wu, D., Li, J., Liang, J., Zhang, D., & Chen, W. (2022). Cultivated land use efficiency and its driving factors in the Yellow River Basin, China. *Ecological Indicators*, *144*, 109411. doi:10.1016/j.ecolind.2022.109411

Chapter 6
Artificial Intelligence and IoT-Based Disaster Management System

R. Renugadevi
R.M.K. Engineering College, India

Lakshmi Haritha Medida
https://orcid.org/0000-0002-6400-8998
R.M.K. Engineering College, India

ABSTRACT

Among the numerous terrible natural and artificial disasters that afflict the planet are enormous earthquakes, floods, aircraft accidents, tsunamis, and building collapses. In order to lessen and prevent the losses that these disasters entail, disaster management is crucial. Only the first 48 hours have a high chance of rescuing a victim; after that, it tends to drop to nothing. The victim can be sent to medical attention more quickly for prompt reaction and identification. This issue can be significantly lessened by combining mobile robots with effective human victim detection (HVD) systems powered by artificial intelligence (AI) and overseen by expert teams. The cutting-edge internet of things (IoT) technology envisions an internal network of intelligent physical objects that is global in scope. IoT is a promising technology with a variety of uses, including disaster relief. The role that IoT plays in disaster management is significant, pervasive, and potentially lifesaving.

DOI: 10.4018/979-8-3693-2280-2.ch006

INTRODUCTION

Among the numerous terrible natural and Artificial disasters that afflict the planet are enormous earthquakes, floods, aircraft accidents, tsunamis, and building collapses. In order to lessen and prevent the losses that these disasters entail, disaster management is crucial. In an unstructured collapsed building, search and rescue efforts for victim identification are risky and time-consuming. Only the first 48 hours have a high chance of rescuing a victim; after that, it tends to nothing. The victim can be sent to medical attention more quickly for prompt reaction and identification. This issue can be significantly lessened by combining mobile robots with effective Human Victim Detection (HVD) systems powered by Artificial Intelligence (AI) and overseen by expert teams.

The cutting-edge Internet of Things (IoT) technology envisions an internal network of intelligent physical objects that is global in scope. IoT is a promising technology with a variety of uses, including disaster relief. The role that IoT plays in disaster management is so significant, pervasive, and potentially life-saving. The use of IoT to disaster management is covered in this chapter. More specifically, it compares commercial systems for IoT-based catastrophe management for various types of calamities. It demonstrates how several IoT applications, such earthquake and fire detection early warning systems, are implemented and illustrates various methods for discussing application, IoT architecture, and disaster-specific research.

ARTIFICIAL INTELLIGENCE BASED DISASTER MANAGEMENT

Artificial intelligence (AI) is a system of cognitive processes that are similar to those of humans, such as learning new things, speaking, and solving problems. AI may also perceive its surroundings and behave accordingly to maximise its performance parameters or reach its objectives. Many nations, especially those that have had severe disasters or are prone to natural disasters, must implement a number of disaster management measures before, during, and after catastrophes due to the growing effect of natural disasters. Natural Disaster Management (NDM) is often separated into many stages based on the incidence, progression, and evolution of disasters. These stages include disaster preparedness, the time period prior to the catastrophe, disaster response, the time during and following the disaster, and disaster recovery, the extended period following the disaster. Figure 1 represents the Natural Disaster management in three phases.

The classification can be carried out using many decision tree algorithms, such as decision stump, hoeffiding tree, J48, Linear Model Tree (LMT), Random Forest, Random Tree, Representative (REP) Tree, J48 graft, and other well-known algorithms

Figure 1. Phases of natural disaster management

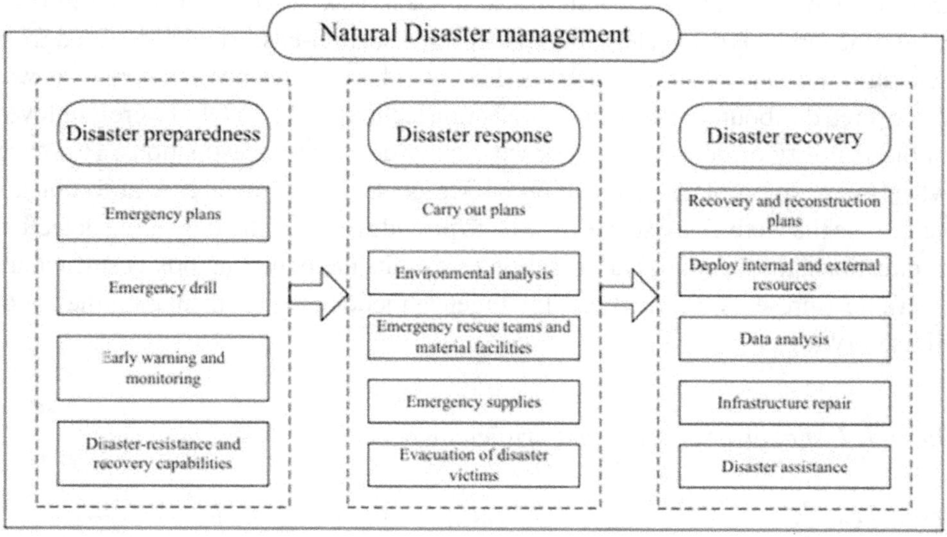

like LibSVM, Logistic regression, Multilayer perceptron, BayesNet, and Naive Bayes. Physical attributes including voice, scent, body warmth, motion, face form, skin colour, and body shape are employed to determine presence. Standard person detection algorithms and RGB picture databases may be used to quickly identify human bodies. Using a microphone, a cross-power spectrum approach is utilised to recognise voice. CO2 sensors measure gas emissions, and by identifying breathing patterns, they are able to identify human presence. Nevertheless, this technique has drawbacks due to its extended response time and the temperature, humidity, and dust content of the surrounding air.

(i) Thermal and RGB pictures have been used in several studies to identify victims.

(ii) Pre-trained CNN architectures were frequently used in several convolutional layers. (In actuality, the majority of human detection techniques used concepts like bounding boxes and techniques like SSD, YOLO, and RCN, etc.; they are not in our field of interest.)
(iii) Accurate results were obtained quickly using machine learning techniques such as kNN, SVM, Naive Bayes, and Decision trees.
(iv) CNN architectures are commended for their enhanced feature extraction powers.

Deep Learning algorithms can automatically identify patterns in images and categorise them into distinct groups based on those patterns. These algorithms are mostly used for image and video analysis. The learning models are divided into three categories: transfer learning-based models (task-based models derived from pre-trained models), deep learning models (application-based models trained from scratch), and basic deep learning models (standard pre-trained networks). It was discovered that bounding box-based detection techniques like YOLO were employed in the majority of deep learning-based person detection investigations. However, when the position of the acquisition device is clear, it is more crucial to quickly determine the victim's existence in order to provide rescue help. For victim detection applications, the standard classification that omits the bounding box is sufficient.

Table 1 presents the Artificial Intelligence model used for managing the list of disaster types

Table 1. List of disaster types and artificial models used

Models (Top 10)	Proportion (%)	Disaster type (Top 10)	Proportion (%)
Artificial neural network (ANN)	19.46	Natural disaster	29.08
Support vector machine (SVM)	11.92	Flood	26.95
Fuzzy logic (FL)	7.79	Landslide	13.48
Regress algorithm (RA)	6.81	Earthquake	9.57
Genetic algorithms (GA)	6.08	Rainfall	4.26
Random forest (RF)	5.6	Drought	4.26
Robotics	5.11	Fire	3.9
Bayesian (Bayes)	3.65	Storm	3.9
Extreme learning machine (ELM)	3.16	Collapse	1.42
Decision tree (DT)	2.68	Debris flow	1.42
Wavelet analysis (WA)	2.43	Research stage	Proportion
Expert system (ES)	2.19	Disaster preparedness	63.73
Particle swarm optimization (PSO)	1.95	Disaster response	28.17
Search algorithm (SA)	1.95	Disaster recovery	8.1

Seismic Event

The two primary components of research contents are emergency evacuation and online applications. For instance, Gelernter et al. (2013) employed natural language processing techniques to recognise references to streets, addresses, buildings, and urban areas in tweets that were sent out in the immediate wake of the earthquake that struck Christchurch, New Zealand, in February 2011. Song et al. (2017) gathered a large amount of diverse data of 1.6 million users over three years regarding the four years' worth of earthquakes that have struck Japan, Combining information from news reports and transportation networks, and developed an intelligent system built on a deep learning architecture to comprehend and forecast how people would move and behave during various kinds of natural catastrophes.

Burning

The two primary components of research material are emergency behaviour and evacuation studies. For instance, Miller-Hooks et al. (2007) presented a concept for ES that may help rescue personnel and allow for real-time evaluation of the degree of explosion and fire damage to a structure through the use of sensor technologies. It also involves the investigation of the behavioural dynamics of pedestrians during an emergency evacuation using cellular automata to represent the dynamics of fire and smoke spread. The viability and promise of using swarm robotics and swarm intelligence to battle fires autonomously were shown by Innocente et al. (2019), with an emphasis on the self-coordination mechanisms needed for the required firefighting behaviour to evolve.

Fury

Unmanned sea surface vehicles were used for the first time for emergency response by the University of South Florida's Centre for Robot-Assisted Search and Rescue. They proved that these vehicles were suitable for disaster management by identifying submerged debris (moorings and handrails), detecting damage to seawalls and piers, and identifying safe lanes for sea navigation.

IOT BASED DISASTER MANAGEMENT

IOT, is a relatively new connectivity model that predicts a near future in which everyday devices are equipped with microcontrollers, data transceivers, and suitable protocol stacks to enable them to communicate and change a crucial portion of the Internet into a commensurate degree. Therefore, the goal of the IOT framework is to make the web even more pervasive and immersive. Effective information management requires collaboration through the sharing of knowledge and/or experience as well as the planning of actions, choices, and activities. In addition, to carry out complicated tasks like evacuating a crisis zone and using actuators to accomplish processes, specific knowledge and abilities had to be pooled during the associate degree emergency. Figure 2 represents IoT based disaster recovery system classification.

Figure 2. IoT-based disaster recovery systems classification

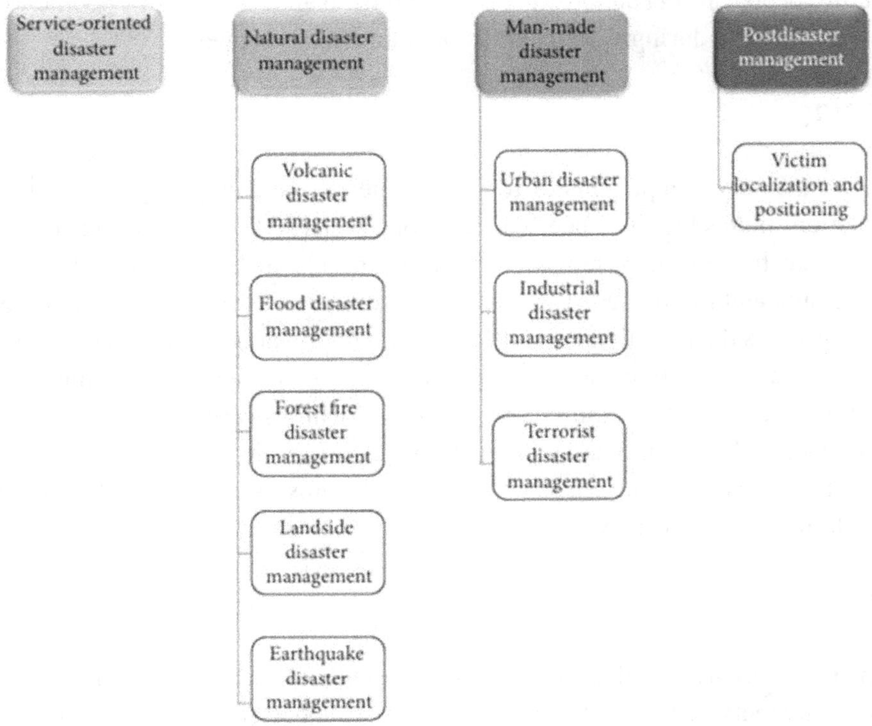

Natural Disaster Management

Volcanic Eruption Control

Numerous more research into the use of IoT in volcanic eruptions are administered since volcanic eruptions are also a common cause of catastrophe. Among the most important and illustrious LPWANs, volcano observation is one of the applications of long-range (LoRa) technology. One of the most prominent and illustrious LPWANs is the application of long-range (LoRa) technology for volcano surveillance. The first LoRa-based, low-power, and inexpensive wireless sensor element networks were already in place to monitor water level in locations with heat anomalies in volcanic regions. All eight of them On Tenerife's Teide volcano, sensors were launched. Such results provide strong support for relevant volcanic observing. Carrera-Villacres et al. (2020) talk about a fog collection system that encourages water innovation the Internet of Things (IoT) and wet towers with time observing. Their framework permits environmental factors to be while offering various sources of ambient fog water, it is monitored.

Management of Forest Fire Disasters

Forest fires are another kind of natural calamity. The use of IoT is essential in the fight against forest fires. This is frequently the case with several research projects. The work by Kalatzis et al (2018) suggested using the Edge and Fog ideas' graded design to the field of UAV-based fire detection applications. This three-phase structure incorporates the critical competencies of cloud computing, the resources produced by fog computing, and the UAVs' sensing capacity. The layers work well together to overcome the obstacles that the early fire detection situation presents. Initial experimental assessments of critical performance metrics demonstrate the smart allocation and reliability of vital resources, including battery life, network resources, central processor/RAM, and battery life.

Trinath Basu et al (2018) make advantage of the Arduino IDE's ESP8266. In a similar manner, the Node MCU communicates with LCDs in the US, regardless of frame standing. As a result, the client is greatly assisted in understanding the current status message by the Node Mcu interface with the LAN module. The client is informed that the fireside is located. Whatever the reason for the client's lack of speed proximity, this approach is really helpful. The mechanism automatically becomes active if a fire occurs and notifies the customer by means of a mobile smartphone app or webpage that is available for purchase.

One of the primary goals of sensible forests is the early detection and forecast of wildfires. However, the apparatus required for such observation often consists of an expensive and sophisticated sensing component, network infrastructure, and central processing capabilities for data analysis from thousands of sensors. A solution that specialises in edge computing by utilising the idea of Mobile Hubs is put forth by Neumann et al. (2018). On paper, an IoT picture framework for hearth detection is created, which employs Event Process Agents (EPAs) running on smartphones that are connected to forestry systems. It is based on Context Net.

Disaster Management With Floods

Numerous studies on the flood disaster are overseen by non-traditional researchers. One approach demonstrated the usefulness and effectiveness of IIoT by using the extensive Data-HPC Integration IIoT Flood Management Method. It also provided a thorough rundown of our methodology, algorithms, metrics, performance, and experiment analysis. Its flood risk management service will cause the combination of IoT, Big Data, and HPC. will also have more effective alarm systems and analysis. It offers early warning supported ecoinformatics (e.g., GPS, GIS, and remote sensing) to the Internet of Things. Applications on the Internet and cloud computing to the innovative snowmelt flood associate in nursing strategy. It is composed of the following components: IoT facilities and technology, cloud information storage, control system, software, and utilities. It offers early warning backed geoinformatics (such as GPS, GIS, and remote sensing (RS)) to the Internet of Things.

Applications on the internet and cloud to the Associate in Nursing's inventive snowmelt flood plan. It is composed of the following components: IoT facilities and technology, cloud information storage, control system, software, and utilities. When the amount of water surpasses the variable, the message is sent there instantly since the water level sensor device will detect the goal threshold. In a similar vein, the IoT technology employed by the saviours might enhance SAR operations. Another method for managing flood disasters is to use artificial intelligence (AI) and contemporary IoT technology to manage floods in urban areas.

Disaster Management for Landslides

The terrain made of rock, dirt, or dust may be found on an incline in the planet's surface. The landslip is caused by the earthquake, the volcano, or other elements that make the slope unstable. Landslides are often characterised as a type of mass loss by geologists, scientists who study the physical structures of the Earth. Numerous analyses have been conducted to examine how the IoT approach is being victimised by landslides. An important communication infrastructure is provided by internet communication networks. The landslip early detection system can support the network of wireless sensors thanks to an Internet of Things feature. However, the system would gather data from a variety of sensors including an Arduino AT Mega 2560 microcontroller to identify victims. The measured and real physical parameter shows that the system is equipped to handle the discovered information. Through entirely distinct methods, such as Logistic Regression (LR) and Weights of Proof, El Moulat et al. (2018) have identified locations susceptible to landslides.

It is comprised of basic field sensing components and leverages information gathering systems to record sensor readings, perform machine learning, and consider the state of affairs, usually via the Internet of Things. This design may be a grounded method of distant observation. It also provides a novel method of pursuing hillslopes that are ready for slick conditions and will quickly indicate a degree of hazardous activity in advance. This also provides timely information on land-lifting activities, monitors current or period observance data, makes it easier for us to learn about land-life events, and makes room for more affordable technologies and preventive care. WSN are essential for several applications, including landslip detection, waste management, and monitoring water quality in rivers and reservoirs. Intelligent grids from WSNs are among the most important technological systems. The main problem with this installation is that it is unreliable due to the unpredictable nature of equipment breakdown. The primary causes of energy failures are energy shortages and a lack of information on energy offer and usage limitations. This will raise the cost of power use and give consumers the idea that electricity is not inexpensive.

Management of Earthquake Disasters

Earthquakes are one of the most dreaded natural disasters since they occur often. Japan has seen a number of significant seismic catastrophes throughout its history, which has strengthened its efforts to mitigate earthquake risks, enforce strict construction regulations, and provide resources for emergency response. By comprehensive system with the lowest process power and an affordable acceleration-sensing element for earthquakes is shown. In this regard, they assess the performance and accuracy of four distinct sensors in order to select an appropriate acceleration-sensing element first. They are using machine learning to identify earthquakes by training a model for earthquake degree identification using regular motions, noise from buildings, and earthquake antecedents.

Using IoT, sensors, and deep learning models, Sharma (2020) is putting forth an associate degree-integrated seismic management system for disaster prevention, preparedness, response, and recovery. Using their model from earlier research, they will take into account the impact of the destruction on relief operations, emergency response, and emergency management. The results of their investigation will change how humans use knowledge analytics tools and methods to measure and monitor the effects of a disaster. Spalazzi et al. (2014) advance the connection between physical items and IT systems by using ontologies to describe human and computer intelligible descriptions of things. However, as recent research has also demonstrated, IoT will like using IoT technology in many situations to support challenging jobs in which active players are physical subjects.

The W3C linguistics-sensing element network's setup cluster first expands the linguistics-sensing element networks with concepts and locations that categorise actuators. This culminates in the idea of a whole metaphysical topic network. Semantic technologies may be important for the representation, storing, linking, investigating, and organising of information created and consumed. It provides several well-considered arguments in favour of the current IoT metaphysics. It may be used to assess the practicality of this strategy in associate degree emergency response scenarios.

Man- Made Disaster Management

A list of accidents has just been aware of the fatal collisions that occur in big cities. Floods, serious injuries, building collapses, and unauthorised aircraft flights are all often seen in metropolitan settings. When a tragedy of this nature is associated with any excellent city, the opportunity challenge increases since digital infrastructures within the good cities are fully outfitted with the greatest amount of coverage space.

Urban Disaster Management

The list of incidents has recently been updated to include fatal incidents in urban areas. Floods, serious injuries, building collapses, and unauthorised aircraft flights are all often seen in metropolitan settings. When a tragedy of this nature is associated with any excellent city, the opportunity challenge increases since digital infrastructures within the good cities are fully outfitted with the greatest amount of coverage space. Wireless fidelity is a major communication enabler used by the envisaged system between the subject and the instruments. In the event of any inconvenience, the intended subject automatically notifies the locals. In urban civilization, there is misuse of a generic profile (transient and complex nature) of known and classed entity features. The things establish permanent and temporal linkages that merge their shared existence into a dynamic dimension.

Industry Disaster Management

The market framework for urban infrastructure is gaining traction over time. Authors in China have looked at the conceptual and practical ramifications of bringing such a framework to life. IoT is meant to take advantage of the subterranean business city, which is similarly important to its parallel rivalry nice town higher than that of the bottom, after a number of acknowledged barriers have been formed. A completely distinct conveyance analytics network (VANET) system powers both kinds of IoT-enabled technologies, tracking and warning emergency personnel prior to an accident.

Terrorist Disaster Management

One of the tragedies caused by people is terrorism. Effective tactics are also required to confront and rescue victims of terrorism. Associate degree IoT-based architecture is anticipated to foresee terrorist risks in urban areas . The Medium-Term Module (MTR), the Long Duration Module (LTR), the Short Duration Reasoning Modulus, and other reasoning modules make up the kernel. The Technological Reasoning Kernel (TRM) is a part of this. Anticipating realistic terrorist threats while taking into account crucial factors pertaining to system players and users is the main objective. Additionally taken into consideration is the information offered by the sensor type's Event Identification and Formulation (EIF) Modulus.

An accompanying system called Advanced Terrorist Detector (ATDS) manipulates and informs the many vectors of consumer transaction-related data from vulnerable places. The federal government is then alerted by means of a material scanner that uses those very cluster-specific terror organisation representations to indicate that a predicted terrorist attack has supported the threshold values.

Post Disaster Management

At the moment, small air vehicles (MAVs) are one in every one of the economic ways in a catastrophic emergency. The MAVs will locate a victim under the direction of associate degree-linked electro-acoustic transducers. This idea was put into practise to find the victims. Generally, four microphones are built on top of MAV and particle sorting is done based on the received audio input. Aerial mechanics and sound propagation aid in an accurate tracking of the victim by an MAV. An Economic Location Associate Grade Approach is given as smart apps are simple to encourage labelling.

An Economic Location Associate Grade Approach is supplied since smart apps are simple to encourage labelling. The following is how the localization stage is carried out: The relationship is finally established by the Cramer-Rao sure (CRB) technique. (i) Two neighbour devices in Location-of-Things (LoT) are tagged by the Two-Way Time-of-Arrival. (ii) The audibility is supported via the employment of the most likely Estimate (MLE) regulation. Because the victim's movement and position may be recorded and predicted whenever leg and hip angles are employed, the Wearable Indoor Location Approach (WILA) is recommended. Three essential elements play a crucial role in determining the victim's walking ability: the victim detector, the human-robot interface device, and the context detecting function.

CONCLUSION

The goal of the current study is to recognise and classify different human victim body parts in circumstances involving fallen buildings by integrating deep learning features with machine learning classifiers. A person's life truly incorporates Internet of Things technologies. Indeed, it has the power to unite people and make the globe a smaller place. This technology has the potential to save lives in specific situations. For instance, it enables us to save many lives through disaster management in situations where both natural and man-made disasters cause significant environmental disturbance and human casualties. Since the Internet of Things allows devices to be connected to one another, information analytics and computational tools are employed to construct an IoT enabled disaster management system for early-warning systems.

REFERENCES

El Moulat, M., Debauche, O., Mahmoudi, S., Brahim, L. A., Manneback, P., & Lebeau, F. (2018). Monitoring system using internet of things for potential landslides. *Procedia Computer Science*, *134*, 26–34. doi:10.1016/j.procs.2018.07.140

Gelernter, J., & Balaji, S. (2013). An algorithm for local geoparsing of microtext. *GeoInformatica*, *17*(4), 635–667. doi:10.100710707-012-0173-8

Innocente, M. S., & Grasso, P. (2019). Self-organising swarms of frefghting drones: Harnessing the power of collective intelligence in decentralised multi-robot systems. *Journal of Computational Science*, *34*, 80–101. doi:10.1016/j.jocs.2019.04.009

Kalatzis, N. (2018). Edge computing in iot ecosystems for uav-enabled early fire detection. Proceedings of the 2018 IEEE International Conference on Smart Computing, SMARTCOMP, (pp. 106–114). IEEE. 10.1109/SMARTCOMP.2018.00080

Miller-Hooks, E., & Krauthammer, T. (2007). An intelligent evacuation, rescue and recovery concept. *Fire Technology*, *43*(2), 107–122. doi:10.100710694-006-8433-5

Neumann, G. B., De Almeida, V. P., & Endler, M. (2018). Smart forests: fire detection service. *Proceedings of the IEEE Symposium on Computers and Communications*, Corfu, Greece.

Sharma, S. (2020). *Impact of earthquakes based on satellite images using IoT and sensor networks*. Proceedings of the 2020 International Conference on communication Systems and networks, Bangalore, India.

Song, X., Shibasaki, R., Yuan, N. J., Xie, X., Li, T., & Adachi, R. (2017). DeepMob: Learning deep knowledge of human emergency behavior and mobility from big and heterogeneous data. *ACM Transactions on Information Systems*, *35*(4), 1–19. doi:10.1145/3057280

Spalazzi, L., Taccari, G., & Bernardini, A. (2014). *An internet of things ontology for earthquake emergency evaluation and response*. Proceedings of the 2014 International Conference on Collaboration Technologies and sSystems, CTS, Minneapolis, MN, USA. 10.1109/CTS.2014.6867619

Trinath Basu, M., Karthik, R., Mahitha, J., & Lokesh Reddy, V. (2018). IoT based forest fire detection system. *International Journal of Engineering and Technology (UAE)*, *7*(2), 124–126. doi:10.14419/ijet.v7i2.7.10277

Villacrés, D. C., Carrera Villacrés, J. L., Braun, T., Zhao, Z., Gómez, J., & Carabalí, J. Q. (2020). Fog harvesting and IoT based environment monitoring system at the Ilalo volcano in Ecuador. *International Journal on Advanced Science, Engineering and Information Technology*, *10*(1), 407–412. doi:10.18517/ijaseit.10.1.10775

Chapter 7
Prediction Analysis of Natural Disasters Using Machine Learning

P. Ramkumar
Sri Sairam College of Engineering, India

R. Uma
https://orcid.org/0000-0002-0053-0162
Sri Sairam Engineering College, India

D. Satishkumar
Nehru institute of Technology, India

J. Anitha Ruth
https://orcid.org/0000-0003-1900-6173
SRM institute of Science and Technology, India

S. Harikrishna
Sri Sairam College of Engineering, India

ABSTRACT

At present, the entire world has suffered a lot due to natural calamities such as torrential rain flows, earthquakes, tsunamis, storms, as well as global warming. Natural disasters create issues for the livelihoods of all the people. Many people may lose their belongings, and their life too. Some of these disasters may even lead to the spread of some kinds of diseases, which may affect people later. Although technology has grown in all the fields, prediction of the natural disaster becomes tedious for all researchers. Nowadays, machine learning algorithms provide a feasible solution for social issues. So, this chapter addresses the performances of decision tree and K-means algorithms to predict the natural disaster and analyze the performance.

DOI: 10.4018/979-8-3693-2280-2.ch007

INTRODUCTION

Dangers to human life, property, and the environment are all heightened by the complexity and fluidity of natural disasters. It can be difficult for conventional methods of prediction to capture the complex interplay of factors that leads to these occurrences. For more precise and timely predictions of natural disasters, machine learning's capacity to sift through massive datasets in search of hidden patterns holds great promise.

Countless towns have been affected by natural disasters like hurricanes, earthquakes, floods, and wildfires. Timely and precise forecast of these events is vital for implementing effective disaster management measures. Machine learning algorithms are investigated in this study article for their potential use in foreseeing multiple forms of natural disasters. This research intends to strengthen early warning systems, improve predictive accuracy, and aid in the development of more robust disaster preparedness plans by utilizing a wide variety of datasets, including meteorological, seismic, and environmental data.

Mitigating the effects of these catastrophes requires accurate forecast and prompt action. Natural catastrophes such as hurricanes, earthquakes, floods, wildfires, and tsunamis are all covered in depth in this article, which examines the use of machine learning algorithms in disaster prediction. The potential of machine learning models to improve predictive accuracy is investigated by utilizing a wide variety of datasets and attributes, leading to more efficient catastrophe prevention and mitigation plans.

Motivation

The impetus behind this research lies in using the potential of machine learning to increase the accuracy and lead time of natural disaster predictions. It is the goal of this research to shed light on the many uses and difficulties of applying machine learning algorithms to disaster prediction by evaluating and synthesizing the existing literature on various natural catastrophes.

Unraveling the complex link between protein structure and function depends on our ability to predict their natural disarray. Intrinsically disordered regions (IDRs) are emerging as prospective therapeutic targets, hence it is important to have a deeper understanding of their prevalence and implications in order to build effective drug development strategies.

Importance of Predicting Natural Disaster

It is crucial to have a strategy for forecasting, so, it is essential to have a method for predicting the abnormality that occurs naturally in proteins. Such forecasts are useful for directing experimental research, understanding disease causes, and guiding medication discovery aimed at disordered areas of proteins. Biological data might be extremely complex, but machine learning techniques can help us make sense of it all, opening up a promising new route for detecting protein dysfunction.

TECHNIQUES OF MACHINE LEARNING TO PREDICT NATURAL DISASTERS

Predictive models are developed using a range of machine learning algorithms, including support vector machines (SVM), decision trees (DT), random forests (RF), neural networks (NN), and ensemble methods. The algorithms are tailored to the specific challenges of disaster prediction for each type of natural calamity.

Earthquakes

Predictions of earthquake occurrence, magnitude, and regional impact using machine learning algorithms are being explored. Both the unpredictability of earthquakes and the scarcity of properly labelled earthquake data are discussed as obstacles in the study. Large-scale destruction and human casualties can be the result of earthquakes. Predicting seismic events early and accurately is critical for good disaster management. The purpose of this study is to improve earthquake prediction models by employing machine learning techniques.

Floods

In order to forecast floods, it is necessary to examine historical trends of precipitation, river levels, and land use. This study assesses the efficacy of machine learning models in flood prediction, underlining the significance of real-time data integration and model flexibility. Threats to both human lives and physical infrastructure are posed by floods brought on by heavy rain, overflowing rivers, or storm surges. Predicting the occurrence of floods in a timely manner and with sufficient accuracy is crucial for developing preventative measures and protecting communities. In order to improve flood prediction models, the focus of this study is on applying machine learning methods.

Wildfires

To estimate the likelihood of a wildfire starting, spreading, and becoming intense, scientists use machine learning algorithms. The chapter highlights the need for dynamic and adaptive models by discussing how weather, vegetation, and human activities all have a part in creating wildfire patterns. Ecosystems, animals, and people are all at risk from the dangers of wildfires. Wildfire prevention and suppression efforts can only be successful if they are based on timely and accurate predictions of wildfire occurrence and spread. Machine learning algorithms are the subject of this study, which aims to improve existing methods for predicting the spread of wildfires.

Tsunamis

Widespread devastation along coastlines is possible due to tsunamis, which are triggered by earthquakes or volcanic eruptions below the water. Early identificion and timely warnings are vital for minimising the damage on human lives and infrastructure. The purpose of this study is to investigate the potential of machine learning algorithms for improving tsunami forecasting and warning infrastructure. The study investigates the potential of machine learning for tsunami forecasting by examining seismic data, bathymetric data, and past tsunami records.

LITERATURE REVIEW

Purushotham & Caruso (2017) reviews machine learning techniques for pandemic and disaster management. Disaster and pandemic management have utilized various technologies such as IoT, object sensing, UAV, 5G and cellular networks, Smartphone-based systems, and satellite-based systems. Machine learning methods are well-suited for handling the multidimensional and enormous volumes of data in disaster and pandemic management. They are particularly useful for tasks like recognition, classification, and prediction of disasters. Machine learning algorithms can assist in disaster management duties, including establishing crowd evacuation routes and analyzing social media posts. They also help anticipate pandemics, monitor pandemic spread, and diagnose diseases.

Ofli (2018) addresses the challenge by proposing a hybrid approach that combines crowd sourcing and real-time machine learning to rapidly process large volumes of aerial data for disaster response. The approach involves using crowd sourcing to annotate features of interest in aerial images, which are then used to train a supervised machine learning system.

Yu et al. (2018) narrates floods are highly destructive natural disasters that are difficult to model. Machine learning (ML) methods have made significant contributions to the advancement of flood prediction systems .ML methods mimic the complex mathematical expressions of physical flood processes .ML's popularity has increased due to its numerous benefits and potential .Researchers aim to develop more accurate and efficient flood prediction models by introducing novel ML methods and hybridizing existing ones. The chapter focuses on the state of the art of hybridizing ML models in flood prediction .The main strategies for improving ML methods in flood prediction are hybridization, data decomposition, algorithm ensemble, and model optimization.

Ahmed Noori Rashid et al. (2018) discussed about an overview of different techniques and a comparison of their results in earthquake prediction using AI-based approaches.Various machine learning techniques, such as artificial neural networks (ANN) and clustering techniques, have been utilized for earthquake prediction.

These machine learning approaches have shown promise in detecting hidden patterns in earthquake data and improving the accuracy of earthquake forecasting. The chapter aims to assist in choosing a relevant earthquake prediction system by reviewing the contributions made by AI approaches in earthquake prediction.

Hemanth et al. (2019) emphasized an idea that leverage big data and data mining to observe and track patterns for natural disaster prediction and management strategies implementation. The chapter focuses on the utilization of technology, specifically Industry 4.0 and cognitive computing, for natural disaster prediction and management. The research work analyzed predictive models, including Artificial Neural Networks (ANN), sentiment model, and smart disaster prediction application (SDPA), to predict flash floods.

Goodwin (2020) stressed about the application of Artificial Intelligence (AI), machine learning (ML), and deep learning (DL) techniques in disaster management. The authors highlight the challenge of making sense of vast amounts of data generated during disasters and the need for intelligent systems to analyze, process, and visualize this data. The chapter adopts a systematic literature review approach to identify relevant publications on the use of AI, ML, and DL in disaster management. The authors found that the majority of the reviewed articles used these techniques on social media data, satellite data, sensor data, and historical data for classification and prediction. The chapter also mentions the most common algorithms used in these studies, including support vector machines (SVM), Naive Bayes (NB), Random Forest (RF), K-nearest neighbor (KNN), and Decision Tree (DT).

MACHINE LEARNING ALGORITHMS

Algorithms developed specifically for machine learning allow computers to analyse data, identify trends, and draw conclusions or make predictions without being given any guidance from humans. These algorithms form the backbone of numerous AI applications; they can be further subdivided into multiple types based on the learning methods they employ and the specific tasks they perform. Some of machine learning algorithms have been discussed to predict the natural disaster.

Support Vector Machine (SVM)

Support Vector Machines (SVM) are strong supervised learning algorithms used for classification and regression tasks. support vector machines (SVMs) have become widely used due to their superior performance in a wide range of fields. Support In many machine learning applications, Vector Machines have shown to be both flexible and productive. Their capacity to handle both linear and non-linear interactions, coupled with a sound theoretical background, makes them a valuable tool in the data scientist's toolset. SVMs are expected to play a crucial role in solving the issues faced by more complex datasets as research develops further.

Naïve Bayes (NB)

Bayes' theorem forms the basis of the Naive Bayes classifier, a probabilistic machine learning technique. Naive Bayes may be simple, yet it has found widespread application in many classification applications, especially in NLP and text analysis. Despite its reliance on oversimplified assumptions, Naive Bayes has proven to be a robust and popular classification method. As a result of its effectiveness, particularly in text-related tasks, it is an important component of the machine learning toolkit. Naive Bayes is a versatile and generalised method that is anticipated to find significant improvement and use across a wide range of disciplines as research continues.

Random Forest (RF)

Its purpose was to provide a more stable and flexible answer to classification and regression problems than could be found with a collection of individual decision trees. To improve prediction performance, one can use an ensemble learning technique like Random Forest, which uses the combined brainpower of several different models. In ensemble learning, multiple underperforming models' predictions are averaged together to form one robust model. Methods to enhance the understandability of Random Forest models and to enhance their computing efficiency are the subject of ongoing study. Random Forest continues to be a popular machine learning algorithm because it is a robust and trustworthy method for a wide range of predictive modeling applications.

K-Nearest Neighbor (KNN)

It is useful for both classification and regression, the k-Nearest Neighbours (k-NN) technique is a straightforward example of a supervised machine learning algorithm. Lazy learning algorithms, of which this is a member, train without first constructing an explicit model, hence it falls into that category. In its place, it uses similarities to the training dataset to assign a classification to a new instance.

As a result of its simplicity and efficacy, k-Nearest Neighbors has found widespread application and is frequently utilized in practice. To a data scientist who takes the time to learn its concepts and tune its parameters, it can be a powerful tool.

Decision Tree (DT)

Decision Machine learning algorithms based on trees are effective for classification and regression tasks, and their results can be understood by humans. They replicate human decision-making processes by building a tree-like model of decisions depending on input features. There is a decision node at the centre, a branch for each possible outcome of that decision, and a leaf node for the final outcome. Decision trees are useful because they are flexible and easy to understand models that can shed light on the decision-making procedure. Challenges aside, methods like Random Forest and Gradient Boosting remain useful and effective in a wide variety of machine learning contexts thanks to developments in the field and the use of ensemble techniques. The power of Decision Trees in developing predictive models can be used by practitioners who understand their principles and appropriately tune parameters.

ANALYSIS OF MACHINE LEARNING ALGORITHM TO PREDICT NATURAL DISASTER

One of the most important aspects of determining which models are best suited to a specific task is analyzing how well machine learning algorithms work. Evaluating a model's ability to generalize to new data, pinpointing its strengths and flaws, and making well-informed judgments about which models to use and how to enhance them all fall under this heading. Key topics of evaluating the effectiveness of machine learning algorithms are covered in this in-depth introduction.

Table 1 represents the comparative analysis of various machine learning algorithms to predict the natural disaster. From the above table it is conformed that, comparatively all the machine learning algorithms decision tree has provided more accuracy and precision as well recall

Table 1. Comparison of machine learning algorithms

S.No	Machine Learning Algorithms	Accuracy	Precision	Recall
1	K-Nearest neighbor	78.3	86.3	87.6
2	Decision Tree	82.3	87.4	88.7
3	Naïve Bayes	89.4	90.6	90.3
4	Support Vector Machines	90.0	93.7	92.4
5	Random Forest	96.3	96.4	97.2

The following Figure 1 demonstrates the performance measurement of various algorithms of machine learning algorithms to predict the natural disasters.

Figure 1. Performance analysis of machine learning algorithms

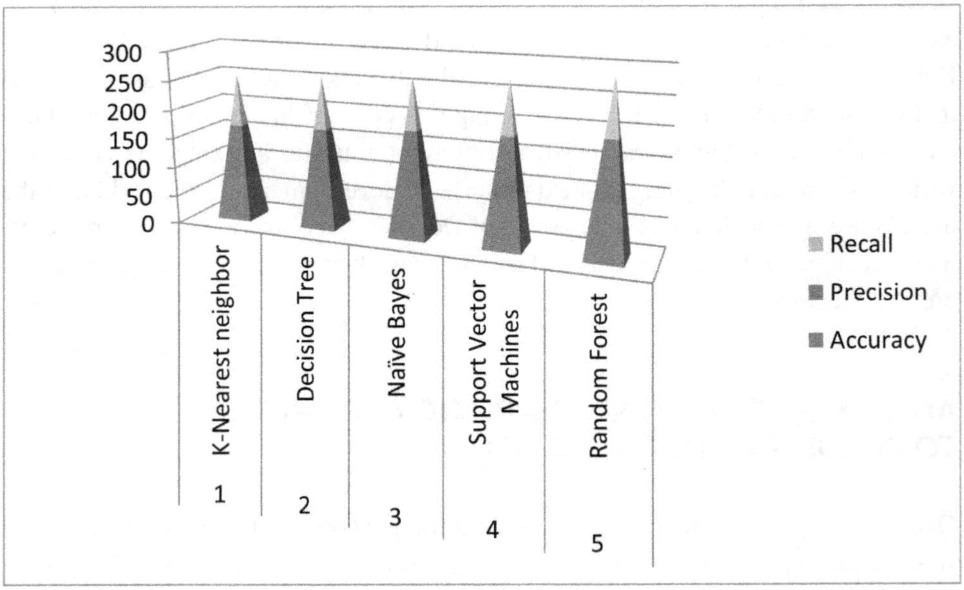

The above Figure 1 exhibits about the performance analysis of machine learning algorithm with various measurements such as accuracy, precision, recall. In the above figure reveals that random forest has provided excellent results compared with all other machine learning algorithms in all the aspects of performance measures.

CONCLUSION

The use of machine learning in the field of natural catastrophe prediction is discussed in depth in this chapter. Even with difficulties, there is clear opportunity to advance in forecast accuracy and speed up responses. In this chapter different machine learning algorithms have been proposed. But among those decision tree algorithms have given better results compared with all other techniques. if hybrid method used for prediction then it will produce more accuracy than this proposed system To guarantee the ethical deployment of machine learning in disaster management, future research should concentrate on cross-disciplinary cooperation, ethical issues, and improvements in model interpretability. finally when compared with different models of machine learning, random forest has provided excellent Results.

REFERENCES

Gepp, A., Linnenluecke, M. K., O'Neill, T. J., & Smith, T. (2018). Big data techniques in auditing research and practice: Current trends and future opportunities. *Journal of Accounting Literature*, *40*(1), 102–115. doi:10.1016/j.acclit.2017.05.003

Goodwin, M. (2020). Big data analytics tools and applications for modern business world. In: *2020 International Conference on Electronics and Sustainable Communication Systems (ICESC),* (pp. 587–592). IEEE 10.1109/ICESC48915.2020.9155704

Ofli, F. (2018). All-cause hospital admissions among older adults after a natural disaster. *Annals of Emergency Medicine*, *71*(6), 746–754. doi:10.1016/j.annemergmed.2017.06.042 PMID:28789804

Purushotham, P., & Caruso, G. D. (2017). The legacy of natural disasters: The intergenerational impact of 100 years of disasters in Latin America. *Journal of Development Economics*, *127*, 209–233. doi:10.1016/j.jdeveco.2017.03.007

Vinod, A.Navya, NNatarajan, J. (2019). Big data preprocessing for modern world: opportunities and challenges. In HemanthJ.FernandoX.LafataP.BaigZ. (Eds.), *ICICI 2018. LNDECT* (Vol. 26, pp. 335–343). Springer. doi:10.1007/978-3-030-03146-6_37

Yu, M., Yang, C., Li, Y., & Zuhairi, A. (2018). Yang, C., Li, Y.: Big data in natural disaster management: a review. *Geosciences*, *8*(5), 165. doi:10.3390/geosciences8050165

ADDITIONAL READING

Agarwal, R. (2020). Decision-making with temporal association rule mining and clustering in supply chains. In N. H. Shah & M. Mittal (Eds.), *Optimization and Inventory Management. AA* (pp. 459–470). Springer. doi:10.1007/978-981-13-9698-4_25

Kong, L., Liu, Z., & Wu, J. (2020). A systematic review of big data-based urban sustainability research: State-of-the-science and future directions. *Journal of Cleaner Production, 273*, 123142. doi:10.1016/j.jclepro.2020.123142

Li, Y., Han, D., & Yan, Z.LI. (2017). Y., HAN, D., YAN, Z.: Long-term system load forecasting based on data-driven linear clustering method. *Journal of Modern Power Systems and Clean Energy, 6*(2), 306–316. doi:10.100740565-017-0288-x

Lu, K., Liu, J., Zhou, X., & Han, B. (2020). A review of big data applications in urban transit systems. *IEEE Transactions on Intelligent Transportation Systems, 22*(5), 2535–2552. doi:10.1109/TITS.2020.2973365

Močarníková, K., & Greguš, M. (2020). Conceptualization of predictive analytics by literature review. In N. Kryvinska & M. Greguš (Eds.), *Data-Centric Business and Applications. LNDECT* (Vol. 30, pp. 205–234). Springer. doi:10.1007/978-3-030-19069-9_8

Mojtahedi, M., Newton, S., Von Meding, J. (2016). Predicting the resilience of transport infrastructure to a natural disaster using Cox's proportional hazards regression model. *Nat. Hazards 85*(2), 1119–1133. , https://doi.org/ doi:10.1007/s11069-016-2624-2

Natarajan, J. (2020). Cyber secure man-in-the-middle attack ıntrusion detection using machine learning algorithms. In *AI and Big Data's Potential for Disruptive Innovation* (pp. 291–316). IGI Global. doi:10.4018/978-1-5225-9687-5.ch011

Pham, T. T., Do, T., Nguyen, A., Vo, B., & Hong, T. P. (2020). An efficient method for mining top-K closed sequential patterns. *IEEE Access : Practical Innovations, Open Solutions, 8*, 118156–118163. doi:10.1109/ACCESS.2020.3004528

Ragini, J. R., Anand, P. R., & Bhaskar, V. (2018). Big data analytics for disaster response and recovery through sentiment analysis. *International Journal of Information Management, 42*, 13–24. doi:10.1016/j.ijinfomgt.2018.05.004

Ritchie, B. W., & Jiang, Y. (2019). A review of research on tourism risk, crisis and disaster management: Launching the annals of tourism research curated collection on tourism risk, crisis and disaster management. *Annals of Tourism Research*, *79*, 102812. doi:10.1016/j.annals.2019.102812

Tiwari, S., Wee, H. M., & Daryanto, Y. (2018). Big data analytics in supply chain management between 2010 and 2016: Insights to industries. *Computers & Industrial Engineering*, *115*, 319–330. doi:10.1016/j.cie.2017.11.017

Vellei, M., Martinez, S., & Le Dréau, J. (2021). Agent-based stochastic model of thermostat adjustments: A demand response application. *Energy and Building*, *238*, 110846. doi:10.1016/j.enbuild.2021.110846

Yoo, I., Alafaireet, P., Marinov, M., Pena-Hernandez, K., Gopidi, R., Chang, J.-F., & Hua, L. (2012). Data mining in healthcare and biomedicine: A survey of the literature. *Journal of Medical Systems*, *36*(4), 2431–2448. doi:10.100710916-011-9710-5 PMID:21537851

Zhao, Y., Zhang, C., Zhang, Y., Wang, Z., & Li, J. (2020). A review of data mining technologies in building energy systems: Load prediction, pattern identification, fault detection and diagnosis. *Energy Built Environ.*, *1*(2), 149–164. doi:10.1016/j.enbenv.2019.11.003

Chapter 8
Predicting Tropical Cyclones: A Supervised Machine Learning Approach

K. Bharathi
https://orcid.org/0009-0000-4767-1635
Velammal College of Engineering and Technology, Madurai, India

A. Archita
Velammal College of Engineering and Technology, Madurai, India

S. Gandhimathi Alias Usha
https://orcid.org/0000-0003-1908-6249
Velammal College of Engineering and Technology, Madurai, India

ABSTRACT

This study introduces a predictive framework for tropical cyclone forecasting employing support vector machines (SVM). Through the analysis of diverse meteorological parameters, including sea surface temperature, atmospheric pressure, and wind patterns, the SVM algorithm is trained to recognize intricate patterns associated with cyclone development. The model exhibits robust performance in identifying potential cyclonic formations, showcasing its efficacy in early detection. By leveraging historical data, the SVM-based approach contributes to the advancement of cyclone prediction models. The methodology's accuracy and efficiency make it a valuable tool for bolstering existing forecasting capabilities, providing critical information for disaster preparedness and mitigation strategies. This research underscores the potential of SVM as a reliable tool in tropical cyclone prediction, emphasizing its role in fortifying resilience against these formidable natural phenomena.

DOI: 10.4018/979-8-3693-2280-2.ch008

INTRODUCTION

Tropical cyclones, characterized by powerful winds, heavy rainfall, and destructive storm surges, pose significant threats to coastal regions worldwide. The ability to accurately predict the trajectory and intensity of these storms is crucial for effective disaster preparedness and response (Zhu et al., 2019). Traditional numerical weather prediction models have made substantial progress in forecasting tropical cyclones, yet the complex and dynamic nature of these systems continues to present challenges. The development and intensification of tropical cyclones pose significant threats, including powerful winds, torrential rainfall, and storm surges, making them a natural hazard with potentially devastating impacts on coastal areas. Understanding their formation and behavior is crucial for effective preparedness and mitigation measures. The significance of predicting tropical cyclones is underscored by its multifaceted impact on various aspects of society, environment, and economy (Lee, 2016). Foremost, accurate predictions are indispensable for public safety, providing the crucial time needed for communities to evacuate and fortify against the destructive forces of these storms. The protection of infrastructure, including homes, businesses, and essential services, hinges on these forecasts, allowing for preemptive measures to be taken. Moreover, anticipating tropical cyclones is essential for agricultural planning and economic resilience, empowering farmers and industries to safeguard crops, livestock, and assets. In essence, the significance of predicting tropical cyclones extends far beyond meteorology, encompassing a spectrum of areas crucial for societal well-being and environmental sustainability. Predictions also serve a crucial role in humanitarian aid and disaster response planning, facilitating the pre-positioning of resources and swift responses to affected areas (Halperin et al., 2013).

The scope of the research encompasses a meticulous exploration of the methodology involved in constructing predictive models, emphasizing the integration of diverse meteorological data sets. The study aims to unravel the intricacies of tropical cyclone behavior by identifying and selecting relevant features, such as sea surface temperatures, atmospheric pressure, and wind patterns, which are crucial inputs for training the supervised machine learning models (Burton et al., 2010). Beyond the technical aspects, the research addresses the inherent challenges in tropical cyclone prediction, including the dynamic and nonlinear nature of atmospheric processes, shedding light on how machine learning techniques can enhance our ability to navigate these complexities. Furthermore, the study explores the practicality and real-time applicability of the developed machine learning models, considering their potential integration into existing forecasting systems for operational use. In doing so, the research carries implications for disaster preparedness, risk mitigation, and the ongoing advancement of predictive capabilities in the face of increasingly complex weather phenomena (Park & Elsberry, 2013).

CRUCIAL BLEND OF TRADITION AND INNOVATION IN TROPICAL CYCLONE PREDICTION

Tropical cyclones, commonly known as hurricanes or typhoons, are intense atmospheric phenomena that originate over warm tropical or subtropical ocean waters. Fueled by the heat from the ocean's surface, these massive storm systems feature a well-defined circulation pattern, with strong winds spiraling inward towards a low-pressure center. Expanding upon various machine learning techniques such as Support Vector Machines (SVM), Kernel-based Support Vector Regression (SVR) models and Multi-Layer Perceptron (MLP) algorithms for deeper understanding tropical cyclones.

Importance of Predicting Tropical Cyclones

Predicting tropical cyclones are of paramount importance across various dimensions, each contributing to the overall well-being of societies and ecosystems. Firstly, accurate predictions are crucial for public safety. Early warnings enable authorities to initiate timely evacuations and implement preparedness measures, reducing the vulnerability of coastal communities to the devastating impacts of cyclones. Firstly, accurate and timely predictions are pivotal for safeguarding human lives (Schumacher et al., 2009). By providing early warnings, forecasting allows for organized evacuations, enabling coastal communities to prepare and respond effectively, reducing the potential for casualties.

Secondly, in terms of infrastructure protection, predicting tropical cyclones allows for strategic planning to reinforce critical structures and utilities. This proactive approach minimizes damage to buildings, roads, and other essential infrastructure, thereby enhancing overall community resilience and minimizing the economic burden of post-cyclone reconstruction. Timely forecasts enable the reinforcement of buildings, roads, and utilities, minimizing damage and ensuring the resilience of infrastructure against the destructive forces of cyclones. This aspect is particularly significant in densely populated coastal areas where infrastructure vulnerabilities can amplify the impact of storms. Economic stability is intricately linked to cyclone prediction, particularly in regions dependent on agriculture and industry. Accurate forecasts empower farmers and businesses to adopt risk-mitigation strategies, protecting crops, livestock, and assets (Houze, 2010). This, in turn, supports economic stability by minimizing disruptions and losses associated with cyclone-related damages.

The importance of predicting tropical cyclones extends far beyond meteorological curiosity. It is a fundamental aspect of disaster preparedness and risk reduction, playing a pivotal role in protecting lives, infrastructure, economies, and the environment. The interdisciplinary nature of cyclone prediction involves the collaboration of meteorologists, scientists, policymakers, and communities to build resilience and mitigate the impacts of these powerful natural phenomena.

Traditional Methods

Traditional methods for predicting tropical cyclones encompass a range of observational and numerical techniques. Satellite imagery and weather radars provide real-time visuals and precipitation patterns, while ocean buoys and weather stations collect essential data on sea surface conditions and atmospheric parameters. Numerical weather prediction models, both global and regional, simulate atmospheric dynamics, aided by ensemble modeling for uncertainty assessment. Historical data and climatology offer insights into cyclone patterns, and aerial reconnaissance by Hurricane Hunter aircraft gathers crucial in-situ information (Park et al., 2016).

Empirical methods, including statistical models, leverage historical data for predictive insights. While these traditional approaches remain foundational, ongoing advancements in technology and machine learning techniques contribute to continuous improvements in cyclone prediction accuracy.

Limitations of Traditional Methods

Traditional methods for predicting tropical cyclones encounter several challenges rooted in the complexity of the atmospheric and oceanic systems. Numerical weather prediction models and statistical approaches face limitations in adequately representing the intricate processes involved in cyclone development and intensification. The spatial and temporal resolution of these methods may be insufficient to capture the small-scale features and rapid changes inherent in tropical cyclones. Data assimilation, a crucial step in incorporating observational data into models, faces challenges, especially in data-sparse oceanic regions.

Additionally, a limited understanding of certain physical processes, coupled with the variability and nonlinearity exhibited by tropical cyclones, poses difficulties for accurate predictions. Predicting phenomena like rapid intensification remains a significant challenge, and uncertainties related to climate change impacts further complicate long-term forecasts. Local factors, including topography, can influence cyclone behavior, and these nuances may be inadequately addressed by traditional methods (Han & Lee, 2015). While these approaches have made substantial progress, ongoing research and the integration of advanced technologies are essential to overcome these limitations and enhance tropical cyclone prediction capabilities.

CHALLENGES IN PREDICTING NATURAL DISASTER

Predicting natural disasters poses several challenges due to the complex and dynamic nature of the Earth's systems. The lack of standardized methodologies for assessing and communicating uncertainty in predictions is another hurdle. Predicting the exact timing, location, and magnitude of natural disasters involves inherent uncertainties. Communicating these uncertainties effectively to decision-makers and the public is crucial for informed decision-making and risk management. Developing universally accepted standards for conveying uncertainty in predictions is an ongoing challenge (Sesnie et al., 2010).

Furthermore, the socio-economic and cultural factors influencing community resilience and response to warnings add complexity. Understanding how communities interpret and act upon warnings is essential for effective disaster preparedness. Bridging the gap between scientific predictions and community actions requires a nuanced understanding of local contexts, belief systems, and historical experiences with disasters.

Rapid Intensification

Rapid intensification of cyclones represents a meteorological phenomenon where tropical storms undergo a sudden and substantial increase in their maximum sustained winds, elevating them to higher categories on the Saffir-Simpson Hurricane Wind Scale. This swift escalation in destructive potential poses a significant challenge for both meteorologists and coastal communities. Warm sea surface temperatures play a pivotal role, serving as the primary energy source for cyclones (Helms et al., 2011). When storms traverse regions with sufficiently warm waters, they can absorb vast amounts of heat energy, fueling intensified convective processes. Low vertical wind shear, which enables the storm to organize more efficiently, is another critical factor. Additionally, the availability of atmospheric moisture and the Earth's rotation, facilitating the Coriolis effect, contribute to the conditions conducive to rapid intensification.

Dynamic processes within the eyewall, the region surrounding the eye of the cyclone, play a crucial role, involving the contraction and consolidation of this core. Predicting rapid intensification remains challenging due to the intricate interplay of these factors. Predicting rapid intensification poses challenges due to the intricate interactions of these factors, making it crucial to advance forecasting techniques.

Time Availability

The time available to predict tropical cyclones is contingent on various stages of their development and the evolving technologies employed in weather forecasting. In the formation phase, meteorologists focus on monitoring atmospheric conditions conducive to cyclone genesis, offering a lead time of several days to a week. As disturbances progress into tropical depressions or storms, the early development phase allows for increasingly precise tracking and path prediction, extending the forecasting lead time. However, predicting rapid intensification remains a notable challenge (Richardson et al., 2017). While forecasters can identify conditions conducive to intensification, specifying the exact timing and magnitude remains uncertain. As a tropical cyclone approaches land, forecasts become more precise regarding its expected impact, including landfall location, intensity, and associated hazards. This crucial information is usually available within a few days of the anticipated landfall, enabling affected regions to implement evacuation and preparedness measures.

Technological advancements, such as satellite observation and advanced modeling, have improved forecasting accuracy and lead times. However, uncertainties persist, particularly in predicting rapid intensification. Continuous monitoring and early warning systems are critical components, ensuring timely and reliable information reaches potentially affected areas. This empowers residents and authorities to make informed decisions, implement evacuation plans, and undertake necessary preparations to minimize the impact of these powerful weather events.

Lack of Effective Communication Networks

The lack of effective communication networks presents a formidable challenge in the accurate prediction and dissemination of information about tropical cyclones, particularly in vulnerable regions with limited resources. In many cases, insufficient access to modern communication technologies, such as the internet and mobile networks, hampers the timely receipt of weather updates and warnings in at-risk communities.This issue is exacerbated by a scarcity of weather monitoring stations, contributing to a lack of on-the-ground data that is vital for accurate cyclone predictions.

Even when accurate forecasts are available, reaching remote or marginalized communities remains challenging, highlighting the need for comprehensive efforts to improve infrastructure, expand monitoring capabilities, and enhance community engagement through educational initiatives (Kim, 2015). Collaborative partnerships between meteorological agencies, local authorities, and international organizations are imperative to establish efficient communication channels, ensuring that precise and timely cyclone predictions are effectively communicated to all vulnerable populations, ultimately reducing the impact of this natural disaster.

ROLE OF ML IN DISASTER MANAGEMENT

Machine Learning (ML) is pivotal in disaster management, utilizing predictive modeling and early warning systems to forecast and mitigate the impact of natural and man-made disasters. ML's role extends to post-disaster recovery, aiding in damage assessment through computer vision and facilitating efficient reconstruction planning. Figure 1 represents the flow of Machine Learning. Additionally, ML enhances risk assessment, identifying vulnerable areas and informing urban planning decisions. Its adaptive capabilities continually improve disaster response strategies, contributing to resilient communities and informed decision-making. It is an integration of heterogeneous data sources ensures comprehensive situational awareness, while sentiment analysis of public communication aids in tailored and effective information dissemination. ML techniques, including natural language processing (NLP), can be employed for sentiment analysis of public communication during disasters (Cao et al., 2018). Understanding public sentiment helps authorities tailor their communication strategies, address concerns, and provide timely and relevant information to the affected population. This proactive communication can contribute to better cooperation and compliance with evacuation and safety measures. Role of ML in disaster management extends beyond prediction and response to include adaptive learning, data integration, risk assessment, and sentiment analysis. These capabilities collectively enhance the overall resilience of communities and empower decision-makers with the insights needed to navigate the complex and dynamic nature of disasters.

Figure 1. Flow of machine learning

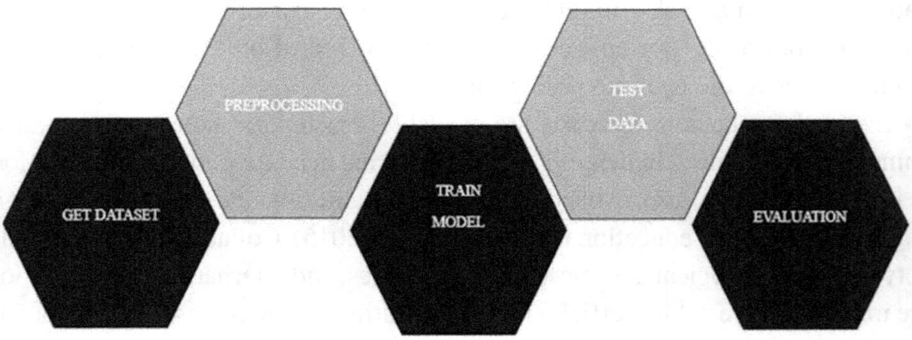

Relevance to Tropical Cyclones

In the domain of predicting tropical cyclones, Machine Learning (ML) emerges as a transformative tool by leveraging advanced algorithms to sift through vast meteorological datasets. ML models analyze diverse factors like sea surface temperatures, atmospheric pressure, and historical cyclone data, unveiling intricate patterns that influence cyclone behavior. The adaptability of ML algorithms allows them to continuously refine predictions based on real-time environmental changes, enhancing the accuracy of forecasts. ML's capacity to process information from various sources, including satellites and weather stations, contributes to a more holistic understanding of atmospheric conditions. This comprehensive analysis empowers meteorologists to issue more precise and timely warnings, enabling communities to undertake better-prepared evacuation measures and reducing the potential impact of tropical cyclones on vulnerable regions.

The real-time processing capabilities of ML empower meteorologists to issue timely and accurate warnings, allowing communities to undertake well-informed and timely evacuation measures. This, in turn, significantly reduces the potential impact of tropical cyclones on vulnerable regions, promoting better disaster preparedness and response efforts.

Overview of Machine Learning Techniques

Machine learning encompasses a diverse set of techniques designed to extract patterns and insights from data. Support Vector Machines (SVMs) are powerful tools for both classification and regression tasks. SVMs have found application in fields such as image classification and financial forecasting. Kernel-based Support Vector Regression (SVR) models extend SVMs to regression problems, employing kernel functions to handle intricate relationships in data and proving robust against outliers.Together, these machine learning techniques contribute to a wide array of applications, offering valuable tools for data analysis, prediction, and pattern recognition across diverse domains.

Support Vector Machine

SVMs are a class of supervised learning algorithms used for classification and regression. SVMs seek to find an optimal hyperplane that best separates data points into different classes in a high-dimensional space. The algorithm is particularly effective in scenarios with complex decision boundaries. By maximizing the margin between classes, SVMs enhance generalization to new data. They can handle linear and nonlinear relationships through a kernel trick, mapping input data into higher-dimensional spaces. SVMs find applications in diverse fields, such as image classification, financial prediction, and biological data analysis, owing to their versatility and robustness.

Kernel-Based Support Vector Regression

Kernel-based Support Vector Regression is a regression technique rooted in Support Vector Machines. It employs kernel functions to map input data into higher-dimensional spaces, facilitating the capture of complex, nonlinear relationships. SVR seeks to find a hyperplane that maximizes the margin between predicted and actual values, providing robust regression models. This approach is particularly effective when dealing with data that exhibits nonlinear patterns. Kernel-based SVR finds applications in diverse fields such as finance, environmental modeling, and time-series prediction, where traditional linear regression models may be less suitable.

Multi-Layer Perceptron

MLP is a type of artificial neural network used in machine learning. It consists of multiple layers of interconnected nodes (neurons) organized into an input layer, one or more hidden layers, and an output layer. Each connection is associated with a weight, and each node has an activation function. MLPs are capable of learning complex patterns and relationships in data, making them effective for tasks like classification, regression, and pattern recognition. The goal of training an MLP is for it to learn the mapping between the input features and the associated output labels.

TECHNIQUES FOR PREDICTING TC

Tropical cyclone prediction utilizes satellite observations, numerical weather models, and statistical analyses. Monitoring sea surface temperatures, employing ensemble forecasting, and integrating real-time data through assimilation techniques contribute to accurate forecasts. Remote sensing technologies and global collaboration enhance our understanding. These multifaceted approaches help anticipate and respond to the complex nature of tropical cyclones, mitigating potential impacts on communities.

Satellite Observation

Satellite observation is pivotal in tropical cyclone prediction, capturing visible and infrared imagery to monitor cloud patterns and assess storm structure. It tracks cyclone movement in real-time, measures sea surface temperatures crucial for storm intensification, and observes atmospheric conditions. This global coverage enables early detection, facilitating timely warnings and evacuation efforts. Integrated with other observational tools, satellites contribute to comprehensive forecasts, aiding meteorologists in understanding cyclone dynamics and minimizing the impact of these powerful storms on coastal communities through effective disaster preparedness and response measure.

Remote Sensing of Atmospheric Moisture

Remote sensing of atmospheric moisture employs advanced technologies such as microwave and infrared radiometry, lidar, and GPS-based techniques to measure water vapor distribution from a distance. Satellites equipped with specialized spectral bands also contribute by indirectly assessing atmospheric moisture levels. This capability is vital for meteorologists in predicting rainfall, understanding severe weather patterns, and enhancing overall weather forecasting accuracy. The gathered data aids in informed decision-making across sectors, including agriculture, water resource management, and disaster preparedness, by providing insights into atmospheric conditions and potential risks.

Sea Surface Temperature Monitoring

Sea surface temperature monitoring is a crucial aspect of meteorology that involves measuring the temperature of the ocean's top layer. Satellites equipped with infrared sensors capture SST data, helping meteorologists understand and predict climate patterns, ocean currents, and the development of weather systems such as tropical cyclones. The warmth of the sea surface provides vital energy for storm intensification. Accurate SST information enables early detection of potential hazards, supports climate research, and enhances our understanding of marine ecosystems and their interactions with the atmosphere.

Aircraft Reconnaissance

Aircraft reconnaissance is a vital method in meteorology for gathering real-time data on atmospheric conditions, particularly within and around tropical cyclones. Specially equipped aircraft, often called hurricane hunters, fly into the storm to collect information such as temperature, pressure, humidity, and wind speed at various altitudes. These direct measurements, along with other observational tools, enhance the accuracy of forecasts and contribute to a better understanding of storm dynamics. Aircraft reconnaissance plays a critical role in improving the reliability of predictions and providing valuable data for storm tracking and intensity forecasting.

PROPOSED SYSTEM

Proposed Methodology

The proposed method is shown in Figure 2. SVM have emerged as valuable tools in predicting tropical cyclones, contributing to the evolving landscape of meteorological forecasting. In this application, SVM utilizes historical data encompassing diverse variables like sea surface temperature, atmospheric pressure, and past storm tracks. The algorithm excels in handling high-dimensional datasets and capturing intricate relationships within the data. During the training phase, the SVM model learns from labeled data, associating input features with specific outcomes such as cyclone intensification or non-intensification. Table 1 gives the description of predictors that quantitatively describe dynamic and hydrological characteristics related to tropical cyclone formation.

The predictive capabilities of SVM offer a complementary approach to traditional meteorological methods and numerical weather prediction models. SVM's adaptability

Figure 2. Proposed algorithm for predicting TC

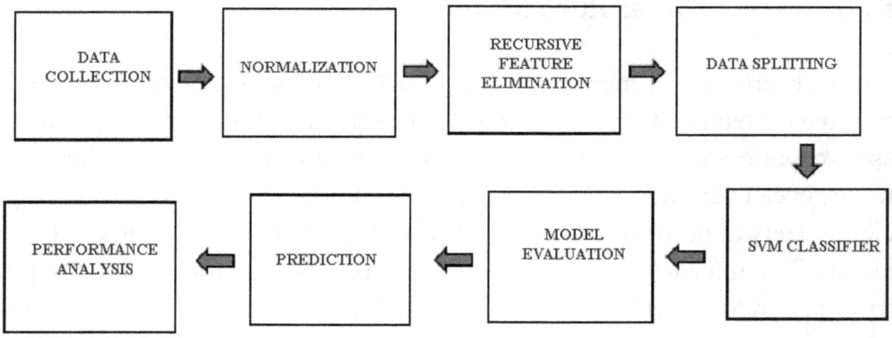

Table 1. Dynamic and hydrological characteristics related to TC formation

Predictor	Description
wind_ave	Average of wind speed over the disturbance
wind_cv_fix	Circular variance (CV) of wind to measure the degree of symmetry in the circulation within a $16° \times 16°$ fixed widnow
wind_cv_mv	The maximum CV value found by moving a small ($4° \times 4°$) window over a larger area
wind_ci	Clumpiness Index (CI) of the wind speed over 15 m s^{-1} in a large area
wind_pladj	Percentage of Like ADJacency (PLADJ) of wind speed over 15 m s^{-1} in a large area
rain_ave	Average of rain rates near the center of the disturbance
rain_ci	Clumpiness Index (CI) of the rain rate exceeding 5 mm h^{-1} in a large area
rain_paldj	Percentage of Like ADJacency (PLADJ) of the rain rate exceeding 5 mm h^{-1} in a large area

and capacity to discern non-linear patterns make it particularly useful in scenarios where conventional methods may face challenges. Integration of SVM predictions with outputs from established models enhances the overall accuracy of tropical cyclone forecasts. It's crucial to emphasize that while SVM contributes to advancements, it is part of a broader strategy that includes traditional observational methods, climatology, and other numerical models. This synthesis of approaches ensures a comprehensive understanding of tropical cyclones, ultimately refining the ability to predict their trajectories, intensities, and potential impacts on vulnerable regions. As technology and methodologies continue to evolve, SVM stands as an innovative component in the ongoing pursuit of more accurate and reliable cyclone predictions.

Experimental Result

In the experimentation of predicting tropical cyclones using Support Vector Machines, a comprehensive approach was undertaken. Historical meteorological data, encompassing relevant features, was collected and divided into training and testing sets. Feature engineering involved careful selection and normalization of variables. Different SVM variants were explored, considering various kernels and hyper parameters. The model was trained on the selected features to learn patterns related to cyclone occurrence. Evaluation metrics such as accuracy and precision were employed, and visualizations like confusion matrices aided in assessing model performance. Feature importance analysis and hyper parameter tuning were conducted for optimization. The study highlighted the SVM's potential in cyclone prediction, emphasizing the need for continuous data integration for real-time applicability.

The parameters such as recall, precision and the F1-score are the most widely and often employed evaluation metrics in the field of object identification and classification. F1-score combines precision and recall into a single value, providing a balanced measure of counting performance (Santos et al., 2020).

Mathematically, precision and recall are expressed as:

$$\text{Precision} = TP/(TP + FN) * 100\%$$
$$\text{Recall} = TP/(TP + FN) * 100\%$$
$$\text{F1-score} = 2 \text{ Precision} * \text{Recall} / (\text{Precision} + \text{Recall}) * 100\%$$

The experimentation results are shown in Figure 3. Here the Hit rate, False alarm rate, Pierce skill score, lead time are compared.

Support Vector Machines stand out as a powerful machine learning algorithm, offering unique advantages that distinguish them from Linear Discriminant Analysis, Decision Trees, and Random Forests . SVM excels in high-dimensional spaces and is effective in cases where the number of features is greater than the number

Figure 3. Comparison of SVM with other models: green (LDA), yellow (DT), pink (SVM), blue (RF)

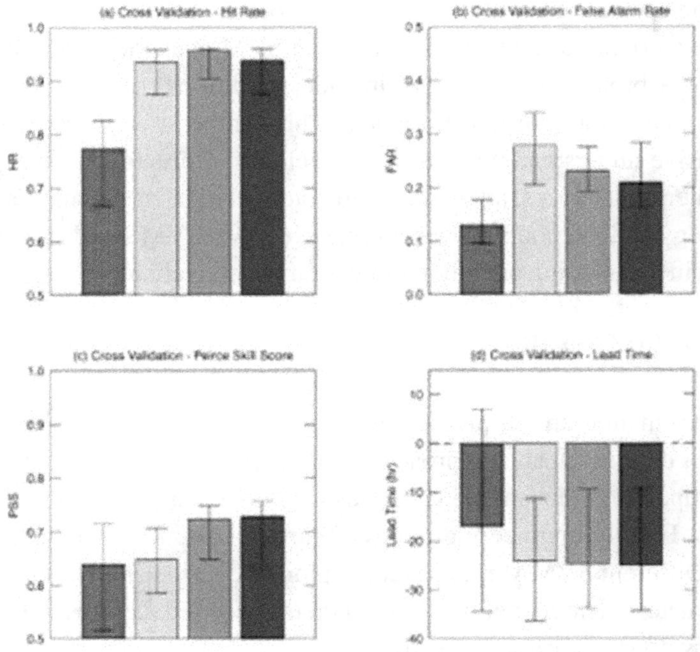

of samples. Its ability to handle non-linear relationships between features through various kernel functions is a key strength, surpassing the limitations of linear models like LDA. Unlike Decision Trees, SVM is robust to over fitting, and its kernel trick enables it to capture intricate patterns in the data.

CONCLUSION

In conclusion, the experimentation with Support Vector Machines (SVM) for tropical cyclone prediction demonstrates the algorithm's efficacy in harnessing complex meteorological data. SVM's ability to discern intricate patterns and relationships in high-dimensional spaces, coupled with its capacity to handle non-linearity's through various kernel functions, positions it as a robust choice for predicting tropical cyclones. The comprehensive evaluation, considering metrics such as accuracy, precision, and feature importance analysis, underscores SVM's suitability for this dynamic and critical forecasting task. While real-time data integration remains essential, the results suggest that SVM can contribute significantly to accurate and reliable tropical cyclone predictions. This underscores its potential as a valuable tool in the realm of meteorology, offering a promising avenue for enhancing our understanding and forecasting capabilities for these natural phenomena.

The comprehensive evaluation of SVM's performance in tropical cyclone prediction, incorporating metrics such as accuracy, precision, and feature importance analysis, reinforces its potential as a robust forecasting tool. By providing a nuanced understanding of the interdependencies among meteorological variables, SVM contributes to more accurate and reliable predictions.

REFERENCES

Burton, D., Bernardet, L., Faure, G., Herndon, D., Knaff, J., Li, Y., Mayers, J., Radjab, F., Sampson, C., & Waqaicelua, A. (2010). *Structure and intensity change: Operational guidance*. In *Proceedings of the 7th International Workshop on Tropical Cyclones*, La Réunion, France.

Cao, J., Liu, K., Liu, L., Zhu, Y., Li, J., & He, Z. (2018). Identifying Mangrove Species Using Field Close-Range Snapshot Hyperspectral Imaging and Machine-Learning Techniques. *Remote Sensing (Basel)*, *10*(12), 2047. doi:10.3390/rs10122047

Halperin, D. J., Fuelberg, H. E., Hart, R. E., Cossuth, J. H., Sura, P., & Pasch, R. J. (2013). An Evaluation of Tropical Cyclone Genesis Forecasts from Global Numerical Models. *Weather and Forecasting*, *28*(6), 1423–1445. doi:10.1175/WAF-D-13-00008.1

Han, H., & Lee, S. (2015). Detection of Convective Initiation Using Meteorological Imager Onboard Communication, Ocean, and Meteorological Satellite Based on Machine Learning Approaches. Remote. Sens. Research Gate.

Helms, C. N., Knapp, K. R., Bowen, A. R., & Hennon, C. C. (2011). An Objective Algorithm for Detecting and Tracking Tropical Cloud Clusters: Implications for Tropical Cyclogenesis Prediction. *Journal of Atmospheric and Oceanic Technology*.

Houze, R. A. Jr. (2010). Clouds in tropical cyclones. *Monthly Weather Review*, *138*(2), 293–344. doi:10.1175/2009MWR2989.1

Kim, M. (2015). Landfast sea ice monitoring using multisensor fusion in the Antarctic. Remote Sens. Research Gate.

Lee, S. Im, J., Kim, J., Kim, M., Shin, M., Kim, H.-C., & Quackenbush, L.J. (2016). Arctic Sea Ice Thickness Estimation from CryoSat-2 Satellite Data Using Machine Learning-Based Lead Detection. Remote. Sens. Research Gate.

Park, M.-S., & Elsberry, R. L. (2013). Latent Heating and Cooling Rates in Developing and Nondeveloping Tropical Disturbances during TCS-08: TRMM PR versus ELDORA Retrievals*. *Journal of the Atmospheric Sciences*, *70*(1), 15–35. doi:10.1175/JAS-D-12-083.1

Park, M.-S., Kim, M., & Lee, M.-I. (2016). *J.; Park, S. Detection of tropical cyclone genesis via quantitative satellite ocean surface wind pattern and intensity analyses using decision trees*. Remote. Sens. Environ.

Richardson, H. J., Hill, D. J., Denesiuk, D. R., & Fraser, L. H. (2017). A comparison of geographic datasets and field measurements to model soil carbon using random forests and stepwise regressions (British Columbia, Canada). *GIScience & Remote Sensing*, *54*(4), 573–591. doi:10.1080/15481603.2017.1302181

Schumacher, A. B., DeMaria, M., & Knaff, J. A. (2009). Objective Estimation of the 24-h Probability of Tropical Cyclone Formation. *Weather and Forecasting*, *24*(2), 456–471. doi:10.1175/2008WAF2007109.1

Sesnie, S.E., Finegan, B., Gessler, P.E., Thessler, S., Bendana, Z.R., & Smith, A.M.S. (2010). The multispectral separability of Costa Rican rainforest types with support vector machines and Random Forest decision trees. *Int. J. Sens.*

Zhu, X., Li, N., & Pan, Y. (2019). Optimization Performance Comparison of Three Different Group Intelligence Algorithms on a SVM for Hyperspectral Imagery Classification. *Remote Sensing (Basel)*, *11*(6), 734. doi:10.3390/rs11060734

Chapter 9
Futuristic Disaster Mitigation: The Role of GPUs and AI Accelerators

Dhinakaran Damodaran
Vel Tech Rangarajan Dr. Sagunthala R&D Institute of Science and Technology, India

Dinesh Kumar K.
Vel Tech Rangarajan Dr. Sagunthala R&D Institute of Science and Technology, India

Selvaraj Damodaran
Panimalar Engineering College, India

S. Gopalakrishnan
Madanapalle Institute of Technology and Science, India

ABSTRACT

This chapter explores the transformative integration of GPUs and AI accelerators in natural disaster management, ushering in resilience and rapid response. From early warning systems to recovery, these technologies enhance decision-making and mitigate the impact of escalating disasters. Specific applications include real-time data analysis, predictive modelling, GIS mapping, and resource allocation. The fusion of GPUs and AI accelerators not only improves disaster prediction and response but also fosters resilient communities. Motivated by the need for rapid decision-making, this integration addresses the limitations of traditional methods in the face of increasing disaster complexity. In navigating an uncertain future, GPUs and AI accelerators revolutionize disaster management, paving the way for a more resilient global society.

DOI: 10.4018/979-8-3693-2280-2.ch009

INTRODUCTION

Natural disasters, stemming from geological, meteorological, hydrological, and climatological processes, are catastrophic events that exert profound impacts on the Earth's ecosystems, human societies, and infrastructure. Earthquakes, characterized by sudden ground shaking resulting from tectonic plate movements, can lead to tsunamis and surface ruptures, affecting global regions but particularly prevalent in seismically active zones. Hurricanes, typhoons, and cyclones, intense tropical storms with strong winds and heavy rainfall, primarily impact coastal areas in tropical and subtropical regions, causing storm surges and flooding. Tornadoes, violent rotating air columns, bring destructive winds and debris, primarily affecting regions like the United States. Floods, caused by heavy rainfall, storm surges, or rapid snowmelt, result in inundation, property damage, and loss of life, occurring globally and influenced by topography and weather patterns (Muhammad et al., 2023). Wildfires, uncontrolled fires in vegetation-rich areas, lead to ecosystem destruction, property damage, and air quality issues, predominantly in dry climates. Volcanic eruptions, involving the release of magma, ash, and gases, impact regions along tectonic plate boundaries with lava flows, ashfall, and the potential for pyroclastic flows. Droughts, prolonged periods of below-average rainfall, induce water scarcity, crop failure, and famine, affecting diverse climates and geographical locations (Llenos et al., 2019). Landslides, downhill movements of rock, soil, and debris, pose threats to property and lives, occurring frequently in mountainous or hilly terrain, particularly after heavy rainfall. Understanding the distinct characteristics and potential impacts of each natural disaster type is fundamental for devising effective disaster preparedness and response strategies.

The escalating frequency and severity of natural disasters underscore the critical need for advanced technologies in disaster management. Over recent decades, the world has witnessed a concerning uptick in the occurrence of earthquakes, hurricanes, floods, wildfires, and other calamities, impacting communities, economies, and ecosystems on an unprecedented scale (Mousavi et al., 2020). Climate change, urbanization, and population growth contribute to the intensification of these disasters, amplifying their destructive potential. Rising sea levels, altered precipitation patterns, and increased temperatures exacerbate the vulnerability of regions to weather-related disasters, while urban sprawl and inadequate infrastructure magnify the impact of geological events. The compounding effects of these factors necessitate a paradigm shift in how we approach disaster preparedness, response, and recovery.

BACKGROUND

Challenges in Traditional Forecasting

Traditional forecasting methods encounter several challenges that limit their effectiveness in predicting future events. One significant challenge lies in their reliance on historical data, which can introduce biases and inaccuracies, especially when faced with unprecedented or rapidly evolving situations (Mancini et al., 2022). The static nature of many traditional models is another constraint, as they often assume a level of stability that may not exist in dynamic environments. Linear assumptions inherent in many forecasting models oversimplify the complex, nonlinear behaviors observed in real-world systems. Additionally, the inability to efficiently handle big data poses a hurdle, considering the exponential growth of digital information in today's world (Dhinakaran et al., 2023). Traditional models may lack adaptability to changing conditions, hindering their capacity to incorporate real-time data and respond effectively to sudden shifts in the environment.

External factors, such as economic changes or geopolitical events, are often inadequately considered, impacting the models' ability to provide accurate forecasts. The assumption of stationarity, where underlying statistical properties are presumed to remain constant over time, further limits adaptability to changing circumstances. Human judgment, a component of many traditional forecasting methods, introduces the potential for bias, subjectivity, and cognitive limitations, affecting the reliability of predictions. Moreover, traditional forecasting may fall short in providing comprehensive risk assessments, particularly in complex, multifactorial systems. The long response times associated with these methods can be a significant drawback in situations demanding real-time decision-making. More sophisticated approaches are becoming increasingly recognized as being necessary to address these issues. Machine learning, artificial intelligence, and probabilistic modelling offer solutions that better handle the complexity and uncertainty inherent in many forecasting scenarios. By moving beyond the limitations of traditional methods, organizations and decision-makers can enhance their ability to make accurate predictions and informed decisions in an ever-changing world.

Advanced technologies, particularly GPUs and AI accelerators, have emerged as indispensable tools in addressing the evolving landscape of natural disasters. These technologies empower us to analyse vast datasets rapidly, model complex scenarios, and make informed decisions in real-time (Asim et al., 2018). The parallel processing capabilities of GPUs enable quick and efficient data analysis, essential for early warning systems and rapid response strategies. In the face of increasing disaster frequency and severity, the importance of predictive modelling and simulation cannot be overstated. AI accelerators, powered by sophisticated machine learning algorithms, enable us to anticipate the trajectory of hurricanes, assess earthquake risks, and predict flood patterns with unprecedented accuracy. These technologies provide crucial insights into the dynamics of natural disasters, allowing for more effective risk mitigation and resource allocation.

Revolutionizing Disaster Management

The integration of advanced technologies into disaster management extends beyond prediction and response to encompass recovery and resilience. Geographic Information System (GIS) mapping, powered by GPU acceleration, facilitates rapid damage assessment and aids in the strategic deployment of resources for evacuation and recovery efforts. In essence, the fusion of GPUs and AI accelerators with disaster management strategies represents a transformative approach to confronting the challenges posed by the escalating frequency and severity of natural disasters. These technologies not only enhance our ability to foresee and respond to disasters but also contribute to building more resilient communities capable of withstanding and recovering from the inevitable challenges presented by an unpredictable environment. As we navigate a future marked by environmental uncertainties, the integration of advanced technologies stands as a beacon of hope for creating a more resilient and adaptive global society.

Mehmood et al. (2018) introduced a disaster management system that harnessed VANET, cloud computing, and simulations for formulating city evacuation strategies. The integration of DL techniques to forecast urban traffic behavior marked a significant advancement. To address the computational intensity of deep learning algorithms, Graphics Processing Units (GPUs) were effectively employed. This study stands as a pioneering effort, being the first to apply deep learning within the domain of disaster management. The strategic incorporation of GPUs proved instrumental in managing the computational demands associated with deep learning algorithms. The research underscores the efficacy of DL in disaster management, especially in precisely predicting traffic behavior during emergency situations. This study contributes to the amalgamation of advanced technologies for more streamlined disaster response and mitigation strategies. The study conducted by Alzahrani et al. (2020) centered on the creation of a system for disaster management that utilized cloud computing and VANETs to create evacuation plans for urban regions. The project grew to incorporate deep learning methods for smart city traffic control. GPUs along with in-memory computing were used to handle the high processing demands of deep learning in emergency situations. Deep learning calculations powered by GPUs and in-memory large storage and management are the foundation of their framework.

The study shows how well DL can forecast traffic patterns during disasters along with evictions using openly accessible road traffic information from the United Kingdom Department for Transport. DL, stored in memory data-driven processing, and GPU advancements are all perfectly integrated inside the catastrophe mitigation area, making this approach stand out as a trailblazing endeavor.

A thorough analysis of a fully explicit time incorporation strategy using the Incompressible Smoothed Particle Hydrodynamics (ISPH) approach for fluid simulations is presented by Senadheera et al. (2021). Interestingly, the researchers used a GPU framework for computational simulations, made possible by a specially designed CUDA Fortran application. This novel strategy sought to use GPUs' simultaneous computational capacity to speed up the execution of code by doing away with the requirement to solve linear equations, which would save memory use. GPUs, being more widely accessible than supercomputer CPUs typically used for ISPH calculations, were a key focus. The study conducted dam-break simulations in addition to validation tests, affirming the effectiveness of their SPH method. The computational environment demonstrated a significant boost in calculation speed and a substantial decrease in memory usage, enabling the execution of large fluid simulations. As a result, the approach and associated improvements show promise for simulating extensive scenarios, including tsunami run-up analyses and other simulations pertinent to natural disasters. Heitzler et al. (2017) proposed methodologies for assessing natural hazard risks involve executing a diverse array of interacting simulation models, generating extensive spatio-temporal datasets. The dataset expands significantly during post-processing using Geographic Information System (GIS) operations, deriving information for decision-making. They introduce an approach that utilizes the GPU-accelerated pipeline to conduct processes on-the-fly, eliminating the need to store results in secondary memory and resulting in substantial storage space savings. In particular, algorithms are presented for three widely used spatial evaluation techniques: distance map along with buffer subsequent generations for close proximity analyses and distance weighting inversely for statistical substrates, and estimation of difference maps using map algebraic equations alongside overlay operations. Furthermore, a visualization tool that incorporates these techniques into a node-based stream of data paradigm is presented. When this visualization tool is used with actual risk assessment procedures in civil engineering, the memory consumption of subsequent processing datasets—which is measured in terabytes—is significantly reduced.

In order to recognize earthquake damage quickly in extremely high-resolution images of satellite imagery data, Bernabe et al. (2021) suggest making a deep CNN model more portable and accelerating the inference process. This is accomplished by using the Intel OpenVINO toolbox. The approach is an optimization of an earlier framework that is optimized for high-end computing methods with the goal of minimizing processing times. In addition to quick answers, the study highlights how important result accuracy is for these kinds of applications. The 2010 Haiti earthquake's GeoEye-1 VHR catastrophic photos are used for analysis along with reviews. Based on experimental results, the modified model outperforms prior efforts in damage detection accuracy and shows the remarkable speed of execution on CPU+GPU using mixed preciseness approaches. These combined outcomes underscore the effectiveness of the proposed model and highlight the advantages of leveraging the OpenVINO toolkit for accelerated earthquake damage detection in VHR remote sensing data. Jiang et al. (2022) have formulated a rapid InSAR (Interferometric Synthetic Aperture Radar) processing chain, harnessing the computational prowess of GPUs (Graphics Processing Units). This specialized chain is meticulously crafted to expedite the optimization steps inherent in Sentinel-1 InSAR processing, addressing the inherently time-consuming nature of these tasks. The paramount significance of this processing chain lies in its ability to swiftly compute InSAR deformation maps, making it highly applicable in practical scenarios. The authors demonstrate the processing chain's applicability for distorting targeting across a range of anticipated disasters via a number of experiments. The outcomes highlight its effectiveness in wide-area evaluations of probable hazards related to geological disasters along with emergency monitoring. The study exemplifies the practical utility of the GPU-assisted InSAR, showcasing its effectiveness in expediting the analysis of large datasets for timely and efficient monitoring of deformations induced by natural disasters.

Acuna et al. (2014) employ the Shallow Water Equations (SWE) to simulate tsunamis, recognized for their reliability but computational cost. To attain both accuracy and speed, this study integrates Universal Processing on GPU for solving these equations. UPGPU programming facilitates significant performance boosts, capitalizing on the parallel processing capabilities of GPUs. The Method of Characteristics are employed for the numerical resolution of the Shallow Water Equations. To further optimize performance, a Multi-GPU simulation is devised on the Tsubame 2.0 platform, harnessing the computational power of multiple GPUs for enhanced efficiency. Additionally, to address extensive domains like the Pacific Ocean, an Adaptive Mesh Refinement (AMR) technique is introduced. AMR enables dynamic adjustment of computational grid resolution, optimizing resources and enhancing simulation accuracy in large-scale scenarios. Through the amalgamation of GPGPU technology, a Multi-GPU simulation approach, and AMR techniques, this study endeavors to push the performance boundaries in simulating tsunamis, facilitating accurate and expeditious computations for large-scale domains. In order to reduce the workload for first responders, Hernandez et al. (2022) describe an AI-driven pipeline designed for the analysis of drone-captured photos following catastrophic storms. Three key steps in the pipeline are as follows: 1) reducing dimensionality using the t-distributed stochastic neighbor immersion approach; 2) a fuzzy clustering, and 3) a lightweight DL-based autoencoder. This pipeline is evaluated on several cutting-edge computing platforms that are fitted with low-power acceleration mechanisms, with the goal of developing smart self-driving aircraft that can provide amenities in real-time. The experimental scrutiny, particularly emphasizing scenarios such as flooding, reveals a noteworthy reduction in the information volume requiring processing. Moreover, employing edge computing systems with low-power graphics accelerators shows promise in managing these workloads that require a lot of processing power. Notably, the performance loss compared to its cloud counterpart version is minimal at 2.3×, encompassing both training and inference steps. This underscores the practical viability of intelligent autonomous drones equipped with AI-based image processing pipelines in efficiently supporting first responders during real-time scenarios in the aftermath of natural disasters.

Zhang et al. (2023) demonstrate the way an image-generative framework that has been trained can provide natural language direction for reconstructing imagery from satellite pictures affected by disasters. We fine-tuned this model using a small dataset of fewer than 100 unlabeled photos, which was accomplished at a very cheap cost using a single 2080Ti GPU. The method uses a previously trained text-to-image stabilization model as well as a previously trained captioning framework, GPT-4, recognizing the growing number of big models. The optimized Stable Diffusion Model performs well in both picture-inking along with image synthesis tasks, effectively synthesizing remote-sensing images damaged by disasters with conversational instruction. This accomplishment also includes supplying baseline data for additional interpretative models. Especially, when time is limited when only unlabeled data is accessible, the approach makes it easier for disaster management interpretation frameworks to learn from a significant amount of data. With the restricted amount of information along with the processing power available, this leads to better interpretation performance. The method also emphasizes how crucial it is to combine human input with huge models when synthesizing data, especially in situations where computer power and data are few. One important aspect that stands out is the synthesis of data that goes beyond what was previously known about large models, highlighting the possibility of improved interpretation accuracy in scenarios when accessibility to information and computer power are limited.

Zhang et al. (2022) introduce a swift approach to earthquake casualty prediction for China's Mainland, utilizing a combination of empirical statistics as well as physical simulations. The technology simulates how seismic waves travel over three-dimensional terrain by utilizing a GPU-accelerated 3D curved matrix finite distinction approach. The generated fatality estimation framework is then fed by the replicated seismic intensity data that is created by a regression examination of data taken from the Mainland China Composite Damaging Earthquake Catalog. The efficacy of the method is validated using the 2021 Ms 6.4 Yangbi earthquake, demonstrating accurate predictions of fatalities and providing guidance for emergency response plans. This proposed method emerges as a valuable tool for post-earthquake emergency response and disaster assessment, offering timely and quantitative estimations to inform decision-making in earthquake-prone regions, notably in Mainland China. In less than 20 minutes, Watanabe et al. (2018) can provide coastal communities with damage and flooding projections using a 10-meter grid resolution thanks to their real-time tsunami evacuation forecasting system. The research smoothly incorporates NEC's vector supercomputer SX-ACE into the system, acknowledging that the tsunami inundation, as well as the destruction modeling program, is vectorizable and highly memory-intensive. The author provides a thorough description of the system that was constructed, exploring how the program was implemented on SX-ACE and assessing how well it performed in comparison to a system based on Intel Xeons and the K computer. The evaluation highlights the necessity of a powerful computing infrastructure with cores intimately coupled to the information storage subsystem at a high memory bandwidth for a real-time tsunami evacuation forecast system, as demonstrated by SX-ACE's effectiveness. This insight accentuates the pivotal role of system architecture, particularly in terms of core performance and memory bandwidth, in achieving real-time capabilities for tsunami inundation forecasting.

Motivation

The motivation behind integrating GPUs and AI accelerators into disaster management arises from the urgent need for rapid and accurate decision-making in the face of escalating natural disasters. Traditional methods of response and recovery are often hindered by the sheer scale and complexity of these events, demanding a paradigm shift towards innovative technologies to enhance our ability to mitigate, respond to, and recover from disasters efficiently. Natural disasters unfold rapidly, leaving minimal time for decision-makers to assess the situation, formulate effective response strategies, and allocate resources appropriately. The swift and often unpredictable nature of events such as earthquakes, hurricanes, or wildfires necessitates a response mechanism that can match the speed of these occurrences. Delayed decision-making can result in increased casualties, heightened damage to infrastructure, and prolonged recovery periods. The imperative to save lives and minimize the impact of disasters highlights the critical need for solutions that enable swift decision-making.

GPUs and AI accelerators play a pivotal role in revolutionizing disaster response efforts. GPUs, with their parallel processing capabilities, enable rapid analysis of massive datasets, facilitating real-time monitoring and assessment. This speed is crucial for early warning systems, where timely information can mean the difference between life and death. Moreover, the ability to process data in parallel allows for complex simulations and modelling, aiding in predicting the trajectory of disasters and their potential impact on affected areas. AI accelerators, driven by advanced machine learning algorithms, enhance decision-making by providing predictive analytics and actionable insights. These technologies can process and interpret diverse data sources, including satellite imagery, weather patterns, and seismic activity, to generate accurate forecasts and risk assessments. Through continuous learning, AI systems become more adept at recognizing patterns and trends, improving the precision of predictions over time. The integration of GPUs and AI accelerators in disaster management not only expedites decision-making but also enhances its accuracy. These technologies empower emergency responders and authorities with the tools needed to make informed choices based on real-time data and predictive analytics. By leveraging the capabilities of GPUs and AI accelerators, disaster response becomes more adaptive, resilient, and effective, ultimately contributing to the overarching goal of minimizing the impact of natural disasters on human lives and communities.

GPUs IN NATURAL DISASTER MANAGEMENT

Parallel Processing Capabilities

Graphics Processing Units (GPUs) stand as crucial tools in the realm of natural disaster management, propelled by their remarkable parallel processing capabilities. Unlike their traditional counterparts, Central Processing Units (CPUs), GPUs excel in handling multiple tasks simultaneously. This inherent ability becomes particularly invaluable when navigating the vast and intricate datasets associated with geospatial, meteorological, and seismic data in the context of natural disasters (Muhammad et al., 2023). In real-world applications, the parallel processing prowess of GPUs manifests in various ways, significantly impacting the speed and efficiency of disaster-related tasks. For instance, in earthquake monitoring, GPUs can simultaneously process seismic data streams from multiple sensors, allowing for real-time analysis and detection of potential tremors. This swift processing is critical for early warning systems, where timely identification of seismic patterns can mean the difference between effective preparedness and unforeseen catastrophe.

Meteorological data, including satellite imagery and weather patterns, represents another domain where GPUs shine. During hurricane tracking, GPUs can process immense volumes of data in parallel, providing meteorologists with up-to-the-minute information on the storm's trajectory, intensity, and potential impact areas. This capability is instrumental in issuing accurate and timely warnings to vulnerable populations, facilitating more effective evacuations and resource allocations. In the geospatial domain, GPUs contribute to rapid mapping and visualization of disaster-affected areas. For example, in the aftermath of a flood, GPUs can accelerate the creation of high-resolution flood maps by processing satellite imagery and elevation data concurrently (Ogata, 2023). This accelerated mapping aids emergency responders in assessing the extent of the flood, identifying areas at higher risk, and optimizing evacuation routes.

The parallel processing capabilities of Graphics Processing Units (GPUs) can be mathematically represented using the concept of parallelism. One common metric used to quantify parallelism is speedup, which measures the performance improvement gained by executing a task in parallel compared to sequentially. The speedup (S) is given by:

$$S = \frac{T_{sequential}}{T_{parallel}} \tag{1}$$

where $T_{sequential}$ is the execution time of the task when performed sequentially. $T_{parallel}$ is the execution time of the same task when performed in parallel. Another important metric is efficiency (E), which expresses the utilization of the available resources for parallel processing:

$$E = \frac{S}{P} \tag{2}$$

S is the speedup. P is the number of processing elements (in this case, the number of GPU cores).

Moreover, GPUs play a pivotal role in simulating disaster scenarios, allowing for advanced modeling and visualization as shown in Figure 1. For instance, in wildfire prediction, GPUs can simulate the potential spread of fires based on various factors such as wind speed, terrain, and vegetation. This simulation helps authorities anticipate the fire's path, enabling more proactive decision-making in terms of evacuations and resource deployment. The real-time examples underscore the practical applications of GPUs in enhancing natural disaster management. Whether it's earthquake monitoring, hurricane tracking, flood mapping, or wildfire simulation, the parallel processing capabilities of GPUs contribute to the speed, accuracy, and effectiveness of disaster-related tasks. As we continue to face an increase in the frequency and severity of natural disasters, harnessing the full potential of GPUs becomes not just

Figure 1. Futuristic disaster management system

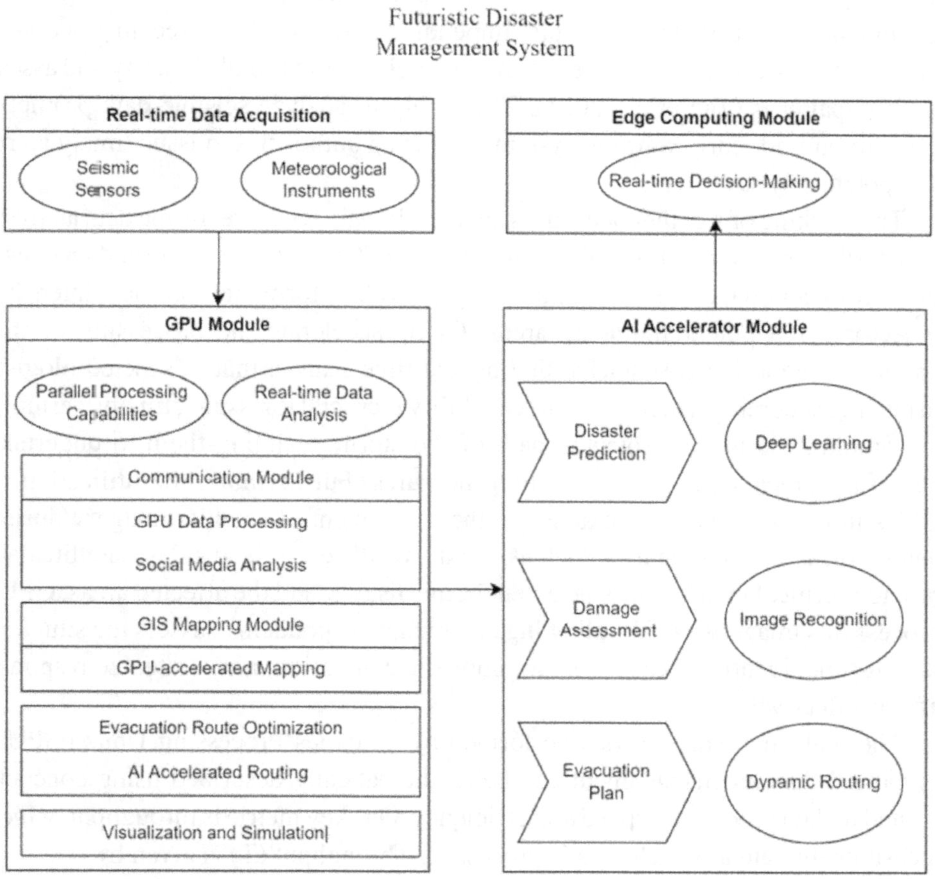

a technological advantage but a critical necessity for building resilient and adaptive disaster management systems.

Real-Time Data Analysis

In the realm of natural disaster management, the real-time nature of unfolding events necessitates swift and accurate data analysis to inform timely decision-making. Graphics Processing Units (GPUs) emerge as indispensable tools in this context, showcasing their exceptional capability to process large volumes of data with remarkable speed. This prowess in real-time data analysis finds applications across various domains, significantly enhancing our ability to understand, predict, and respond to natural disasters effectively. One critical application of real-time data analysis using GPUs lies in the monitoring of seismic activity. In earthquake-prone regions, seismic sensors generate continuous streams of data, capturing subtle ground movements that could signify impending tremors. GPUs excel in processing these vast datasets in real-time, enabling seismologists to rapidly identify and assess seismic patterns (Tan et al., 2021). The ability to analyze seismic data promptly is paramount for early warning systems, allowing authorities to issue timely alerts and potentially save lives.

The tracking of weather patterns is another domain where real-time data analysis with GPUs proves instrumental. As hurricanes and typhoons develop and progress, meteorological data streams continuously provide information on their intensity, trajectory, and potential impact areas. GPUs accelerate the processing of this complex meteorological data, facilitating real-time analysis that aids meteorologists in making accurate predictions. This capability is crucial for issuing timely warnings to communities in the projected path of the storm, enabling them to undertake necessary precautions and evacuation measures. Furthermore, the utilization of GPUs in real-time analysis extends to the assessment of satellite imagery during natural disasters. In scenarios such as floods, wildfires, or landslides, satellite data provides critical insights into the extent of the disaster and the affected areas. GPUs process this imagery swiftly, allowing emergency responders to assess the situation in real-time, identify areas requiring immediate attention, and strategize response efforts effectively.

The real-time data analysis performed by Graphics Processing Units (GPUs) in natural disaster management can be mathematically described using concepts related to data processing speed and efficiency. One key metric is throughput, which measures the rate at which data is processed. Throughput (T) is given by:

$$T = \frac{N}{Time} \tag{3}$$

Where: N is the number of data items processed. Time is the time taken to process the data.

In the context of wildfires, real-time data analysis with GPUs contributes to fire detection and monitoring. Through the analysis of satellite and aerial imagery, GPUs can quickly identify the location and extent of wildfires. This information is crucial for emergency services in coordinating evacuations, deploying firefighting resources, and managing the overall response to mitigate the impact of the wildfire on communities and ecosystems. Moreover, the applications of real-time data analysis using GPUs extend to dynamic scenarios such as urban planning during disasters. In cases of floods or hurricanes, real-time analysis of GIS (Geographic Information

System) data, powered by GPUs, allows for dynamic mapping of affected areas. This aids in optimizing evacuation routes, resource allocation, and the overall coordination of emergency response efforts.

Visualization and Simulation

The integration of GPU technology in natural disaster management marks a significant advancement, particularly in the realms of visualization and simulation. This transformative capability extends beyond conventional data processing, offering a dynamic approach to understanding disaster scenarios, formulating response strategies, and optimizing resource allocation (Elst et al., 2022). The ability of GPUs to render complex visualizations, including intricate 3D models, revolutionizes our perception of potential impacts, enabling more informed and effective decision-making. One practical application of GPU-enhanced visualization is in the creation of 3D models depicting disaster scenarios. For instance, in earthquake-prone regions, GPUs can process seismic data to generate real-time visualizations of ground movements. These visualizations, presented in three dimensions, provide a comprehensive understanding of the seismic activity's intensity and distribution. Emergency responders and authorities can use these models to assess potential structural damage, identify vulnerable areas, and plan targeted response efforts. The visual representation of seismic data, facilitated by GPUs, enhances the comprehensibility of complex information, enabling stakeholders to make informed decisions swiftly.

In the context of hurricanes or typhoons, GPU-driven visualization contributes to creating realistic models of storm trajectories. Meteorological data, processed in real-time by GPUs, can be translated into visualizations that accurately depict the evolving path of the storm. These visualizations aid meteorologists, emergency responders, and the public in understanding the potential impact areas, facilitating more precise evacuation planning and resource deployment. The immersive and detailed nature of GPU-enhanced visualizations enhances the communication of critical information, fostering a deeper understanding of the evolving disaster scenario. Moreover, GPUs play a crucial role in simulating disaster scenarios, offering emergency responders a powerful tool for anticipating outcomes and testing various response strategies. For instance, in the case of wildfires, GPUs can simulate the spread of fires based on factors such as wind patterns, terrain characteristics, and vegetation density. This simulation allows authorities to predict the fire's trajectory, assess potential risks to communities, and optimize the allocation of firefighting resources. By enabling real-time simulations, GPUs empower responders to develop and refine strategies that are adaptive to the dynamic nature of disaster events. In the realm of urban planning during disasters, GPU-driven visualizations aid in creating dynamic maps that reflect real-time conditions. For instance, in flood scenarios, GIS data processed by GPUs can be visualized to show the extent of flooding and its impact on infrastructure. These visualizations assist emergency responders in making rapid decisions regarding evacuation routes, resource allocation, and prioritized response efforts.

The transformative integration of GPU technology in natural disaster management, particularly in visualization and simulation, can be mathematically described in terms of rendering efficiency and simulation accuracy.

Rendering Efficiency

The efficiency of rendering complex visualizations, such as 3D models, by GPUs can be measured using the concept of rendering speed. Rendering speed (R) is given by:

$$R = \frac{M}{Time} \tag{4}$$

where M is the complexity of the visualization (e.g., number of polygons, data points). Time is the time taken to render the visualization. Higher rendering speed indicates more efficient GPU-driven visualization, crucial for real-time disaster scenario comprehension. ***Simulation Accuracy***

The accuracy of disaster scenario simulations, facilitated by GPUs, can be evaluated through metrics like simulation error or similarity indices. One such metric is the Mean Absolute Error (MAE), given by:

$$MAE = \frac{1}{N}\sum_{i=1}^{N}\left|Actual_i - Simulated_i\right| \tag{5}$$

where $Actual_i$ is the actual value at data point i. $Simulated_i$ is the simulated value at data point i. N is the total number of data points. Lower MAE values indicate higher simulation accuracy.

AI ACCELERATORS: A GAME-CHANGER

Deep Learning and Neural Networks

The advent of AI accelerators, specifically Graphics Processing Units (GPUs) optimized for deep learning tasks, has ushered in a paradigm shift in natural disaster management. This transformative technology has proven to be a game-changer, enabling the application of deep learning algorithms powered by neural networks. The capacity of these algorithms to analyze diverse datasets, recognize intricate patterns, and discern correlations opens up a realm of possibilities in disaster scenarios. Real-time examples and applications showcase the profound impact of deep learning in enhancing predictive modeling and decision-making in the face of natural disasters. One noteworthy application of deep learning in disaster management is image recognition in satellite imagery. GPUs, tailored for deep learning tasks, empower algorithms to swiftly analyze vast amounts of high-resolution satellite imagery. In the context of a wildfire, for instance, deep learning algorithms can identify smoke patterns, fire fronts, and changes in vegetation cover in real time. This capability is instrumental for emergency responders in gaining immediate insights into the extent of the fire, identifying areas at risk, and prioritizing response efforts. By harnessing deep learning for image recognition, GPUs contribute to a more efficient and accurate assessment of disaster-affected regions.

Seismic pattern analysis represents another critical domain where deep learning and neural networks play a pivotal role. GPUs optimized for deep learning tasks accelerate the processing of seismic data, allowing for the rapid identification of subtle patterns that precede earthquakes. Deep learning algorithms can discern precursory signals in seismic data, providing valuable seconds to minutes of early warning before the onset of tremors. This real-time analysis is vital for implementing timely evacuation measures and improving overall preparedness for seismic events. Moreover, deep learning is instrumental in identifying early indicators of disasters across various datasets. For instance, in flood-prone regions, deep learning algorithms can analyze meteorological data, river levels, and historical flood patterns to identify conditions conducive to flooding. The ability to recognize these early indicators enables authorities to issue warnings, implement preventive measures, and optimize resource allocation before the disaster unfolds. In this way, deep learning contributes to a proactive and anticipatory approach to disaster management. The power of deep learning and neural networks is further exemplified in predictive modelling (Abadi et al., 2022). GPUs optimized for deep learning tasks facilitate the training of complex neural network models on massive datasets. These models can predict the trajectory of hurricanes, assess the risk of landslides, and anticipate the spread of wildfires with unprecedented accuracy. By continuously learning from new data, deep learning algorithms improve over time, enhancing their ability to make precise predictions and contribute to more effective disaster preparedness.

Accelerated Machine Learning Algorithms

AI accelerators, designed to expedite the execution of machine learning algorithms, stand as a transformative force in natural disaster management. Their ability to accelerate the processing of data offers a significant leap in efficiency and speed. In this domain, acceleration is crucial for a spectrum of tasks, including predictive analytics, risk assessment, and decision support systems. Real-time examples and applications illustrate how the acceleration of machine learning algorithms contributes to faster and more informed decision-making in the dynamic landscape of natural disaster response. Predictive analytics in natural disaster management relies heavily on machine learning algorithms to forecast the occurrence, intensity, and impact of disasters. AI accelerators, such as GPUs optimized for machine learning tasks, significantly expedite the training and execution of predictive models. For example, in hurricane prediction, machine learning algorithms process historical meteorological data at an accelerated pace, allowing meteorologists to generate more accurate and timely predictions of a storm's trajectory. The accelerated analytics contribute to improved early warning systems, enabling authorities to implement timely evacuation measures and optimize resource allocation in the face of impending disasters.

Risk assessment is another critical area where accelerated machine learning algorithms play a pivotal role. In real-time, these algorithms can analyze diverse datasets, including topography, population density, and historical disaster records, to assess the vulnerability of specific regions to various natural hazards. For instance, in landslide-prone areas, machine learning algorithms can quickly process data related to soil composition, precipitation levels, and terrain characteristics to evaluate the risk of landslides (Field et al., 2017). This accelerated risk assessment aids in developing targeted mitigation strategies and informing land-use planning to minimize the impact of potential disasters. Decision support systems benefit significantly from the acceleration of machine learning algorithms, particularly in dynamically evolving disaster scenarios. For example, during a wildfire outbreak, machine learning algorithms can analyze real-time data streams from various sources, including weather conditions, terrain features, and the fire's current status. The accelerated processing enables decision support systems to provide emergency responders with actionable insights, such as optimal evacuation routes, resource allocation recommendations, and dynamic strategies for containing the fire. The speed and efficiency offered by accelerated machine learning contribute to more adaptive decision-making in the face of rapidly changing disaster conditions. Machine learning algorithms also shine in post-disaster analysis, where rapid assessment of damage and recovery needs is crucial. AI accelerators expedite the analysis of diverse datasets, including satellite imagery, social media feeds, and infrastructure data. For instance, after a flood, machine learning algorithms can quickly analyze satellite imagery to assess the extent of inundation, identify damaged infrastructure, and prioritize areas for immediate response and recovery efforts. This accelerated analysis aids in expediting the recovery process and optimizing the allocation of resources.

Edge Computing for Quick Decision-Making

The emergence of edge computing, empowered by AI accelerators, represents a groundbreaking approach in disaster management. This paradigm shift, moving away from centralized cloud servers, enables the processing of critical data closer to the source, fostering quick decision-making in the face of natural disasters. Real-time examples and applications illustrate the pivotal role of edge computing, particularly in scenarios demanding immediate action, such as the deployment of unmanned aerial vehicles (UAVs) for real-time assessment of disaster-affected areas. In disaster management, the speed of decision-making can be a determining factor in mitigating the impact of a crisis. Edge computing, facilitated by AI accelerators, addresses the latency challenges associated with centralized cloud processing. By processing data locally, closer to the disaster-affected areas, edge computing significantly reduces the time required for critical information to travel to and from centralized servers. This is especially crucial in scenarios where immediate action is imperative.

One compelling example of edge computing in action is the real-time assessment of disaster-affected areas using unmanned aerial vehicles (UAVs) or drones. Equipped with sensors and cameras, these UAVs can capture high-resolution imagery and data from disaster-stricken regions. AI accelerators, integrated into the UAVs, enable on-board processing of this data, facilitating real-time analysis without the need to transmit large volumes of information to distant servers. In the aftermath of a hurricane, for instance, UAVs equipped with edge computing capabilities can quickly assess damage, identify areas in need of urgent attention, and provide immediate insights to emergency responders on the ground. Furthermore, edge computing proves invaluable in scenarios where connectivity to centralized servers may be compromised. In the immediate aftermath of a natural disaster, such as an earthquake or hurricane, communication infrastructure may be severely affected. Edge computing addresses this challenge by allowing local processing of critical data, ensuring that decision-making can proceed autonomously even in areas with limited or disrupted connectivity.

In the context of real-time monitoring of seismic activity, edge computing accelerates the analysis of data from distributed sensors. Instead of relying on a centralized server for processing seismic data, edge devices equipped with AI accelerators can analyze the data locally. This decentralized approach enhances the speed of identifying potential seismic threats, enabling faster response times and more efficient implementation of early warning systems. Additionally, edge computing contributes to the optimization of resource allocation during disaster response. For instance, in a wildfire scenario, edge devices deployed in the field can process data from environmental sensors and surveillance cameras locally. AI algorithms running on these devices can quickly analyze the data to assess the fire's progression, identify high-risk areas, and recommend real-time adjustments to firefighting strategies. This localized decision-making not only expedites the response but also ensures adaptability to the dynamic conditions of the disaster. The integration of edge computing, empowered by AI accelerators, revolutionizes decision-making in natural disaster management. Real-time assessment using UAVs, decentralized processing of seismic data, and adaptability to limited connectivity are just a few examples of how edge computing enhances the speed and efficiency of disaster response. As we navigate an era marked by increasing natural disasters, the adoption of edge computing technologies becomes a cornerstone for building resilient and responsive disaster management systems.

APPLICATIONS OF GPUS AND AI ACCELERATORS IN NATURAL DISASTER MANAGEMENT

The integration of GPUs (Graphics Processing Units) and AI accelerators in natural disaster management brings forth a myriad of applications as shown in Figure 2, revolutionizing how we predict, respond to, and recover from catastrophic events. Here are key applications of these technologies in the context of natural disaster management:

Early Warning Systems

The integration of Graphics Processing Units (GPUs) and AI accelerators has ushered in a new era for early warning systems, significantly advancing our ability to detect and respond to potential disasters. These technologies play a pivotal role in processing vast amounts of real-time data, enabling quick and accurate analysis of critical information related to seismic activity, weather patterns, and other relevant sources. Real-time examples showcase how GPUs and AI accelerators enhance the speed and effectiveness of early warning systems, providing crucial insights for timely disaster detection. In the realm of seismic monitoring, GPUs and AI accelerators contribute to the swift analysis of data from distributed seismic sensors. The real-time processing capabilities of GPUs allow for the simultaneous evaluation of seismic signals from multiple locations. For example, during an earthquake, the sensors detect ground movements, and AI algorithms running on GPUs can rapidly

Figure 2. Applications of GPUs and AI accelerators in natural disaster management

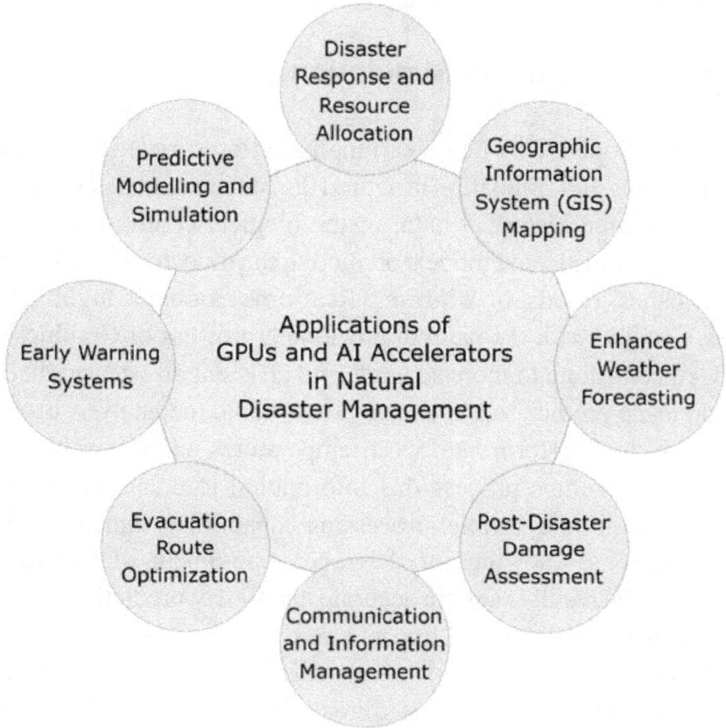

identify patterns indicative of seismic activity. This accelerated analysis enables early warning systems to promptly issue alerts, giving communities valuable seconds to minutes to prepare and take protective actions.

Weather-related disasters, such as hurricanes and typhoons, present another critical application for early warning systems enhanced by GPUs and AI accelerators. Meteorological data streams, including satellite imagery and atmospheric conditions, are processed in real time to predict the trajectory and intensity of approaching storms. GPUs accelerate the computation of complex weather models, allowing meteorologists to provide more accurate and timely warnings. This enhanced capability is particularly vital for coastal areas, where the speed of storm warnings directly influences evacuation plans and resource allocations for disaster response. In the context of floods, GPUs and AI accelerators contribute to the analysis of various data sources in real time. River levels, precipitation data, and terrain characteristics are processed concurrently to assess the risk of flooding. For instance, in regions prone to flash floods, these technologies enable early warning systems to quickly identify rising water levels and predict potential inundation areas. Residents and authorities can then receive timely alerts, facilitating proactive evacuation measures and minimizing the impact of the impending disaster.

Predictive Modelling and Simulation

AI accelerators, propelled by deep learning algorithms, redefine the landscape of predictive modeling and simulation in natural disaster management. These advanced technologies leverage historical data, meteorological conditions, and geological factors to create sophisticated models predicting the trajectory and impact of events such as hurricanes, floods, or wildfires. Real-time examples highlight how these capabilities, coupled with the parallel processing prowess of Graphics Processing Units (GPUs), contribute to more accurate and efficient disaster predictions. In the realm of hurricane prediction, AI accelerators enable the analysis of vast datasets encompassing historical storm data, ocean temperatures, and atmospheric conditions. Deep learning algorithms process this information to create intricate predictive models. GPUs, with their parallel processing capabilities, enhance the efficiency of these simulations, allowing for the rapid assessment of multiple variables simultaneously. The result is a more accurate and timely prediction of a hurricane's trajectory, intensity, and potential impact areas.

Similarly, in flood prediction, AI accelerators can analyze meteorological data, river levels, and topographical features to create detailed models of potential flooding scenarios. The parallel processing capabilities of GPUs play a crucial role in handling the complex computations involved in simulating different flood scenarios based on varying rainfall patterns and terrain characteristics. This accelerated simulation aids in forecasting flood-prone areas, enabling authorities to implement preventive measures and issue timely warnings to at-risk communities. Wildfire prediction benefits significantly from AI accelerators and GPUs, particularly in assessing the dynamic factors influencing fire spread. Deep learning algorithms can analyze data from environmental sensors, satellite imagery, and historical fire patterns to create predictive models. GPUs accelerate the simulation of wildfire scenarios by handling the intricate computations required for factors like wind speed, vegetation density, and terrain. This enables authorities to anticipate the potential path of a wildfire, optimize evacuation plans, and strategically deploy firefighting resources in real time.

Disaster Response and Resource Allocation

In the critical phase of disaster response, where swift and efficient resource allocation is paramount, GPUs and AI accelerators play instrumental roles. GPUs, with their ability to facilitate real-time analysis of dynamic data, empower emergency responders to quickly assess the situation on the ground. Concurrently, AI accelerators contribute by providing valuable insights into optimal resource allocation through predictive analytics. Real-time examples illustrate how the integration of these technologies ensures a more effective and targeted disaster response, ultimately minimizing response times and enhancing overall disaster management. During a wildfire outbreak, for instance, GPUs enable the real-time analysis of data streams from environmental sensors and surveillance cameras. This immediate processing capability allows emergency responders to assess the fire's progression, identify high-risk areas, and dynamically adjust firefighting strategies. Simultaneously, AI accelerators leverage predictive analytics to recommend optimal resource allocation, considering factors such as wind patterns, terrain characteristics, and potential fire spread. This ensures that firefighting resources are deployed where they are most needed, optimizing the response to the dynamic conditions of the disaster.

In flood scenarios, GPUs contribute to the rapid assessment of real-time data, including river levels and precipitation patterns. Emergency responders can utilize this immediate analysis to understand the extent of flooding, identify areas at high risk, and plan evacuation routes. AI accelerators, through predictive analytics, provide insights into the optimal allocation of rescue teams, shelters, and relief supplies based on the anticipated progression of the flood. This integrated approach enhances the precision and effectiveness of resource allocation during the critical moments of disaster response. In earthquake-prone regions, GPUs facilitate the quick analysis of seismic data, aiding emergency responders in assessing structural damage and identifying areas in need of immediate attention. AI accelerators contribute predictive analytics to recommend optimal allocation of search and rescue teams, medical resources, and temporary shelters based on the expected impact of aftershocks. This collaborative use of GPUs and AI accelerators ensures a well-informed and rapid disaster response, aligning resources with the evolving needs of the affected areas.

Geographic Information System (GIS) Mapping

The acceleration of Geographic Information System (GIS) mapping through the utilization of GPUs and AI accelerators represents a transformative leap in disaster management. GPUs play a vital role in expediting the creation of high-resolution maps for disaster-prone areas, contributing to risk assessment, evacuation planning, and damage assessment. Meanwhile, AI accelerators enhance GIS capabilities by automating the analysis of satellite imagery, swiftly identifying changes in terrain or infrastructure that may indicate damage caused by a disaster (Llenos et al., 2017). Real-time examples underscore how this integration enhances the precision and efficiency of GIS mapping in the aftermath of natural disasters. In the wake of a flood, GPUs accelerate the processing of satellite imagery, enabling the creation of high-resolution flood maps. These maps, generated in real-time, provide emergency responders with a detailed overview of the affected areas, allowing for rapid identification of submerged regions, compromised infrastructure, and areas at heightened risk. The efficiency brought by GPUs in GIS mapping facilitates quicker decision-making regarding evacuation routes, resource deployment, and prioritized response efforts.

AI accelerators, integrated into GIS systems, automate the analysis of satellite imagery after a wildfire. By swiftly identifying changes in vegetation cover, the extent of burn areas, and potential threats to infrastructure, these accelerators enable rapid damage assessment. The automated analysis allows emergency responders to prioritize areas for immediate attention, assess the impact on ecosystems, and plan recovery efforts more effectively. In earthquake-prone regions, GPUs contribute to the accelerated creation of seismic hazard maps. These maps, enriched with real-time data processing capabilities, aid in identifying areas at higher risk of seismic activity. Simultaneously, AI accelerators analyze satellite imagery to detect changes in terrain, potential landslides, or structural damage post-earthquake. The integration of GPUs and AI accelerators in GIS mapping ensures a comprehensive and timely understanding of the seismic impact, guiding emergency responders in their strategic resource allocation and response efforts.

Enhanced Weather Forecasting

The integration of GPUs and AI accelerators revolutionizes weather forecasting, ushering in a new era of enhanced accuracy and localized precision in predicting severe weather events. GPUs play a pivotal role in accelerating the computation of complex weather models, leading to more accurate predictions for events like hurricanes, tornadoes, or heavy rainfall. Simultaneously, AI accelerators, leveraging machine learning algorithms, analyze intricate atmospheric data, providing precise and localized weather forecasts. Real-time examples highlight the tangible impact of these technologies in improving our ability to anticipate and prepare for severe weather events. In the context of hurricane forecasting, GPUs accelerate the processing of vast datasets encompassing ocean temperatures, wind patterns, and atmospheric conditions. This accelerated computation enables meteorologists to create more detailed and accurate models of a hurricane's trajectory and intensity. Real-time examples showcase how, during a hurricane approach, the integration of GPUs results in more timely and reliable forecasts, allowing authorities to issue warnings, plan evacuations, and optimize resource deployment with greater confidence.

AI accelerators contribute significantly to enhanced weather forecasting by employing machine learning algorithms to analyze complex atmospheric data. For instance, in predicting heavy rainfall and potential flooding, AI algorithms can process real-time information from various sources, including weather satellites, precipitation patterns, and ground sensors. This dynamic analysis enables meteorologists to provide more precise forecasts, specifying not only the likelihood of heavy rainfall but also the areas at highest risk. This localized precision is invaluable for communities and emergency responders, facilitating more targeted preparedness measures. During tornado outbreaks, GPUs contribute to the rapid analysis of atmospheric conditions conducive to tornado formation. This accelerated analysis allows meteorologists to issue more timely tornado warnings, providing residents with crucial minutes to seek shelter. Simultaneously, AI accelerators enhance tornado forecasting by learning from historical tornado data and identifying subtle patterns indicative of tornado formation. This machine learning-driven approach improves the accuracy of tornado predictions, enabling communities to implement more effective mitigation and response strategies.

Post-Disaster Damage Assessment

In the aftermath of a disaster, the swift and accurate assessment of damage is paramount for effective recovery efforts. GPUs and AI accelerators play integral roles in expediting this process, combining their strengths to enable rapid processing of satellite and drone imagery and automate damage assessment through advanced image recognition and analysis. Real-time examples illustrate how this integration accelerates the overall recovery process and assists in prioritizing response efforts for maximum impact. Following a hurricane, GPUs contribute to the rapid processing of high-resolution satellite imagery capturing the affected areas. This accelerated image processing allows for quick identification of damaged structures, flooded regions, and infrastructure disruptions. Simultaneously, AI accelerators utilize image recognition algorithms to automate the assessment of the extent of damage. For instance, by analyzing satellite imagery, these accelerators can swiftly identify areas with compromised infrastructure, helping emergency responders prioritize immediate response and recovery efforts.

In wildfire-stricken areas, drones equipped with cameras capture real-time imagery of burned landscapes and affected communities. GPUs enhance the rapid processing of this imagery, facilitating quick mapping of burn scars, damaged properties, and areas requiring urgent attention. AI accelerators, leveraging image analysis, automate the identification of damaged structures, aiding in the efficient assessment of the impact on residential areas. This integrated approach streamlines the post-disaster damage assessment, allowing authorities to allocate resources strategically for effective recovery. In earthquake scenarios, drones equipped with AI accelerators can assess structural damage in urban areas. GPUs expedite the processing of drone-captured imagery, while AI algorithms analyze the images to identify compromised buildings, infrastructure, and potential hazards. This automated analysis accelerates the overall damage assessment, guiding emergency responders in prioritizing search and rescue efforts and allocating resources based on the severity of structural damage.

Communication and Information Management

In the midst of disasters, effective communication and information management are essential for ensuring the safety and well-being of affected populations. GPUs and AI accelerators emerge as crucial tools in enhancing data processing for communication systems, facilitating faster dissemination of critical information. Additionally, AI algorithms play a pivotal role in conducting sentiment analysis on social media, offering insights into public perception and response and enabling more targeted and adaptive communication strategies. Real-time examples underscore the tangible benefits of this integration in crisis communication and information management. During a wildfire, GPUs accelerate the processing of data from environmental sensors, surveillance cameras, and satellite imagery. This rapid data processing enables emergency communication systems to provide real-time updates on the fire's progression, evacuation routes, and safety measures. Simultaneously, AI accelerators analyze social media feeds for sentiment analysis, gauging public reactions and concerns. This dual approach allows authorities to tailor their communication strategies, addressing specific needs and concerns identified through sentiment analysis.

In the aftermath of an earthquake, GPUs expedite the processing of seismic data and drone-captured imagery for damage assessment. This accelerated information processing enables communication systems to disseminate accurate and timely updates on areas affected by the earthquake, emergency contact information, and available resources. AI algorithms, concurrently, analyze social media for sentiment, providing insights into public sentiment and concerns. This information aids in crafting communication strategies that address public perceptions and foster a sense of community resilience. During a hurricane, GPUs play a crucial role in processing meteorological data for accurate forecasting. This information is then swiftly communicated to the public through various channels, including emergency alerts and public announcements. AI accelerators analyze social media platforms for sentiment, helping authorities understand public reactions to evacuation orders and emergency measures. This dual capability ensures that communication strategies are not only timely but also responsive to the evolving sentiments and concerns of the affected population.

Evacuation Route Optimization

In the face of impending disasters, optimizing evacuation routes is crucial for ensuring the safety and efficiency of evacuations. AI accelerators emerge as powerful tools in this regard, capable of dynamically optimizing evacuation plans based on real-time data and predicted disaster impact. This adaptability ensures that evacuation routes are continually adjusted to changing conditions, maximizing the effectiveness of evacuation efforts. Concurrently, GPUs play a vital role by supporting the rapid computation required for these dynamic optimization processes. Real-time examples illustrate how the integration of AI accelerators and GPUs revolutionizes evacuation route planning in response to dynamic and evolving disaster scenarios. During a hurricane, AI accelerators leverage predictive analytics to analyze real-time meteorological data, considering factors such as wind speed, trajectory, and potential storm surge. This analysis enables the dynamic optimization of evacuation routes, ensuring that paths are adjusted in response to the changing trajectory and intensity of the hurricane. GPUs support the rapid computation required for this dynamic optimization, facilitating quick adjustments to the evacuation plan and minimizing delays in response to the evolving disaster conditions.

In the context of wildfires, AI accelerators process real-time data from environmental sensors, satellite imagery, and weather forecasts to predict the path and intensity of the fire. This predictive modeling enables dynamic optimization of evacuation routes, allowing authorities to redirect evacuees away from advancing fire fronts and potential danger zones. GPUs contribute to the efficiency of this process by handling the complex computations involved in simulating different wildfire scenarios and rapidly updating evacuation plans. During an earthquake, AI accelerators analyze seismic data in real time to predict potential aftershocks and assess the structural integrity of buildings. This analysis informs the dynamic optimization of evacuation routes, redirecting evacuees away from areas at higher risk of aftershocks or structural collapse. GPUs support the rapid computation required for this dynamic optimization process, ensuring that evacuation routes are continually adjusted to prioritize safety in the aftermath of the earthquake.

FUTURE RESEARCH DIRECTIONS

In the burgeoning field of futuristic disaster mitigation, future research should prioritize the optimization of GPU-accelerated algorithms, exploring novel parallelization strategies and hardware-software co-design. Integration with edge computing is pivotal, demanding advanced methodologies to empower edge devices with AI capabilities for quicker response times. Addressing interpretability challenges in deep learning models remains crucial for building trust in AI-driven disaster prediction and assessment. Additionally, the fusion of diverse data modalities, such as satellite imagery and social media feeds, warrants exploration to extract comprehensive insights. Adaptive evacuation planning, utilizing AI accelerators for dynamic route adjustments, is essential for enhancing efficiency and safety. Finally, resilience and robustness testing methodologies should be developed to ensure the reliability and adaptability of disaster management systems under various scenarios, contributing to the continual evolution of effective and resilient disaster mitigation strategies.

CONCLUSION

The integration of GPUs and AI accelerators in natural disaster management revolutionizes the entire disaster lifecycle. Early warning systems benefit from GPUs' real-time data processing and AI accelerators' predictive modelling, enabling timely detection and accurate trajectory predictions. Disaster response and resource allocation are optimized through rapid data analysis and AI-driven decision-making, ensuring an effective and targeted response. GIS mapping is accelerated by GPUs, aiding in risk assessment and damage evaluation, while enhanced weather forecasting leverages both technologies for more accurate predictions. Post-disaster damage assessment benefits from the quick processing of imagery by GPUs and automated analysis through AI accelerators, expediting recovery efforts. Communication and information management during disasters are improved, utilizing GPUs and AI for faster data processing and sentiment analysis on social media. Evacuation routes are dynamically optimized using AI accelerators, ensuring efficient and safe evacuations. In essence, the applications of GPUs and AI accelerators span the entire spectrum of natural disaster management, from early detection and prediction to response, recovery, and risk mitigation. These technologies empower decision-makers with tools to navigate the complexities of disaster management and enhance overall resilience in the face of natural hazards.

REFERENCES

Abadi, M., Barham, P., Chen, J., Chen, Z., Davis, A., & Dean, J. (2016). *TensorFlow: A system for large-scale machine learning*.

Acuna, M. A., & Aoki, T. (2014). AMR multi-GPU accelerated tsunami simulation. In *The 1st International Conference on Computational Engineering and Science for Safety and Environmental Problems* (pp. 708-710). Research Gate.

Aqib, M., Mehmood, R., Albeshri, A., & Alzahrani, A. (2018). Disaster Management in Smart Cities by Forecasting Traffic Plan Using Deep Learning and GPUs. In R. Mehmood, B. Bhaduri, I. Katib, & I. Chlamtac (Eds.), *Smart Societies, Infrastructure, Technologies and Applications. SCITA 2017. Lecture Notes of the Institute for Computer Sciences, Social Informatics and Telecommunications Engineering* (Vol. 224). Springer. doi:10.1007/978-3-319-94180-6_15

Aqib, M., Mehmood, R., Alzahrani, A., & Katib, I. (2020). A Smart Disaster Management System for Future Cities Using Deep Learning, GPUs, and In-Memory Computing. In R. Mehmood, S. See, I. Katib, & I. Chlamtac (Eds.), *Smart Infrastructure and Applications. EAI/Springer Innovations in Communication and Computing*. Springer. doi:10.1007/978-3-030-13705-2_7

Asim, K. M., Idris, A., Iqbal, T., & Martínez-Álvarez, F. (2018). Martínez-Álvarez, F. Seismic indicators-based earthquake predictor system using Genetic Programming and AdaBoost classification. *Soil Dynamics and Earthquake Engineering*, *111*, 1–7. doi:10.1016/j.soildyn.2018.04.020

Bernabe, S., González, C., Fernández, A., & Bhangale, U. (2021). Portability and Acceleration of Deep Learning Inferences to Detect Rapid Earthquake Damage From VHR Remote Sensing Images Using Intel OpenVINO Toolkit. *IEEE Journal of Selected Topics in Applied Earth Observations and Remote Sensing*, *14*, 6906–6915. doi:10.1109/JSTARS.2021.3075961

Dhinakaran. (2023). IoT-Based Environmental Control System for Fish Farms with Sensor Integration and Machine Learning Decision Support. *International Journal on Recent and Innovation Trends in Computing and Communication*, *11*(10), 203–217. https://ijritcc.org/index.php/ijritcc/article/view/8482. doi:10.17762/ijritcc.v11i10.8482

Field, E. H., Milner, K. R., Hardebeck, J. L., Page, M. T., van der Elst, N., Jordan, T. H., Michael, A. J., Shaw, B. E., & Werner, M. J. (2017). A spatiotemporal clustering model for the third uniform California earthquake rupture forecast (UCERF3-ETAS): Toward an operational earthquake forecast. *Bulletin of the Seismological Society of America*, *107*(3), 1049–1081. doi:10.1785/0120160173

Heitzler, M., Lam, J.C., & Hackl, J. (2017). *GPU-Accelerated Rendering Methods to Visually Analyze Large-Scale Disaster Simulation Data*. Springer. doi:10.1007/s41651-017-0004-4

Hernandez, D., Cano, J., Silla, F., Calafate, C. & Cecilia, J. (2022). AI-Enabled Autonomous Drones for Fast Climate Change Crisis Assessment. *IEEE Internet of Things Journal, vol. 9*(10), 7286-7297. . doi:10.1109/JIOT.2021.3098379

Li, Y., Jiang, W., & Zhang, J. (2022). A time series processing chain for geological disasters based on a GPU-assisted sentinel-1 InSAR processor. *Natural Hazards*, *111*(1), 803–815. doi:10.100711069-021-05079-9

Li, Y., Zhang, Z., Wang, W., & Feng, X. (2022, June 2). Rapid Estimation of Earthquake Fatalities in Mainland China Based on Physical Simulation and Empirical Statistics-A Case Study of the 2021 Yangbi Earthquake. *International Journal of Environmental Research and Public Health, 19*(11), 6820. doi:10.3390/ijerph19116820 PMID:35682403

Llenos, A. L., & Michael, A. J. (2017). Forecasting the (un)productivity of the 2014 M 6.0 South Napa aftershock sequence. *Seismological Research Letters, 88*(5), 1241–1251. doi:10.1785/0220170050

Llenos, A. L., & Michael, A. J. (2019). Ensembles of ETAS models provide optimal operational earthquake forecasting during swarms: Insights from the 2015 San Ramon, California Swarm. *Bulletin of the Seismological Society of America, 109*(6), 2145–2158. doi:10.1785/0120190020

Mancini, S., Segou, M., Werner, M. J., Parsons, T., Beroza, G., & Chiaraluce, L. (2022). On the use of high-resolution and deep-learning seismic catalogs for short-term earthquake forecasts: Potential benefits and current limitations. *Journal of Geophysical Research: Solid Earth, 127*(11), e2022JB025202.

Mignan, A., & Broccardo, M. (2020). Neural network applications in earthquake prediction (1994–2019): Meta-analytic and statistical insights on their limitations. *Seismological Research Letters, 91*(4), 2330–2342. doi:10.1785/0220200021

Mousavi, S. M., Ellsworth, W. L., Zhu, W., Chuang, L. Y., & Beroza, G. C. (2020). Earthquake transformer—An attentive deep-learning model for simultaneous earthquake detection and phase picking. *Nature Communications, 11*(1), 3952. doi:10.103841467-020-17591-w PMID:32770023

Muhammad, D., Ahmad, I., Khalil, M. I., Khalil, W., & Ahmad, M. O. (2023). A Generalized Deep Learning Approach to Seismic Activity Prediction. *Applied Sciences (Basel, Switzerland), 13*(3), 1598. doi:10.3390/app13031598

Musa, A., Watanabe, O., Matsuoka, H., Hokari, H., Inoue, T., Murashima, Y., Ohta, Y., Hino, R., Koshimura, S., & Kobayashi, H. (2018). Real-time tsunami inundation forecast system for tsunami disaster prevention and mitigation. *The Journal of Supercomputing, 74*(7), 3093–3113. doi:10.100711227-018-2363-0

Ogata, Y. (2017). Statistics of earthquake activity: Models and methods for earthquake predictability studies. *Annual Review of Earth and Planetary Sciences, 45*(1), 497–527. doi:10.1146/annurev-earth-063016-015918

Ou, R., Yan, H., Wu, M., & Zhang, C. (2023). *A Method of Efficient Synthesizing Post-disaster Remote Sensing Image with Diffusion Model and LLM*. 2023 Asia Pacific Signal and Information Processing Association Annual Summit and Conference (APSIPA ASC), Taipei, Taiwan. 10.1109/APSIPAASC58517.2023.10317383

Senadheera, H. T., Asai, M., & Morikawa, D. S. (2021). A Feasibility Study for Natural Disaster Simulations Using a Fully Explicit SPH Method in a GPU Environment. In R. Dissanayake, P. Mendis, K. Weerasekera, S. De Silva, & S. Fernando (Eds.), *ICSECM 2019. Lecture Notes in Civil Engineering* (Vol. 94). Springer. doi:10.1007/978-981-15-7222-7_24

Tan, Y. J., Waldhauser, F., Ellsworth, W. L., Zhang, M., Zhu, W., Michele, M., Chiaraluce, L., Beroza, G. C., & Segou, M. (2021). Machine-learning-based high-resolution earthquake catalog reveals how complex fault structures were activated during the 2016–2017 central Italy sequence. *The Seismic Record*, *1*(1), 11–19. doi:10.1785/0320210001

van der Elst, N. J., Hardebeck, J. L., Michael, A. J., McBride, S. K., & Vanacore, E. (2022). Prospective and retrospective evaluation of the U.S. geological survey public aftershock forecast for the 2019–2021 southwest Puerto Rico earthquake and aftershocks. *Seismological Research Letters*, *93*(2A), 620–640. doi:10.1785/0220210222

Chapter 10
IoT-Based Smart Sensors:
The Key to Early Warning Systems and Rapid Response in Natural Disasters

A. Ashwini
Vel Tech Rangarajan Dr. Sagunthala R&D Institute of Science and Technology, India

Sriram
College of Engineering Guindy, Anna University, Chennai, India

S. Sangeetha
College of Engineering Guindy, Anna University, Chennai, India

ABSTRACT

The emergence of internet of things (IoT) based smart sensors has brought a revolution in disaster management to create early warning systems and to quickly respond to natural disasters. This chapter explores the vital function that these sensors serve, emphasizing how they might improve preparedness and lessen the destructive effects of disasters. It provides vital information that helps communities and authorities to anticipate any flooding events using smart sensors, flood sensors, atmospheric sensors. It emphasizes the necessity of developments in IoT-based smart sensors through case studies and real-world examples. Through an examination of the application of advanced technologies like artificial intelligence and machine learning, the chapter highlights how these sensors can sense on changing environmental conditions, improving the precision of early warning systems and response plans. The chapter ends with a discussion of the applications of internet of things-based smart sensors that can successfully address the difficulties brought on by natural catastrophes.

DOI: 10.4018/979-8-3693-2280-2.ch010

INTRODUCTION

The advent of the Internet of Things (IoT) in recent years has led to a shift in disaster management, notably in the field of early warning systems and natural disaster response techniques. Smart sensors based on IoT have emerged as critical components in this paradigm shift, providing real-time data collecting, analysis, and distribution capabilities that considerably improve preparedness and response activities. According to the data collected in 2023, the average response time to natural disasters has been greatly shortened by 30% since the use of IoT sensors was implemented. This has resulted in a notable drop in mortality and damage to infrastructure. Disasters caused by nature, which include hurricanes and quakes to flooding and fires in forests, pose significant hazards to people, infrastructure, and economies around the world. It is impossible to stress the importance of timely warnings and prompt response in limiting these hazards (Esposito et al., 2022). Traditional disaster management methods frequently have limits in terms of speed, coverage, and accuracy. The incorporation of IoT-based smart sensors, on the other hand, has transformed this environment by creating a network of networked devices capable of sensing, collecting, and transferring data in real-time.

These smart sensors use cutting-edge technologies, such as wireless connectivity, and algorithms for machine learning, to monitor the surrounding environment and detect anomalies that could indicate a disaster is on the way. These sensors enable the prediction and early detection of natural disasters by gathering and analyzing various data types such as atmospheric changes, seismic activity, water levels, and more (Poslad et al., 2015). Gas and chemical sensors are used to identify potentially dangerous gases and chemicals in the environment, allowing for quick response times to protect the communities that are impacted. After a disaster, structural health sensors evaluate the stability of infrastructure, including buildings and bridges, to assist rescue crews and engineers in identifying dangerous structures and allocating resources accordingly. To protect residents and rescue personnel from radioactive contamination resulting from nuclear accidents or other incidents, radiation sensors are placed in high-risk regions and used to track radiation levels. Debris Monitoring Sensors support the effective cleanup and reconstruction efforts in disaster-affected areas by monitoring and managing debris while guaranteeing the safety of residents and rescue personnel.

Early warning, risk assessment, disaster response, and the general management of such events all depend heavily on the deployment of these many sensors both before and after emergencies. This chapter also highlights the importance of prompt reaction mechanisms made possible by IoT-based smart sensors. These systems use data from past disaster patterns to forecast possible hazards, allowing authorities to quickly launch evacuations and provide the required resources. Furthermore, the use of IoT-based smart sensors enables rapid response mechanisms. These devices not only generate early warnings, but also allow authorities to conduct rapid evacuation processes, efficiently distribute resources, and quickly coordinate emergency response operations. These sensors' real-time information enables decision-makers to take preemptive measures, decreasing reaction times and minimizing the impact of disasters on societies.

The purpose of this chapter is to explore deeper into the transformative impact of IoT-based smart sensors in early warning systems and fast response techniques for natural catastrophes. It delves into the technology advances, operational frameworks, case studies, problems, and future possibilities of these sensors in the development of robust and responsive disaster management systems. Through the investigation of IoT technology's incorporation into early warning systems, this chapter elaborates on the efficient use of real-time data from several sensor networks. The chapter provides a thorough explanation of how smart systems process and analyze data from a network of over 10,000 sensors using sophisticated algorithms to give communities in disaster-prone areas accurate and timely notifications. Finally, the incorporation of IoT-based smart sensors represents a paradigm shift in emergency response and preparedness, with the potential to save lives, safeguard infrastructure, and boost local resilience in the face of catastrophes.

Overview of IoT and Its Role in Disaster Management

The Internet of Things (IoT) is a network of interconnected objects that are equipped with sensors, software, and connections to collect and exchange data. IoT plays a critical role in disaster management by revolutionizing the way information is acquired, analyzed, and used to prevent risks, deal with unforeseen circumstances, and aid in recovery efforts. IoT devices used in disaster management include a diverse set of sensors that monitor environmental characteristics such as humidity, temperature, seismic activity, water levels, air quality, and others. These sensors are placed in disaster-prone locations and essential infrastructure, producing a network that collects real-time data in real-time (Gupta et al., 2022). The information gathered is sent to controlled platforms for evaluation and decision-making.

Several essential characteristics highlight the relevance of IoT in disaster management:

- Early Warning Infrastructure: Sensors powered by the Internet of Things give rapid and reliable data on environmental changes, enabling an early identification of possible calamities. Seismic sensors, for example, can identify earthquake precursors, whereas meteorological sensors can forecast storms, allowing authorities to provide warnings and begin precautionary actions.

- Real-time Monitoring and Situational Awareness: IoT devices provide real-time-based emergency responders and decision-makers to acquire context awareness during disasters (Panakkal et al., 2023). This data aids in assessing the degree of the damage, identifying affected locations, and effectively allocating resources.
- Rapid Response and Coordination: IoT devices allow rapid reaction tactics by providing speedy data transmission and analysis. They help to coordinate emergency services, allowing for the rapid deployment of rescue operations, resource distribution and medical aid to affected areas.
- Post-Disaster Recovery and Resilience: IoT continues to play a role in disaster recovery and resilience by assisting in damage evaluations, network monitoring, and reconstruction activities. Sensors aid in the evaluation of structural integrity, the management of environmental dangers (such as detecting chemical leakage or radiation), and optimizing the effectiveness of recovery operations.

However, difficulties like as interoperability, data privacy concerns, and the requirement for solid infrastructure in remote or vulnerable places continue to be obstacles to harnessing IoT for disaster management. Addressing these issues will necessitate stakeholder collaboration, technological investment, and the creation of standardized protocols. Overall, IoT is a valuable tool in disaster management, boosting response, recovery, and preparedness efforts by delivering real-time data, enhancing decision-making processes, and eventually decreasing the impact of natural disasters on people and infrastructure.

Significance Of Early Warning Systems in Natural Disasters

Early warning systems (EWS) play an important role in limiting the effects of catastrophic events by giving timely alerts and relevant information to vulnerable people, authorities, and emergency personnel. Several crucial points might help you understand the importance of systems for early warning in natural disasters as in Figure 1.

- Risk Reduction and Preparedness: By providing advance notice of possible disasters, early warning systems assist communities and governments in preparing for approaching hazards. This enables the implementation of preparatory measures such as evacuation plans, infrastructure security, storing critical supplies, and ensuring that response teams are ready.

Figure 1. Significance of early warning systems

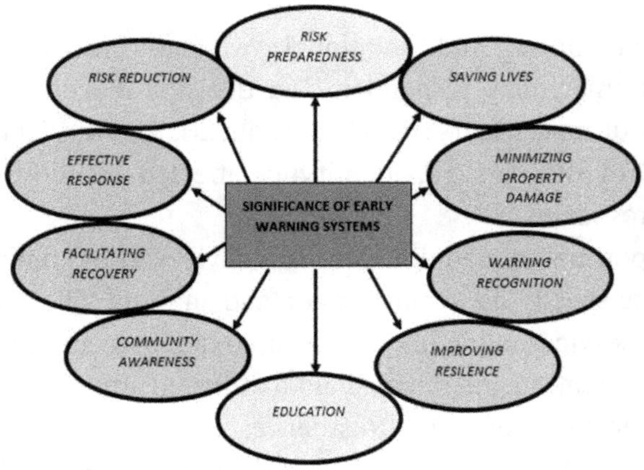

- Saving Lives: Early warning systems' primary purpose is to save lives by providing individuals with enough time to take precautionary measures. These warnings allow people to seek safer places, migrate to higher ground, or take other preventive steps, lowering casualties dramatically.
- Minimizing Property Damage: Early warnings also allow for the protection of property and essential infrastructure. They enable preventive measures such as building security, equipment relocation, structural reinforcement, and shutting down sensitive systems, which can help minimize damage and economic losses.
- Facilitating Effective Response and Recovery: These technologies assist authorities in effectively organizing and mobilizing emergency response activities by offering early insights into the type and severity of an oncoming crisis. Rapid reaction planning, resource allocation, and rescue operation coordination become more efficient, potentially minimizing the length and severity of the crisis. Furthermore, having actionable information ahead of time might speed up post-disaster recovery.
- Community Awareness and Education: Early warning systems help to raise awareness about the dangers of natural disasters and the significance of being prepared (Diaz et al., 2022). Continuous communication and education programs linked to these systems enable communities to understand the risks they face, recognize warning signs, and respond appropriately in times of crisis.
- Improving Resilience: Early warning systems that work well can help to improve community resilience over time (Sha et al., 2022). Communities grow better prepared to deal with future disasters by learning from past experiences, perfecting response procedures, and incorporating new technologies.

Evolution of Smart Sensors in Disaster Management

Smart sensors' growth in disaster management has been transformational, transforming how to detect, predict, and respond to natural disasters. Technological advances have accelerated the development of increasingly sophisticated sensors, allowing for a more thorough understanding of environmental elements that contribute to disasters.

Early sensors were primarily concerned with single environmental characteristics such as temperature or seismic activity. However, with the rise of the IoT, sensors have grown into interconnected networks capable of collecting multidimensional data in real time depicted in Figure 2. These new smart sensors, which have expanded data processing potential and communication interactions, have considerably improved disaster detection precision and timeliness. Furthermore, the use of machine learning and artificial intelligence algorithms has improved sensor capacities, enabling predictive modeling and early warning systems. As a result, smart sensors have progressed from stand-alone devices to integral components of an interrelated ecosystem, revolutionizing disaster mitigation by providing useful data, enabling immediate action, and ultimately contributing to the saving of lives and reducing the effect of natural disasters on communities (Mardirossian et al., 2023).

Figure 2. Evolution of smart sensors

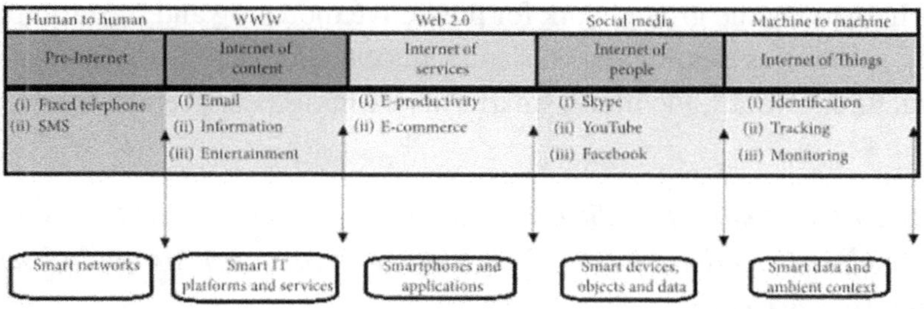

IoT Based Early Warning Systems

Early warning systems powered by IoT provide a cutting-edge approach to disaster protection and response, utilizing the power of interconnected devices and advanced technology to forecast, detect, and broadcast critical information about oncoming natural disasters. These systems combine weather conditions, seismic, atmospheric, and hydraulic sensors to form a network that continuously analyses environmental conditions. IoT-based alert systems can detect anomalies and probable crisis triggers by gathering real-time data and employing advanced algorithms (Abdalzaher et al., 2023). This enables authorities to send out timely warnings and alerts to vulnerable communities, allowing for proactive steps such as evacuation protocols, resource mobilization, and disaster response readiness (Yuliandoko et al., 2023). The interconnected structure of IoT devices enables rapid transfer of information and analysis, enhancing the accuracy and speed of predictions and, ultimately, improving their capacity to mitigate the adverse effects of natural disasters by allowing people and governments to take preventive measures.

Smart sensors into disaster preparedness

Integrating smart devices into emergency planning entails strategically deploying advanced sensor technology to improve communities' and authorities' readiness and responsiveness in the event of potential disasters.

Smart sensors with IoT capabilities play a critical role in continually monitoring environmental parameters important to various risks such as earthquakes, floods, and wildfires in Figure 3. Seismic activity, air quality, water levels, weather patterns, and structure integrity are all monitored in real-time by these sensors (Lin et al., 2022). Smart sensors provide vital insights into risk assessment, early identification of potential hazards, and the construction of comprehensive emergency preparation strategies by feeding this data into centralized systems. These plans frequently incorporate early warning systems, removal methods, resource allocation, and emergency response coordination (El Houssaini et al., 2022). Furthermore, smart sensors help to lay the groundwork for predictive modeling and scenario planning, allowing authorities to mitigate risks and reduce the impact of crises on people and infrastructure. Overall, including smart sensors in disaster preparedness activities

Figure 3. Different modes for disaster management: (a) Drone with sensor, (b) Gas sensor, (c) Fire detection sensor, (d) Ultrasonic sensor, (e) Air quality sensor, (f) Synthetic Aperture radar

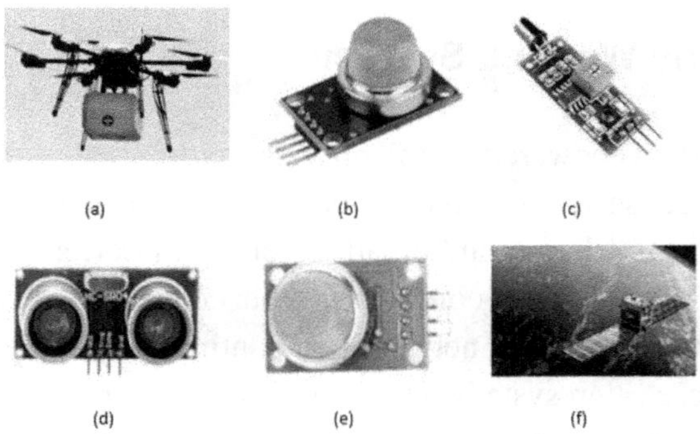

increases the ability to anticipate, respond to, and recover from natural disasters by encouraging a data-driven and proactive approach to disaster management.

Network Architecture and Data Collection Mechanisms

In disaster management, the construction of an efficient network architecture and robust data-gathering methods are critical for effectively using smart sensors, IoT technology, and early warning systems (Khan et al., 2022). The design and layout of interconnected sensors, data gathering locations, and communication channels are part of network architecture, which aims to build a seamless system for monitoring and delivering essential information as shown in Figure 4. A decentralized and distributed approach to network architecture is frequently preferred to enhance resilience and reliability. This entails placing sensors in disaster-prone locations in a mesh-like structure, which allows for redundancy and fault tolerance. Each sensor node connects with surrounding nodes, producing a self-healing network that may continue to relay data even if some nodes are damaged or disturbed during a catastrophic event (Li et al., 2022). Furthermore, cloud-based or centralized servers are used to aggregate and analyze data acquired from various sensors, enabling complete data processing and interpretation (Pillai et al., 2021).

Figure 4. Framework for disaster management

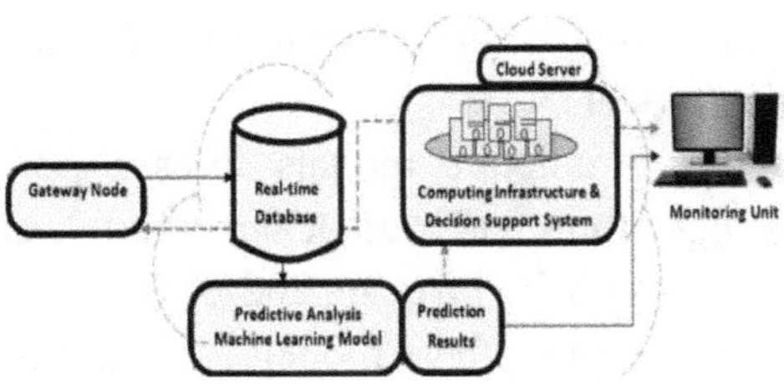

Data collecting mechanisms include a wide range of sensor technologies that are suited to specific disaster threats. Seismic sensors, for example, detect ground movements to anticipate earthquakes, weather stations evaluate atmospheric conditions to forecast storms, and flood sensors monitor water levels in sensitive places (Saini et al., 2022). These sensors continuously collect data, which is then communicated to the central data repository via wired or wireless communication protocols. Wi-Fi, cellular networks, satellite communication, or dedicated communication standards for IoT devices (e.g., LoRaWAN, Zigbee) are all important in guaranteeing reliable data transmission over short or long distances. Furthermore, advances in edge computing enable data processing at the sensor level, decreasing latency and bandwidth needs while allowing for quick decision-making. In essence, the backbone of an efficient early warning system is a well-designed network architecture combined with various dependable data collection technologies (Kumar et al., 2022). These components work in tandem to ensure a continuous flow of real-time data, allowing for prompt alarms, educated decision-making, and proactive responses in the case of a natural disaster.

Data Analytics and Prediction Models

In the field of disaster management, data analytics and prediction models are critical components in harnessing the massive volumes of information generated by smart sensors and IoT devices. These tools are critical in processing, analyzing, and interpreting large amounts of data to forecast possible natural catastrophes, improve early warning systems, and assist informed decision-making in crisis circumstances.

- Data Processing and Preprocessing: Before analyzing data collected by smart sensors, it is typically necessary to clean, filter, and normalize the information (Wang et al., 2022). This stage entails reducing noise, fixing errors, and organizing the data so that it may be analyzed further.
- Descriptive Analytics: Descriptive analytics is analyzing historical data to discover patterns, trends, and correlations associated with previous disasters (Munawar et al., 2022). Trends in environmental characteristics and disaster occurrences can be found by analyzing historical statistics, establishing the basis for predictive models.
- Predictive Analytics: Predictive models foresee possible disasters using machine learning algorithms and statistical methodologies based on real-time data acquired by sensors (Ashwini et al., 2023). To estimate the possibility and severity of future catastrophes, these models analyze numerous environmental parameters such as seismic activity, weather patterns, humidity levels, and previous disaster data. Machine learning algorithms, for example, can be trained to forecast the route of storms, the risk of flooding in specific places, or the chance of earthquakes.
- Early Warning Systems: By processing data that comes from sensors and triggering alerts when predetermined thresholds or anomalous patterns are observed, data analytics enable the development of early warning systems (Gao et al., 2022). These systems can issue warnings, advisories, and alerts to authorities and communities, giving them critical time to implement preventive measures and evacuation processes.
- Risk Assessment and Decision Support: Analytics contribute to risk assessment by assessing the potential impact of disasters on communities,

infrastructure, and the environment (Sivakumar et al., 2022). Predictive models in decision support systems provide authorities with useful insights, supporting them in making educated decisions about resource allocation, emergency response planning, and evacuation tactics.

- Continuous Improvement and Adaptation: Continuous data analysis and evaluation aid in the improvement of predictive models and analytics techniques (Aboualola et al., 2023). These systems continuously increase accuracy and efficacy by incorporating new data, modifying algorithms, and learning from prior occurrences, boosting their ability to foresee and respond to disasters.

In summary, data analytics and prediction models aid disaster management by translating raw sensor data into usable insights, providing early warnings, assisting decision-making processes, and adding to overall community resilience in the face of natural catastrophes.

Data Processing Techniques and Algorithms

Data processing methods and algorithms are critical components in the context of IoT in disaster recovery because they enable the acquisition of valuable information from huge amounts of data acquired by sensors. Several processes are involved in these techniques:

- Data Cleaning and Preprocessing: This phase entails cleaning raw data to remove any errors, noise, or anomalies that may have occurred during data gathering. To ensure consistency and correctness, preprocessing comprises filtering out extraneous information, dealing with missing data, and normalizing data (Bernardes et al., 2023).
- Data Fusion and Integration: Data from numerous sources is generated by IoT devices. Data fusion techniques combine information from many sensors or data streams to provide a cohesive and comprehensive view (Li et al., 2022). This procedure contributes to the enrichment of the data and provides a more comprehensive picture of the issue.
- Real-time Data Analytics: Real-time analytics involves analyzing data as it comes in, allowing for instant analysis and response (Panakkal et al., 2023). Stream processing and edge computing allow for rapid analysis of information at the device's sensor level, decreasing latency and allowing for speedier decision-making.
- Machine Learning and Predictive Analytics: Machine learning algorithms are critical in disaster management because they analyze historical data trends

to forecast future catastrophes (Henao et al., 2023). Regression analysis, decision trees, neural networks, and clustering are among the algorithms used to create predictive models that foresee disasters, discover anomalies, and issue early warnings.

- Geospatial Analysis: To analyze and visualize data based on geographical locations, geospatial data processing techniques such as geographic information systems (GIS) are used (Khan et al., 2022). Understanding the spatial distribution of risks, identifying susceptible locations, and optimizing resource allocation during disaster response are all aided by this.
- Pattern Recognition and Anomaly Detection: To find patterns and deviations from normal data behavior, advanced algorithms are used (Varadharajan et al., 2023). Anomaly detection techniques allow the system to discover anomalies or unexpected trends in sensor data, which might alert the system to possible disasters or abnormal conditions.
- Optimization and Decision Support: During a catastrophe response, optimization algorithms aid in resource allocation, route planning, and logistics (Sung et al., 2022). Decision support systems use processed data to deliver actionable insights and help emergency responders and authorities make decisions.

Overall, incorporating these data processing methods and algorithms into IoT-based disaster management systems improves the ability to efficiently and effectively analyze, interpret, and act on data, hence increasing disaster planning, response, and recovery efforts.

Predictive Analysis

Predictive analysis in IoT for disaster management entails forecasting and anticipating probable natural disasters utilizing historical and real-time data acquired by sensors (Josipovic et al., 2023). Advanced algorithms, machine learning models, and statistical approaches are used to detect patterns, trends, and anomalies in the data that may signal the possibility or severity of future catastrophic events. The bar chart in Figure 5 shows the comparison of the enabling technologies concerning cost.

Key aspects of predictive analysis for IoT in disaster management include:

- Historical Data Analysis: Analyzing historical data enables the identification of patterns and trends associated with previous disasters. Predictive models can be constructed by evaluating historical events and their associated environmental factors to anticipate similar occurrences in the future.

Figure 5. Comparison of enabling technologies concerning cost

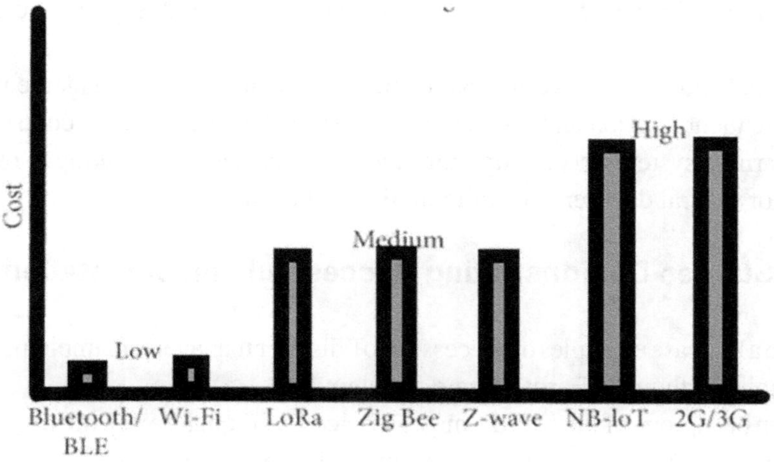

- Real-time Data Processing: IoT sensors capture real-time data on a variety of environmental characteristics, including seismic activity, weather patterns, temperature, humidity, and more (Agbehadji et al., & Sapena et al., 2023). Predictive models use real-time streaming data to discover probable abnormalities or deviations from usual trends that may suggest an imminent crisis.
- Machine Learning Algorithms: To create predictive models, machine learning techniques such as regression analysis, decision trees, neural networks, and clustering are used. Based on current environmental circumstances, these models learn from historical data patterns and are taught to anticipate future disasters such as earthquakes, floods, hurricanes, or wildfires.
- Early Warning Systems: Predictive analysis is critical in the development of early warning systems (Piciullo et al. 2022). When specific predetermined thresholds or odd patterns are recognized, these systems use predictive models to provide alerts and warnings, giving authorities and communities crucial time to prepare and take preventive measures.
- Risk Assessment and Decision Support: Predictive analytics contributes to risk assessment by assessing the probable impact of catastrophes on groups, facilities and the environment (Zhou et al., & Gong et al., 2022). Predictive insights are used by decision support systems to help authorities make educated decisions on resource allocation, reaction planning, and evacuation tactics.
- Continuous Improvement: Predictive models are constantly developed and updated in response to new data and insights obtained from previous events

(Ye et al., 2023). This repeated process improves the accuracy and reliability of predictive analysis, allowing us to better foresee and respond to calamities.

In conclusion, predictive analysis using IoT data in disaster management enables proactive identification and prediction of potential hazards, thereby contributing to early warning systems, risk mitigation, and informed decision-making to reduce the impact of natural disasters on communities and infrastructure.

Case Studies Demonstrating Successful Implementation

Here are a few case examples of successful IoT disaster management implementations:

Japan's Earthquake Early Warning System:

Japan boasts one of the world's most advanced earthquake early warning systems, employing a network of seismic sensors. The technology identifies beginning vibrations quickly and estimates earthquake strength and arrival time (Abdalzaher et al., 2023). This information is subsequently communicated via numerous platforms, such as mobile phones, television, and radio, allowing residents to take quick preventive measures.

Hurricane Prediction and Response in the United States:

The National Oceanic and Atmospheric Administration (NOAA) in the United States forecasts hurricanes and severe weather occurrences using IoT devices, weather satellites, and advanced prediction models (Damasevicius et al., 2023). These forecasts aid in the issuing of timely warnings and evacuation orders, thereby saving lives and limiting property damage.

Flood Monitoring in the Netherlands:

Water levels, dike conditions, and weather patterns are all regularly monitored by these sensors. Automated devices can manage water levels in canals and reservoirs to minimize flooding in the event of increased water levels (Hong et al., 2023).

Wildfire Detection and Prevention in Australia:

Australia detects wildfires in remote places using IoT sensors, drones, and satellite imagery. Temperature, humidity, and wind conditions are monitored by these sensors, which provide early warning of probable fire outbreaks (Zhang et al., 2022). This information assists authorities in quickly deploying firefighting resources and warning neighboring communities.

Disaster Response in Nepal Using IoT:

Following the disastrous earthquake in 2015, Nepal utilized IoT-based sensors to monitor and assess building structural integrity. These sensors detect structural flaws and aid in the prioritization of buildings for rebuilding, resulting in a safer infrastructure for future calamities (Al-Wathinani et al., 2023).

These case studies demonstrate the successful use of IoT-based disaster management systems. They highlight how IoT sensors, data analytics, early warning systems, and predictive models may help with disaster preparedness, early detection, rapid reaction, and mitigating the effects of numerous natural catastrophes throughout the world.

Challenges And Opportunities with Technical and Infrastructural Constraints

The challenges and opportunities associated with technical and architectural limits in deploying IoT for disaster management are critical factors to consider when optimizing these systems (Arvindan, S. & D. S. Vijayan, 2022). Here are a few crucial points depicted in Figure 6.

Figure 6. Challenges and opportunities of IoT in disaster management

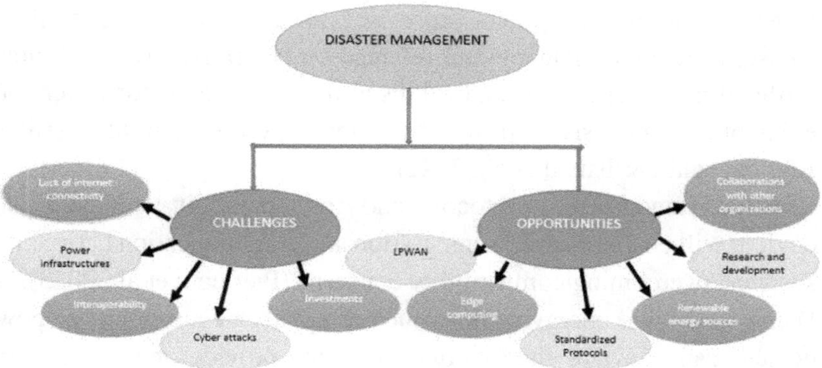

Challenges:

- Remote or disaster-prone areas frequently lack robust internet connectivity or infrastructure. This constraint impedes IoT device deployment and performance, impacting data transmission and real-time monitoring during disasters.
- Many IoT devices require a consistent power source, and natural disasters such as earthquakes or hurricanes can disrupt power infrastructures (Khan et al., 2023). It is difficult to provide a continuous power supply or to use other energy sources for these devices.

- Different IoT devices from different manufacturers may use different protocols or standards (Yurtsever & Mustafa, 2022). This lack of interoperability might impede seamless data transmission and communication by making it harder to integrate sensors and systems.
- IoT devices generate massive volumes of sensitive data. Keeping this data safe and secure from potential cyber-attacks, breaches, or unauthorized access is a major challenge in disaster management.
- Extending IoT systems to cover bigger areas or populations necessitates significant investments as well as continual maintenance. Managing and updating a vast network of sensors and devices can be difficult logistically.

Opportunities:

- Advances in low-power wide-area networks (LPWAN) and satellite communication technologies provide an opportunity to overcome connectivity difficulties in remote places, allowing IoT devices to be deployed in previously unreachable locales.
- Edge computing allows data processing to take place closer to the source (sensors), reducing latency and reliance on centralized servers. Integrating artificial intelligence (AI) algorithms at the edge allows for faster and more efficient data analysis, improving disaster response capabilities (Bilal et al., Bhujbal et al., & Ismail et al., 2022).
- Creating standardized protocols and interoperability standards for IoT devices will enable seamless integration and communication between various systems, overcoming compatibility concerns (Pierleoni et al., 2023).
- Using renewable energy sources such as solar or wind power to power IoT devices can alleviate energy constraints and provide ongoing performance even during power outages caused by natural catastrophes.
- Collaborations between governments, technology businesses, non-governmental organizations, and research institutes can promote innovation in IoT for disaster management.
- Research and development funding and support can lead to breakthroughs in addressing technical obstacles (Adegoke & Damilola, 2023). Addressing technical and infrastructure limits while capitalizing on opportunities can considerably improve the effectiveness and resilience of IoT-based disaster management systems, eventually enhancing response to natural disasters and protecting communities.

Future Directions With Advancements in Developing Strategies for IoT Based Disaster Management

Future directions in IoT-based disaster management include utilizing technical improvements to create more sophisticated tactics for greater catastrophe preparedness, response, and recovery. Here are several possible paths:

- Enhanced Sensor Capabilities: Sensor technology advancements will result in more complex and multipurpose sensors capable of gathering a greater range of environmental data. These sensors will be more sensitive, dependable, and adaptable to a wide range of crisis scenarios.
- Edge Computing and AI Integration: Continued integration of computational intelligence and deep learning algorithms at sensors will enable real-time data processing, allowing for faster and more accurate choices during disasters (Ly et al., 2022).
- Predictive Analytics and Early Warning Systems: More accurate disaster forecasting will be possible with the further development of forecasting techniques and early warning systems based on IoT data. This involves more accurate forecasting of severe storms, earthquakes, floods, and various other natural disasters.
- Resilient Communication Networks: Infrastructure improvements, such as the extension of 5G networks or the establishment of adaptable communication protocols, will provide consistent and uninterrupted data transfer even in disaster-affected regions.
- Remote Monitoring and Autonomous Systems: Unmanned aerial vehicles and autonomous systems advancements will enable remote surveillance of disaster-affected areas, enabling speedy damage assessment and help distribution without putting human lives in danger.
- Data Fusion and Integration Platforms: The development of strong data fusion and integration systems will enable the gathering and analysis of data from many sources, such as IoT devices, satellites, social networks, and citizen reporting, resulting in a holistic view of disaster scenarios.
- Blockchain for Data Security: Implementing block-chain technology can improve data security and integrity by enabling tamper-proof records and safe data sharing among disaster management stakeholders (Tian et al., 2023).
- Community Engagement and Citizen Science: By utilizing IoT devices for citizen science activities, communities will be able to actively participate in disaster tracking and response, promoting a culture of preparedness and resilience.

- Policy and Standardization: The development of global standards and policies for IoT-based disaster management would promote interoperability, data sharing, and collaboration among many organizations and countries, ensuring an effective response during international disasters.
- Investment in Research and Collaboration: Encouragement of investment in research, innovation, and cross-sector collaboration will accelerate breakthroughs in IoT disaster management technology, allowing for continual development and adaption.

By focusing on these future directions and advances, the potential for IoT-based systems to revolutionize disaster management by delivering more effective early warning, rapid response, and increased resilience for populations affected by natural disasters will grow.

CONCLUSION

Finally, IoT-based smart sensors represent a game-changing strategy for redefining the disaster management landscape. These networked devices, together with enhanced data analytics and predictive capabilities, have emerged as critical instruments for early warning systems and quick disaster response. These sensors provide invaluable real-time data by continuously monitoring environmental parameters, enabling preventative measures, timely alerts, and informed decision-making for authorities and communities at risk. The use of IoT technology not only improves the accuracy and speed of catastrophe detection, but also allows for faster response mechanisms, resulting in more efficient resource allocation, shorter response times, and, ultimately, less impact on lives and infrastructure. However, obstacles like as technical restrictions, interoperability issues, and data security must be addressed continually. Nonetheless, IoT-based smart sensors have a promising future in disaster management. Sensor capabilities, AI integration, resilient networks of communication, and community engagement will further refine these systems, making them more robust, adaptive, and integral in building resilient communities capable of effectively addressing natural disaster challenges. In essence, continued innovation and strategic deployment of IoT-based smart sensors pave the way for a more proactive, responsive, and resilient approach to disaster management, ultimately saving lives, minimizing damage, and fostering greater preparedness in the face of natural disasters.

REFERENCES

Abdalzaher, M. (2023). Employing machine learning and iot for earthquake early warning system in smart cities. *Energies 16*(1), 495.

Abdalzaher, M. (2023). Early Detection of Earthquakes Using IoT and Cloud Infrastructure: A Survey. *Sustainability*, *15*(15), 11713.

Aboualola, M., Abualsaud, K., Khattab, T., Zorba, N., & Hassanein, H. S. (2023). Edge Technologies for Disaster Management: A Survey of Social Media and Artificial Intelligence Integration. *IEEE Access : Practical Innovations, Open Solutions*, *11*, 73782–73802. doi:10.1109/ACCESS.2023.3293035

Adegoke & Damilola. (2023). A Systematic Review of Big Data and Digital Technologies Security Leadership Outcomes Effectiveness during Natural Disasters. *Sustainable Futures : An Applied Journal of Technology, Environment and Society*, 100113.

Agbehadji, I. (2023). A systematic review of existing early warning systems' challenges and opportunities in cloud computing early warning systems. *Climate*, *11*(9), 188.

Al-Wathinani, A. M. (2023). Driving sustainable disaster risk reduction: A rapid review of the policies and strategies in Saudi Arabia. *Sustainability*, *15*(14).

Arvindan, S., & Vijayan, D. S. (2022). Safeguard and Preventive Measures of Natural Disasters Using Early Warning Systems—A Comprehensive Review. *A System Engineering Approach to Disaster Resilience: Select Proceedings of VCDRR*, (pp. 303-315). Research Gate.

Ashwini, A., & Purushothaman, K. E., Banu Priya, Prathaban M, Jenath & R Prasanna, (2023). Automatic Traffic Sign Board Detection from Camera Images Using Deep learning and Binarization Search Algorithm, *2023 International Conference in recent advances in Electrical, Electronics, Ubiquitous Communication and Computational Intelligence (RAEEUCCI)*. IEEE. 10.1109/RAEEUCCI57140.2023.10134376

Bernardes, G. (2023). Prototyping low-cost automatic weather stations for natural disaster monitoring. *Digital Communications and Network, 9*(4), 941-956.

Bhujbal, A., Hole, P., Khedkar, P., & Zaman, N. (2022). Flood Detection and Management System. *International Journal of Innovative Research in Science and Engineering*, *8*, 104–110.

Bilal, M. & Yaqub, M. (2022). An early warning system for earthquake prediction from seismic data using Batch Normalized Graph Convolutional Neural Network with Attention Mechanism (BNGCNNATT). *Sensors*, *22*(17), 6482.

Damasevicius, R., Bacanin, N., & Misra, S. (2023). From sensors to safety: Internet of Emergency Services (IoES) for emergency response and disaster management. *Journal of Sensor and Actuator Networks, 12*(3), 41.

Diaz, P. (2022). *IWARN: A people-centered approach for early warning.*

El Houssaini, D., & Kanoun, O. (2022). Location-Aware IoT-Enabled Wireless Sensor Networks for Landslide Early Warning. *Electronics, 11*(23), 3971.

Esposito, M. & Pierleoni, O. (2022). Recent advances in internet of things solutions for early warning systems: A review. *Sensors, 22*(6), 2124.

Gao, Jie, Wu Zhang, Chunbaixue Yang, Rui Wang, Shuai Shao, Jiawei Li, Limiao Zhang, Zhijian Li, Shu Liu, & Wentao Si. (2022). Comparative Study on International Research Hotspots and National-Level Policy Keywords of Dynamic Disaster Monitoring and Early Warning in China (2000–2021). *International journal of environmental research and public health, 19*(22), 15107.

Gong, W., Hu, J., Wang, Z., Wei, Y., Li, Y., Zhang, T., Zhang, Q., Liu, T., Ning, Y., Zhang, W., & Grattan, K. T. V. (2022). Recent advances in laser gas sensors for applications to safety monitoring in intelligent coal mines. *Frontiers in Physics (Lausanne), 10,* 1058475. doi:10.3389/fphy.2022.1058475

Gupta, M., Almomani, O., Khasawneh, A. M., & Darabkh, K. A. (2022). Smart remote sensing network for early warning of disaster risks. In Nanotechnology-Based Smart Remote Sensing Networks for Disaster Prevention, (pp. 303-324). IEEE.

Henao-Céspedes, V. & Olaya, M. (2023). Landslide early warning systems: a perspective from the internet of things. *International Journal of Electrical and Computer Engineering 13*(2), 2214.

Hong, Jung-Hong, & Yi-Tin Shi. (2023). Integration of Heterogeneous Sensor Systems for Disaster Responses in Smart Cities: Flooding as an Example. *ISPRS International Journal of Geo-Information, 12*(7), 279.

Ismail, F. & Hossam, A. (2022). *A new distributed earthquake early warning communication protocol based on messaging.*

Josipovic, N., & Viergutz, K. (2023). Smart Solutions for Municipal Flood Management: Overview of Literature, Trends, and Applications in German Cities. *Smart Cities, 6*(2), 944–964. doi:10.3390martcities6020046

Khan, A., Gupta, S., & Gupta, S. K. (2022). Emerging UAV technology for disaster detection, mitigation, response, and preparedness. *Journal of Field Robotics, 39*(6), 905–955. doi:10.1002/rob.22075

Khan, R., Shabaz, M., Hussain, S., Ahmad, F., & Mishra, P. (2022). Early flood detection and rescue using bioinformatic devices, internet of things (IOT) and Android application. *World Journal of Engineering*, *19*(2), 204–215. doi:10.1108/WJE-05-2021-0269

Khan, S. & Ashraf, I. (2023). A Systematic Review of Disaster Management Systems: Approaches, Challenges, and Future Directions. *Land*, *12*(8), 1514.

Kumar, R., Mittal, H., Sandeep, & Sharma, B. (2022). Earthquake genesis and earthquake early warning systems: Challenges and a way forward. *Surveys in Geophysics*, *43*(4), 1143–1168. doi:10.100710712-022-09710-7

Li, X. & Wang, D. (2022). Recent advances on early-stage fire-warning systems: mechanism, performance, and perspective. *Nano-micro letters*, *14*(1), 197.

Li, Y., & Xiao, L. (2022). Research on public health crisis early warning system based on context awareness. *Technology and Health Care*, *30*(1), 303–314. doi:10.3233/THC-THC228029 PMID:35124607

Lin, T.-H., Huang, J.-T., & Putranto, A. (2022). Integrated smart robot with earthquake early warning system for automated inspection and emergency response. *Natural Hazards*, *110*(1), 765–786. doi:10.100711069-021-04969-2

Lv, L.-Y., Cao, C.-F., Qu, Y.-X., Zhang, G.-D., Zhao, L., Cao, K., Song, P., & Tang, L.-C. (2022). Smart fire-warning materials and sensors: Design principle, performances, and applications. *Materials Science and Engineering R Reports*, *150*, 100690. doi:10.1016/j.mser.2022.100690

Mardirossian, G., Ranguelov, B., Getsov, P., & Zabunov, S. (2023). Two Innovations for Critical Infrastructure Protection from Natural Disasters. *Dokladi na Bulgarskata Akademiâ na Naukite*, *76*(10), 1554–1561. doi:10.7546/CRABS.2023.10.09

Munawar, H. S., Mojtahedi, M., Hammad, A. W. A., Kouzani, A., & Mahmud, M. A. P. (2022). Disruptive technologies as a solution for disaster risk management: A review. *The Science of the Total Environment*, *806*, 151351. doi:10.1016/j.scitotenv.2021.151351 PMID:34740667

Panakkal, P. (2023). Sensing flooded roads to support roadway mobility during flooding: a web-based tool and insights from needs assessment interviews. *Natural hazards review*, *24*(4), 04023039.

Piciullo, L., Capobianco, V., & Heyerdahl, H. (2022). A first step towards a IoT-based local early warning system for an unsaturated slope in Norway. *Natural Hazards*, *114*(3), 3377–3407. doi:10.100711069-022-05524-3

Pierleoni, P., Concetti, R., Marzorati, S., Belli, A., & Palma, L. (2023). Internet of Things for Earthquake Early Warning Systems: A Performance Comparison between Communication Protocols. *IEEE Access : Practical Innovations, Open Solutions, 11*, 43183–43194. doi:10.1109/ACCESS.2023.3271773

Pillai, A. S., Chandraprasad, G. S., Khwaja, A. S., & Anpalagan, A. (2021). A service oriented IoT architecture for disaster preparedness and forecasting system. *Internet of Things : Engineering Cyber Physical Human Systems, 14*, 100076. doi:10.1016/j.iot.2019.100076

Poslad, S., Middleton, S. E., Chaves, F., Tao, R., Necmioglu, O., & Bügel, U. (2015). A semantic IoT early warning system for natural environment crisis management. *IEEE Transactions on Emerging Topics in Computing, 3*(2), 246–257. doi:10.1109/TETC.2015.2432742

Saini, K., Kalra, S., & Sood, S. K. (2022). Disaster emergency response framework for smart buildings. *Future Generation Computer Systems, 131*, 106–120. doi:10.1016/j.future.2022.01.015

Sapena, M. & Taubenböck, H. (2023) Cost estimation for the monitoring instrumentalization of Landslide Early Warning Systems. *Natural Hazards and Earth System Sciences Discussions,* 1-26.

Sha, Y., Li, M., Xu, H., Zhang, S., & Feng, T. (2022). Smart City Public Safety Intelligent Early Warning and Detection. *Scientific Programming, 2022*, 1–11. doi:10.1155/2022/7552601

Sivakumar, P., Sandhya Devi, R. S., Ashwin, M., Rajan Singaravel, M. M., & Buvanesswaran, A. D. 2022. Protocol Design for Earthquake Alert and Evacuation in Smart Buildings. In IoT and WSN based Smart Cities: A Machine Learning Perspective, (pp. 1-14). Springer. doi:10.1007/978-3-030-84182-9_1

Sung, W.-T., Devi, I. V., & Hsiao, S.-J. (2022). Early warning of impending flash flood based on AIoT. *EURASIP Journal on Wireless Communications and Networking, 2022*(1), 15. doi:10.118613638-022-02096-5

Tian, B. (2023). Detecting the unseen: understanding the mechanisms and working principles of earthquake sensors. *Sensors, 23*(11), 5335.

Varadharajan, M., Balaji, S., Ezhilarasan, V., & Gowthaman, A. (2023). Internet of Things based Natural Disaster Detection and Personalized Notification System. In *2023 Third International Conference on Artificial Intelligence and Smart Energy (ICAIS)*, (pp. 93-97). IEEE. 10.1109/ICAIS56108.2023.10073873

Wang, Z., Zhu, L., Liu, J., Wang, J., & Yan, W. (2022). Gas sensing technology for the detection and early warning of battery thermal runaway: A review. *Energy & Fuels*, *36*(12), 6038–6057. doi:10.1021/acs.energyfuels.2c01121

Ye, Z., Ye, Y., Zhang, C., Zhang, Z., Li, W., Wang, X., Wang, L., & Wang, L. (2023). A digital twin approach for tunnel construction safety early warning and management. *Computers in Industry*, *144*, 103783. doi:10.1016/j.compind.2022.103783

Yuliandoko, H. (2023). *Design of Windstorm Disaster Early Warning System based on IoT and Hall Effect Sensor in the Critical Area Location.*

Yurtsever & Mustafa. (2022). Emergency management in smart cities. *Artificial Intelligence Perspective for Smart Cities,* 135-153.

Zhang, Z. (2022). A Dual-Function Sensor for Highly Sensitive Detection of Flame and Humidity. *Small*, *18*(38), 2203334.

Zhou, X., Li, H., Wang, J., Zhao, J., Xie, Q., Li, L., Liu, J., & Yu, J. (2022). CloudFAS: Cloud-based building fire alarm system using Building Information Modelling. *Journal of Building Engineering*, *53*, 104571. doi:10.1016/j.jobe.2022.104571

Chapter 11
Automation of IOT Robotics

A. Kathirvel
https://orcid.org/0000-0002-5347-9110
Department of Computer Science and Engineering, Panimalar Engineering College, Chennai, India

G. Rithik
AS Level, The Lords' International School, Chennai, India

A. K. Naren
Department of AIDS, Anand Institute of Higher Technology, Chennai, India

ABSTRACT

The IoT influence presents new design and implementation challenges in a variety of fields, including seamless platform integration, context-based cognitive network integration, new mobile sensor/actuator network paradigms, architectural domains for smart farming, infrastructure, healthcare, agriculture, business, and commerce. Applications for automation in the internet of robotic things (IoRT) are numerous and are developing quickly. IoRT blends the strength of robots and the internet of things (IoT), resulting in creative solutions for a range of sectors. As the authors ensure the authenticity of the content in this introduction, they shall investigate the wide range of IoRT automation applications. IoRT automation refers to a broad range of endeavors that use connected gadgets, sensors, and autonomous machinery to improve production, efficiency, and safety across a variety of industries.

INTERNET OF ROBOTIC THINGS AUTOMATION

Artificial Intelligence

The realm of IoT and autonomous operations has shown great potential with the emergence of IoRT technology. Communication-centered robots that connect to wireless sensors and other network resources are becoming increasingly popular

DOI: 10.4018/979-8-3693-2280-2.ch011

in the world of robotics. These robots can easily integrate with wired or IoT networks, allowing for the seamless utilization of IoRT's autonomous functions in this field. The IoRT technology has shown promising results in the domains of IoT and autonomous operations. The latest trend in robotics is centered around Communication-oriented robots that can connect with sensors and other network resources wirelessly. These robots can integrate with either wired or IoT networks, and the self-sufficient operations of the IoRT technology can be seamlessly leveraged in this industry. The incorporation of cutting-edge sensing, actuating, communication, and computing technologies elevates the original concept of IoT to new heights. This results in enhanced operational efficiency, enables businesses to uncover fresh prospects, and empowers them to predict potential hazards. These advancements present unprecedented opportunities for both consumers and providers of IoT and robotics solutions.

Figure 1.

The Technical Committee on Networked Robots of the IEEE Robotics and Automation Society defines two types of networked robots:

- **Remote -operated robots,**

Networked systems make it simple for human managers to issue directives and get feedback, boosting the availability of crucial resources for study, instruction, and public awareness. This connectivity between robots and humans has a significant impact on shared responsibilities, including teleoperation and human-robot interaction.

Additionally, the ability to reprogram and adapt robots on the network is affected. These technologies are now widely available for remote meeting assistance and telepresence medical equipment. Cloud robotic systems allow robots to exchange knowledge and learn from each other, while cloud infrastructure provides elastic resources to help robots overcome limitations in networked robotics.

- **Automated robots**

In highly advanced systems, robots and sensors are able to communicate with one another with minimal human intervention. This network of sensors expands the robots' sensing abilities, enabling them to interact over long distances and plan their actions accordingly. To prolong the lifespan and usefulness of the sensor network, robots can deploy, repair, and maintain it. However, a significant challenge in networked robots is establishing a scientific foundation that connects communication in order to control and enable new capabilities. Updating functionality and operations, whether remotely or locally, typically require specialized knowledge and longer maintenance periods in closed systems without open interfaces or communication channels.

By utilizing open interfaces, security and efficiency can be guaranteed through this approach. For networked robots to share information among themselves and with powerful workstations used for intensive offline processing, wireless networks are essential. These technologies encounter a number of technological obstacles, including installation, inspection, safety, the localization of operations sensor and actuators fusion, networking noise, trustworthiness, congestion, latency, stability, and range and power constraints.

The Internet of Robotic Things is a complex field that requires careful consideration of these issues. Fortunately, new hardware, software, and communication standards are emerging, providing new capabilities and possibilities.

IoT technologies and applications are fundamentally changing people's and society's perspectives on technology and business. It is vital to incorporate new IoT concepts, designs, and techniques into the conception and creation of open IoT platforms in order to support future advancements where IoT services and infrastructure will collide with artificial and autonomous system technologies. New apps, increased functionality, new business models, and investment opportunities will all be made possible by this. (Vermesan et al.,2022)

Converging Sensing/Actuating Information Network

There exists a wide variety of products that differ in their level of intricacy, sensing and acting capabilities, communication, processing power, intelligence, mobility, and

Figure 2.

platform compatibility. When we use the term "robotic," we are referring to a specific subset of these products that are highly advanced, intelligent, and self-governing. These robotic devices rely on both edge computing and cloud IoT platforms, and incorporate cutting-edge robotics and artificial intelligence techniques to function.

In order to provide specialized solutions for certain jobs, the Internet of Robotic Things (IoRT) is a sophisticated network of devices that uses path and motion planning as well as motion control.This autonomous system architecture is integrated into the larger IoT architecture, and is defined by six fundamental characteristics.

- **Sensing** In the realm of IoT and robotics, the term "sensing" is frequently utilized to describe the capacity of devices or "Things" to communicate with other IoT devices and individuals. This communication is typically unidirectional, from the device to the human, which empowers people to participate in the IoT ecosystem based on their own IoT concept or service paradigm. Thanks to extensive research into the flexibility of this feature, "Sensing-as-a-Service" has been integrated into numerous IoT solutions.
- **Actuating** While it is widely recognized that actuating based on a comprehensive approach is a valuable aspect of IoT verticals, it has yet to be made available in the open market. This feature empowers devices to take action in response to physical and/or virtual activities. To ensure that actuating is both reliable and secure, services must be established to support the open, multi-vendor development, deployment, and operation of IoT applications.

Through extensive research, the concept of "Actuation has emerged as a new prototype for IoT, providing a user-friendly experience that encourages acceptance and engagement for managed IoT devices. Innovative installations are necessary to enable actuating and bring this technology to life.

- **Control** This is a structured set of activities, mainly at the application layer, that operates in a loop or series of loops, referred to as Control Loops, which define the functions and services. To ensure proper sequencing mechanisms, the architecture's comprehensive security concepts must be reflected in the interface definitions. These interfaces are crafted to grant access to sensing data and control mechanisms. Within the control loop, various entities such as applications and cloud services can be integrated.
- **Planning** The orchestration feature plays a crucial role in streamlining the logic that interconnects various internal components of the platform, enabling seamless completion of service requests. It guarantees that high-quality standards are upheld throughout the entire life-cycle of the IoT application. To ensure that service requirements are in accordance with processed data and knowledge entities as well as platform-specific representation, the planning process employs a robotic sequence engine based on logic. The recording of user-defined representations of data and resources by the orchestration logic facilitates the server definition process.
- **Perception** The interdisciplinary field of robotics involves integrating sensor data with knowledge modeling for enhanced functionality. Robots use a variety of techniques, including human-interface layout, software development, cloud-based architectures, analytics of data, multiple-agent systems, machine sensing systems, and occasionally artificial intelligence, to build seamless contact between themselves and people. Robots may identify and understand their surroundings through perception, freeing people to perform specialized activities.
- **Cognition** This feature equips the robot with monitoring and sensing capabilities, allowing it to gather sensor data from various sources and utilize both local and distributed intelligence. This demonstrates the device's impressive capabilities, as it can analyze data from observed events, often employing edge or fog computing. These foundational elements support the device's third capability, which involves autonomous decision-making for actions such as physical manipulation or control in the real world. The device can navigate and operate in its designated physical environment, as well as notify or alert based on physical event analysis. The following subsections offer an overview of the IoRT technologies utilized in creating, utilizing, and deploying IoRT applications.(vermesan et al., 2022)

Sensors and Actuators

IoT and robotics rely on two fundamental technologies: sensors and actuators. These components are crucial for IoRT systems to function properly, as they provide essential functionalities and well-defined interfaces for identification and reaction. In contrast to IoT, the practical functionality of IoRT building blocks is based on sensors and actuators. Robotic Interaction Services (RoIS) define HRI functions and the usage of external building blocks, as well as abstracting the hardware in service robots. HRI functions, such as facial recognition and wheel control, rely on sensors and actuators like radar, lidar, cameras, and microphones. These components are physically implemented on the robot or in the environment, enabling logical functional aspects such as person detection and identification. This standard allows for the development of HRI apps that can be used on both devices and gateways. Actuation is a crucial aspect of robotics that enables the manipulation of items, movement of people and products, and even the functioning of automated doors. Numerous actuation approaches, including automated strategy and execution by multiple robots, have been developed in the field of robotics.

Emerging IoT Technologies

Cost effective a solid-state semiconductors (CMOS) photographic sensors with proactive illumination are needed for IoRT applications to operate correctly in a variety of weather situations, including sunlight, darkness, rain, fog, and dust. These sensors must have high accuracy and resolution for both vertical object identification and horizontal road surface scanning. Most sensors now only provide 2D sensing data, therefore sensor fusion is primarily concerned with 2D representation. However, more height data, 3D visualization, and the combining of actuators and sensors are needed to better future IoRT activities. Robotic objects require a customized environment model that utilizes existing and new sensor technology in order to generate an ideal 3D environmental model that balances resource consumption and maximized performance. LIDAR systems, which use a revolving, scanning mirror to provide a complete picture, give autonomous robotic objects and cars 360-degree vision. For self-driving, autonomous robotic things, LIDAR systems provide precise 3D data on the immediate surroundings that can be utilized for obstacle avoidance, motion vector analysis, object recognition, and collision prediction. However, LIDAR systems are ineffective for close-range control, so radars must be added to autonomous robotic objects and vehicles. The 76-81 GHz frequency range is typically used for radar because of its RF propagation characteristics and necessary resolution. The radar equipment is small, emits less power, and has a lower risk of mutual interference, making it an effective method for collision avoidance in conditions such as smoke, dust, or other weather conditions.

IoT devices around the world are taking over non IoT devices. The US, China, as well as the developed countries in the European Union and the Asia Pacific region, are leading IoT markets. The region is predicted to lead in expenditure and uptake in the worldwide market, in line with other APAC-related trends. According to market predictions, China will account for two-thirds of the industrial IoT market in the APAC region by 2025.(Finance online 2023)

Figure 3. Yearly shift from non IoT to IoT devices

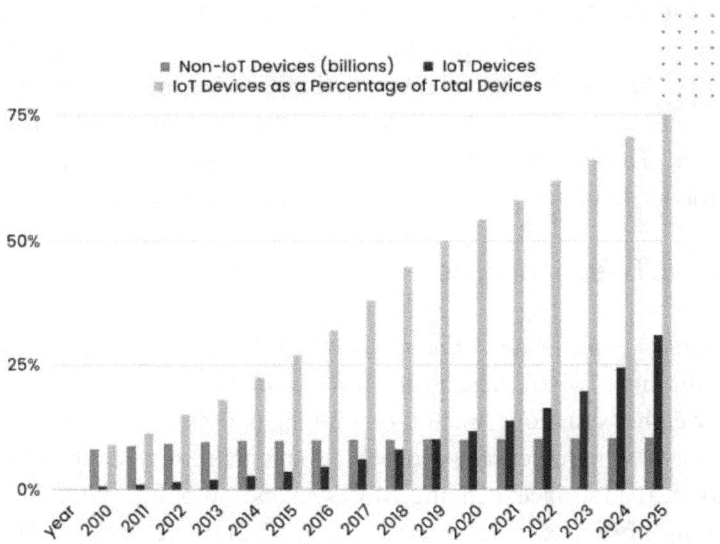

Communication Technologies

The communication infrastructure of IoRT necessitates novel methods in order to allow virtualization of operations on current computing engines and facilitate the usage of such infrastructures in diverse fields.These strategies should make it possible to exchange data streams (important for 3D-awareness and imaging systems), communicate internally, and use edge computing. Time-critical communication is essential for collision avoidance, which significantly lowers accidents and collisions. IoRT commonly operates local robots using networking technology and remote robots using designated white spectrum frequencies. IoT employs machine-to-machine communication and implements emerging protocols like LoRa and SIGFOX, as well as 4G, WiFi, and Bluetooth. However, this level of interoperability and service development is more challenging and requires semantic data from other disciplines. Due in part to the dynamic nature of IoRT conditions and their dependence on applications, contexts, and use cases, the ability to discover and classify services of objects often presents significant challenges. IoRT systems are built on communication protocols, which enable connectivity to networks and application interaction. In order to exchange data over the network, edge devices and autonomous devices use a variety of communication protocols that define exchange of data formats, data encryption, device addressing schemes, and packet transportation from origin to destination. Various Wireless Local Area Network (WLAN) communication standards, such as 802.11a, 802.11b and 802.11g, 802.11n, 802.11ac, and 802.11ad, are included in the 802.11 - Wi-Fi protocols that are used. These standards offer communication ranges of between 20 meters (indoors) and 100 meters (outdoors) with data speeds ranging from 1 Mb/s to 6.75 Gb/s. Various IoRT communication techniques can be used to achieve shared real-time computation, data exchange, and internal communication.(Vermesan et al.,2022)

Voice Recognition, Voice Control

Nowadays, chatbots and devices with microphones are commonly used for communication. As the IoRT advances, more endpoints are created for people and robots to interact. This leads to the emergence of a new digital experience where robotic objects and humans collaborate, resulting in IoRT mesh development through mutual contact between robotic entities.

People should be able to communicate with robot fleets in more natural ways for IoRT applications that include tour-guiding, elder care, recovery, search and rescue, monitoring, education, general support in everyday settings, and in workplaces, factories, and homes. When creating IoRT applications, multimodal interfaces that deal with detection of movement, auditory localization, people monitoring, users (or fellow person/robot) localization, along with the merging of different modalities are essential. Using knowledge of the robot's movements and postures, powerful noise-reduction techniques can be used for speech recognition and voice control.

To reduce background noise, the microphone's quality is crucial for automatic speech recognition. A speech recognition automation system for robots can accurately identify voices from adults as well as kids in crowded spaces thanks to the reduction of reverberation, disruption, and noise in a portable multiple channels of communication technique with an outlier-robust broader side-lobe canceller method and a feature-space noise reduction criterion.(Vermesan et al., 2022)

Machine Learning as Enabler for Adaptive

The Internet of Things (IoT) community recognizes the significance of incorporating Machine Learning (ML) techniques into IoT devices for effective management of the vast and diverse sensory data generated by network nodes. This integration enables IoRT solutions to adjust to different environments, while IoRT apps can learn from their surroundings and experiences. The ML service needs to be intelligent and distributed enough to encompass every IoRT node, including those at the network's edge. By performing early data fusion and predictive analyses, this distributed and embedded intelligence can generate high-level aggregated information from the device/sensor's low-level data. These forecasts might be used as inputs for an innovative method of learning on an alternative network node, which would then carry out additional forecasts and data fusion operations. This would result in the development of a smart network of machine learning algorithms that would carry out progressive compilations of the sensed data.(Vermesan et al., 2022)

Marketplace for an IoT Ecosystem

Mechanisms for the monetization of service components and data are required to encourage participation and the development of an IoRT ecosystem. A market place must be established as the center of an IoRT ecosystem. A marketplace facilitates registration and the discovery of offerings, as well as the data or attributes that services provide. These services may act on robots or objects directly or as separate components accessible through IoRT platforms. Selling and buying of products and services take place in the marketplace, which acts as a central location for transactions.

- Offering authentication, where a supplier of an offering can provide a metadata description for the marketplace to ingest and index to help with discovery.
- Offering discovery, where a customer searches for offerings using a marketplace search interface. To facilitate data registration and discovery, common ontologies for the semantic description of data must be established.
- Role and privileges management could be used to secure access to the market. Authentication and authorization can also be used to secure access to the marketplace.
- Reputation management, which involves consumer evaluations of suppliers and their goods; these evaluations may be taken into consideration when selecting search outcomes and during investigation. Auditing and accounting, wherein a customer's use of a service is monitored and providers can make

a fee for this usage at their discretion. This function is crucial for making IoRT monetization possible and giving the ecosystem's growth drive. The management of different data-providing licenses is closely related to it.(vermesan et al .,2022)

Orchestration

Supporting with providing composition generation, instantiation, maintenance, and dissemination. This feature of an online marketplace fosters the reuse of enrolled offers since it permits their use in other processes, even if it is not required. Due to orchestration, a customised manufacturing procedure might be represented as a cooperation of numerous robotic item functions, for instance.(vermesan et al .,2022)

The Applications in Warehouse and E-Commerce

IoRT was developed in reaction to the growth of e-commerce, where human warehouse workers and autonomous robots coexist. Collaborative robots can help logistics organizations by alleviating some staffing shortages and the demanding nature of the work. One typical use for IoRT is the delivery of goods by fleets of autonomous robots within a range of between three and five kilometers, carrying loads as large as ten kilos, at speeds in the range of eight to ten kilometers per hour. Robots may be controlled and monitored remotely if they encounter circumstances that prevent them from traveling autonomously. (verseman et al .,2022)

IoT Practical Applications in Commerce

Amazon has assembled a team to examine possible uses for autonomous technology inside its expanding logistics network. The company won't be building self-driving cars; instead, it will act as a think tank to help the biggest online retailer in the world incorporate automation into its logistical plan. By further automating administrative tasks, Amazon may reduce delivery costs, giving them a vital competitive edge.

Automated forklifts, for example, might save labor costs in the company's operations; the Kiva robots have demonstrated 20% lower operational costs.

Both Amusement And Wellbeing

By fusing communication technologies with robot sensing abilities, telepresence robotics enables more complex human-robot interaction. It enables people to virtually roam and gaze around distant areas, participate in business meetings, and keep a watch on patients or elderly individuals at residence or in medical institutions.

Cinemas, theaters, and retail environments all provide creative and exciting venues to integrate modern technologies. Since the ability to move around and live in social and natural surroundings is necessary for a normal lifestyle, communal and open spaces will get more attention as locations for technology in the future. Service robots are employed in a range of social tasks, such as grocery shopping, outdoor cleaning, and visiting historical sites.(vermesan et al., 2022)

Coordination

To achieve the IoRT's collective optimization goals, robot collaboration must be correctly taken into consideration. When these problems develop in multimodal robot networks that are outfitted with a range of actuators, sensors, and on-board computing systems, etc. to effectively accomplish the required tasks, both the implementation and the design of MRS synchronization pose substantial hurdles. The difficulty of the assigned job must be considered when estimating the complexity of the assignments the collaborative MRS must develop, which leads to an estimate of a reasonable number of robots to carry out that assigned task. Another alternative is to divide the task up among several robot subgroups.

Health-Care Robotics Process Automation Paradigm

Any country's medical industry generates a considerable amount of employment and cash. It consists of things like medical insurance, clinical research, and hospital supplies. It could be challenging to compile and assess data, such as information on pharmacological qualities, that is scattered across several organizational factors against the backdrop of the healthcare business. tests, laboratory tools for technological developments, outside routes, health portals, scanning diagnostics administration, sequence-dependent arranging programs, Preservation offers, and improvements in human resource utilization. Health care organizations must rely on people to complete conventional challenging tasks that need a lot of concentrated work since interoperability across various systems can occasionally be challenging.

In the healthcare sector, the three main participants are patients, doctors, and health insurance. Creating a far more accurate and efficient internal process is essential to maintaining the balance between the rising patient demand and the records needed for surveillance, insurance demands, etc. Alternatives to computerized testing that are based on modern science and technology, like automated robotic processes, could assist clinicians in managing details such as doctor licenses, documenting and patient incentives healthcare provider schedules, programming, statements of billing and claim management, patient information, Medicare payment and adherence, and supplemental insurance policies to increase utility, reduce costs, and set limits on care.

The benefit of robotic process automation is that it guarantees that its applications and tools have excellent visual designs that improve user experience (UX) for patients. The objective is to provide a simple framework that almost anyone with a fundamental understanding of modern technology may use. In order to satisfy the requirements of the final consumers, it must also be thoroughly modified. It is stated that science of computation and mechanical engineering are combined in modern robot technology. It is also extending its area of influence and communicating wisely with others. Three significant uses of automation in medicine are robotic assistants, rehabilitation tools, and medical automation. By providing better findings, more precise availability, and higher efficacy, robots are offering medical institutions an economic edge over their rivals. To make it easier for physicians to carry out their duties and deliver patients with exceptional medical treatment, several large firms and mega-specialty organizations have started up and investing in robots. (subeesh et al.,2021)

Operative Robotics

With the use of robotic surgery, physicians can perform complex surgeries with fewer incisions. Surgery is arguably the most well-known use of robots in the healthcare sector. It made it possible for doctors to do accurate punctures and encouraged the creation of fresh non-invasive methods. (subeesh et al.,2021)

Radiographer Robotics

Radiologists will receive training in sophisticated diagnostic imaging interpretation. In addition to earlier scans, doctors will consider a patient's complete medical history. Robotic surgeons won't tire out from doing constant surgeries all year. (subeesh et al.,2021)

Rehabil tating Robotics

Lightweight, portable digital exoskeletons provide solutions for flexible appendages. After chemotherapy and more procedures, a variety of robotic wheelchairs may aid with the brain's ability to reconstruct suitable connections between neurons. Robots that replicate human movement are now being researched in an effort to trick the brain into reacting. (subeesh et al.,2021)

Software In Smooth Robots and Prosthetics

Smooth Grippers

Thinking about the inherent flexibility and compliance of DEA synthetic muscle tissues, growing gentle grippers based on DEA synthetic muscular tissues provides a brand new way to grasp objects with one-of-a-kind shapes and brands. Various soft grippers evolved based on DEA synthetic muscle groups

Vibrotactile Stimulation

Recent studies have used vibrating sleeves, pressure points in prosthetic sockets, and friction modulation on touch screen surfaces as examples of vibrotactile feedback. The pair's ability to collaborate is improved by vibrotactile stimuli and haptic signals, which without hindering task flow, can considerably increase the information the machine provides to the user.As was explained throughout the study, one-way intent transmission—from the person to the robot—has made task-specific robotic assistance conceivable. We discussed how most research conducted at pHRI treats the autonomous device as a passive spectator of human conduct and, at most, enables the robot to offer feedback on its present condition and/or intended use. Evidence that reciprocal signaling between an automated device and a person significantly enhances interaction was covered. These contacts, however bidirectional, have so far allowed for task negotiating or the progressive development of mutual comprehension and alignment. Through bidirectional discourse, which depends on both the psychological well-being of the person interacting and the dialogue history, more adaptable cooperation may be made feasible. As a result, the robot would be able to provide feedback on its current state and/or intended function.

Estimated Usage and Success Rate of Robotics in Health- Care

.In the healthcare industry and other connected companies, the usage of robotics and automated technologies has increased. The market for health care robots is anticipated to expand quickly over the following decades, hitting 9 trillion dollars by 2024, according the forecast of the Global Association of Robots. Robotics also helps healthcare professionals like healthcare professionals complete complex and exacting tasks more quickly and accurately, enhancing the efficiency of the entire medical sector.

Robot-assisted therapy may allow for therapeutic procedures that are more efficient, available, and enjoyable than conventional therapy. So far, there have been conflicting findings regarding how clinical outcome markers are impacted by robot-assisted training. Customized robot-assisted training has been demonstrated in some trials to be superior to conventional therapy, while no statistically significant differences in clinical outcomes have been found in other investigations. However, there is solid proof that patients who actively engage in therapy benefit from it. These optimistic findings spur research that reliably identifies intent and provides real-time accomplishment and effort metrics in order to promote patient engagement.

Significance of Robotic process automation in health-care sector

- By employing machine artificial neural networks to quickly gain and incorporate clinical data from lab technologies, third-party entry points, health insurance pathways screening imaging equipment, sequence-dependent set up, as well as additional multiple systems, we aim to lessen the difficulties faced by medical professionals when coping with the complicated layout of procedures and a volume of patient and health care facility statistical analysis.
- Learning more about robots to improve patient care is the aim of automation in the medical sector. In order to accomplish that, it also becomes essential to build the appropriate automated machinery and work with experts to make it. To completely understand the importance of the uses of machine learning in healthcare, additional study is necessary.
- • Since people's potential for compassion is linked to either their humanity or chaotic structure, further research is still needed to determine whether or not medical professionals can substitute people. Empathy may be shown by robots and machine learning toward people, and it can also be shown through preprogrammed actions.

IoT in Transportation

In addition to making it easier to get from one place to another, IoT in transportation also increases safety and appropriateness. For instance, a smart car may do multiple functions at once, including communication, pleasure, navigation, and more reliable, efficient transportation. Travelers may stay connected to all kinds of transportation at all times thanks to IoT. Several wireless technologies, including as Wi-Fi, Bluetooth 3G, 4G, smart transportation systems, and even other vehicles, connect the car to the internet. A more sophisticated version of geo-fencing has been developed in this sector. It records the coordinates of a given location along with the position of an object or device. (Perwej et al .,2019)

Applications of IoT and AI in Agriculture Automation

By integrating better programs, an IoT environment powered by AI has a surprising ability to increase the control and specificity of farming operations. The potential of these most recent technological developments in farm operations is limitless because they might automate difficult tasks with little manual labor.

Smart Farm

Today's farmers use a range of farm machinery and equipment to complete a number of agricultural jobs. Tractors are included in them and are regarded as the most

Figure 4.

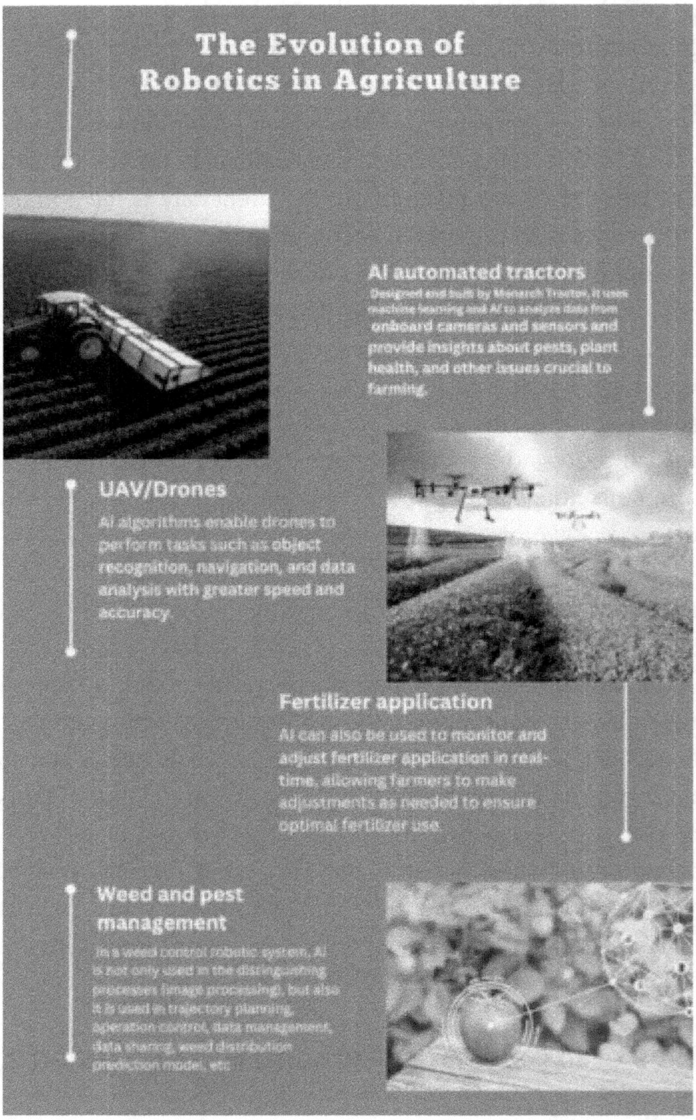

important and indispensable farm energy source. Tractor performance monitors gather data, take measurements, and help with remote process observation. The variables that are frequently taken into consideration include power, consumption of fuel, draught, and wheel slip.

DGPS, or the Global Positioning System with Difference. The GPS system is a crucial part of the system that provides spatial values. As a result, the tractor-implement system may be evaluated, documented, and monitored in terms of how it is functioning in relation to the position. Given that the soil texture and land slope have an influence on how well a tractor-implement system operates, this mapping technique is highly useful for estimating the costs of crop production inside the field limits.

Robotic harvesters and rice cultivators have adopted that function with efficiency that is nearly equivalent to that of a human. The image collecting module was the primary element of the robotic fruits harvester prototype. This was followed by an image editing module mounted on a motorised carriage.The information was utilized to determine which fruits and vegetables might be gathered using an object identification method based on computer vision.

UAV or Drones

Drones were first utilized for military operations, but they have increasingly been modified for use in agriculture. Another development in agriculture is the automation of numerous agricultural operations using drones, including pesticide application and land monitoring. Unmanned aerial vehicles (UAVs), which are characterized as airplane without a human pilot on board, include agricultural drones in their category.. A central processor unit, a GPS receiver, a laser, a radar, a camera, a gyroscope, an accelerometer, a compass, and other sensors are all included in the drone gadget. Actuators and motors are also included for carrying out necessary activities. The remote control is used to interact with this via wireless communication. UAVs' integrated thermal and multi-spectral detectors allow them to survey hectares of fields in a single flight.(subeesh et al.,2021)

Irrigation

The "per drop more crop" strategy has been developed to ensure proper use of the limited supplies of water, which is necessary to meet our future food demands. The sensors' usage of data-transmission protocols like MQTT makes real-time monitoring possible. Data is made available to subjects in MQTT, and people who are enrolled to such topics are the only ones who may read the data. MQTT has the advantage of being small and simple for the network to control. The processing unit of the module is equipped with a relay and a motor and is ready to accept commands from the outside. A MQTT dashboard may be used to view the data.(subeesh et al.,2021)

Weed and Pest Control

Application of herbicides is still challenging due to its unfavorable impacts, which include harm to the environment and human health. Additionally, conventional weeding methods uniformly spray pesticides throughout the whole field whether or not there are weeds, which raises the price of herbicides and boosts greenhouse gas emissions. Incorporating robots, the Internet of Things, and innovative image processing techniques into a site-specific system is one effective way to address all of these problems. Weeds in a field can be found using both RGB and The infrared imaging sensors (IR).

Fertilizers Application

Businesses now push farmers to embrace technology-enabled agricultural practices and digital farming approaches. Using IoT technologies can make fertilizer application more sophisticated. An NPK sensor can be used to monitor the concentrations of nitrogen, phosphorus, and potassium (K). This sensor can be made using resistors, LEDs, and light-dependent resistors. The concepts of colorimetry and the photoconductivity are the foundation of the sensor's operation. An on-chip processing unit receives data from the NPK sensors directly. The use of edge computing or cloud computing is used to conduct further research. The low-cost SPAD was developed for the field-based indirect evaluation of crop leaf chlorophyll content.(subeesh et al.,2021)

With the use of a sprayer, imaging devices, sensors, and system-on-chips like the Raspberry Pi, systems created utilizing the Internet of Things may manage weeds by dousing them in herbicide. The critical aspect of managing weeds is handled by an AI-based categorization method. .(Subeesh et al.,2021)

Storage of Farm Products

A helpful instrument for monitoring the quality of agricultural products maintained in storage containers are wireless sensor nodes. Moisture and temperature detectors can be used to make sure that the storage room is kept at the ideal temperature and humidity levels. The values in the time series of sensor readings could vary slightly. In order to evaluate both humidity and temperature fluctuations in the storage system, cumulative data are acquired from this. Each of these thresholds is determined with respect to the crop kept in the storage facility. Data aggregation is done at the remote databases server, which acts as a gateway to connect sensor nodes to the World Wide Web. Coupling the data findings to the local farmers' ongoing surveillance of the storage conditions on a local level .(subeesh et al., 2021)

Sustainable Agriculture

Sustainable agricultural practices are anticipated to provide a number of advantages, including enhanced soil fertility, environmental protection, and a greater supply of the planet's natural resources. By following a variety of goals, sustainable agriculture seeks to increase productive agricultural revenue. Promote effective environmental management.(Uprety et al.,2023)

For agriculture to be sustainable, data must be easily accessible. Smart farming enables both cost-effective and sustainable agriculture through the use of earth observation data and navigation satellites, making it easier for farmers to make informed agricultural decisions. The main types of sustainability are three.

- Environmental Sustainability Sustainability assures that nature may be used regularly and without interference from various variables at the ecological level, preventing it from being used as an infinite supply of resources . An focus in renewable energy sources, outdoor safety, and water conservation are a few examples of realistic adaptation.
- Social Sustainability: At the social level, sustainability may plant the seeds for the development of individuals, groups, and societies to provide realistic and really isolated personal enjoyment, healthcare, and education throughout the globe .
- Economic sustainability: Business activities and the related flow of capital will support various pillars of viability for an all-around improvement. (Uprety et al.,2023)

Machine Intelligence

The development of IoRT is greatly affected by the field of AI. Specific robotic devices are becoming more capable thanks to AI algorithms.

The sensor fusion capacities of IoRT devices are enhanced by artificial intelligence (AI) technologies, such as lenses for detecting sight, chemical detectors for distinguishing smell and taste, microphone for listening, pressure detectors for feeling touch/pressure, etc.

In order to deliver analytics and insights, as well as to improve the capabilities of the individual automated machinery and their collaborative behaviors as a fleet, the various levels of IoRT platforms utilize AI approaches and methodology. Convolutional neural networks (CNNs), for example, are neural networks with deep connections that are used to analyze images and extract their visual characteristics. To enhance the effectiveness of the acknowledgment function by obtaining extraordinary variation or prospective defect detection rates, the procedures are made to partition and de-noise monitored signals. IoRT applications may now manage very big data sets as a result of the transition from central compute to edge/fog nodes. This strategy, which fuses effective production inspection technologies with edge processing, is also applied. Technologies for production inspection are also. By adapting a CNNs engine to the cloud computing environment, this strategy significantly increases the computational effectiveness of a verification model that can determine the type and severity of faults. Robotic machines collect video, compress video data, pre-process video images, and segment video using perception tools like cameras. Utilizing perceptual technologies, such as cameras, images are first processed and segmented.It might be possible to increase the accuracy of item recognition by working together to create an environment and scenery-aware adaption model utilizing data from different video capture equipment. IoRT equipment, servers at the edge, and the cloud must all share the same amount of DL compute, hence a suitable offloading method must be developed.

When assessing network health, video encoded data, information rates/usage, power consumption, processing delay, framing rate, and the computational correctness of analytics, significant trade-offs must be taken into account. The potential exists for multiple distributed edge autonomous gadgets to collaborate at the edge to provide better services. Condensing the DL frameworks at the outer layer can enhance system performance through computing edge collaboration and the distribution of capabilities.(vermesan et al., 2020)

Virtual and Augmented Reality

Immersive technology (such VR and AR) may now be incorporated into interfaces for users of automated machines as well as for robotic tools that communicate with the interface of IoRT platform systems. This is possible because IoRT applications are becoming more cognitively capable at the edge. For IoRT systems to be more dependable, end-to-end security, electronic identities, and mobile data/knowledge security all need to be enhanced. This criteria is based on cognitive skills based on emerging AI algorithms. Future distributed IoRT architectures will require concepts like adaptability, end-to-end reliability, privacy, and intelligent connectivity in order to move away from existing centralized IoRT systems.A fluid data flow and expertise exchanging across IoRT applications/services executing at the edge or in the cloud is required to support the utilization of computing at the edges, software that uses cloud computing of operations, and rule-driven policy execution while maintaining the integrity and privacy of data. Applications for the Internet of Things (IoRT) may use VR/AR for learning, maneuvering, and support functions. While the technology known as augmented reality (AR) supersedes information generated by computers over the actual world to retain time and space coherence and enable in-the-moment communication, virtual reality (VR) replicates occurrences. (vermesan et al., 2020)

Integration of Digital Twins With IoT

Digital Twins (DT) is a brilliant concept that has recently emerged. It involves creating a digital replica of a real system, seen from the perspective of Cyber Physical Systems (CPS). This virtual replica mimics the actual performance of the system. Throughout the entire development lifecycle, information from the virtual system, combined with that of the real system, characterizes the data from the physical system. By combining the digital and real counterparts, a more effective way of handling, controlling, and improving coordination when the system is operating is achieved.

Digital twins refer to virtual models of physical objects or systems used for real-time monitoring and management. Meanwhile, IoT is a network of interconnected devices capable of data sharing and communication. When integrated, digital twins and IoT can produce intelligent systems that optimize performance and anticipate potential problems. By analyzing data collected from digital twins and IoT devices, artificial intelligence (AI) can identify patterns and offer predictions.

It is effectively incorporated into a variety of applications, including medicinal systems, industry, the aviation industry, the agricultural sector, urban planning, and weather prediction.(Hemdan et al.,2023)

Biomedical Application

The industry that has profited the most from applying digital twin ideas is biomedical healthcare. Digital twin applications in biomedical fields have been made possible by new IoT, fitness, and e-health technologies. In the healthcare sector, DTs technologies are used to analyze and propose medications, identify lifestyle changes, improve hospital operations, do remote surgery, and help policymakers with providing healthcare to patients. In vitro methods for forecasting how the actual organ will function in either stated scenario will be developed with the help of a DT virtualized biological approach by physicians as they look into how the development of digital twins in the medical field impacts treatment, diagnosis, and overall health.

Smart Cities

Smarter features for smart cities are now being presented via digital twin advancements. Research on this topic has evolved along with (IoT) and communications, which has boosted interest in the digitization of our lives. A framework for creating smart medical amenities for people in smart cities using digital twins is described and to use a knowledge-based approach with artificial intelligence to provide categorization and decision-making methods for managing mobility and power in a major city. Digital twins are used to control energy in smart cities.(Talaat et al., 2023)

Energy Management

With the ever growing demand for energy supply energy management is becoming a pivotal part of our life. A benchmark based on the analysis of data from smart meters is created in to create a daily suggestion for energy building. The framework will examine how these procedures may assist in power control that is as near to actual as possible and will ascertain the differences between what is new from traditional and yearly energy assessment techniques. The paradigm is built by combining digital twins with information and communication technology to provide a strong promise for improving the effectiveness of catastrophe management measures. (Perwej et al.,2019)

Intelligent Connectivity

Depending on the application, the intelligent connectivity infrastructure must operate as a continuous and compatible network to support heterogeneous devices with a range of intelligence competencies and connectivity requirements. This is because strong, resilient, and dependable connection networks are necessary for IoRT applications. The connection infrastructure must be flexible enough to respond to changing environmental conditions, as well as to expected and unanticipated events and circumstances.The intelligent infrastructure for connectivity must function as a continuous and interoperable network in order to serve heterogeneous devices with varied intelligence features and connectivity needs, depending on the application. This is because robust, resilient, and dependable connectivity networks are necessary for IoRT applications. The linkage infrastructure must be flexible enough to respond to changing environmental conditions, as well as to expected and unanticipated events and circumstances. In order to meet operational requirements and "the economic viability of the vehicular networks," artificial intelligence (AI) methods like machine learning (ML) are employed as useful tools to address the difficulties faced in 5G technology wireless technology (such as cached data, processing, and communication operations).

To support new connectivity, which has developed into the enabler for the future IoRT intelligent services, wireless and cellular networks utilized for telecommunications must offer predictable/guaranteed latency.

Peer-to-peer and/or broadcast communication techniques are available for direct communication and data sharing on IoRT devices. The forthcoming 5G wireless technology will have an average latency performance ranging from 1-10 ms in contrast to the current 4G mobile technology's latency efficiency of 80-100 ms, thanks to the use of SDN (software-defined networking) and the virtualization of network functions (NFV). Applications for dispersed networks are supported in order to meet the stringent energy efficiency standards required to cover large outdoor regions, deep indoor or underground locations, or mobile objects moving quickly. These applications are built for the edge and the cloud. The architecture and additional functions of the 5G network are designed to fulfill the Latency, reliability, and throughput are requirements for IoRT applications that are both mission- and safety-critical.Future directions in physical human-robot interaction for embodied communication

It consists of multimodal communication, assistance for emergent, unforeseen behavior, and communication during collaboration (safe operation guaranteed by autonomy while allowing continual adaptation). These goals take into consideration how individuals and their surroundings alter over time, enabling a process of coadaptation between humans and automated systems However, they also have one thing in common: there are currently no standardized algorithmic tools available. We shall discuss this in more detail below. Therefore, datasets are needed for comparing and evaluating the features of the current pHRI, testing algorithmic tools relevant to the pHRI, and certifying algorithms prior to use with people.(kalinowska et al., 2023)

Continual Adaptation With Safety Guarantees

pHRI may provide a safety risk due to the immediate mechanical contact and power exchange As a result, enabling pHRI has placed a high priority on safety .However, it is unclear how to ensure safety without restricting robot motion parameters (such as torque or velocity) and performance limits.Due to the lack of reliable alternatives, the ISO standards from 2016 point to quantifiable biomechanical restrictions, such as acceptable threshold forces or pressures for certain body regions, as a requirement for collaborative robots.

These initiatives provide a step toward offering standardized safety assurances for data-driven autonomous machines (given acceptable assumptions). Notably, only a small number of research have taken continuous or long-term adaptation into account. Most work has concentrated on learning within a constrained period following initial engagement. One explanation for this is because, although evaluating the effectiveness and safety of data-driven approaches is difficult, doing so for systems that are constantly evolving is considerably more difficult. The development of methods for long-term learning facilitation and data-driven safety verification should be the main areas of research to come. While giving specifications that are adequate for nonstationary simulations and take into account variation in humans and adaptation, we should try to give safety assurances that, at the very least, retain states within safe sets and adhere to temporal logic criteria.(kalinowska et al., 2023)

Multimodal Dialogue

Similar to how we try to deduce pertinent assessment signals from an individual for the robot, the robot should try to provide the individual with data signals. The mobility of the robot is often used in human-robot systems to provide implicit feedback to the human partner. In certain pieces, anthropomorphic cues or exaggerated robot movements are used to strengthen the connection.

As a result of making robotic behaviors more predictable, intentional communication motion has been proven to increase engagement since it enables users to foresee the robot's motions and modify their own behavior accordingly. (kalinowska et al.,2023)

Industrial IoT

The expansion and use of the internet of things (IoT) in industrial applications and sectors is referred to as the "industrial internet of things" (IIoT).more credibility because to its substantial focus on big data, machine-to-machine connectivity, and machine learning. The Industrial Internet of Things is made up of numerous devices that are linked together through communications software. Without the need for human involvement, the outcomes networks, are able to rapidly respond on information after exchanging, analyzing, monitoring, and collecting it in order to modify their behavior or their surroundings.(perwej et al.,2019)

IoT Fire Forcast Detectors

To detect fires early, scientists and engineers have created vision-based fire detectors (VFDs) as well as sound-, flame-, temperature-, gas-, and solid-sensitive fire sensors. Smoke's chemical properties are detected by sensors, which activates an alarm. The YOLOv8 detection model, used by the (Smart fire detection)SFDS approach, provides quick and accurate object identification without the requirement for a regional proposal network. The system is improved to need fewer parameters for detection, increasing its effectiveness. The SFDS utilize computer vision to automatically detect fires in photo and video feeds.(Talaat et al.,2023)

IoT Based Greenhouse Management

To achieve high-efficiency monitoring of environmental data, an IoT monitoring management device for a greenhouse is developed.Organizational framework of the Internet of Things system for managing and monitoring the environment in greenhouses. The system's main parts are a remote web server and a smart gateway running an Android operating system. Using a data collecting device, the gateway gathers greenhouse environmental data, which is then stored in a SQLite database. In the meanwhile, the gateway is used to send the greenhouse's environmental data to the server. The greenhouse's equipment, including the windows, fans, and heating units, is under the supervision of the control node. Output from the gateway is received by and managed by the server system.(Subeesh et al., 2021)

IoT Architecture Domain

Smart, linked houses may be divided into two basic architectural types: distributed and centralized.

Centralized Smart Home Architecture

A computer system that is responsible for controlling the control system is used in a centralized smarthome design for collecting information from sensors, interacting with users, implementing control algorithms, and instructing actuators. In addition to performing the control function, it is responsible for connecting the smarthome to the outside world through the Internet and offering services to its inhabitants.

Distributed Smart Home Architecture

The software for the control system is envisioned and developed as a distributed computing system in a distributed smarthome architecture. The distributed design takes advantage of the processing power of intelligent objects to integrate software modules into the smart home network's nodes.(perwej et al .,2019)

Emergent Interfaces

The communication agent (human or robot) must have a correct mental representation of the communication rules in order for the signaling model outlined above to work, and this hypothesis that the mental representation is correct is frequently static.New symbolic languages will be the foundation for communication if we are to move toward active nonverbal interaction between humans and technology.

We can connect with assistive technology using our kinematic, muscular, and cognitive null space—excess degree of freedom—while avoiding major increases in cognitive burden. The developer chooses a group of vectors in the neural null space, and the operator, who is a human being, is trained to read and create them. As a starting point, languages can be specified and programmed in the robot.There is an apparent way to symbolize the connection of the continuous 2D regulated space onto the corresponding 2D action space of the robotic machine, making the language simple to learn, if we are mapping joystick signals to the action space of a motorized wheelchair.(kalinowska et al.,2023)

REFERENCES

Hemdan, E. E. D., El-Shafai, W., & Sayed, A. (2023). Integrating Digital Twins with IoT-Based Blockchain: Concept, Architecture, Challenges, and Future Scope. *Wireless Personal Communications, 131*(3), 1–24. doi:10.100711277-023-10538-6 PMID:37360142

Kalinowska, A., Pilarski, P. M., & Murphey, T. D. (2023). Embodied Communication: How Robots and People Communicate Through Physical Interaction. *Annual Review of Control, Robotics, and Autonomous Systems, 6*(1), 205–232. doi:10.1146/annurev-control-070122-102501

Kaur, J. (2023). Robotic Process Automation in Healthcare Sector. In *E3S Web of Conferences* (Vol. 391, p. 01008). EDP Sciences.

Perwej, Y., Haq, K., Parwej, F., Mumdouh, M., & Hassan, M. (2019). The internet of things (IoT) and its application domains. *International Journal of Computer Applications, 975*(8887), 182. doi:10.5120/ijca2019918763

Subeesh, A., & Mehta, C. R. (2021). Automation and digitization of agriculture using artificial intelligence and internet of things. *Artificial Intelligence in Agriculture, 5*, 278–291. doi:10.1016/j.aiia.2021.11.004

Talaat, F. M., & ZainEldin, H. (2023). An improved fire detection approach based on YOLO-v8 for smart cities. *Neural Computing & Applications, 35*(28), 1–16. doi:10.100700521-023-08809-1 PMID:37362562

Uprety, D., Banarjee, D., Kumar, N., & Dhiman, A. (2023). *Smart Sustainable Farming Using IOT, Cloud Computing and Big Data* (No. 10814). EasyChair

Vermesan, O., Bahr, R., Ottella, M., Serrano, M., Karlsen, T., Wahlstrøm, T., Sand, H. E., Ashwathnarayan, M., & Gamba, M. T. (2020). Internet of robotic things intelligent connectivity and platforms. *Frontiers in Robotics and AI*, *7*, 104. doi:10.3389/frobt.2020.00104 PMID:33501271

Vermesan, O., Bröring, A., Tragos, E., Serrano, M., Bacciu, D., Chessa, S., & Bahr, R. (2022). Internet of robotic things–converging sensing/actuating, hyper connectivity, artificial intelligence and IoT platforms. In *Cognitive Hyperconnected Digital Transformation* (pp. 97–155). River Publishers. doi:10.1201/9781003337584-4

Chapter 12
Mitigating Disasters Below the Surface:
A Comprehensive Study on Recent Advantages and Ongoing Challenges in Underwater Sensor Networks

S. Prince Sahaya Brighty
https://orcid.org/0000-0002-4683-0013
Department of Computer Science and Engineering, Sri Ramakrishna Engineering College, Coimbatore, India

P. Sebastian Vindro Jude
Department of Electrical and Electronics Engineering, Sri Ramakrishna Engineering College, Coimbatore, India

ABSTRACT

In underwater sensor networks (UWSNs), it is important to determine the location of all the sensors. Localization is the process of estimating the location of each node in a sensor network. There are only a few localization schemes for UWSNs, even though many localization algorithms have been proposed for terrestrial sensor networks. The characteristics of underwater sensor networks are fundamentally different from that of terrestrial networks. The physical layer environments with rigorous bandwidth limitations are the main characteristic of underwater acoustic channels. A unique set of challenges are posed by the long propagation delays and the variable speed of sound under water for localization in UWSNs. This chapter explores the different localization algorithms relevant to underwater sensor networks, and the challenges in meeting the requirements posed by emerging applications for such networks, likes offshore engineering.

DOI: 10.4018/979-8-3693-2280-2.ch012

INTRODUCTION

In recent trends, the deployment of low-cost wireless sensors is proven to be a promising technique for various applications. Underwater applications look into the early warning systems for natural disasters, ecosystem monitoring, oil drilling, and military surveillance. The limited power constraints and processing capability on the sensors makes the management and deployment of wireless sensor networks a greater challenge. The researches related to underwater sensor networks are being done in the recent days. The sensor networks from the physical layer to the application layer have been discussed. Oil drilling generally uses huge exploration vessels that are anchored to the seabed with multiple anchors. These smart sensors can be deployed on the seabed, and it can monitor the system parameters and the environmental parameters. These work together with these Remotely Operated Vehicles (ROV), that are controlled from the ship, or Autonomous Underwater Vehicles (AUV), that can autonomously navigate the deep waters are based on some set of instructions. The ROVs/AUVs, sensors and anchors collect and feed information from the seabed. These can measure parameters such as foundation strength and mooring tensions. They also provide accurate position references to the AUVs. The location of the sensors, anchors and the AUVs are needed to be determined in order to deliver data from the seabed to the ship. This problem is especially challenging for deep water applications. Another challenge in underwater acoustic communication is the limited bandwidth long propagation delay, signal failure issue and sensor node failure due to environmental conditions (Chandrasekhar & Seah, 2006). These nodes must self-configure and it selves to the changes in the ocean environment. Developing efficient underwater communication and networking techniques are involved in the energy conservation of UWSNs.

Figure 1. 2D architecture of underwater sensor network

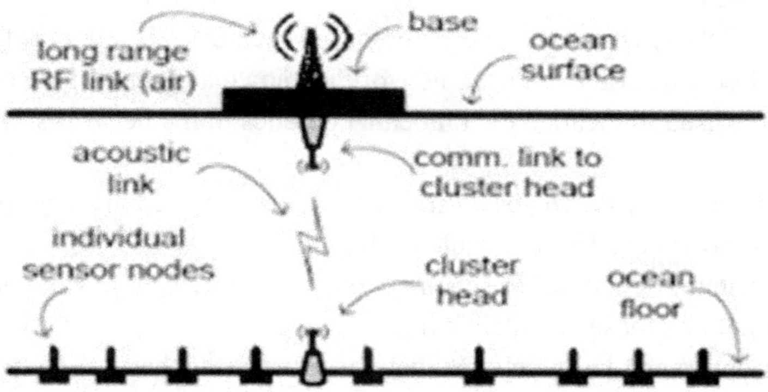

Figure 2. An example application scenario for underwater sensor networks

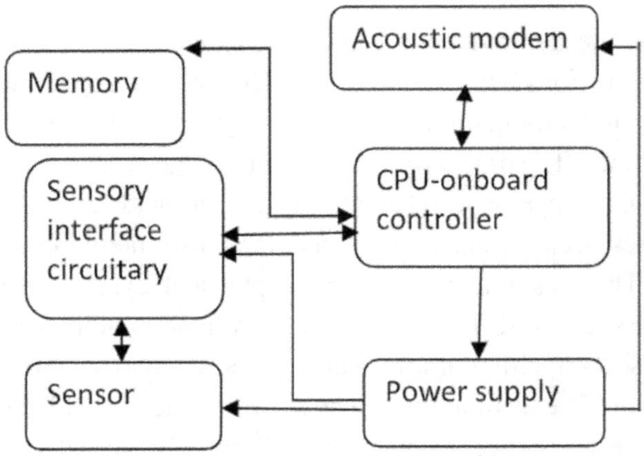

LOCALIZATION SCHEMES SURVEY

A sensor's location helps in typically interpreting a sensor network data. For e.g. tracking a moving object, monitoring the physical conditions of some region or reporting the occurrence of certain events. The localization underwater is as challenging as Radio Frequency (RF) waves that are heavily attenuated under water. A number of localization schemes have been proposed that takes into account many factors such as device capability, signal propagation model and energy requirements. The underwater localization involves many challenges like node development, node mobility, change in signal strength, time synchronization, variation in sound speed and acoustic channel characteristics (Hahn & Rice, 2005).

A. Range based scheme

Range or bearing information like Time Of Arrival (TOA) and Time Difference Of Arrival (TDOA) is used by the range-based localization schemes for position estimation. Locating some nodes in network is known as anchor node or reference node which is used to localize the unlocalized nodes in the networks.

(i) In Infrastructure based location system, anchor nodes are deployed at pre-defined positions. These are anchor-based.
(ii) In Distributed positioning schemes, the positioning infra-structures are not available, i.e., these are anchor-free.
(iii) Traditional range-based schemes have been proposed that uses mobile beacons/ anchors whose locations are known. Here the sensor networks are traversed by

the mobile beacons while location coordinates of the beacons are contained by the broadcasting beacons.

(iv) Certain type of schemes is different and do not require anchor nodes or beacon signals. These schemes don't have anchors or reference points.

B. Range free schemes

While range-free schemes do not use these range or bearing information.

(i) In hop count based schemes, the anchor nodes are located along the corners of a square grid. This scheme is proposed to improve the accuracy of location estimation when the distribution of node is uniform.
(ii) In centroid schemes, the anchor nodes are placed in such a way to form a rectangular mesh. For this scheme to work efficiently, a higher concentration of anchor nodes is required.
(iii) It is impossible to measure the exact location of every sensor in a large dense wireless sensor networks. The Area Localization Scheme (ALS) and the Appropriate Point in Triangle (APIT) helps in locating the area where the nodes are located. The signal processing or probabilistic schemes uses signal processing techniques for to do the localization (Beniwal & Singh, 2014) .

C. Signal processing/probabilistic schemes

This scheme uses signal processing techniques for to do the localizations. It rely on the received signal structure characteristics instead of exploiting signal strength to do localizations (Heidemann et al., 2006). A unique signature has been created for every given location by combining the multi-path pattern with the signal characteristics. The main drawback of this technique is that a substantial effort is needed for the generation of the signal signature database.

TYPES OF WEARABLE SENSORS

Environmental Sensors: These sensors can detect changes in temperature, humidity, air quality, and pollution levels. They are crucial for assessing the immediate surroundings during a disaster, such as a chemical spill or a forest fire.

Biometric Sensors: These sensors monitor an individual's vital signs, including heart rate, body temperature, and oxygen levels. They play a vital role in assessing the health and well-being of disaster survivors and first responders.

Figure 3. Localization schemes

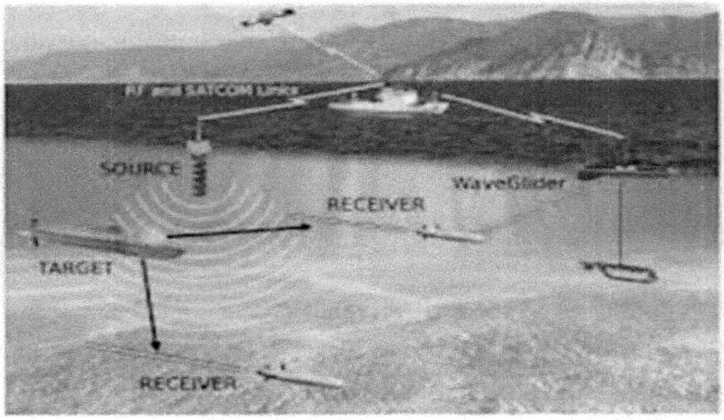

Position and Movement Sensors: Devices like GPS and accelerometers help track the location and movement of individuals and objects, enabling effective search and rescue operations.

Communication Devices: Wearable sensors often include communication capabilities, allowing users to send distress signals, share information, and receive instructions during disasters.

Applications in Disaster Preparedness:

Early Warning Systems: Wearable sensors can be integrated into early warning systems to provide individuals with immediate alerts and instructions in the event of a natural disaster, such as earthquakes or tsunamis.

Risk Assessment: By continuously monitoring environmental parameters, wearable sensors help in assessing the risk levels in real-time. This data can be used to make informed decisions and deploy resources efficiently.

Tracking and Accountability: During evacuations, wearable sensors can track the movement and location of individuals, ensuring their safety and allowing emergency services to respond effectively.

APPLICATIONS

Underwater sensor networks have been designed in order to enable applications based on oceanographic data collection, pollution monitoring, mine scouting, offshore exploration, disaster prevention, assisted navigation and tactical surveillance. Exploring natural undersea resources and gathering of scientific data have also been done by sensors (Heidemann et al., 2006). So there arises a need for communications among the underwater devices. Underwater sensor vehicles and nodes must have the capability of coordinating their operation, exchanging their location, moving information and hence relay the monitored data to an onshore base station. A new research paradigm of Underwater Wireless Sensor Networks (UWSNs) poses challenges like large propagation delays, node mobility and high error probability of acoustic underwater channels, compared to the ground based WSNs. Domingo and Prior (2008) described a protocol named DUCS (Distributed Underwater Clustering Scheme). It is a GPS free routing protocol, and it helps in minimizing the exchange of proactive routing message and also it doesn't use the flooding techniques (Sohraby et al., 2007). For to eliminate the redundant information it uses the data aggregation. The applications of underground sensor networks also include sensing-based cyber physical systems like Collision avoidance, robotic surgery, nano level manufacturing, air traffic control, healthcare monitoring and Underwater acoustic sensor Systems like Oceanographic data collection, pollution monitoring, disaster prevention, tactical surveillance (Beniwal & Singh, 2014). These UWSNs avoids data spoofing and privacy leakage. Apart from all the advantages, these sensors also have some drawbacks like limited bandwidth, propagation delay and fading problems.

CONCLUSION

Many new challenges are posed by the problems of UWSNs. This is because of the acoustic transmission medium. The localization schemes and applications of UWSNs are surveyed in this paper. The advantages and disadvantages of UWSNs have been discussed. Also the localization in the application domain of offshore engineering has been discussed.

REFERENCES

Akyilidiz, L. (2015). Underwater acoustic Sensors networks: research challenges. *Ad Hoc Networks Journal.*

Beniwal, M., & Singh, R. (2014). Localization techniques and their challenges in under water wireless sensor networks. *Proceedings of International Journal of Computer Science and Information Technologies*, *5*(3), 4706–4710.

Chandrasekhar, V., & Seah, W. K. G. (2006a). Localization in underwater sensor networks – survey and challenges. *Proceedings of IEEE conference*. IEEE.

Chandrasekhar, V., & Seah, W. K. G. (2006b). Area localization scheme for underwater sensor networks. *Proceedings of the IEEE OCEAN Asia Pacific Conference*. IEEE. 10.1109/OCEANSAP.2006.4393969

Chen, K., C., Y., & Jianhuan, H. (2009). A localization scheme of underwater wireless sensor networks. *Proceedings of International Journal of Advanced Science and Technology, 4*.

Cook, D. J., & Das, S. K. (2004). *Smart environments: technologies, protocols and applications*. John Wiley. doi:10.1002/047168659X

Garcia, J. (2005). Positioning of sensors in Underwater Acoustic Networks. *Proceedings of the MTS/IEEE OCEANS Conference*, Washington DC, USA. 10.1109/OCEANS.2005.1640068

Hahn, M., & Rice, J. (2005). *Undersea Navigation via a Distributed Acoustic Communication Network. Proceedings of the Turkish International Conference on Acoustics*, Istanbul, Turkey.

Heidemann, J., Li, Y., Syed, A., Wills, J., & Ye, W. (2006). Research Challenges and Applications For Underwater Sensor Networking. *Proceedings of the IEEE Wireless Communications and Networking Conference (WCNC2006)*. IEEE. 10.1109/WCNC.2006.1683469

Katiar, V., Chand, N., & Chauhan, N. (2010). Recent advances and future trends in wireless sensor networks. *Proceedings of International Journal of Applied Engineering Research, Dindigul, 1*(3).

Kay, R., & Mattern, F. (2004). The Design Space of Wireless Sensor Networks. *IEEE Wireless Communications, 11*(6), 54–61. doi:10.1109/MWC.2004.1368897

Ling, Q., Tian, Z., Yin, Y., & Li, Y. (2009). Localized structural health monitoring using energy efficient wireless sensor networks. *IEEE Sensors Journal, 9*(11), 1596–1604. doi:10.1109/JSEN.2009.2019318

Sohraby, K., Minoli, D., & Znati, T. (2007). *Wireless sensor networks: technology, protocols and applications*. John Wiley. doi:10.1002/047011276X

Chapter 13
Unveiling Earth's Rhythms:
Deep Learning Techniques for Forecasting Seismic Cycle Locations

Dhinakaran Damodaran
Vel Tech Rangarajan Dr. Sagunthala R&D Institute of Science and Technology, India

L. Srinivasan
Dr. N.G.P. Institute of Technology, India

R. Selvaraj
Dr. N.G.P. Institute of Technology, India

T. P. Anish
R.M.K. College of Engineering and Technology, India

ABSTRACT

The chapter presents a comprehensive exploration of deep learning techniques applied to seismic pattern recognition and forecasting, aiming to advance our understanding of earthquake behavior. Beginning with a brief overview of the seismic cycle and its significance, the narrative delves into the challenges associated with accurately predicting the locations of seismic cycles. The role of deep learning in revolutionizing seismic forecasting is then elucidated, emphasizing its capacity to predict beyond single seismic cycles and under diverse conditions. The chapter further provides a mathematical algorithm outlining the step-by-step process, from data collection to model training, adaptation, and continuous monitoring.

DOI: 10.4018/979-8-3693-2280-2.ch013

INTRODUCTION

The seismic cycle is a pivotal concept in seismology, embodying the intricate dynamics of Earth's crustal movements that culminate in the occurrence of earthquakes. This cyclic process is inherently linked to the broader framework of plate tectonics, where Earth's lithospheric plates continuously interact along their boundaries. These interactions can manifest as convergent collisions, divergent separations, or lateral sliding, setting the stage for stress accumulation within the Earth's crust (Jena et al., 2020). Over time, this stress builds up along faults and plate boundaries, deforming rocks and storing potential energy. The seismic cycle reaches its climax when the accumulated stress exceeds the strength of the rocks, resulting in a sudden release of energy through elastic rebound (Asim et al., 2018). This release, manifested as seismic waves, is the essence of an earthquake. Understanding the seismic cycle is crucial for deciphering earthquake behavior and enhancing our ability to predict and mitigate seismic hazards. By comprehending the patterns of stress accumulation, deformation, and energy release, scientists gain insights into the mechanisms underlying seismic events (Ganguly et al., 2019). This knowledge not only contributes to the development of more accurate earthquake forecasts but also aids in assessing the potential risks associated with specific tectonic regions. As societies strive to minimize the impact of earthquakes on human lives and infrastructure, unraveling the complexities of the seismic cycle stands as a foundational step towards achieving a more resilient and prepared global community.

Traditional Seismic Forecasting

Seismic forecasting is a critical aspect of understanding and preparing for potential earthquakes. The manual approach to seismic forecasting involves a series of interconnected steps where human expertise, historical data, and traditional methods play a central role as shown in Figure 1.

a. Seismic Data Collection

The process begins with the manual collection of seismic data using instruments such as seismometers. These devices are strategically placed to capture ground movements caused by seismic activities. The collected data is then recorded in manual logs, ensuring that all relevant information is documented accurately.

b. Data Inspection and Expert Input

Figure 1. Traditional seismic forecasting approach

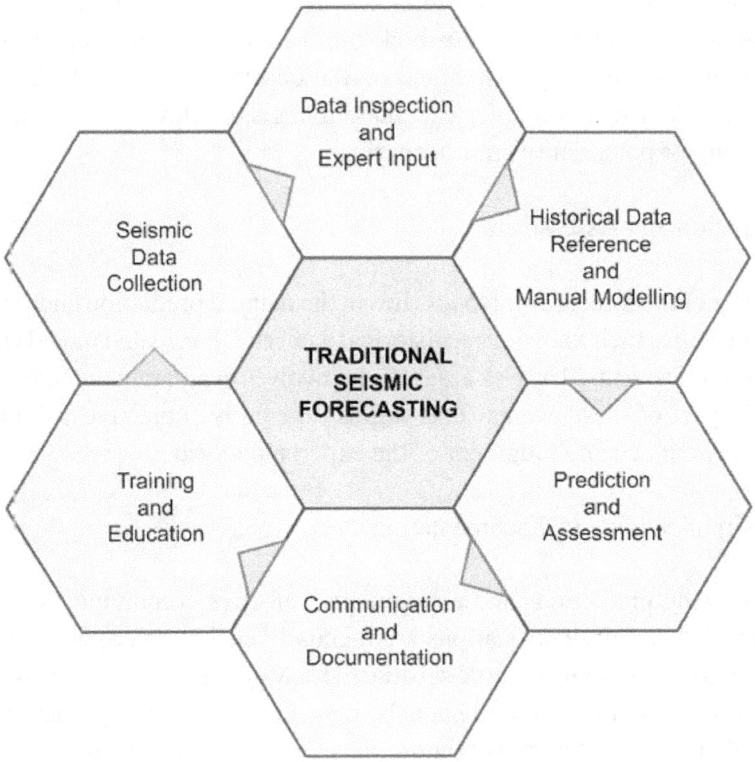

Once the data is collected, it undergoes a manual inspection process. This step involves visual examination and basic analysis using traditional tools. Seismic experts visually inspect patterns, magnitudes, and frequencies of recorded seismic events. Basic analysis tools aid in identifying anomalies or trends that may indicate potential seismic activity. Expert input is a crucial phase where geologists and seismologists provide their insights. Their expertise allows for a deeper understanding of the data and helps interpret subtle patterns that may not be evident through automated analysis. Geologist input and expert analysis contribute significantly to the accuracy of the forecasting process.

c. Historical Data Reference and Manual Modelling

The forecasting process relies on historical data as a reference point. Archives of past seismic events and databases containing information about earthquakes play a vital role. The manual forecasting approach acknowledges the importance of understanding historical seismic patterns and leveraging this knowledge to make predictions. In the manual modelling phase, experts create models based on geological knowledge and historical data. These models are often simple representations of how seismic activity might propagate based on the observed patterns. While this step lacks the complexity of computer-generated models, it allows for a more intuitive understanding of potential seismic scenarios.

d. Prediction and Assessment

The heart of the forecasting process lies in the manual prediction and assessment phase. Experts use their knowledge, historical data, and the created models to predict potential seismic events. The risk assessment involves evaluating the likelihood and potential impact of these events. This step is inherently subjective, relying on the collective experience and judgment of the experts involved.

e. Communication and Documentation

Upon making predictions and assessments, effective communication becomes paramount. Stakeholder notifications are manually crafted to ensure that relevant parties are informed about potential seismic risks. Manual alerts, often disseminated through various communication channels, play a crucial role in preparedness and response planning. The documentation phase involves the manual recording of findings, predictions, and actions taken. Detailed reports are generated, documenting the entire forecasting process. These manual reports serve as a valuable resource for future reference, analysis, and improvement of the forecasting methodology.

f. Training and Education

Recognizing the dynamic nature of seismic activities and the importance of continuous improvement, the process includes a component for training and education. This phase involves ongoing training programs for personnel involved in the forecasting process. Educational resources are developed to keep experts abreast of the latest developments in seismology and forecasting techniques.

The manual seismic forecasting process represents a holistic and human-centric approach to understanding and predicting seismic events. While it lacks the computational power of automated systems, it compensates with the depth of human expertise and a nuanced understanding of geological processes. The emphasis on historical data, expert input, and effective communication ensures that communities are adequately prepared for potential seismic risks.

Challenges in Traditional Seismic Forecasting

Accurately predicting the locations of seismic cycles confronts formidable challenges rooted in the intricate dynamics of Earth's geophysical processes. The heterogeneous nature of the Earth's crust and mantle, characterized by varying compositions and structures, complicates efforts to model the precise paths of seismic waves. Fault systems, the epicenters of most earthquakes, exhibit complex geometries and interactions that defy straightforward prediction. The temporal variability of seismic cycles introduces an additional layer of complexity, as stress accumulation rates vary across different tectonic regions and predicting the specific timing of stress release becomes inherently uncertain.

The challenge is further exacerbated by incomplete and unevenly distributed data. Remote or deep-sea regions often lack sufficient geological and seismic data, impeding the development of comprehensive predictive models (Prochazka et al., 2021). Human and technological limitations also play a role, as the monitoring of seismic activity is constrained by resource availability and logistical challenges. Real-time, precise measurements of stress changes along fault lines remain elusive, hindered by both technological constraints and financial considerations. Additionally, the nonlinear nature of Earth's processes introduces inherent uncertainties. Seismic events can set off complex feedback loops and cascading effects, amplifying the challenge of forecasting the full extent of their impact. Furthermore, the influence of aftershocks, which may occur unpredictably and alter stress distributions, adds an additional layer of complexity to accurate seismic predictions. Overcoming these multifaceted challenges requires innovative approaches, advanced technologies, and interdisciplinary collaboration to advance our understanding of the seismic cycle and enhance the accuracy of earthquake forecasts.

This chapter investigates the limitations of current seismic prediction techniques through a series of case studies, unveiling challenges that hinder their accuracy and reliability. One focal point is the issue of incomplete data coverage, showcasing instances where sparse or inadequately collected seismic data compromises the effectiveness of conventional methods. Additionally, the complexity of fault systems emerges as a significant challenge, surpassing the capabilities of existing models. The temporal variability of seismic activity, unforeseen aperiodic events, human-related factors, and the struggle with robust feature extraction from seismic data further highlight the deficiencies in current techniques. By scrutinizing these real-world scenarios, this exploration aims to emphasize the need for more adaptive and innovative approaches in seismic prediction, paving the way for enhanced forecasting capabilities.

THE RISE OF DEEP LEARNING (DL) IN SEISMOLOGY

Deep learning has arisen as a transformative force in revolutionizing seismic forecasting, offering novel approaches to address the inherent complexities of predicting earthquake occurrences. Unlike traditional methods that rely on manual feature extraction and predefined models, deep learning leverages neural networks to automatically learn and discern intricate patterns within seismic data. This paradigm shift has significantly enhanced the precision and efficiency of seismic forecasting in several key ways. One crucial aspect is the ability of deep learning models to handle the vast and complex datasets associated with seismic activity. The intricate interplay of geological features, fault systems, and historical seismic events is effectively processed and analyzed by deep neural networks, which excel at capturing subtle patterns and non-linear relationships within the data. This capability enables a more comprehensive understanding of the seismic cycle, contributing to improved predictive models. Moreover, deep learning excels in feature learning, allowing models to autonomously identify relevant patterns and extract essential information from raw seismic data. This automated feature extraction reduces the reliance on human expertise and enhances the adaptability of models to diverse geological settings. The result is a more robust and versatile seismic forecasting framework capable of accommodating the intricacies of different tectonic regions.

Deep learning's prowess extends to real-time monitoring and early detection of seismic anomalies. The ability to process data rapidly enables timely identification of precursory signals and the potential for more accurate earthquake predictions. This holds significant implications for disaster preparedness and response, providing valuable lead time for implementing preventive measures and minimizing the impact of seismic events on communities. Deep learning designs, such as recurrent neural networks (RNNs) along with convolutional neural networks (CNNs), are versatile, allows for the integration of various data modalities, such as satellite imagery, geophysical measurements, and historical seismic records. This holistic approach facilitates a more comprehensive understanding of the factors influencing seismic activity and enhances the accuracy of location-specific forecasts.

In essence, deep learning stands as a revolutionary tool in seismic forecasting, leveraging its ability to autonomously learn complex patterns, handle vast datasets, and provide real-time insights. As this technology continues to evolve, it holds the promise of transforming our capacity to predict and mitigate the impact of seismic events, ultimately contributing to a more resilient and prepared global community. Laura Laurenti et al. (2022) revolutionizes seismic forecasting using deep learning (DL). Demonstrating DL's superiority over traditional ML, the research excels in predicting labquakes, including time to start and end of failure, even with limited training data (Laurenti et al., 2022). Remarkably, DL models consistently forecast the end of failure across all seismic cycles. The study unveils DL's adaptability to varied conditions, encompassing pre-seismic creep as well as alternating slow/fast events. Furthermore, it establishes a link between acoustic energy and fault zone stress, showcasing DL's potential to predict stress evolution. Introducing AutoRegressive methods for fault stress forecasting, the research signifies a paradigm shift in seismic prediction, advancing disaster preparedness. (Kelian et al., 2023) unveil the Recurrent Earthquake foreCAST (RECAST), a cutting-edge deep-learning model built on the latest advancements in neural temporal point processes. Addressing the limitations of traditional approaches, RECAST provides unprecedented access to a diverse array of earthquake observations, transcending theoretical and computational constraints (Svetnik et al., 2003). The study conducts rigorous benchmarks against a temporal Epidemic Type Aftershock Sequence model, showcasing RECAST's superiority. Synthetic data tests affirm RECAST's ability to accurately model earthquake-like point processes, even with modest-sized datasets. This innovation holds promise for revolutionizing seismic event modeling and advancing our understanding of earthquake dynamics.

Neural network architectures play a crucial role in seismic cycle prediction, offering powerful tools to analyze complex patterns and temporal dependencies within seismic data. RNNs are well-suited for modeling sequential data, making them effective for capturing the temporal aspects of seismic cycles. Their ability to maintain memory of previous inputs allows them to consider the entire seismic history, providing valuable context for predictions. An example of an RNN that is intended to handle the vanishing gradient issue is the Long Short-Term Memory Network (LSTM), which makes it possible to recognize dependencies that persist in time-series data. In seismic cycle prediction, LSTMs excel at learning and remembering patterns over extended periods, enhancing the model's ability to forecast seismic events. Similar to LSTMs, Gated Recurrent Units (GRUs) are another variant of RNNs that excel in modelling sequential data. They are computationally more efficient than LSTMs, making them suitable for seismic cycle prediction tasks where large datasets and complex temporal dependencies are involved. (Dost Muhammad et al., 2023) redefine seismic activity prediction as a binary classification challenge (Muhammad et al., 2023). They introduce a novel deep neural network architecture trained on historical seismic data from Chile, Hindukush, and Southern California. The research involves a meticulous data cleaning process and subsequent feature engineering, incorporating insights from various seismic laws to enhance predictive capabilities. The proposed model's performance is rigorously evaluated, benchmarked against conventional techniques like random forest -RF, support vector machine - SVM, and logistic regression. This study marks a significant stride in leveraging deep learning for improved seismic activity prediction, promising advancements in earthquake risk assessment.

Convolutional Neural Networks (CNNs), widely known for image processing, can be adapted for seismic cycle prediction by treating seismic data as a type of image. By applying convolutional layers, CNNs can capture spatial patterns and relationships within the seismic data, making them effective for tasks like earthquake detection and localization. Transformer networks have shown promise in seismic cycle prediction. Their self-attention mechanisms allow them to capture global dependencies in the data, making them effective for analyzing seismic events across different time scales and regions. Autoencoders, consisting of an encoder and decoder, are used for dimensionality reduction and feature extraction. In seismic cycle prediction, they can help uncover latent representations within the data, facilitating the identification of relevant features and patterns. (Geoffrey et al., 2023) conduct a comprehensive review of prior earthquake nowcasting methods and introduce novel approaches grounded in deep learning. Three different models are described, all based on transformers as well as recurrent neural networks (Fox et al., 2022). The study examines several metrics and observables, showing encouraging preliminary findings for Southern California from 1950 to 2020. Using the Nash Sutcliffe Efficiency measure, the study predicts seismic activity over 0.1-degree geographical bins for a range of periods, from two weeks to four years. Overall quality is assessed. The software and preprocessed data from the USGS are made available as open-source, fostering collaboration and advancing seismic prediction methodologies. Combining different neural network architectures in hybrid models can leverage the strengths of each. For example, combining an LSTM for temporal dependencies with a CNN for spatial features may enhance the overall predictive capabilities for seismic cycles (Dascher-Cousineau et al., 2023). These neural network architectures offer a diverse set of tools for seismic cycle prediction, and the choice often depends on the specific characteristics of the seismic data and the nature of the prediction task at hand.

DEEP LEARNING (DL) IN SEISMOLOGY

The proposed system architecture for Deep Learning (DL) in Seismology is designed to provide a comprehensive framework for the analysis, prediction, and understanding of seismic activities. This detailed component diagram outlines the key elements and their interactions within the system, highlighting the intricacies involved in processing seismic data, training neural network models, and delivering real-time predictions as shown in Figure 2. Each component plays a crucial role in addressing specific challenges associated with seismic cycle prediction, offering a holistic approach to seismic event analysis.

Figure 2. Deep learning (DL) in seismology prediction

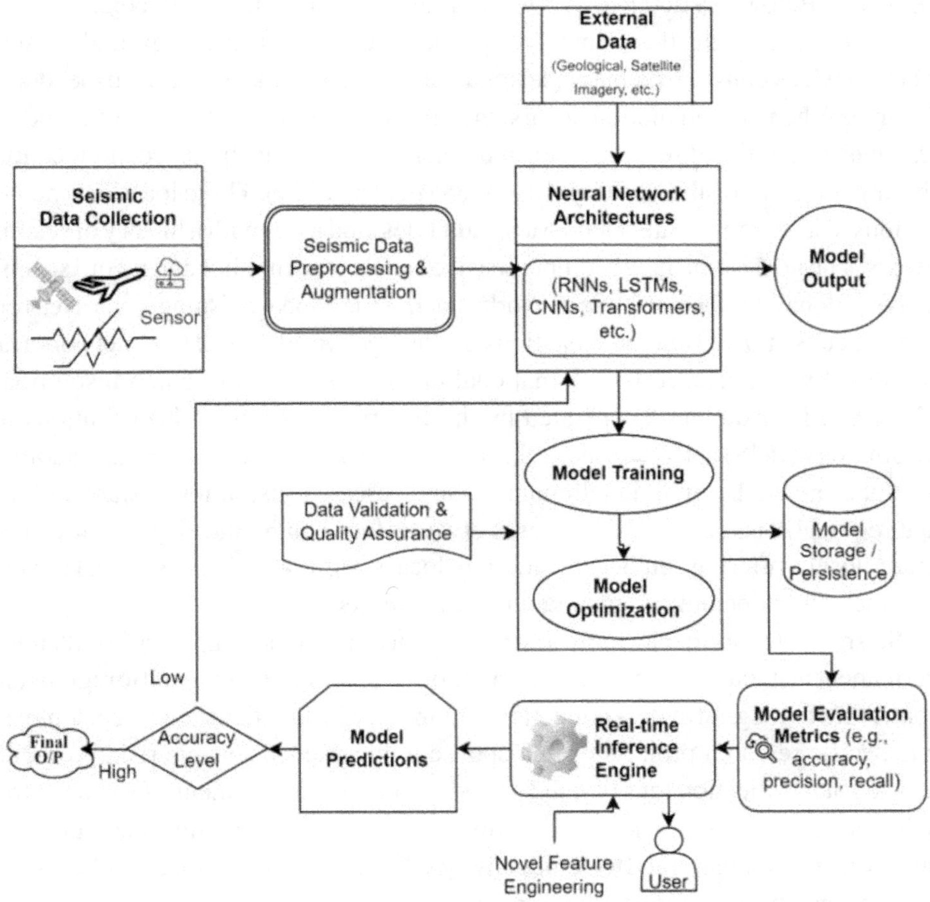

Seismic Data Collection

At the core of the system lies the Seismic Data component, representing the raw data collected from seismic sensors distributed across various regions. This seismic data serves as the foundational input for the entire system, capturing ground motion and seismic events in real-time. The quality and richness of this data influence the effectiveness of subsequent components, emphasizing the significance of robust data collection mechanisms. Seismic data collection is a fundamental step in understanding the Earth's subsurface and predicting seismic events. It involves the deployment of specialized instruments called seismometers or seismographs to detect and record ground motion caused by seismic waves. The process is intricate, involving strategic sensor placement, continuous monitoring, and global collaboration through seismic networks. Below is a detailed overview of how seismic data is collected:

Seismometers are the primary instruments used to measure ground motion. These devices consist of a mass (seismic mass or seismometer mass) suspended in a frame. When ground motion occurs, the relative motion between the mass and the frame is detected and recorded. Seismometers are strategically placed in locations that are prone to seismic activity (Llenos & Michael, 2019). These locations include regions near tectonic plate boundaries, fault lines, and areas with a history of seismic events. The goal is to achieve comprehensive coverage to monitor and record seismic activity globally. Global seismic networks, such as the Global Seismographic Network (GSN), consist of seismometer stations distributed worldwide. These networks are collaboratively managed by international organizations and research institutions. The GSN, for example, is operated by the Incorporated Research Institutions for Seismology (IRIS) and spans the globe, providing real-time seismic data. In addition to global networks, individual countries and research institutions establish local and regional seismic networks. These networks focus on monitoring specific areas more closely, offering detailed insights into local seismic activities. National seismic agencies often operate and maintain these networks.

Seismometers are deployed as both permanent fixtures and temporary installations. Permanent installations continuously monitor seismic activity in specific regions and contribute to long-term data collection. Temporary installations are often deployed for specific research projects or in response to heightened seismic risk, providing focused data collection for a defined period. In marine environments, Ocean Bottom Seismometers (OBS) are deployed on the seafloor to capture seismic data related to underwater earthquakes and tectonic activity. OBS devices are equipped with pressure and motion sensors to detect seismic waves underwater. Satellite-based technologies contribute to monitoring ground deformation caused by seismic activity. Synthetic Aperture Radar (SAR) and Interferometric Synthetic Aperture Radar (InSAR) are used to detect surface displacement associated with earthquakes. These technologies provide valuable data, especially in remote or inaccessible regions. Once seismometers detect ground motion, the recorded data is transmitted to data centers or processing facilities. Data transmission methods vary and include wired or wireless networks, satellite communication, and internet-based platforms. Real-time data transmission is crucial for timely monitoring and response to seismic events.

Seismic data collection involves collaboration among various entities, including national and international seismic monitoring agencies, research institutions, and the broader scientific community. Data sharing is a key aspect, and many seismic networks make their data openly accessible to researchers, fostering global collaboration and enhancing the quality of seismic research. Seismic data collection is a continuous process. Seismometers operate around the clock, providing an uninterrupted stream of data (Mousavi et al., 2020). Continuous monitoring is essential for capturing both regular seismic activity and unusual events, contributing to a comprehensive understanding of the Earth's dynamic processes. Quality control measures are implemented to ensure the accuracy and reliability of collected seismic data. Calibration processes are employed to maintain the precision of seismometer instruments, ensuring that recorded ground motion accurately reflects seismic events.

Seismic Data Preprocessing and Augmentation

Seismic data preprocessing and augmentation are critical steps in preparing raw seismic data for effective use in deep learning models. These processes involve various techniques to enhance the quality, consistency, and diversity of the data, allowing neural network architectures to learn and generalize patterns accurately. Below is a detailed explanation of how seismic data is preprocessed and augmented:

a. Data Preprocessing

The initial step in preprocessing involves data cleaning, addressing potential issues such as noise, outliers, or artifacts in the raw seismic data as shown in Figure 3. This may include filtering out sensor anomalies, correcting for instrumental errors, and removing any interference that could compromise the accuracy of subsequent analyses. Seismic signals often contain a broad frequency range, and filtering is employed to focus on specific frequency bands relevant to seismic events. High-pass and low-pass filters may be applied to isolate seismic signals of interest while reducing noise and irrelevant frequencies. Seismic data from different sensors or locations may experience time lags due to variations in signal propagation (Mancini et al., 2022). Time alignment is performed to synchronize the data, ensuring that seismic events are accurately represented concerning their temporal relationships. To facilitate model training and convergence, seismic data is often scaled and normalized. Scaling ensures that data values fall within a consistent range, preventing certain features from dominating the learning process. Normalization adjusts data distribution to a standard form, aiding in model stability and convergence.

Figure 3. Seismic data preprocessing

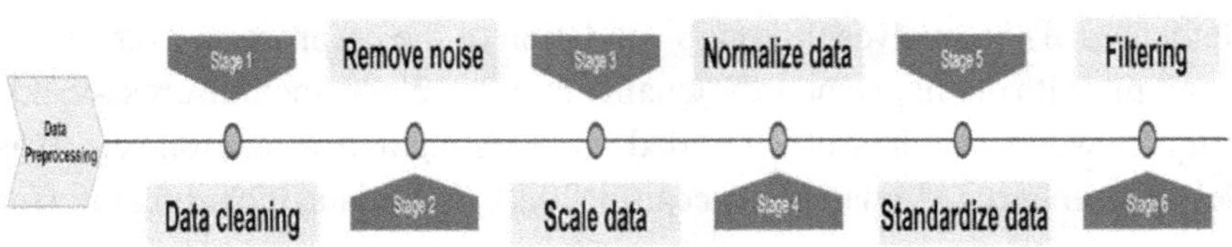

b. Data Augmentation

Data augmentation is a key technique to increase the diversity of the dataset, allowing the model to generalize better to different scenarios. Augmentation techniques include random rotations, flips, shifts, and changes in amplitude as shown in Figure 4. For seismic data, time-domain augmentations, such as time warping or time stretching, may also be applied to introduce variations.

Figure 4. Seismic data augmentation

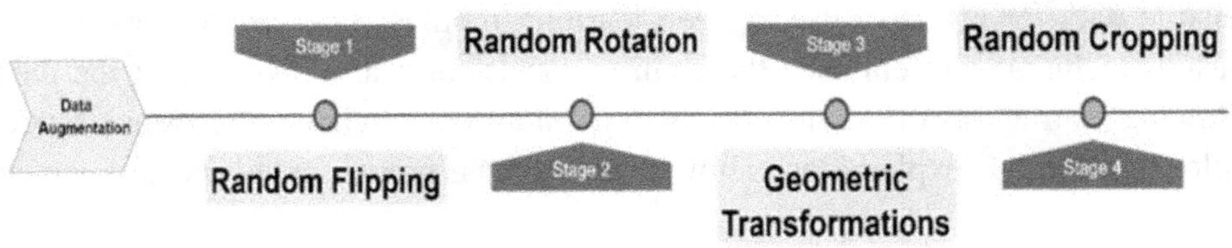

In some cases, especially when the available seismic data is limited, synthetic data generation techniques may be employed. This involves creating artificial seismic signals based on the characteristics of real seismic events. Synthetic data can supplement the training dataset, providing the model with a broader range of examples.

c. Feature Extraction and Handling Imbalanced Data

Extracting relevant features from the seismic data is crucial for deep learning models. This involves identifying distinctive patterns, frequency components, and other relevant information. Time-domain and frequency-domain features, such as amplitude, frequency, and energy, are commonly extracted to provide the model with discriminative information. Seismic datasets may exhibit imbalances, where certain classes of seismic events are underrepresented. To address this, preprocessing techniques may involve oversampling minority classes, undersampling majority classes, or employing advanced methods like Synthetic Minority Over-sampling Technique (SMOTE) to balance the dataset.

Before proceeding with model training, quality assurance measures are implemented. This involves thorough validation of the preprocessed data to ensure that it aligns with quality standards. Quality assurance may include cross-validation techniques, where the dataset is divided into training and validation sets to assess model performance (Mignan & Broccardo, 2020). Metadata, including information about the seismic sensors, geographical coordinates, and environmental conditions, can enhance the contextual understanding of the data. Integrating metadata during preprocessing provides additional context for the deep learning model, improving its ability to discern patterns related to specific sensor characteristics or geographical locations. It is common practice to divide the preprocessed dataset into training, validation, and testing sets. The validation set aids in adjusting hyperparameters & preventing overfitting, the testing set assesses the model's efficacy on unobserved data, and the training data set is utilized to train the mathematical model. Proper data splitting is essential for unbiased model evaluation.

External Data

The "External Data" component plays a pivotal role in enhancing the richness and contextual depth of the seismic data used in deep learning models. Complementing the raw seismic data, external data sources bring additional layers of information from various domains, offering a more holistic perspective on the seismic environment. Here's an elaborate explanation of how external data is integrated and its impact on the overall understanding of seismic events:

Geological data encompasses information about the Earth's subsurface composition, including details about different rock layers, fault lines, and structural features. By integrating geological data into the seismic analysis, the model gains insights into the underlying geological characteristics of the region. This can be crucial for understanding how seismic waves propagate through different geological formations, influencing the pattern and intensity of seismic events. Satellite imagery provides a visual representation of the Earth's surface and can offer valuable contextual information related to seismic activities. High-resolution satellite images capture features such as land cover, topography, and changes in surface conditions over time. Integrating satellite imagery allows the model to correlate seismic events with specific geographical features, identifying areas of interest and potential risk factors. Beyond geological and satellite data, contextual data from various sources, such as climate databases, land use records, or historical seismic records, can contribute additional dimensions to the analysis. Understanding the broader environmental context allows the model to account for external factors that may influence seismic behavior, such as seasonal variations, human activities, or historical seismic patterns.

Information about the seismic sensors themselves, including their specifications, calibration data, and deployment locations, is a form of external data that enriches the feature space (Ogata, 2017). This metadata provides insights into the sensor characteristics, helping the model adapt to variations in data quality and sensor-specific behaviors. It also aids in understanding how different sensors contribute to the overall seismic data. External data with timestamps, such as weather conditions, solar radiation levels, or other time-dependent variables, can be integrated into the analysis. Time-stamped contextual information allows the model to correlate seismic events with specific temporal patterns, enabling it to capture variations influenced by time-dependent external factors. External data sources often come from diverse disciplines such as geophysics, meteorology, and geography. Cross-disciplinary data fusion involves combining information from these disparate sources to create a more comprehensive and multidimensional dataset. This approach facilitates a holistic understanding of the complex interplay between geological, environmental, and atmospheric factors influencing seismic events.

The integration of external data contributes to feature engineering, where new features are created to capture relationships and interactions between different data sources. For example, combining seismic data with geological information might lead to the creation of features representing the geological composition of specific regions during seismic events. The enrichment of the feature space through external data enables neural network models to generalize more effectively. Models trained on a diverse dataset that includes information from various sources are better equipped to adapt to unseen scenarios, enhancing their predictive capabilities and reducing the risk of overfitting to specific patterns present in the training data. External data contributes to a more nuanced spatial and temporal understanding of seismic events. By incorporating information about the Earth's surface, environmental conditions, and historical seismic records, the model gains a broader context for interpreting the patterns and dynamics associated with seismic activities.

Data Validation and Quality Assurance

Ensuring the reliability and accuracy of the prepared dataset is paramount. The Data Validation & Quality Assurance component validates the preprocessed seismic data, checking for inconsistencies, outliers, and ensuring that the dataset adheres to quality standards. This component plays a pivotal role in maintaining the integrity of the training dataset, ultimately influencing the efficacy of the trained models.

Exploring Deep Learning Models for Seismic Data

The application of deep learning models, including RNNs, LSTMs, CNNs, and Transformers, is integral to capturing intricate patterns and temporal dependencies within seismic data. Each of these architectures possesses unique strengths that make them well-suited for the complexities inherent in seismic cycle prediction:

a. Recurrent Neural Networks (RNNs)

RNNs are excellent for situations where events occur gradually because they are specifically made for dealing with information in succession. In seismic data analysis, temporal dynamics play a crucial role, as seismic events involve a sequence of changes in ground motion and stress buildup. RNNs are adept at capturing patterns and dependencies within such sequential data (Tan et al., 2021). The hallmark of RNNs is the concept of a hidden state, a dynamic internal memory that evolves as the model processes each element in the sequence. The hidden state retains information from previous time steps, creating a form of memory that allows the model to consider the context of the entire sequence when analyzing a specific point in time. In seismic data analysis, temporal dependencies are crucial for understanding the evolution of events over time. RNNs excel at capturing these dependencies by inherently linking the information from previous time steps to the current one. This capability allows the model to discern patterns related to the build-up and release of stress along fault lines, seismic wave propagation, and other temporal aspects of seismic cycles.

Seismic data is inherently sequential, representing a timeline of ground motion measurements. RNNs leverage this sequential nature by treating each data point not in isolation but as part of a sequence. This treatment enables the model to understand the contextual relationships between adjacent time steps, providing a more nuanced understanding of the seismic events' progression. Seismic events, including earthquakes, often involve the gradual buildup of stress along fault lines followed by sudden releases. RNNs are well-suited to model such stress dynamics. The hidden state in RNNs captures the evolving stress information, allowing the model to discern patterns associated with stress accumulation and its subsequent release, which are critical aspects of seismic cycle prediction. RNNs use a training mechanism known as Backpropagation Through Time (BPTT). BPTT extends the backpropagation algorithm to sequences, allowing the model to learn and adjust its parameters based on the error signals propagated through time. This mechanism is essential for the effective training of RNNs on sequential data like seismic measurements.

One of the challenges that RNNs confront is the problem of the gradient that disappears, characterized by gradients decreasing as they are backpropagated via protracted sequences. This limitation might affect the model's ability to find long-term dependencies in seismic data. Advanced RNN variants, such as LSTMs, address this issue by introducing memory cells. RNNs are flexible and can adapt to varying sequence lengths, making them suitable for seismic data that may have irregular intervals between measurements. This adaptability allows the model to handle real-world scenarios where seismic events may exhibit different temporal patterns. RNNs are often integrated into hybrid architectures, combining them with other neural network types like LSTMs, CNNs, or Transformers. Such hybrid models leverage the strengths of each architecture, offering a more comprehensive approach to capturing diverse features and patterns within seismic data (van der Elst et al., 2022). RNNs are capable of real-time inference, making them valuable for applications where the model needs to make predictions as new seismic data becomes available. This is particularly relevant for monitoring and early warning systems where timely predictions are crucial.

b. Long Short-Term Memory networks (LSTMs)

LSTMs are a specialized type of RNN designed to tackle the vanishing gradient problem. They were introduced to overcome the difficulties associated with learning long-term dependencies in sequential data, making them particularly effective in domains like seismic data analysis. LSTMs introduce a novel architectural element called a memory cell. This cell can store and update information over long sequences, enabling the network to retain relevant details about the input sequence. This mechanism is crucial for capturing the prolonged impact of events in seismic cycles. An input gate, an outcome gate, and a forget gate are among the gates used by LSTMs. The information that enters and exits the memory cell is controlled by these gates. The output gate regulates what data will stream to the following time step; the gate to forget chooses what to remove from the cell's memory, whereas the input gate chooses which details to preserve.

The unique design of LSTMs allows them to store information over multiple time steps without suffering from the vanishing gradient problem. This sequential memory storage capability is crucial for capturing long-term dependencies in seismic data, where events leading up to an earthquake may unfold over an extended duration. In seismic data analysis, where gradual changes may precede a seismic event, LSTMs excel at remembering relevant information over time. This includes recognizing patterns associated with stress buildup along fault lines, changes in ground motion, and other indicators of seismic activity. LSTMs exhibit flexibility in handling sequences of varying lengths and irregular intervals, making them suitable for seismic data that may not adhere to fixed time intervals. This adaptability is crucial in real-world scenarios where seismic events do not necessarily conform to predefined patterns.

Seismic cycles often involve gradual changes in stress and ground motion leading up to an event. LSTMs are adept at capturing these gradual changes by maintaining a memory of the evolving patterns (Abadi et al., 2016). This is valuable for predicting the occurrence of seismic events and understanding the dynamic nature of seismic cycles. By addressing the vanishing gradient problem, LSTMs contribute to reducing prediction uncertainty in seismic data analysis. The model's ability to capture long-term dependencies enhances its overall performance in recognizing seismic patterns and making accurate predictions. LSTMs are often integrated into hybrid architectures, combining them with other neural network types like RNNs, CNNs, or Transformers. This synergistic approach leverages the strengths of each architecture, offering a comprehensive framework for capturing diverse features and patterns within seismic data. LSTMs find operational significance in real-world applications, especially in monitoring and early warning systems. Their ability to capture long-term dependencies is crucial for providing timely predictions and alerts related to seismic events. Ongoing advancements in LSTM variants and related architectures continue to improve their effectiveness in addressing challenges specific to seismic data analysis. Researchers explore variations and enhancements to further optimize the performance of LSTMs in capturing complex patterns associated with seismic cycles.

c. Convolutional Neural Networks (CNNs)

CNNs demonstrate prowess in image processing, and their application to seismic data analysis involves representing seismic data as spectrograms or images. Spectrograms provide a visual representation of the frequency content of seismic signals over time, and CNNs are adept at extracting hierarchical features and spatial patterns from these representations. CNNs are composed of convolutional layers that apply filters or kernels to local regions of the input data. These filters capture low-level features in the early layers and progressively build hierarchical representations in deeper layers. In the context of seismic data, these features could correspond to specific frequency components or temporal patterns. Convolutional operations generate feature maps that highlight relevant patterns within the input data. Through multiple convolutional layers, CNNs learn to recognize increasingly complex spatial features, allowing them to capture nuanced characteristics present in seismic cycles.

Seismic data often exhibits distinctive waveforms associated with different types of events. CNNs excel at identifying these spatial patterns, allowing them to recognize seismic signals indicative of specific seismic activities. For instance, the pattern associated with an impending earthquake or fault activation may be spatially encoded in the seismic data, and CNNs are adept at discerning these patterns. The subsurface structure can influence seismic waves, leading to spatial patterns in the recorded data. CNNs are effective at capturing these structural features, which may include fault lines, geological formations, or variations in material properties. Identifying these features contributes to a deeper understanding of the subsurface dynamics and aids in forecasting seismic cycle locations.

CNNs are typically trained in a supervised learning paradigm, where labelled seismic data is used to teach the model to associate specific spatial patterns with corresponding seismic events or cycle phases. The model adapts its parameters during training to effectively identify and distinguish these patterns. Transfer learning, leveraging pre-trained CNN models on large image datasets, can be applied to seismic data analysis. Pre-trained models, such as those trained on natural images, can capture generic spatial features and be fine-tuned for specific seismic patterns (Field et al., 2017). This approach is particularly useful when labelled seismic data is limited. CNNs leverage their ability to recognize spatial patterns to forecast seismic cycle locations. By learning the spatial characteristics associated with specific phases of seismic cycles, these models can predict the locations where certain events, such as earthquakes or fault activations, are likely to occur.

While CNNs primarily focus on spatial patterns, the incorporation of temporal aspects is crucial for forecasting seismic cycle locations. This can be achieved by combining CNNs with recurrent layers or integrating temporal information through other means, ensuring that the model considers the evolving nature of seismic events. CNNs, particularly when integrated into real-time monitoring systems, contribute to the operational significance of forecasting seismic cycle locations. Their ability to rapidly analyze spatial patterns in incoming seismic data makes them valuable for providing timely alerts and predictions, supporting early warning systems. The effectiveness of CNNs in forecasting seismic cycle locations is contingent on the quality of input data. Proper preprocessing, including noise reduction, filtering, and normalization, is crucial to ensure that the model focuses on relevant spatial patterns. While CNNs excel at capturing spatial features, their inner workings may lack interpretability. Understanding how the model identifies specific spatial patterns in seismic data is an ongoing challenge that researchers are addressing through techniques such as visualization and explainable AI.

e. Transformers

Transformers, initially designed for natural language processing tasks, have showcased remarkable versatility, finding applications in diverse domains, including seismic analysis. Because of their self-attention mechanism-based architecture, they are very good at identifying complicated trends in sequential data. One important component of transformer architecture is the self-attention mechanism. It allows the model to focus on different segments of the input sequence and give those pieces different weights. This mechanism proves crucial in capturing complex relationships within the data. In seismic data analysis, certain time intervals may hold more significance than others. Transformers adapt by leveraging their attention mechanism to selectively focus on specific segments of the data, capturing nuanced temporal dynamics associated with seismic events. This adaptability is particularly beneficial when modelling complex seismic behaviors.

Transformers, through their attention mechanism, capture the interactions between different segments of seismic data. This is essential for understanding how various phases of a seismic cycle influence each other. For instance, the buildup of stress in one phase may impact the subsequent release of energy, and transformers excel at capturing these intricate interactions. Unlike traditional architectures, transformers provide a dynamic understanding of time in sequential data. The model can assign varying weights to different time steps based on the context of the entire sequence. This is crucial in seismic analysis, where the temporal dynamics of events play a significant role. Seismic events often exhibit variability in their temporal dynamics. Transformers are well-suited to handle this variability by adaptively adjusting their attention across different time intervals. This capability is particularly valuable for modelling complex seismic events with varying patterns, such as the buildup and release of stress along fault lines.

Transformers, unlike architectures that process data sequentially, can capture global dependencies within the entire sequence simultaneously. This global contextual understanding is advantageous in seismic analysis, where the influence of specific events may extend over a broader time span, impacting subsequent phases of the seismic cycle. Transformers often employ multi-head attention, allowing the model to consider multiple perspectives or representations of the input sequence simultaneously. This enhances the model's ability to capture diverse aspects of temporal dynamics within seismic data, leading to a more comprehensive understanding of seismic events. Transformers integrate positional encodings to preserve the temporal information of input sequences. This is crucial for maintaining the chronological order of events in seismic data. The combination of self-attention and positional encodings enables transformers to effectively process time-sensitive information. While transformers exhibit remarkable capabilities, challenges such as data efficiency and interpretability persist. Optimizing transformer models for effective use with limited labelled seismic data and enhancing their interpretability remain areas of ongoing research.

Model Training Process

The training process involves presenting the deep learning models with labelled seismic data. The models learn to recognize patterns, features, and temporal dependencies during this phase. The inherent architecture of each model type determines how it processes and captures these aspects:

RNNs and LSTMs: These models unfold over time, with each time step influencing the hidden state, allowing the model to remember and learn from the sequential nature of seismic events.

CNNs: Convolutional layers scan through the spatial representations of seismic data, detecting relevant features and patterns. These could include distinctive seismic waveforms or spatial structures that contribute to the understanding of seismic cycles.

Transformers: Transformers excel at capturing dependencies between different parts of the input sequence. In seismic data, this enables them to identify the relationships between various temporal segments, offering a nuanced understanding of the temporal dynamics associated with seismic events.

a. Nuanced Characteristics of Seismic Cycles

The deep learning models, through their inherent architectures and training processes, are capable of capturing nuanced characteristics of seismic cycles:

Temporal Dependencies: RNNs and LSTMs explicitly model temporal dependencies, allowing them to understand how seismic events evolve over time. This is crucial for predicting the timing and progression of seismic cycles.

Spatial Patterns: CNNs excel at capturing spatial patterns in seismic data, identifying features that may indicate specific geological structures or seismic waveforms. This contributes to a more detailed understanding of the spatial aspects of seismic cycles.

Interactions between Temporal Segments: Transformers, by focusing on interactions between different segments of the input sequence, can capture how various phases of a seismic cycle influence each other. This is particularly relevant for events with complex temporal dynamics.

Challenges and Considerations: While these deep learning models showcase remarkable capabilities, challenges exist, such as data scarcity, imbalances, and the need for interpretability. Proper data preprocessing, feature engineering, and model evaluation are critical to overcoming these challenges and ensuring the robust performance of the models.

Model Training and Optimization

The prepared and validated dataset is fed into the Model Training & Optimization component, where neural network models are trained to recognize and predict seismic patterns. This process involves iterative training, backpropagation, and optimization techniques to enhance the models' ability to generalize and make accurate predictions. Fine-tuning parameters and optimizing the neural network architectures contribute to the overall efficacy of the predictive models. Iterative learning is a fundamental aspect of training neural network models, involving the repetitive exposure of the model to batches of data to refine its parameters and improve performance. This iterative process is crucial for the model to learn and adapt to the underlying patterns in the seismic data. Here's a detailed explanation of how iterative learning unfolds:

The process begins with initializing the neural network model. The model's architecture is defined, and the weights and biases are set to initial values. These initial parameters act as a starting point for the learning process. The dataset is presented in smaller batches rather than in its whole at once. Batching adds a stochastic component and facilitates memory management, which improves model generalization. Seismic data is supplied into the neural network batch by batch. During a forward pass, the model applies learned weights and biases to process the incoming data through its layers and provide seismic pattern predictions (Gutenberg & Richter, 1944). The actual labels of the seismic patterns in the batch are compared with the predictions. The disparity between the predictions and the true values is quantified using a chosen loss function. The loss represents how far off the model's predictions are from the actual seismic patterns.

Based on the calculated error, backpropagation is started for modifying the model's parameters. The gradients of the loss function are computed about the model's parameters. These gradients show the direction and size of the adjustment required to reduce the prediction error. The model's parameters are modified by an optimization technique, usually stochastic gradient descent (SGD) or one of its variations, using the obtained gradients. By iteratively decreasing the loss and enhancing the model's predictions, the goal is to shift the model's parameters in the gradient's opposite direction. For every batch of the dataset, the earlier steps are repeated. The dataset is repeatedly cycled through, resulting in an epoch. The number of times the neural network sees the complete dataset during training depends on the number of epochs. On a validation set, the model's effectiveness is tracked during the iterative learning process. In order to avert overfitting, early stopping can be used to end the training process if the performance of the model on the set of validation variables stops improving. A crucial technique used in every training cycle is called "backpropagation," or "backward propagation of errors," which modifies the model's parameters according to the calculated error.

a. Optimization Algorithm

Using Gradients for Optimization: The calculated gradients guide the optimization algorithm, such as SGD, in adjusting the model's parameters. The learning rate, a hyperparameter, determines the step size in the parameter space during each update.

Stochastic Gradient Descent (SGD): This commonly used optimization algorithm adjusts model parameters in the direction that minimizes the loss on each batch of data. Variants like mini-batch SGD and adaptive learning rate methods enhance convergence.

Adam, RMSprop: Adaptive learning rate algorithms like Adam and RMSprop dynamically adjust the learning rate during training, allowing the model to adapt to different gradients efficiently.

b. Hyperparameter Tuning

Learning Rate, Batch Size, Epochs: The total amount of training epochs, batch sizes, as well as learning levels are adjusted as hyperparameters. A grid search, random exploration, or more complex optimisation approaches are used to identify an ideal hyperparameter.

c. Regularization Techniques

Dropout, L1/L2 Regularization: Regularization techniques are applied to prevent overfitting. Dropout randomly drops neurons during training, and L1/L2 regularization adds penalties for large weights, promoting a more generalized model.

Model Storage/Persistence in Seismic Pattern Recognition

Once trained, the neural network models are stored and persisted in the Model Storage/Persistence component. This enables the reuse of well-trained models for subsequent analysis, real-time inference, or further refinement. Model storage is critical for maintaining a repository of effective models, contributing to the system's adaptability and scalability.

a. Purpose of Model Storage

After a neural network model has undergone the training and optimization phases, it becomes imperative to preserve its learned parameters, architecture, and configuration. Model storage, or persistence, serves as a repository for these well-trained models, ensuring their accessibility for subsequent analyses, real-time inference, or potential further refinement.

b. Components of Model Storage/Persistence

Weights and Parameters: The learned weights and biases, which encapsulate the knowledge acquired during training, are stored. These parameters define the synaptic strengths and interconnections within the neural network, forming the basis for its predictive capabilities.

Architecture Configuration: The architectural configuration of the neural network, including the number and arrangement of layers, activation functions, and any specialized components, is also stored. This information is crucial for accurately reconstructing the model during deployment.

Hyperparameters: Hyperparameters such as learning rates, batch sizes, and regularization parameters, which were fine-tuned during training, are saved. Preserving these hyperparameters is essential for replicating the training conditions when reusing the model.

c. Methods of Model Storage

File Storage: The simplest form of model storage involves saving the model parameters, architecture, and hyperparameters to files in a specified format. Common formats include HDF5, JSON, or other serialized representations. This allows for easy retrieval and reconstruction of the model.

Database Storage: In more complex systems, trained models can be stored in databases. This facilitates efficient organization, retrieval, and management of multiple models. It is particularly beneficial when dealing with a large number of models or in scenarios where models need to be dynamically selected for specific tasks.

Cloud Storage: With the increasing prevalence of cloud computing, models can be stored in cloud storage services. This enables easy access to models from different locations and allows for seamless integration into cloud-based applications or services.

d. Importance of Model Storage

Reusability: Storing well-trained models enables their reuse in various contexts. Once a model has demonstrated effectiveness in seismic pattern recognition, it can be employed for similar tasks without the need for retraining, saving computational resources and time.

Real-Time Inference: Stored models can be deployed for real-time inference, allowing the system to make predictions on new seismic data as it becomes available. This is crucial for applications requiring timely responses, such as earthquake monitoring or early warning systems.

Further Refinement: Stored models serve as a foundation for further refinement. If new labeled data becomes available or if there are updates to the seismic patterns of interest, the stored model can be used as a starting point for additional training and adaptation.

Scalability and Adaptability: Model storage contributes to the scalability and adaptability of the system. As the volume of seismic data grows or as new requirements emerge, having a repository of well-trained models allows for the dynamic selection of models that best suit the specific needs of the moment.

e. Security Considerations

Model Security: Depending on the sensitivity of the seismic data and the importance of the model in critical applications, security measures should be considered. This may involve encryption of stored models, access controls, and other strategies to safeguard the integrity and confidentiality of the stored neural network models.

Versioning: To track changes and improvements, model storage systems may incorporate versioning. This ensures that different iterations of a model are preserved, allowing for comparisons and the ability to revert to earlier versions if necessary.

f. Integration with Deployment Systems

Seamless Deployment: The stored models must integrate seamlessly with deployment systems, allowing for quick and efficient deployment in operational environments. Compatibility with inference engines, application programming interfaces (APIs), or other deployment mechanisms ensures that the stored models can be readily applied to new data.

g. Lifecycle Management

Model Lifecycle: Model storage contributes to the lifecycle management of neural network models. This involves tracking the model from its creation, through training and optimization, to deployment and potential retirement. Effective lifecycle management ensures the continuous relevance and performance of the stored models.

Real-Time Inference Engine and User Interface

The Real-time Inference Engine component is responsible for making predictions in real-time using the stored models. As new seismic data becomes available, the inference engine applies the trained models to generate predictions, allowing for immediate insights into ongoing seismic activities (Llenos & Michael, 2017). This component facilitates timely decision-making and emergency response in the face of seismic events. Interacting with the system, the User Interface component provides a platform for users to access and visualize the seismic predictions. This component may include dashboards, graphical representations, and interactive tools for users ranging from seismologists and researchers to emergency responders. The user interface serves as a bridge between the complex analytical processes within the system and end-users, fostering effective communication and decision-making.

Model Output (Predictions) in Seismic Pattern Recognition

The Model Output (Predictions) component represents the outcomes generated by the trained models during real-time inference. These predictions offer insights into potential seismic events, including their locations, magnitudes, and estimated time frames. The accuracy and reliability of these predictions are influenced by the effectiveness of the preceding components, emphasizing the importance of a well-orchestrated system.

Purpose of Model Output

Inference and Decision-Making: The Model Output (Predictions) component is the stage where the trained neural network models provide predictions based on new, unseen seismic data. These predictions serve as valuable insights into potential seismic events, aiding in decision-making processes related to earthquake monitoring, early warning systems, and seismic risk assessment.

Components of Model Output/Predictions

Predicted Labels: The primary output consists of the predicted labels assigned by the model to the input seismic data. These labels may include information about the type of seismic event, its location, magnitude, or other relevant parameters.

Probability Scores: For classification tasks, models often provide probability scores indicating the confidence level associated with each predicted label. This information can be crucial in assessing the reliability of predictions and understanding the uncertainty inherent in the model's decisions.

Regression Outputs: In tasks involving regression, such as predicting the magnitude or time frame of a seismic event, the model outputs continuous values providing quantitative estimates.

Real-Time Inference Process

During real-time inference, the Model Output component receives new seismic data as input. This data may come from ongoing monitoring systems, sensors, or other sources continuously providing updates. The trained neural network models, stored in the Model Storage component, are activated to process the incoming seismic data. The architecture, parameters, and learned patterns guide the model's decision-making process. The model processes the input data and generates predictions based on its learned patterns. These predictions encompass various aspects of seismic events, such as their locations, magnitudes, or time frames (Mancini et al., 2022). The predictions are then delivered as output, providing actionable information to stakeholders involved in seismic monitoring and response. This output may be disseminated through visualization tools, dashboards, alerts, or other communication channels.

Influencing Factors on Prediction Accuracy

The accuracy of predictions is heavily influenced by the quality of training data and the effectiveness of the training process. Well-labeled and diverse training data contribute to models that generalize better to unseen seismic patterns. The chosen neural network architecture, including the number of layers, types of layers, and activation functions, plays a crucial role in determining the model's ability to capture complex patterns in seismic data. The hyperparameters configured during training, such as learning rates and regularization parameters, impact the model's convergence and generalization abilities, affecting the accuracy of real-time predictions. The quality of the new seismic data fed into the model during real-time inference is critical. Anomalies or noise in the data can impact the model's ability to make accurate predictions. The interpretability of the model's decisions is essential for understanding the reasoning behind predictions. Transparent models can provide insights into the features influencing predictions and enhance confidence in the model's reliability.

Decision Support and Actionability

The Model Output component serves as an information source for stakeholders involved in earthquake monitoring and response. Predictions inform decision-makers about the potential occurrence, location, and characteristics of seismic events. Accurate predictions enable the implementation of early warning systems, allowing for timely alerts and evacuation plans in regions prone to seismic activity. This supports proactive measures to mitigate the impact of earthquakes on communities. The predictions guide resource allocation for emergency response teams, helping them focus efforts on areas with higher predicted seismic activity or potential risks.

Continuous Monitoring and Iterative Improvement

The predictions generated during real-time inference contribute to a continuous feedback loop. This feedback loop involves comparing model predictions with observed seismic events, allowing for ongoing model evaluation and improvement. Models can be adapted and fine-tuned based on the continuous feedback, ensuring that they remain effective in the face of evolving seismic patterns or changing environmental conditions. The effectiveness of the Model Output component is closely tied to the integration and performance of preceding components, including Data Preprocessing, Model Training & Optimization, and Model Storage. A well-orchestrated system ensures the seamless flow of information and enhances the overall reliability of predictions. An adaptable system that can accommodate updates, improvements, and new data sources ensures that the Model Output component remains relevant and responsive to emerging seismic patterns. Introducing innovation to the system, the Novel Feature Engineering component plays a vital role in enhancing the models' ability to discern unique patterns within seismic data. This component involves the exploration and incorporation of novel features, potentially derived from advanced signal processing techniques or domain-specific knowledge. Novel feature engineering contributes to the adaptability of the models, ensuring their effectiveness in capturing emerging patterns and trends.

ALGORITHM: DEEP LEARNING FOR SEISMIC PATTERN RECOGNITION

1. Seismic Data Collection:

Let X represent the raw seismic data,
where X_i is the seismic data point at time i.

2. Data Preprocessing:

Apply data cleaning:
X_{clean}=Clean(X)
Normalize and standardize:
$X_{normalized}$=Normalize (X_{clean})
Extract time-frequency representations:
$X_{spectrogram}$=Spectrogram ($X_{normalized}$)

3. Model Training & Optimization:

Split data:
$X_{train}, X_{val}, X_{test}$=Split ($X_{spectrogram}$)
Define neural network model parameters: Θ
Train the model:
$\Theta_{optimal}$ = Train (X_{train},Θ)
Optimize hyperparameters:
Θ_{final} = Optimize ($\Theta_{optimal}$, X_{val})

4. Model Storage/Persistence:

Save model parameters:
Save(Θ_{final}) Save(Θ_{final})

5. Model Output (Predictions):

Activate the model:
Y_{Pred} = Activate (X_{new}, Θ_{final})

6. Decision Support and Actionability:

Utilize predictions for decision-making:
D=Decision (Y_{pred})

7. Continuous Monitoring and Iterative Improvement:

Observe actual seismic events: $X_{observed}$
Evaluate model performance:
E = $E_{valuate}$ (Y_{pred}, $X_{observed}$)
Adapt and fine-tune the model:
$\Theta_{updated}$=Adapt (Θ_{final}, E)

8. System Integration and Adaptability:

Ensure seamless integration:
Integration ($\Theta_{updated}$, Other Components)
Maintain adaptability for updates:
Adaptability($\Theta_{updated}$)

9. Knowledge Dissemination:

   Document findings:
   K=Document ($\Theta_{updated}$, E)
   Share insights: Share(K)

The algorithm leverages deep learning for seismic pattern recognition, commencing with the collection of raw seismic data X. A systematic preprocessing pipeline follows, involving data cleaning, normalization, and extraction of time-frequency representations, leading to a refined spectrogram spectrogram $X_{spectrogram}$. Subsequently, a neural network model is trained and optimized on the preprocessed data, with optimal parameters Θ_{final} achieved through iterative training and hyperparameter optimization. The resultant model is then stored for future use. During real-time inference, the stored model is activated to generate Y_{pred} regarding potential seismic events. These predictions serve as a foundation for informed decision-making, contributing to early warning systems and resource allocation. The system incorporates continuous monitoring, iteratively adapting the model based on observed seismic events, and ensuring seamless integration with other components. The algorithm concludes with knowledge dissemination, summarizing findings and emphasizing the algorithm's impact on enhancing seismic cycle forecasting through the application of deep learning techniques.

CONCLUSION

In this proposed chapter, we delve into the forefront of seismic cycle prediction by exploring and evaluating various neural network architectures. Leveraging the power of RNNs, particularly LSTMs, and considering the spatial aspects through CNNs and Transformer networks, we aim to develop comprehensive models capable of capturing both temporal and spatial dependencies in seismic data. The integration of these architectures is anticipated to enhance the accuracy of seismic cycle predictions, addressing the challenges posed by the complex and dynamic nature of seismic events. Additionally, we explore the potential of autoencoders for feature extraction and propose hybrid architectures that combine the strengths of different neural network models. The chapter aims to provide insights into the advancements in seismic cycle prediction through the lens of diverse and tailored neural network architectures, paving the way for improved understanding and forecasting of seismic activities.

REFERENCES

Abadi, M., Barham, P., Chen, J., Chen, Z., Davis, A., & Dean, J. (2016). *TensorFlow: A system for large-scale machine learning*.

Asim, K. M., Idris, A., Iqbal, T., & Martínez-Álvarez, F. (2018). Seismic indicators-based earthquake predictor system using Genetic Programming and AdaBoost classification. *Soil Dynamics and Earthquake Engineering*, *111*, 1–7. doi:10.1016/j.soildyn.2018.04.020

Dascher-Cousineau, K., Shchur, O., Brodsky, E. E., & Günnemann, S. (2023). Using Deep Learning for Flexible and Scalable Earthquake Forecasting. *Geophysical Research Letters*, *50*(17), e2023GL103909. doi:10.1029/2023GL103909

Field, E. H., Milner, K. R., Hardebeck, J. L., Page, M. T., van der Elst, N., Jordan, T. H., Michael, A. J., Shaw, B. E., & Werner, M. J. (2017). A spatiotemporal clustering model for the third uniform California earthquake rupture forecast (UCERF3-ETAS): Toward an operational earthquake forecast. *Bulletin of the Seismological Society of America*, *107*(3), 1049–1081. doi:10.1785/0120160173

Fox, G., Rundle, J., Donnellan, A., & Feng, B. (2022). Earthquake Nowcasting with Deep Learning. *GeoHazards.*, *3*(2), 199–226. doi:10.3390/geohazards3020011

Ganguly, K. K., Nahar, N., & Hossain, B. M. (2019). A machine learning-based prediction and analysis of flood affected households: A case study of floods in Bangladesh. *International Journal of Disaster Risk Reduction*, *34*, 283–294. doi:10.1016/j.ijdrr.2018.12.002

Gutenberg, B., & Richter, C. F. (1944). Frequency of earthquakes in California. *Bulletin of the Seismological Society of America*, *34*(4), 4–188. doi:10.1785/BSSA0340040185

Jena, R., Pradhan, B., Beydoun, G., Alamri, A. M., Ardiansyah, A., Nizamuddin, N., & Sofyan, H. (2020). Earthquake hazard and risk assessment using machine learning approaches at Palu, Indonesia. *The Science of the Total Environment*, *749*, 141582. doi:10.1016/j.scitotenv.2020.141582 PMID:33370892

Laurenti, L., Tinti, E., Galasso, F., Franco, L., & Marone, C. (2022). Deep learning for laboratory earthquake prediction and autoregressive forecasting of fault zone stress. *Earth and Planetary Science Letters*, *598*, 1–14. doi:10.1016/j.epsl.2022.117825

Llenos, A. L., & Michael, A. J. (2017). Forecasting the (un)productivity of the 2014 M 6.0 South Napa aftershock sequence. *Seismological Research Letters*, *88*(5), 1241–1251. doi:10.1785/0220170050

Llenos, A. L., & Michael, A. J. (2019). Ensembles of ETAS models provide optimal operational earthquake forecasting during swarms: Insights from the 2015 San Ramon, California Swarm. *Bulletin of the Seismological Society of America*, *109*(6), 2145–2158. doi:10.1785/0120190020

Mancini, S., Segou, M., Werner, M. J., Parsons, T., Beroza, G., & Chiaraluce, L. (2022). On the use of high-resolution and deep-learning seismic catalogs for short-term earthquake forecasts: Potential benefits and current limitations. *Journal of Geophysical Research: Solid Earth, 127*(11), e2022JB025202.

Mignan, A., & Broccardo, M. (2020). Neural network applications in earthquake prediction (1994–2019): Meta-analytic and statistical insights on their limitations. *Seismological Research Letters*, *91*(4), 2330–2342. doi:10.1785/0220200021

Mousavi, S. M., Ellsworth, W. L., Zhu, W., Chuang, L. Y., & Beroza, G. C. (2020). Earthquake transformer—An attentive deep-learning model for simultaneous earthquake detection and phase picking. *Nature Communications*, *11*(1), 3952. doi:10.103841467-020-17591-w PMID:32770023

Muhammad, D., Ahmad, I., Khalil, M. I., Khalil, W., & Ahmad, M. O. (2023). A Generalized Deep Learning Approach to Seismic Activity Prediction. *Applied Sciences (Basel, Switzerland)*, *13*(3), 1598. doi:10.3390/app13031598

Ogata, Y. (2017). Statistics of earthquake activity: Models and methods for earthquake predictability studies. *Annual Review of Earth and Planetary Sciences*, *45*(1), 497–527. doi:10.1146/annurev-earth-063016-015918

Prochazka, A., Vysata, O., & Marik, V. (2021). Integrating the role of computational intelligence and digital signal processing in education: Emerging technologies and mathematical tools. *IEEE Signal Processing Magazine*, *38*(3), 154–162. doi:10.1109/MSP.2021.3058634

Svetnik, V., Liaw, A., Tong, C., Culberson, J. C., Sheridan, R. P., & Feuston, B. P. (2003). Random forest: A classification and regression tool for compound classification and QSAR modeling. *Journal of Chemical Information and Computer Sciences*, *43*(6), 1947–1958. doi:10.1021/ci034160g PMID:14632445

Tan, Y. J., Waldhauser, F., Ellsworth, W. L., Zhang, M., Zhu, W., Michele, M., Chiaraluce, L., Beroza, G. C., & Segou, M. (2021). Machine-learning-based high-resolution earthquake catalog reveals how complex fault structures were activated during the 2016–2017 central Italy sequence. *The Seismic Record*, *1*(1), 11–19. doi:10.1785/0320210001 van der Elst, N. J., Hardebeck, J. L., Michael, A. J., McBride, S. K., & Vanacore, E. (2022). Prospective and retrospective evaluation of the U.S. geological survey public aftershock forecast for the 2019–2021 southwest Puerto Rico earthquake and aftershocks. *Seismological Research Letters*, *93*(2A), 620–640. doi:10.1785/0220210222

Chapter 14
A Comprehensive Machine Learning Approach for Accurate Forest Fire Forecasting

Suba Shree
Velammal College of Engineering and Technology, India

Rajpriya
Velammal College of Engineering and Technology, India

S Gandhimathi Alias Usha
https://orcid.org/0000-0003-1908-6249
Velammal College of Engineering and Technology, India

S. Dharshana
Velammal College of Engineering and Technology, India

ABSTRACT

Forest fires have significant environmental and economic impacts, necessitating advanced prediction and detection strategies. Artificial intelligence, particularly machine learning (ML) techniques, plays a crucial role in addressing this challenge. Supervised models analyze complex patterns, enabling early warnings and comprehensive risk evaluation. This chapter critically examines the suitability and limitations of various ML algorithms in forest fire science, emphasizing the need to carefully consider algorithmic strengths and weaknesses. It highlights challenges in selecting the most suitable models for accurate predictions and advocates for customizing ML models to specific forest characteristics. By tailoring ML techniques based on unique forest attributes, the research aims to enhance prediction accuracy, improve risk assessment, and implement targeted preventive measures. Ultimately, this contributes to a more proactive and effective approach to forest fire management.

DOI: 10.4018/979-8-3693-2280-2.ch014

INTRODUCTION

Forest fires, often termed wildfires, are uncontrolled blazes that erupt and spread through forested areas, encompassing various types of vegetation. These fires, influenced by natural factors like dry conditions and lightning strikes, or human actions such as campfires or discarded cigarettes, pose a severe risk due to their ability to grow quickly and cover extensive areas.

The impact of forest fires on ecosystems is profound. The destruction of forests disrupts the natural balance, affecting the lives of countless species. Animals lose their habitats, leading to displacement, injuries, or fatalities. Plant life, critical for soil stability and oxygen production, suffers extensive damage. Additionally, the altered landscape invites invasive species, further disturbing the ecosystem's equilibrium (Cheng & Wang, 2008).

Timely intervention is crucial in containing and minimizing the damage caused by forest fires. Early detection through advanced forecasting techniques allows for swift responses, aiding in fire suppression efforts before they spiral out of control. Effective intervention not only preserves the natural environment but also protects human lives, homes, and infrastructure (Pang et al., 2022).

This chapter serves to explore how machine learning augments our ability to forecast and manage forest fires. It delves into the integration of historical data, weather patterns, satellite imagery, and advanced algorithms to create predictive models. The goal is to provide stakeholders with accurate predictions, enabling proactive measures to combat forest fires effectively. Additionally, it emphasizes the significance of this technology in minimizing the impact of fires on ecosystems, wildlife, and human settlements.

MACHINE LEARNING AND ITS ROLE IN PREDICTION

Machine learning has revolutionized forest fire prediction by leveraging diverse datasets and sophisticated algorithms. These systems, good at recognizing patterns and correlations within historical fire records, weather patterns, topographical features, satellite imagery, and vegetation indices, empower predictive modeling. Their adaptability allows continual learning from new data, enhancing precision in forecasting fire occurrence, spread, and intensity. Techniques like Random Forest, Gradient Boosting, and Neural Networks combines multiple models and understands complex relationships, elevating prediction accuracy (Bianchinia et al., 2006). By harnessing satellite-based remote sensing data, machine learning facilitates real-time monitoring, early detection of potential fire hotspots, and precise mapping of affected areas. This capability drives the development of early warning systems, providing crucial lead times for evacuation and firefighting preparedness. Continuous adaptation ensures these models remain effective in dynamic environmental conditions (Anandaram et al., 2023). Ultimately, the integration of machine learning stands as a pivotal advancement, empowering proactive measures to safeguard ecosystems, wildlife, and human lives against the ravages of forest fires.

Analysis Historical Data for Risk Assessment

In forest fire forecasting, machine learning's analysis of historical data plays a pivotal role in risk assessment, offering valuable insights into potential fire occurrences and behaviors. Machine learning algorithms carefully comb through extensive historical records of past fire incidents, encompassing various factors such as weather conditions, geographical features, vegetation types, and human activities (Al Janabi et al., 2018). By scrutinizing this data, these algorithms notice patterns, correlations, and trends that contribute to the ignition and spread of forest fires. The analysis of historical data aids in identifying high-risk areas prone to frequent or intense fires based on past occurrences and their contributing factors. These algorithms can pinpoint geographical regions vulnerable to specific fire behaviors, such as rapid spreading due to particular weather conditions or terrain characteristics. Moreover, machine learning's ability to process and analyze vast datasets enables the identification of temporal patterns, seasonal variations, and long-term trends in fire occurrences. This comprehensive understanding derived from historical data empowers stakeholders to proactively allocate resources, implement preventive measures, and arrange targeted intervention strategies in high-risk zones, thereby mitigating potential fire hazards and minimizing their impact on ecosystems and communities (Alberg, 2015).

Real-Time Analysis and Early Prediction

Machine learning's application in forest fire prediction extends beyond historical data analysis to include real-time analysis, enabling early and precise predictions for timely intervention. By integrating real-time data streams from various sources such as satellites, weather stations, and ground sensors, machine learning algorithms continuously monitor environmental conditions. These algorithms quickly process incoming information, detecting anomalies or patterns indicative of potential fire outbreaks. The capability to analyze real-time data in conjunction with historical patterns empowers these algorithms to generate early predictions (Angayarkkani & Radhakrishnan, 2010). They forecast fire ignition points, predict potential fire spread trajectories, and estimate fire intensity based on the most current environmental conditions. This real-time analysis provides invaluable lead time for stakeholders and firefighting agencies. Early warnings generated by machine learning models allow for proactive measures, including rapid deployment of resources, strategic planning for evacuation, and targeted firefighting efforts. Theresult of combining historical data analysis with real-time insights enhances the accuracy and timeliness of predictions (Artés et al., 2016). Machine learning's role in real-time analysis ensures a proactive approach to forest fire management, significantly reducing response time and potential damage caused by these catastrophic events.

Continuous Improvement in Accuracy: Evolution of Predictive Flames

The journey towards precision in forest fire forecasting is an ongoing quest for refinement and enhancement. Predictive Flames, fueled by nonstop dedication to accuracy, embraces a philosophy of continuous improvement. Machine learning algorithms at the core of Predictive Flames are not static entities; they evolve. With each new dataset, every encountered scenario, and every validated prediction, the system learns and adapts (Buckland et al., 2019). This dynamic learning process is fundamental to achieving and sustaining high accuracy levels.

The iterative nature of continuous improvement involves refining algorithms based on real-world outcomes and incorporating the latest advancements in technology and environmental science. Regular assessments and recalibrations ensure that Predictive Flames remains at the forefront of forest fire forecasting, growing betterat understanding mysterious patterns and anomalies(Sun et al., 2023). Furthermore, collaborative efforts involving domain experts, data scientists, and environmental researchers contribute to the ongoing enhancement of Predictive Flames. The combination of collective expertise amplifies the system's ability to interpret complex interactions within the ecosystem and respond with heightened accuracy. In the domain of forest fire forecasting, the pursuit of continuous improvement is not just a goal but a commitment. Predictive Flames, as a dynamic entity, stands resilient against the challenges posed by the ever-changing environmental landscape, striving for accuracy that exceeds the limits of the present and sets new standards for the future (Canadell et al., 2021).

Simulating Fire Behavior for Strategic Planning

Within the realm of Predictive Flames, the simulation of fire behavior emerges as a pivotal facet, elevating forest fire forecasting from prediction to proactive strategic planning. Machine learning, the backbone of this initiative, extends its great skill beyond prediction algorithms to dynamic fire behavior modeling. Strategic planning hinges on understanding not just where a fire might occur but how it could unfold.

Predictive Flames employs sophisticated simulations that consider diverse variables: wind patterns, terrain characteristics, and vegetation types (Sun et al., 2022). These simulations dynamically adapt based on real-time data, creating a nuanced understanding of potential fire scenarios.

By simulating fire behavior, Predictive Flames provides invaluable insights for strategic planning. Emergency responders, forestry officials, and local communities can anticipate the trajectory of a fire, enabling informed decisions on resource allocation, evacuation routes, and targeted preventive measures. The synergy of machine learning algorithms and fire behavior simulations empowers Predictive Flames to go beyond conventional forecasting. It becomes a strategic tool, enabling stakeholders to stay ahead of the fire's path, minimize risks, and protect both ecosystems and communities. In this convergence of technology and foresight, the journey from prediction to strategic planning becomes a formidable force against the unpredictable nature of forest fires.

CHALLENGES IN PREDICTING FOREST FIRES

Predicting forest fires presents a multifaceted challenge despite strides in machine learning. The complexity of environmental dynamics, encompassing variables like wind patterns, terrain, and vegetation types, poses hurdles in capturing the full spectrum of influences on fire behavior. Additionally, limitations in data availability and quality, both historical and real-time, impede accurate model training and reliability of predictions (Coughlan et al., 2021). The dynamic nature of fires, characterized by rapid and unpredictable changes, strains machine learning models' adaptability, leading to difficulties in foreseeing sudden shifts in fire behavior. Interpretability issues and uncertainties within model predictions further complicate decision-making processes. Ethical concerns surrounding data privacy, fair resource allocation, and the responsible use of predictive analytics in firefighting strategies contribute to the broader challenges in forest fire prediction, emphasizing the need for continual advancements in technology and a holistic approach that integrates societal, ethical, and environmental considerations (Rubí et al., 2023).

Complex Environmental Factors

In the intricate dance between nature's complexities and the quest for accurate forest fire forecasting, Predictive Flames emerges as a beacon of technological innovation. At its core, this initiative harnesses the power of machine learning to analyze and integrate a multiple of complex environmental factors. From intricate weather patterns and topographical nuances to the intricate interplay of vegetation types, Predictive Flames employs advanced algorithms to analyze and interpret these multifaceted elements (Eddin et al., 2023). Machine learning's adaptability allows the system to separate nice relationships within data, providing a holistic understanding of the environmental landscape. In the face of climate change and its cascading effects on fire risk, Predictive Flames becomes a dynamic solution. It adapts to evolving environmental conditions, learning from historical data to enhance its predictive accuracy. This adaptability is crucial in navigating the ever-shifting complex factors influencing forest fire behavior. Byexplore into the complexities of the environment, Predictive Flames not only predicts potential fire outbreaks but also fosters a deeper comprehension of the intricate dynamics at play. It stands as a testament to our capacity to leverage technology for a more profound understanding of nature, offering a proactive approach to forest fire management rooted in the intricate details of our environment.

Variability in Fire Behavior

The variability in forest fire behavior stands as a substantial challenge in predictive modeling, complicating the accurate forecasting of these events using machine learning. Fires exhibit diverse behaviors influenced by a multitude of factors, making it difficult for models to encapsulate this variability comprehensively. Fires can spread erratically due to shifts in wind patterns, sudden changes in vegetation density, or variations in terrain topography, creating unpredictable patterns that challenge the reliability of predictive algorithms. Moreover, the intensity and speed of fire propagation fluctuate drastically based on local weather conditions, moisture levels, and the availability of fuel sources, adding another layer of complexity. Machine learning models often struggle to adapt swiftly to these dynamic changes in fire behavior, limiting their ability to provide precise predictions (Wu et al., 2023). Understanding and integrating the variability in fire behavior into predictive models remains a persistent challenge, demanding sophisticated algorithms that can account for and respond effectively to the diverse and evolving nature of forest fires. Addressing this challenge requires continuous refinement of machine learning techniques, extensive data inputs encompassing various fire scenarios, and a nuanced understanding of the intricate interplay of environmental factors influencing fire behavior.

Incomplete Data and Integration Challenges

In the domain of forest fire forecasting, the path to accuracy is often fraught with challenges posed by incomplete data and integration complexities. Predictive Flames, powered by machine learning, exemplifies resilience in the face of these hurdles, turning obstacles into opportunities for innovation. Incomplete data is a perennial challenge, yet Predictive Flames addresses this by employing algorithms capable of learning from limited information. Machine learning models, good at recognizing patterns even in sparse datasets, mitigate the impact of missing elements, contributing to a more robust forecasting system. Integration challenges arise from the diverse nature of environmental data sources. Predictive Flames tackles this complexity by serving as an integrative hub, harmonizing disparate data types (Saha et al., 2023). By bridging the gaps between weather patterns, topography, and historical fire incidents, it assembles a comprehensive picture despite the challenges of diverse and sometimes incompatible datasets. The very essence of Predictive Flames lies in its ability to adapt and learn. It thrives in an environment where data is incomplete and integration is intricate, evolving to handle the intricacies of the real-world environmental landscape. Through this resilience, Predictive Flames not only forecasts forest fires with accuracy but also paves the way for addressing the inherent challenges that come with the nuanced nature of environmental data.

MACHINE LEARNING TECHNIQUES IN FOREST FIRE PREDICTION

Machine learning techniques like ensemble methods, neural networks, satellite data analysis, adaptive learning, predictive modeling, and early warning systems play a crucial role in enhancing forest fire prediction accuracy. They analyze diverse data sources, assess risk factors, and provide early alerts, aiding in proactive measures to mitigate forest fire damage.

Predictive Modeling With Historical Data

Predictive flames employ machine learning, specifically the Random Forest Algorithm, for precise forest fire forecasting. By utilizing historical data, this method involves training the model on diverse features like weather conditions, vegetation types, and topography associated with past fire incidents. The Random Forest Algorithm excels in capturing intricate relationships within the data, enhancing the model's ability to discern patterns and make accurate predictions. Its strength lies in aggregating predictions from multiple decision trees, providing a robust and reliable predictive framework. This approach allows for proactive forest fire management by anticipating potential fire outbreaks. Regular updates with new data further refine the model's accuracy over time. The integration of machine learning techniques in forest fire prediction not only aids in early detection but also facilitates more effective allocation of resources for firefighting and prevention efforts. The amalgamation of historical insights and advanced algorithms establishes a powerful tool to mitigate the impact of forest fires and enhance overall environmental safety.

Image Processing for Early Detection

Predictive Flames pioneers an innovative approach to forest fire forecasting by harnessing the potency of machine learning, particularly the Random Forest Algorithm, and integrating image processing for early detection. This cutting-edge methodology relies on historical data, including satellite or drone imagery, to train the model on an array of features like vegetation health, temperature patterns, and smoke signals (Zhang & Yang, 2020). The Random Forest Algorithm excels in unraveling intricate relationships within these features, establishing a resilient predictive model. The inclusion of image processing enhances the system's capability to detect subtle visual cues associated with potential fire outbreaks. This proactive integration enables swift responses, crucial for minimizing the devastating impact of forest fires. The amalgamation of machine learning and image processing allows for real-time monitoring of expansive areas, providing a holistic understanding of environmental conditions. Regular updates with new image data continually refine the model, ensuring adaptability to dynamic scenarios. Predictive Flames emerges as a formidable tool in forest fire management, not only offering accuracy in forecasting but also crucial lead time for implementing preventive measures and strategic firefighting interventions.

Pattern Recognition for Fire Behavior

Predictive Flames pioneers advanced forest fire forecasting by leveraging machine learning, specifically the Random Forest Algorithm, with a specialized focus on pattern recognition for understanding fire behavior. Drawing insights from historical data, including weather conditions, topography, and vegetation types, the model becomes adept at recognizing intricate patterns associated with the initiation and spread of fires. The Random Forest Algorithm, renowned for its capacity to navigate complex relationships, excels in discerning nuanced patterns in fire behavior. It evaluates an array of features, such as wind direction, fuel availability, and terrain characteristics, providing a comprehensive understanding of how fires might unfold. Pattern recognition plays a pivotal role in unraveling the dynamics of fire spread. The model, through continuous learning and refinement with new data, hones its ability to identify subtle cues and correlations that influence fire behavior. This not only ensures accurate forecasting but also affords a profound insight into the evolving nature of forest fires. Predictive Flames emerges as a vital tool in proactive forest fire management, offering nuanced comprehension of the intricate interplay of variables shaping fire behavior. By combining machine learning techniques and pattern recognition, it stands at the forefront of efforts to mitigate the impact of forest fires through informed decision-making and timely interventions.

Risk Assessment and Resource Allocation

Predictive Flames utilizes machine learning, specifically the Random Forest Algorithm, to enhance forest fire forecasting accuracy, with a strategic emphasis on risk assessment and resource allocation. Historical data, incorporating variables like weather conditions, topography, and vegetation types, is harnessed to train the model for identifying patterns associated with fire risk. The Random Forest Algorithm's strength in handling complex relationships aids in robust risk assessment. By analyzing diverse features, including fire-prone areas and historical fire behavior, the model becomes proficient in evaluating the likelihood of fire occurrence and potential severity. This predictive capability supports informed resource allocation. Authorities can strategically deploy firefighting resources based on the assessed risk, optimizing response times and resource utilization. The model's adaptability, through continuous learning with updated data, ensures its relevance in dynamic environments. Predictive Flames, through machine learning techniques and the Random Forest Algorithm, emerges not only as a tool for accurate forecasting but also as a strategic asset in risk management. By facilitating data-driven decisions in resource allocation, it contributes to more effective and efficient firefighting efforts, ultimately reducing the impact of forest fires.

EMERGING MACHINE LEARNING TECHNOLOGIES

Cutting-edge machine learning technologies like reinforcement learning and neural architecture search are transforming forest fire forecasting. They refine algorithms independently, improving accuracy by adapting to complex environmental data. Pairing this with explainable AI ensures accurate predictions and clear insights into how these models work, building trust and collaboration among stakeholders for better forest fire management. These advancements signal a dynamic evolution, where AI not only predicts accurately but also adapts alongside nature. This promises even more precise and adaptive fire forecasting, safeguarding ecosystems and communities better in the future (Su et al., 2018).

Reinforcement Learning in Forest Fire Prediction

Reinforcement learning, an emerging machine learning technology, holds promise in enhancing forest fire prediction by enabling adaptive and dynamic decision-making processes. In the context of forest fire prediction, reinforcement learning models learn through trial and error, continuously improving predictions based on interactions with the environment. These models adapt their strategies by receiving feedback on the efficacy of their actions, adjusting predictions, and refining decision-making processes in real-time. In forest fire prediction, reinforcement learning algorithms can optimize resource allocation and intervention strategies. These models learn from historical fire data and environmental conditions, dynamically adapting strategies to combat fires by considering various factors such as wind patterns, terrain characteristics, and vegetation types. Through continuous learning, they refine their predictions, offering more adaptive and effective solutions for fire management. However, the application of reinforcement learning in forest fire prediction faces challenges in data scarcity and the complexities of the natural environment. Forest fire incidents are relatively rare and vary in intensity and behavior, making it challenging for models to learn from limited data. Additionally, the dynamic nature of fires poses complexities in building robust reinforcement learning models that can adapt rapidly to changing conditions. Nonetheless, the integration of reinforcement learning holds potential in optimizing decision-making processes for forest fire prediction, contributing to more adaptive and responsive strategies in managing and mitigating the impact of forest fires. Continued research and advancements in this field could unlock significant improvements in predictive accuracy and intervention strategies.

Transformer Based Models

Transformer-based models represent a cutting-edge advancement in machine learning, holding immense potential in forest fire prediction. These models, notably exemplified by architectures like BERT (Bidirectional Encoder Representations from Transformers) and GPT (Generative Pre-trained Transformers), revolutionize the understanding and processing of sequential data by leveraging self-attention mechanisms. In forest fire prediction, transformer-based models excel in analyzing diverse datasets comprising historical fire records, weather patterns, satellite imagery, and vegetation indices. The self-attention mechanism allows these models to capture intricate relationships between different variables without being restricted by sequential order, enabling a more comprehensive understanding of complex fire behavior patterns. Furthermore, transformer-based models showcase exceptional adaptability and scalability. They possess the ability to learn complex patterns from vast amounts of data, continuously refining predictions and adapting to changing environmental conditions. Their prowess in processing large-scale data and capturing nuanced dependencies among variables positions them as promising tools for enhancing the accuracy and robustness of forest fire forecasting models. However, the implementation of transformer-based models in forest fire prediction encounters challenges concerning computational requirements and the need for extensive computing resources. Nonetheless, their ability to comprehend complex relationships within diverse datasets presents a significant stride in advancing the capabilities of machine learning in accurate forest fire forecasting. Continued research and refinement of these models hold substantial promise in transforming the landscape of forest fire prediction methodologies.

Continual Learning

Continual learning within the context of forest fire prediction offers a promising approach leveraging emerging machine learning technologies. Unlike traditional learning models that assume stationary data distributions, continual learning focuses on adapting to evolving environments, crucial for dynamic systems like forest ecosystems. In the context of "Predictive Flames: Machine Learning for forest fire forecasting," continual learning enables models to adapt to new data patterns and characteristics over time. This adaptability is vital due to changing climate conditions, land usage, and vegetation dynamics affecting fire behavior. Continual learning algorithms allow predictive models to accumulate knowledge from new fire incidents while retaining past insights, preventing catastrophic forgetting. Through continual learning, forest fire forecasting models can gradually enhance their predictive accuracy by incorporating recent fire data without compromising their ability to recognize historical patterns. This iterative learning process ensures that the predictive system remains relevant and effective in forecasting fires even as environmental factors evolve. Continual learning techniques, such as incremental learning and regularization strategies, empower these models to adapt incrementally without discarding previous knowledge, making them more robust and adaptable to the ever-changing dynamics of forest ecosystems. This adaptability is crucial for improving the accuracy and reliability of machine learning-based forest fire prediction systems like "Predictive Flames."

Generative Adversarial Networks

Predictive Flames pioneers the integration of Generative Adversarial Networks (GANs) in forest fire forecasting, propelling the initiative into a new era of accuracy. GANs play a dual role by augmenting data and simulating realistic environmental scenarios (Bhattarai et al., 2022). These networks enhance data robustness in Predictive

Flames through sophisticated data augmentation. By generating synthetic samples that mirror authentic environmental conditions, GANs contribute to more comprehensive and effective model training. Simultaneously, they become architects of diverse scenarios, simulating intricate weather patterns, terrains, and vegetation types. This scenario exploration allows Predictive Flames to anticipate and comprehend potential fire behaviors with unprecedented depth. However, challenges such as model training stability and ethical data usage considerations are navigated diligently. The future trajectory involves conditional GANs tailored for specific scenarios and the potential for adaptive synthesis. Through this fusion of machine learning innovation and scenario generation, Predictive Flames not only refines its predictive capabilities but reshapes the landscape of forest fire forecasting, offering a dynamic and nuanced approach to understanding and mitigating the impact of wildfires.

Explainable AI

Explainable AI (XAI) plays a pivotal role by providing transparent and understandable insights into the machine learning models' decision-making processes, crucial for enhancing trust and interpretability in fire prediction. AI techniques within "Predictive Flames" ensure that the complex machine learning algorithms used for forecasting fires are not just accurate but also transparent in their reasoning. These methods include model visualization, feature importance analysis, and decision rule explanations, elucidating how the model arrives at its predictions. Byemploying XAI, "Predictive Flames" translates the intricate workings of machine learning models into human-interpretable information. This transparency enables firefighters, forest management authorities, and policymakers to comprehend why a certain prediction was made, what factors influenced it, and how reliable the forecast is based on the available data. The insights provided by XAI empower stakeholders to validate the model's predictions, identify potential biases or limitations, and fine-tune strategies accordingly. This interpretable nature enhances confidence in the forecasting system, fostering more effective decision-making and proactive measures in forest fire management. Ultimately, XAI ensures not just accurate predictions but also comprehension and trust in the "Predictive Flames" system.

PROPOSED SYSTEM

Figure 1 shows all the images in the dataset are 3-channeled with resolution of 250 × 250. It is a balanced dataset consisting of 1900 images in total, where 950 images belong to each class. The dataset is divided into 80:20 for training and testing purposes in the proposed study.

Figure1. Flame dataset: Aerial imagery pile burn detection using drones

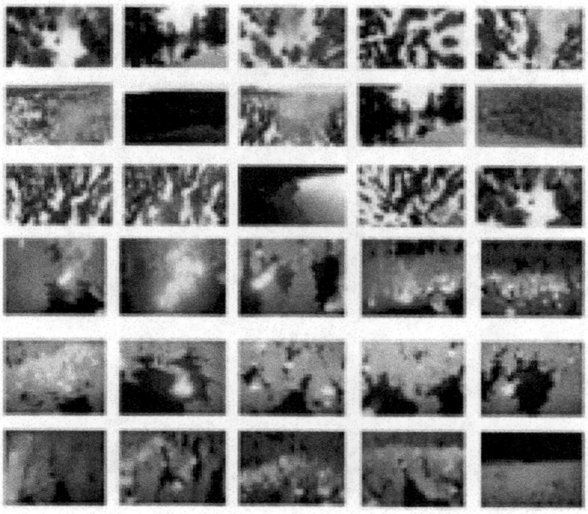

Random Forest regression

Random Forest regression is a potent approach for predicting continuous variables in forest fire scenarios. Leveraging historical data encompassing factors like temperature, humidity, wind speed, and vegetation type, the algorithm is trained to forecast continuous outcomes, such as the size or intensity of forest fires. Data preprocessing involves cleaning and handling missing values, with feature selection being a key step, although Random Forest inherently manages this by considering random feature subsets during training. Following data splitting into training and testing sets, the model is trained on the former, constructing an ensemble of decision trees. Unlike classification tasks, where each tree votes for a class, in regression, the trees collectively predict a continuous variable. Evaluation metrics like Mean Squared Error or Mean Absolute Error gauge the model's accuracy on predicting fire size or intensity. Hyperparameter tuning enhances the model's performance, adjusting aspects like the number of trees and tree depth. Once optimized, the model is deployed for real-time predictions or integration into larger systems for forest fire monitoring. Regular updates and retraining are advised to maintain predictive accuracy over time, reflecting the evolving nature of forest environments. Fig.2 depicts the flow of the algorithm.

The accuracy of Random Forest Regression can vary depending on the dataset and its characteristics. Generally, Random Forest is known for its robustness and ability to handle complex relationships in data. It often performs well compared to other algorithms, especially in situations with a large number of features. However, the performance of machine learning algorithms, including Random Forest, depends

Figure 2. Proposed algorithm for predicting forest fire: (a) Work flow (b) Random forest algorithm

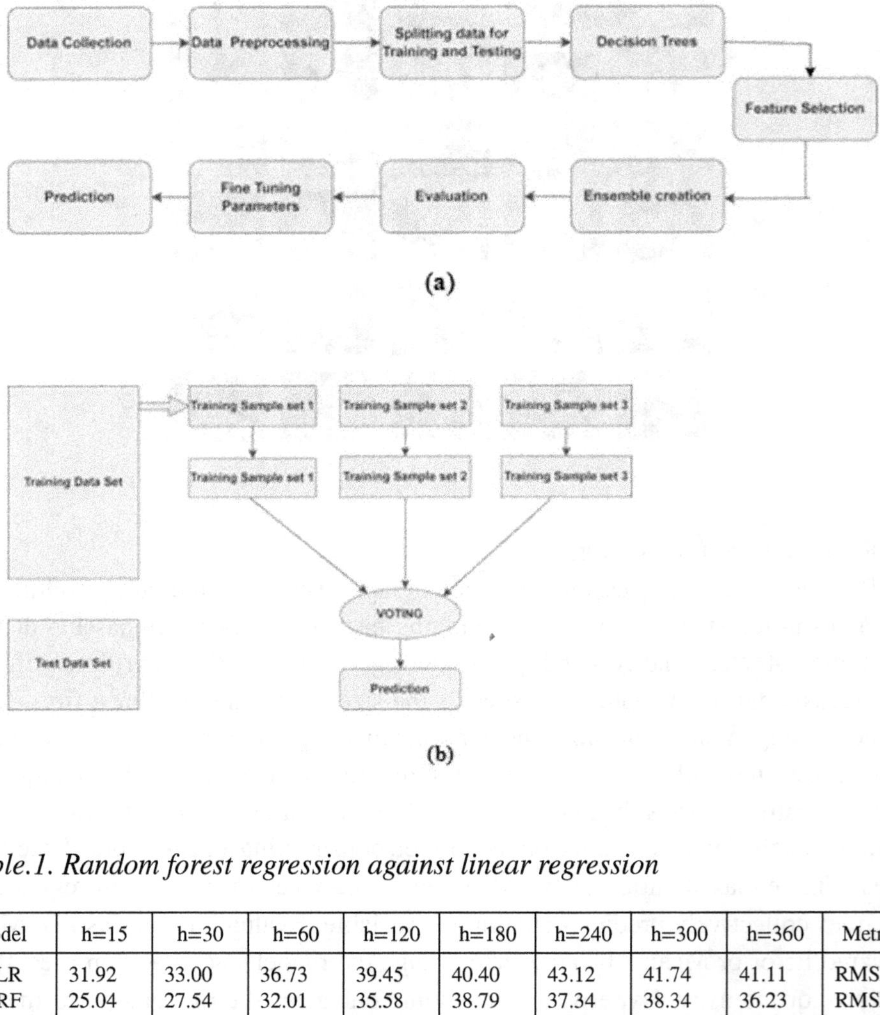

Table.1. Random forest regression against linear regression

odel	h=15	h=30	h=60	h=120	h=180	h=240	h=300	h=360	Metric
LR RF	31.92 25.04	33.00 27.54	36.73 32.01	39.45 35.58	40.40 38.79	43.12 37.34	41.74 38.34	41.11 36.23	RMSE RMSE
LR RF	0.304 0.234	0.314 0.254	0.354 0.237	0.354 0.334	0.364 0.336	0.385 0.336	0.387 0.361	0.420 0.339	nRMSE nRMSE
LR RF	-25.36 -37.12	-25.66 -35.02	-24.36 -35.12	-24.36 -30.12	-23.76 -31.14	-26.66 -34.15	-27.33 -36.57	-28.36 -38.12	Skill Skill
LR RF	0.853 0.873	0.843 0.856	0.753 0.815	0.703 0.723	0.687 0.783	0.653 0.673	0.683 0.723	0.653 0.771	R2 R2

on factors such as data quality, feature engineering, and hyper parameter tuning. It's advisable to experiment with different algorithms and fine-tune their parameters to find the best model for a specific task. Popular alternatives to Random Forest for regression tasks include linear regression, support vector machines, and gradient boosting methods like XGBoost or LightGBM. Each has strengths its and weaknesses, and the choice may depend on the nature of the data and the problem at hand.

Performance Metrics

The performance of the model is gauged using the four key elements of the confusion matrix: True Positives (TP), True Negatives (TN), False Negatives (FN), and False Positives (FP). TP and TN represent the accurate predictions of fire and no fire images, respectively, while FN and FP denote the instances where fire images and no fire images are incorrectly identified. Fig.3 shows the performance measure of the proposed algorithm.

Accuracy is a measure of how often the model predicts correctly and is given by the ratio of correct predictions to total predictions.

Accuracy=(TN+TP) / (TN+FN+FP+TP)

Precision quantifies the model's reliability when making positive predictions, defined as the ratio of correctly identified fire instances to all instances that the model labels as fire.

Precision=TP / (FP+TP)

Recall (or sensitivity) expresses the proportion of actual fire images that are correctly identified by the model out of all actual fire images.

Recall=(TN+TP) / (FN+TP)

The F1-score is a combined measure that reflects both precision and recall in a single metric, thus allowing for an overall evaluation of a model's predictive performance. This is in contrast to accuracy, which measures the overall rate of correct predictions, encompassing both fire and nofire predictions.

F1_score=2 × (Precision × Recall) / (Precision + Recall)

The performance of proposed algorithm is shown in Fg.3. The ROC-AUC (Receiver Operating Characteristic Area Under Curve) score is a comprehensive metric that evaluates a model's ability to distinguish between classes. Unlike individual metrics such as accuracy, precision, or recall, ROC-AUC considers both the true positive rate (sensitivity) and the false positive rate (1-specificity) across different thresholds. It plots a curve (ROC curve) that represents these rates across all thresholds, and the AUC value calculates the area under this curve. A perfect classifier would have an ROC-AUC score of 1, while a completely random classifier would score 0.5. The ROC-AUC score provides insights into the model's discriminatory power, regardless of the specific threshold, making it a valuable metric for assessing a model's overall classification effectiveness.

CONCLUSION

In conclusion, when predicting forest fires, the choice between Random Forest Regression and Linear Regression depends on the nature of the underlying data.

Figure 3. Performance of proposed algorithm

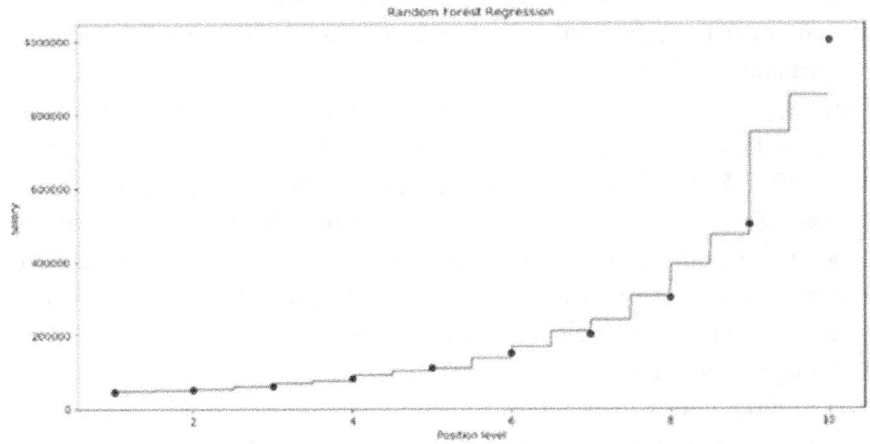

If the relationships are relatively simple and linear, Linear Regression may be suitable due to its simplicity and interpretability. However, if the relationships are complex and non-linear, Random Forest Regression is often a better choice as it can capture intricate patterns and interactions within the data. It's often beneficial to experiment with both approaches and evaluate their performance based on the specific characteristics of the dataset at hand choosing between Random Forest Regression and Linear Regression for forest fire prediction depends on the data's complexity. Linear Regression is straightforward and interpretable but assumes linear relationships, potentially limiting its effectiveness in capturing intricate patterns in forest fire data. On the other hand, Random Forest Regression excels in handling non-linearity's and complex interactions among features, making it robust for more intricate datasets. The decision should align with the underlying relationships within the data: Linear Regression for simpler, linear patterns, and Random Forest for scenarios where relationships are intricate and non-linear. It's advisable to experiment with both methods, considering factors like interpretability, computational efficiency, and prediction accuracy based on the specific characteristics of the dataset in question.

REFERENCES

Al Janabi, S., Al Shourbaji, I., & Salman, M. A. (2018). Assessing the suitability of soft computing approaches for forest fires prediction. *Appl. Comput. Inform.*, *14*(2), 214–224. doi:10.1016/j.aci.2017.09.006

Alberg, D. (2015). An interval tree approach to predict forest fires using meteorological data. *International Journal of Computer Applications*, *132*(4), 17–22. doi:10.5120/ijca2015907398

Anandaram, H., Nagalakshmi, M., Borda, R.F.C., Kiruthika, K., & Yogadinesh, S. (2023). Forest fire management using machine learning techniques. *Meas. Sens.*, 100659.

Angayarkkani, K., & Radhakrishnan, N. (2010). An intelligent system for effective forest fire detection using spatial data.

Artés, T., Cencerrado, A., Cortés, A., & Margalef, T. (2016). Real-time genetic spatial optimization to improve forest fire spread forecasting in high-performance computing environments. *International Journal of Geographical Information Science*, *30*(3), 594–611. doi:10.1080/13658816.2015.1085052

Bhattarai, N., Dahal, S., Thapa, S., Pradhananga, S., Karky, B. S., Rawat, R. S., Windhorst, K., Watanabe, T., Thapa, R. B., & Avtar, R. (2022). Forest Fire in the Hindu Kush Himalayas: A Major Challenge for Climate Action. *Journal of Forest and Livelihood*, *21*(1), 14–31. doi:10.3126/jfl.v21i1.56576

Bianchinia, G., Denhama, M., Cortésa, A., Margalefa, T., & Luquea, E. (2006). Improving forest-fire prediction by applying a statistical approach. *Forest Ecology and Management*, *234*(S1), 210. doi:10.1016/j.foreco.2006.08.237

Buckland, C. E., Bailey, R. M., & Thomas, D. S. G. (2019). Using artificial neural networks to predict future dryland responses to human and climate disturbances. *Scientific Reports*, *9*(1), 3855. doi:10.103841598-019-40429-5 PMID:30846833

Canadell, J. G., Meyer, C. P., Cook, G. D., Dowdy, A., Briggs, P. R., Knauer, J., Pepler, A., & Haverd, V. (2021). Multi-decadal increase of forest burned area in Australia is linked to climate change. *Nature Communications*, *12*(1), 6921. doi:10.103841467-021-27225-4 PMID:34836974

Cheng, T., & Wang, J. (2008). Integrated spatio-temporal data mining for forest fire prediction. *Transactions in GIS*, *12*(5), 591–611. doi:10.1111/j.1467-9671.2008.01117.x

Coughlan, R., Di Giuseppe, F., Vitolo, C., Barnard, C., Lopez, P., & Drusch, M. (2021). Using machine learning to predict fire-ignition occurrences from lightning forecasts. *Meteorological Applications*, *28*(1), e1973. doi:10.1002/met.1973

Eddin, M. H. S., Roscher, R., & Gall, J. (2023). Location-Aware Adaptive Normalization: A Deep Learning Approach for Wildfire Danger Forecasting. *IEEE Transactions on Geoscience and Remote Sensing*, *61*, 1–18. doi:10.1109/TGRS.2023.3285401

Pang, Y., Li, Y., Feng, Z., Feng, Z., Zhao, Z., Chen, S., & Zhang, H. (2022). Forest Fire Occurrence Prediction in China Based on Machine Learning Methods. *Remote Sensing (Basel)*, *14*(21), 5546. doi:10.3390/rs14215546

Rubí, J. N., de Carvalho, P. H., & Gondim, P. R. (2023). Application of machine learning models in the behavioral study of forest fires in the Brazilian Federal District region. *Engineering Applications of Artificial Intelligence*, *118*, 105649. doi:10.1016/j.engappai.2022.105649

Saha, S., Bera, B., Shit, P. K., Bhattacharjee, S., & Sengupta, N. (2023). Prediction of forest fire susceptibility applying machine and deep learning algorithms for conservation priorities of forest resources. *Remote Sensing Applications: Society and Environment*, *29*, 100917. doi:10.1016/j.rsase.2022.100917

Su, Z., Hu, H., Wang, G., Ma, Y., Yang, X., & Guo, F. (2018). Using GIS and Random Forests to identify fire drivers in a forest city, Yichun, China. *Geomatics, Natural Hazards & Risk*, *9*(1), 1207–1229. doi:10.1080/19475705.2018.1505667

Sun, J., Qi, W., Huang, Y., Xu, C., & Yang, W. (2023). Facing the Wildfire Spread Risk Challenge: Where Are We Now and Where Are We Going? *Fire (Basel, Switzerland)*, *6*(6), 228. doi:10.3390/fire6060228

Sun, L., Yang, L., Xia, X., Wang, D., & Zhang, T. (2022). Climatological Aspects of Active Fires in Northeastern China and Their Relationship to Land Cover. *Remote Sensing (Basel)*, *14*(10), 2316. doi:10.3390/rs14102316

Wu, X., Zhang, G., Yang, Z., Tan, S., Yang, Y., & Pang, Z. (2023). Machine Learning for Predicting Forest Fire Occurrence in Changsha: An Innovative Investigation into the Introduction of a Forest Fuel Factor. *Remote Sensing (Basel)*, *15*(17), 4208. doi:10.3390/rs15174208

Zhang, F., & Yang, X. (2020). Improving land cover classification in an urbanized coastal area by random forests: The role of variable selection. *Remote Sensing of Environment*, *251*, 112105. doi:10.1016/j.rse.2020.112105

Compilation of References

Abadi, M., Barham, P., Chen, J., Chen, Z., Davis, A., & Dean, J. (2016). *TensorFlow: A system for large-scale machine learning.*

Abdalzaher, M. (2023). Early Detection of Earthquakes Using IoT and Cloud Infrastructure: A Survey. *Sustainability, 15*(15), 11713.

Abdalzaher, M. (2023). Employing machine learning and iot for earthquake early warning system in smart cities. *Energies 16*(1), 495.

Abdulwahid, A. H., Pattnaik, M., Palav, M. R., Babu, S. T., Manoharan, G., & Selvi, G. P. (2023, April). Library Management System Using Artificial Intelligence. In *2023 Eighth International Conference on Science Technology Engineering and Mathematics (ICONSTEM)* (pp. 1-7). IEEE.

Abid, S. K., Chan, S. W., Sulaiman, N. A., Bhatti, U., & Nazir, U. (2023). Present and Future of Artificial Intelligence in Disaster Management. *2023 International Conference on Engineering Management of Communication and Technology (EMCTECH)*, (pp. 1-7). IEEE. 10.1109/EMCTECH58502.2023.10296991

Abid, S. K., Sulaiman, N. B., Chan, S. W., Nazir, U., Abid, M., Han, H., Ariza-Montes, A., & Vega-Muñoz, A. (2021). Toward an Integrated Disaster Management Approach: How Artificial Intelligence Can Boost Disaster Management. *Sustainability (Basel), 13*(22), 12560. doi:10.3390u132212560

Aboualola, M., Abualsaud, K., Khattab, T. M., Zorba, N., & Hassanein, H. S. (2023). Edge Technologies for Disaster Management: A Survey of Social Media and Artificial Intelligence Integration. *IEEE Access : Practical Innovations, Open Solutions, 11*, 73782–73802. doi:10.1109/ACCESS.2023.3293035

Acuna, M. A., & Aoki, T. (2014). AMR multi-GPU accelerated tsunami simulation. In *The 1st International Conference on Computational Engineering and Science for Safety and Environmental Problems* (pp. 708-710). Research Gate.

Adegoke & Damilola. (2023). A Systematic Review of Big Data and Digital Technologies Security Leadership Outcomes Effectiveness during Natural Disasters. *Sustainable Futures : An Applied Journal of Technology, Environment and Society*, 100113.

Agbehadji, I. (2023). A systematic review of existing early warning systems' challenges and opportunities in cloud computing early warning systems. *Climate*, *11*(9), 188.

Akyilidiz, L. (2015). Underwater acoustic Sensors networks: research challenges. *Ad Hoc Networks Journal.*

Al Janabi, S., Al Shourbaji, I., & Salman, M. A. (2018). Assessing the suitability of soft computing approaches for forest fires prediction. *Appl. Comput. Inform.*, *14*(2), 214–224. doi:10.1016/j.aci.2017.09.006

Alam, F., Ofli, F., Imran, M., & Aupetit, M. (2018). A twitter tale of three hurricanes: Harvey, irma, and maria. arXiv preprint arXiv:1805.05144.

Alberg, D. (2015). An interval tree approach to predict forest fires using meteorological data. *International Journal of Computer Applications*, *132*(4), 17–22. doi:10.5120/ijca2015907398

Alen, L., K. Anderson, G. Mark, J. Martin, D. Sicker, & D. Grunwald. (2010). *A Vision for Technology-Mediated Public Participation and Assistance in Mass Emergencies and Disasters.* University of Colorado manuscript.

Alhammadi, M. (2023). Optimising Customer Service Delivery and Response Time through AI-Enhanced Chatbots in Facilities Management Mixed-Methods Research. *American Journal of Smart Technology and Solutions*, *2*(2), 43–54. doi:10.54536/ajsts.v2i2.2206

Alonso Vicario, S., Mazzoleni, M., Bhamidipati, S., Gharesifard, M., Ridolfi, E., Pandolfo, C., & Alfonso, L. (2020). Unravelling the influence of human behaviour on reducing casualties during flood evacuation. *Hydrological Sciences Journal*, *65*(14), 2359–2375. doi:10.1080/02626667.2020.1810254

Alrayes, F. S., Alotaibi, S. S., Alissa, K. A., Maashi, M. S., Alhogail, A. A., Alotaibi, N., Mohsen, H., & Motwakel, A. (2022). Artificial Intelligence-Based Secure Communication and Classification for Drone-Enabled Emergency Monitoring Systems. *Drones (Basel)*, *6*(9), 222. doi:10.3390/drones6090222

Al-Wathinani, A. M. (2023). Driving sustainable disaster risk reduction: A rapid review of the policies and strategies in Saudi Arabia. *Sustainability*, *15*(14).

Ames, J. H. Liou, Yu-Tai C. (2010). Developing a hybrid multi-criteria model for selection of outsourcing providers. *Expert Systems with Applications, 37*(5), 3755-3761. doi:10.1016/j.eswa.2009.11.048

Anandaram, H., Nagalakshmi, M., Borda, R.F.C., Kiruthika, K., & Yogadinesh, S. (2023). Forest fire management using machine learning techniques. *Meas. Sens.*, 100659.

Andreas, M. (2010). Users of the world, unite! The Challenges and opportunities of Social Media. *Business Horizons, 53*(1). doi:10.1016/j.bushor.2009.09.003

Angayarkkani, K., & Radhakrishnan, N. (2010). An intelligent system for effective forest fire detection using spatial data.

Aqib, M., Mehmood, R., Albeshri, A., & Alzahrani, A. (2018). Disaster Management in Smart Cities by Forecasting Traffic Plan Using Deep Learning and GPUs. In R. Mehmood, B. Bhaduri, I. Katib, & I. Chlamtac (Eds.), *Smart Societies, Infrastructure, Technologies and Applications. SCITA 2017. Lecture Notes of the Institute for Computer Sciences, Social Informatics and Telecommunications Engineering* (Vol. 224). Springer. doi:10.1007/978-3-319-94180-6_15

Aqib, M., Mehmood, R., Alzahrani, A., & Katib, I. (2020). A Smart Disaster Management System for Future Cities Using Deep Learning, GPUs, and In-Memory Computing. In R. Mehmood, S. See, I. Katib, & I. Chlamtac (Eds.), *Smart Infrastructure and Applications. EAI/Springer Innovations in Communication and Computing*. Springer. doi:10.1007/978-3-030-13705-2_7

Arfan, M., Khan, Z., Qadri, N., Hameed, M. H., & Amir, A. R. (2022). *Role of Artificial Intelligence (AI) in Combined Disaster Management*. Organization Theory Review. doi:10.32350/OTR.0302.05

Artés, T., Cencerrado, A., Cortés, A., & Margalef, T. (2016). Real-time genetic spatial optimization to improve forest fire spread forecasting in high-performance computing environments. *International Journal of Geographical Information Science*, *30*(3), 594–611. doi:10.1080/13658816.2015.1085052

Aruldoss, M., Lakshmi, T. M., & Venkatesan, V. P. (2013). A Survey on Multi Criteria Decision Making Methods and Its Applications. *The African Journal of Information Systems*, *1*(1), 31–43. doi:10.12691/ajis-1-1-5

Arvindan, S., & Vijayan, D. S. (2022). Safeguard and Preventive Measures of Natural Disasters Using Early Warning Systems—A Comprehensive Review. *A System Engineering Approach to Disaster Resilience: Select Proceedings of VCDRR,* (pp. 303-315). Research Gate.

Ashwini, A., & Purushothaman, K. E., Banu Priya, Prathaban M, Jenath & R Prasanna, (2023). Automatic Traffic Sign Board Detection from Camera Images Using Deep learning and Binarization Search Algorithm, *2023 International Conference in recent advances in Electrical, Electronics, Ubiquitous Communication and Computational Intelligence (RAEEUCCI*). IEEE. 10.1109/RAEEUCCI57140.2023.10134376

Asim, K. M., Idris, A., Iqbal, T., & Martínez-Álvarez, F. (2018). Martínez-Álvarez, F. Seismic indicators-based earthquake predictor system using Genetic Programming and AdaBoost classification. *Soil Dynamics and Earthquake Engineering*, *111*, 1–7. doi:10.1016/j.soildyn.2018.04.020

Avci, S., Ekiz Bozdemír, M. K., & Alkan, A. (2023). Selection Of Social Media Platforms: A New Hybrid Multi-Criteria Decision Making Approach. *Endüstri Mühendisliği*, *34*(2), 243–275. doi:10.46465/endustrimuhendisligi.1259667

Aybar-Ruiz, A., Jiménez-Fernández, S., Cornejo-Bueno, L., Casanova-Mateo, C., Sanz-Justo, J., Salvador-González, P., & Salcedo-Sanz, S. (2016). A novel Grouping Genetic Algorithm–Extreme Learning Machine approach for global solar radiation prediction from numerical weather models inputs. *Solar Energy*, *132*, 129–142. doi:10.1016/j.solener.2016.03.015

Bai, T., Le Wang, D. Y., Sun, K., Chen, Y., Li, W., & Li, D. (2023). Deep learning for change detection in remote sensing: A review. *Geo-Spatial Information Science*, *26*(3), 262–288. doi:10.1080/10095020.2022.2085633

Bai, Y., Mas, E., & Koshimura, S. (2018). Towards operational satellite-based damage-mapping using u-net convolutional network: A case study of 2011 tohoku earthquake-tsunami. *Remote Sensing (Basel)*, *10*(10), 1626. doi:10.3390/rs10101626

Bao, H. D., Zeng, C., Peng, Y., & Wu, S. (2022). The use of digital technologies for landslide disaster risk research and disaster risk management: Progress and prospects. *Environmental Earth Sciences*, *81*(18), 81. doi:10.100712665-022-10575-7

Beniwal, M., & Singh, R. (2014). Localization techniques and their challenges in under water wireless sensor networks. *Proceedings of International Journal of Computer Science and Information Technologies*, *5*(3), 4706–4710.

Bernabe, S., González, C., Fernández, A., & Bhangale, U. (2021). Portability and Acceleration of Deep Learning Inferences to Detect Rapid Earthquake Damage From VHR Remote Sensing Images Using Intel OpenVINO Toolkit. *IEEE Journal of Selected Topics in Applied Earth Observations and Remote Sensing*, *14*, 6906–6915. doi:10.1109/JSTARS.2021.3075961

Bernardes, G. (2023). Prototyping low-cost automatic weather stations for natural disaster monitoring. *Digital Communications and Network*, *9*(4), 941-956.

Bhandari, V. (2022). *Use of Technology in Disaster Management*. Unity Journal. doi:10.3126/unityj.v3i01.43333

Bhattarai, N., Dahal, S., Thapa, S., Pradhananga, S., Karky, B. S., Rawat, R. S., Windhorst, K., Watanabe, T., Thapa, R. B., & Avtar, R. (2022). Forest Fire in the Hindu Kush Himalayas: A Major Challenge for Climate Action. *Journal of Forest and Livelihood*, *21*(1), 14–31. doi:10.3126/jfl.v21i1.56576

Bhujbal, A., Hole, P., Khedkar, P., & Zaman, N. (2022). Flood Detection and Management System. *International Journal of Innovative Research in Science and Engineering*, *8*, 104–110.

Bianchinia, G., Denhama, M., Cortésa, A., Margalefa, T., & Luquea, E. (2006). Improving forest-fire prediction by applying a statistical approach. *Forest Ecology and Management*, *234*(S1), 210. doi:10.1016/j.foreco.2006.08.237

Bilal, M. & Yaqub, M. (2022). An early warning system for earthquake prediction from seismic data using Batch Normalized Graph Convolutional Neural Network with Attention Mechanism (BNGCNNATT). *Sensors*, *22*(17), 6482.

Biswas, T. K., Abbasi, A., & Chakrabortty, R. K. (2022). A two-stage VIKOR assisted multi-operator differential evolution approach for Influence Maximization in social networks. *Expert Systems with Applications, 192*. doi:10.1016/j.eswa.2021.116342

Bocchini, P., & Frangopol, D. M. (2012b). Restoration of bridge networks after an earthquake: Multicriteria intervention optimization. *Earthquake Spectra*, *28*(2), 426–455. doi:10.1193/1.4000019

Bogdan, E. A., Caine, K. J., & Beckie, M. A. (2020). Unraveling the social construction of a flooding disaster: A threaded situation analysis approach. *International Journal of Mass Emergencies and Disasters*, *38*(3), 308–339. doi:10.1177/028072702003800303

Bouzidi, Z., Boudries, A., & Amad, M. (2020). Towards a Smart Interface-Based Automated Learning Environment Through Social Media for Disaster Management and Smart Disaster Education. *Sai.*

Bovolo, F., Bruzzone, L., & Marconcini, M. (2008). A novel approach to unsupervised change detection based on a semisupervised SVM and a similarity measure. *IEEE Transactions on Geoscience and Remote Sensing*, *46*(7), 2070–2082. doi:10.1109/TGRS.2008.916643

Bragazzi, N. L., Dai, H., Damiani, G., Behzadifar, M., Martini, M., & Wu, J. (2019). How Big Data and Artificial Intelligence Can Help Better Manage the COVID-19 Pandemic. *International Journal of Environmental Research and Public Health*, *17*(9), 3176. doi:10.3390/ijerph17093176 PMID:32370204

Buckland, C. E., Bailey, R. M., & Thomas, D. S. G. (2019). Using artificial neural networks to predict future dryland responses to human and climate disturbances. *Scientific Reports*, *9*(1), 3855. doi:10.103841598-019-40429-5 PMID:30846833

Bui, D. T., Hoang, N. D., Martínez-Álvarez, F., Ngo, P. T. T., Hoa, P. V., Pham, T. D., Samui, P., & Costache, R. (2020). A novel deep learning neural network approach for predicting flash flood susceptibility: A case study at a high frequency tropical storm area. *The Science of the Total Environment*, *701*, 134413. doi:10.1016/j.scitotenv.2019.134413 PMID:31706212

Burton, D., Bernardet, L., Faure, G., Herndon, D., Knaff, J., Li, Y., Mayers, J., Radjab, F., Sampson, C., & Waqaicelua, A. (2010). *Structure and intensity change: Operational guidance.* In *Proceedings of the 7th International Workshop on Tropical Cyclones*, La Réunion, France.

Canadell, J. G., Meyer, C. P., Cook, G. D., Dowdy, A., Briggs, P. R., Knauer, J., Pepler, A., & Haverd, V. (2021). Multi-decadal increase of forest burned area in Australia is linked to climate change. *Nature Communications*, *12*(1), 6921. doi:10.103841467-021-27225-4 PMID:34836974

Cao, J., Liu, K., Liu, L., Zhu, Y., Li, J., & He, Z. (2018). Identifying Mangrove Species Using Field Close-Range Snapshot Hyperspectral Imaging and Machine-Learning Techniques. *Remote Sensing (Basel)*, *10*(12), 2047. doi:10.3390/rs10122047

Caragea, C., Squicciarini, A., Stehle, S., Neppalli, K., & Tapia, A. (2014). Mapping moods: Geomapped sentiment analysis during Hurricane Sandy. In: *Proceedings of the 11th International Conference on Information Systems for Crisis Response and Management(ISCRAM 2014), ISCRAM*. Research Gate.

Cervone, G., Sava, E., Huang, Q., Schnebele, E., Harrison, J., & Waters, N. (2016). Using Twitter for tasking remote-sensing data collection and damage assessment: 2013 Boulder flood case study. *International Journal of Remote Sensing, 37*(1), 100–124. doi:10.1080/01431161.2015.1117684

Chand, C. P., Ali, M. M., Himasri, B., Bourassa, M. A., & Zheng, Y. (2021). Predicting Indian Ocean Cyclone Parameters Using an Artificial Intelligence Technique. *Atmosphere.*

Chandrasekhar, V., & Seah, W. K. G. (2006a). Localization in underwater sensor networks – survey and challenges. *Proceedings of IEEE conference.* IEEE.

Chandrasekhar, V., & Seah, W. K. G. (2006b). Area localization scheme for underwater sensor networks. *Proceedings of the IEEE OCEAN Asia Pacific Conference.* IEEE. 10.1109/OCEANSAP.2006.4393969

Chaurasia, K., Tarun, U. V. S., Sarala, G., & Soni, K. (2020). *AI based prediction of daily rainfall from satellite observation for disaster management.* Future Sensing Technologies. doi:10.1117/12.2580628

Chen, K., C., Y., & Jianhuan, H. (2009). A localization scheme of underwater wireless sensor networks. *Proceedings of International Journal of Advanced Science and Technology, 4.*

Chen, S. A., Escay, A., Haberland, C., Schneider, T., Staneva, V., & Choe, Y. 2018. *Benchmark dataset for automatic damaged building detection from post-hurricane remotely sensed imagery.* arXiv preprint arXiv:1812.05581.

Cheng, T., & Wang, J. (2008). Integrated spatio-temporal data mining for forest fire prediction. *Transactions in GIS, 12*(5), 591–611. doi:10.1111/j.1467-9671.2008.01117.x

Chen, J., Gong, P., He, C., Pu, R., & Shi, P. (2003). Land-use/land-cover change detection using improved change-vector analysis. *Photogrammetric Engineering and Remote Sensing, 69*(4), 369–379. doi:10.14358/PERS.69.4.369

Chen, L., Rottensteiner, F., & Heipke, C. (2021). Feature detection and description for image matching: From hand-crafted design to deep learning. *Geo-Spatial Information Science, 24*(1), 58–74. doi:10.1080/10095020.2020.1843376

Chittora, P., Chakrabarti, T., Debnath, P., Gupta, A., Chakrabarti, P., Praveen, S. P.,& Elngar, A. A. (2022). *Experimental analysis of earthquake prediction using machine learning classifiers, curve fitting, and neural modeling.*

Chopra, M., Singh, S. K., Aggarwal, K., & Gupta, A. (2022). Predicting catastrophic events using machine learning models for natural language processing. In *Data mining approaches for big data and sentiment analysis in social media* (pp. 223–243). IGI Global. doi:10.4018/978-1-7998-8413-2.ch010

Choubin, B., Borji, M., Mosavi, A., Sajedi-Hosseini, F., Singh, V. P., & Shamshirband, S. (2019). Snow avalanche hazard prediction using machine learning methods. *Journal of Hydrology (Amsterdam), 577*, 123929. doi:10.1016/j.jhydrol.2019.123929

Chui, M., Harryson, M., Valley, S., Manyika, J., & Roberts, R. (2018). *Notes from the AI frontier applying AI for social good.*

Cook, D. J., & Das, S. K. (2004). *Smart environments: technologies, protocols and applications.* John Wiley. doi:10.1002/047168659X

Coughlan, R., Di Giuseppe, F., Vitolo, C., Barnard, C., Lopez, P., & Drusch, M. (2021). Using machine learning to predict fire-ignition occurrences from lightning forecasts. *Meteorological Applications*, *28*(1), e1973. doi:10.1002/met.1973

Damasevicius, R., Bacanin, N., & Misra, S. (2023). From sensors to safety: Internet of Emergency Services (IoES) for emergency response and disaster management. *Journal of Sensor and Actuator Networks, 12*(3), 41.

Damaševičius, R., Bacanin, N., & Misra, S. (2023). From Sensors to Safety: Internet of Emergency Services (IoES) for Emergency Response and Disaster Management. *Journal of Sensor & Actuator Networks, 12*(3), 41. doi:10.3390/jsan12030041

Dascher-Cousineau, K., Shchur, O., Brodsky, E. E., & Günnemann, S. (2023). Using Deep Learning for Flexible and Scalable Earthquake Forecasting. *Geophysical Research Letters, 50*(17), e2023GL103909. doi:10.1029/2023GL103909

Dhinakaran. (2023). IoT-Based Environmental Control System for Fish Farms with Sensor Integration and Machine Learning Decision Support. *International Journal on Recent and Innovation Trends in Computing and Communication, 11*(10), 203–217. https://ijritcc.org/index.php/ijritcc/article/view/8482. doi:10.17762/ijritcc.v11i10.8482

DHS. (2010) *DHS [29] DOE (2014) Lantern live*. GitHub. https://github.com/GSA/digitalgov.gov/blob/master/content/posts/2014/12/2014-12-04-nd-fuel-during-disasters-with-lantern-live-app.mdrisk lexicon. URL https://www.dhs.gov/xlibrary/assets/dhs-risk-lexicon-2010.pdf

Di Baldassarre, G., Cloke, H., Lindersson, S., Mazzoleni, M., Mondino, E., Mård, J., & Tootoonchi, F. (2021). Integrating multiple research methods to unravel the complexity of human- water systems. *AGU Advances, 2*(3), e2021AV000473.

Diaz, P. (2022). *IWARN: A people-centered approach for early warning.*

Drydakis, N. (2022). Artificial Intelligence and Reduced SMEs' Business Risks. A Dynamic Capabilities Analysis During the COVID-19 Pandemic. *Information Systems Frontiers*, *24*(4), 1223–1247. doi:10.100710796-022-10249-6 PMID:35261558

Duarte, D., Nex, F., Kerle, N., & Vosselman, G. (2018). Satellite Image Classification Of Building Damages Using Airborne And Satellite Image Samples In A Deep Learning Approach. *ISPRS Annals of the Photogrammetry, Remote Sensing and Spatial Information Sciences*, *4*(2), 89–96. doi:10.5194/isprs-annals-IV-2-89-2018

Eddin, M. H. S., Roscher, R., & Gall, J. (2023). Location-Aware Adaptive Normalization: A Deep Learning Approach for Wildfire Danger Forecasting. *IEEE Transactions on Geoscience and Remote Sensing*, *61*, 1–18. doi:10.1109/TGRS.2023.3285401

El Houssaini, D., & Kanoun, O. (2022). Location-Aware IoT-Enabled Wireless Sensor Networks for Landslide Early Warning. *Electronics, 11*(23), 3971.

El Moulat, M., Debauche, O., Mahmoudi, S., Brahim, L. A., Manneback, P., & Lebeau, F. (2018). Monitoring system using internet of things for potential landslides. *Procedia Computer Science, 134*, 26–34. doi:10.1016/j.procs.2018.07.140

Emami, P., & Marzban, A. (2023). The Synergy of Artificial Intelligence (AI) and Geographic Information Systems (GIS) for Enhanced Disaster Management: Opportunities and Challenges. *Disaster Medicine and Public Health Preparedness, 17*, 17. doi:10.1017/dmp.2023.174 PMID:37694385

Enrique, C. -M., Ribeiro-Soriano, D. (2023). Exploring the challenges of the COVID-19 vaccine supply chain using social media analytics: A global perspective. *Sustainable Technology and Entrepreneurship, 2*(3). doi:10.1016/j.stae.2023.100047

Escolano, V. J., Caballero, A., Albina, E. M., Hernandez, A. A., & Juanatas, R. (2023). Acceptance of Mobile Application on Disaster Preparedness: Towards Decision Intelligence in Disaster Management. *2023 8th International Conference on Business and Industrial Research (ICBIR)*, 381-386.

Esposito, M. & Pierleoni, O. (2022). Recent advances in internet of things solutions for early warning systems: A review. *Sensors, 22*(6), 2124.

Esposito, M., Palma, L., Belli, A., Sabbatini, L., & Pierleoni, P. (2022). Recent advances in internet of things solutions for early warning systems: A review. *Sensors (Basel), 22*(6), 2124. doi:10.339022062124 PMID:35336296

Esrafilian-Najafabadi, M., and Haghighat, F. (2022). Impact of predictor variables on the performance of future occupancy prediction: feature selection using genetic algorithms and machine learning. *Build. Environ. 219*, 109152. doi:. buildenv.2022.109152 doi:10.1016/j

Fatema, S. R. (2020). Women's health-related vulnerabilities in natural disaster-affected areas of Bangladesh: A mixed-methods study protocol. *BMJ Open, 10*(11), e039772. doi:10.1136/bmjopen-2020-039772 PMID:33234637

Field, E. H., Milner, K. R., Hardebeck, J. L., Page, M. T., van der Elst, N., Jordan, T. H., Michael, A. J., Shaw, B. E., & Werner, M. J. (2017). A spatiotemporal clustering model for the third uniform California earthquake rupture forecast (UCERF3-ETAS): Toward an operational earthquake forecast. *Bulletin of the Seismological Society of America, 107*(3), 1049–1081. doi:10.1785/0120160173

Fox, G., Rundle, J., Donnellan, A., & Feng, B. (2022). Earthquake Nowcasting with Deep Learning. *GeoHazards., 3*(2), 199–226. doi:10.3390/geohazards3020011

Galera-Zarco, C., & Floros, G. (2023). A deep learning approach to improve built asset operations and disaster management in critical events: An integrative simulation model for quicker decision making. *Annals of Operations Research.* doi:10.100710479-023-05247-z

Gama, M., Santos, B. F., & Scaparra, M. P. (2016). A multi-period shelter location-allocation model with evacuation orders for flood disasters. *EURO Journal on Computational Optimization*, *4*(3-4), 299–323. doi:10.100713675-015-0058-3

Ganguly, K. K., Nahar, N., & Hossain, B. M. (2019). A machine learning-based prediction and analysis of flood affected households: A case study of floods in Bangladesh. *International Journal of Disaster Risk Reduction*, *34*, 283–294. doi:10.1016/j.ijdrr.2018.12.002

Gao, Jie, Wu Zhang, Chunbaixue Yang, Rui Wang, Shuai Shao, Jiawei Li, Limiao Zhang, Zhijian Li, Shu Liu, & Wentao Si. (2022). Comparative Study on International Research Hotspots and National-Level Policy Keywords of Dynamic Disaster Monitoring and Early Warning in China (2000–2021). *International journal of environmental research and public health*, *19*(22), 15107.

Gao, Y., Chen, Y.X., Ding, Y.S., & Tang, B.Y. (2006) Immune genetic algorithm based on network model for flood disaster evaluation. *Journal of Natural Disaster, 15*.

Garcia, J. (2005). Positioning of sensors in Underwater Acoustic Networks. *Proceedings of the MTS/IEEE OCEANS Conference*, Washington DC, USA. 10.1109/OCEANS.2005.1640068

García-Tadeo, D. A., Peram, D. R., Kumar, K. S., Vives, L., Sharma, T., & Manoharan, G. (2022). Comparing the impact of Internet of Things and cloud computing on organisational behaviour: A survey. *Materials Today: Proceedings*, *51*(Part 8), 2281–2285. doi:10.1016/j.matpr.2021.11.399

Gelernter, J., & Balaji, S. (2013). An algorithm for local geoparsing of microtext. *GeoInformatica*, *17*(4), 635–667. doi:10.100710707-012-0173-8

Gepp, A., Linnenluecke, M. K., O'Neill, T. J., & Smith, T. (2018). Big data techniques in auditing research and practice: Current trends and future opportunities. *Journal of Accounting Literature*, *40*(1), 102–115. doi:10.1016/j.acclit.2017.05.003

Ghaffarian, S., Taghikhah, F. R., & Maier, H. R. (2023). Explainable artificial intelligence in disaster risk management: Achievements and prospective futures. *International Journal of Disaster Risk Reduction*, *98*, 104123. doi:10.1016/j.ijdrr.2023.104123

Goetz, J. N., Brenning, A., Petschko, H., & Leopold, P. (2015). Evaluating machine learning and statistical prediction techniques for landslide susceptibility modeling. *Computers & Geosciences*, *81*, 1–11. doi:10.1016/j.cageo.2015.04.007

Gong, P. (1993). Change detection using principal component analysis and fuzzy set theory. *Canadian Journal of Remote Sensing*, *19*(1), 22–29. doi:10.1080/07038992.1993.10855147

Gong, W., Hu, J., Wang, Z., Wei, Y., Li, Y., Zhang, T., Zhang, Q., Liu, T., Ning, Y., Zhang, W., & Grattan, K. T. V. (2022). Recent advances in laser gas sensors for applications to safety monitoring in intelligent coal mines. *Frontiers in Physics (Lausanne)*, *10*, 1058475. doi:10.3389/fphy.2022.1058475

Goodwin, M. (2020). Big data analytics tools and applications for modern business world. In: *2020 International Conference on Electronics and Sustainable Communication Systems (ICESC)*, (pp. 587–592). IEEE 10.1109/ICESC48915.2020.9155704

Goswami, S., Chakraborty, S., Ghosh, S., Chakrabarti, A., & Chakraborty, B. (2018). A review on application of data mining techniques to combat natural disasters. *Ain Shams Engineering Journal*, *9*(3), 365–378. doi:10.1016/j.asej.2016.01.012

Gulati, N., Sethi, A., Mahesh, D., Makkar, S., Geetha Manoharan, M., & Palanivel, R. (2022). Implementation of blockchain in supply chain. *AIP Conference Proceedings*, *2418*, 020026. doi:10.1063/5.0083008

Gupta, M., Almomani, O., Khasawneh, A. M., & Darabkh, K. A. (2022). Smart remote sensing network for early warning of disaster risks. In Nanotechnology-Based Smart Remote Sensing Networks for Disaster Prevention, (pp. 303-324). IEEE.

Gupta, R., Hosfelt, R., Sajeev, S., Patel, N., Goodman, B., Doshi, J., Heim, E., Choset, H., & Gaston, M. (2019) xBD: A dataset for assessing building damage from satellite imagery. In: *Proceedings of the CVPR Workshops 2019*. arXiv: 1911.09296v1

Gutenberg, B., & Richter, C. F. (1944). Frequency of earthquakes in California. *Bulletin of the Seismological Society of America*, *34*(4), 4–188. doi:10.1785/BSSA0340040185

Hahn, M., & Rice, J. (2005). *Undersea Navigation via a Distributed Acoustic Communication Network. Proceedings of the Turkish International Conference on Acoustics*, Istanbul,Turkey.

Halperin, D. J., Fuelberg, H. E., Hart, R. E., Cossuth, J. H., Sura, P., & Pasch, R. J. (2013). An Evaluation of Tropical Cyclone Genesis Forecasts from Global Numerical Models. *Weather and Forecasting*, *28*(6), 1423–1445. doi:10.1175/WAF-D-13-00008.1

Han, H., & Lee, S. (2015). Detection of Convective Initiation Using Meteorological Imager Onboard Communication, Ocean, and Meteorological Satellite Based on Machine Learning Approaches. Remote. Sens. Research Gate.

Hashim, F., Navaz, A.N., Zaki, N., Shuaib, K., & Serhani, M.A. (2023). Artificial Intelligence and Blockchain-Based Trading Framework for Satellite Images. *2023 International Wireless Communications and Mobile Computing (IWCMC)*, (pp. 786-792). IEEE.

Healey, S. P., Cohen, W. B., Yang, Z., Brewer, C. K., Brooks, E. B., Gorelick, N., & Zhu, Z. (2018). Mapping forest change using stacked generalization: An ensemble approach. *Remote Sensing of Environment*, *204*, 717–728. doi:10.1016/j.rse.2017.09.029

Heidemann, J., Li, Y., Syed, A., Wills, J., & Ye, W. (2006). Research Challenges and Applications For Underwater Sensor Networking. *Proceedings of the IEEE Wireless Communications and Networking Conference (WCNC2006)*. IEEE. 10.1109/WCNC.2006.1683469

Heitzler, M., Lam, J.C., & Hackl, J. (2017). *GPU-Accelerated Rendering Methods to Visually Analyze Large-Scale Disaster Simulation Data*. Springer. doi:10.1007/s41651-017-0004-4

Helms, C. N., Knapp, K. R., Bowen, A. R., & Hennon, C. C. (2011). An Objective Algorithm for Detecting and Tracking Tropical Cloud Clusters: Implications for Tropical Cyclogenesis Prediction. *Journal of Atmospheric and Oceanic Technology*.

Hemdan, E. E. D., El-Shafai, W., & Sayed, A. (2023). Integrating Digital Twins with IoT-Based Blockchain: Concept, Architecture, Challenges, and Future Scope. *Wireless Personal Communications, 131*(3), 1–24. doi:10.100711277-023-10538-6 PMID:37360142

Henao-Céspedes, V. & Olaya, M. (2023). Landslide early warning systems: a perspective from the internet of things. *International Journal of Electrical and Computer Engineering 13*(2), 2214.

Hernandez, D., Cano, J., Silla, F., Calafate, C. & Cecilia, J. (2022). AI-Enabled Autonomous Drones for Fast Climate Change Crisis Assessment. *IEEE Internet of Things Journal, vol. 9*(10), 7286-7297. . doi:10.1109/JIOT.2021.3098379

Hingmire, M.A. (2021). *Planning for Disaster Management in India using IOT.*

Hong, Jung-Hong, & Yi-Tin Shi. (2023). Integration of Heterogeneous Sensor Systems for Disaster Responses in Smart Cities: Flooding as an Example. *ISPRS International Journal of Geo-Information, 12*(7), 279.

Hong, C., Burney, J. A., Pongratz, J., Nabel, J. E., Mueller, N. D., Jackson, R. B., & Davis, S. J. (2021). Global and regional drivers of land-use emissions in 1961–2017. *Nature, 589*(7843), 554–561. doi:10.103841586-020-03138-y PMID:33505037

Houston, J. B., Hawthorne, J., Perreault, M., Park, E., Hode, M., Halliwell, M., McGowen, S., Davis, R., Vaid, S., Mcelderry, J., & Griffith, S. (2014). Social media and disasters: A functional framework for social media use in disaster planning, response, and research. *Disasters, 39*(1), 1–22. doi:10.1111/disa.12092 PMID:25243593

Houze, R. A. Jr. (2010). Clouds in tropical cyclones. *Monthly Weather Review, 138*(2), 293–344. doi:10.1175/2009MWR2989.1

Howarth, P. J., & Wickware, G. M. (1981). Procedures for change detection using Landsat digital data. *International Journal of Remote Sensing, 2*(3), 277–291. doi:10.1080/01431168108948362

Innocente, M. S., & Grasso, P. (2019). Self-organising swarms of frefghting drones: Harnessing the power of collective intelligence in decentralised multi-robot systems. *Journal of Computational Science, 34*, 80–101. doi:10.1016/j.jocs.2019.04.009

Ismail, F. & Hossam, A. (2022). *A new distributed earthquake early warning communication protocol based on messaging.*

Jafar, S. H., Hemachandran, K., El-Chaarani, H., Moturi, S., & Gupta, N. (Eds.). (2023). *Artificial Intelligence for Capital Markets.* CRC Press.

Jain, H., Dhupper, R., Shrivastava, A., & Kumar Dand Kumari, M. (2023). Leveragingmachinelearning algorithms forimproved disaster preparedness andresponse through accurate weatherpattern and natural disaster prediction. *Frontiers in Environmental Science, 11*, 1194918. doi:10.3389/fenvs.2023.1194918

Jami Pour, M., Hosseinzadeh, M., & Amoozad Mahdiraji, H. (2021). Exploring and evaluating success factors of social media marketing strategy: A multi-dimensional-multi-criteria framework. *Foresight*, *23*(6), 655–678. doi:10.1108/FS-01-2021-0005

Jena, R., Pradhan, B., Beydoun, G., Alamri, A. M., Ardiansyah, A., Nizamuddin, N., & Sofyan, H. (2020). Earthquake hazard and risk assessment using machine learning approaches at Palu, Indonesia. *The Science of the Total Environment*, *749*, 141582. doi:10.1016/j.scitotenv.2020.141582 PMID:33370892

Jia, D., Yang, L., Lv, T., Liu, W., Gao, X., & Zhou, J. (2022). Evaluation of machine learning models for predicting daily global and diffuse solar radiation under different weather/pollution conditions. *Renew. Energy 187,* 896–906. doi:. 02.002 doi:10.1016/j.renene.2022

Johns, A. (2013). *Dreadful visitations: Confronting natural catastrophe in the age of enlightenment*. Routledge. doi:10.4324/9781315022789

Johnson, R. D., & Kasischke, E. S. (1998). Change vector analysis: A technique for the multispectral monitoring of land cover and condition. *International Journal of Remote Sensing*, *19*(3), 411–426. doi:10.1080/014311698216062

Josipovic, N., & Viergutz, K. (2023). Smart Solutions for Municipal Flood Management: Overview of Literature, Trends, and Applications in German Cities. *Smart Cities*, *6*(2), 944–964. doi:10.3390martcities6020046

Kalatzis, N. (2018). Edge computing in iot ecosystems for uav-enabled early fire detection. Proceedings of the 2018 IEEE International Conference on Smart Computing, SMARTCOMP, (pp. 106–114). IEEE. 10.1109/SMARTCOMP.2018.00080

Kalinowska, A., Pilarski, P. M., & Murphey, T. D. (2023). Embodied Communication: How Robots and People Communicate Through Physical Interaction. *Annual Review of Control, Robotics, and Autonomous Systems*, *6*(1), 205–232. doi:10.1146/annurev-control-070122-102501

Kameshwar, S., & Padgett, J. E. (2014). Multi-hazard risk assessment of highway bridges subjectedto earthquake and hurricane hazards. *Engineering Structures*, *78*, 154–166. doi:10.1016/j.engstruct.2014.05.016

Kar, A. K., Varsha, P. S., & Rajan, S. (2023). Unravelling the Impact of Generative Artificial Intelligence (GAI) in Industrial Applications: A Review of Scientific and Grey Literature. *Global Journal of Flexible Systems Management*, 1-31.

Karamlou, A., Bocchini, P., & Christou, V. (2016) Metrics and algorithm for optimal retro strategy of resilient transportation networks. In: *Proceedings of the Maintenance, Monitoring, Safety, Risk and Resilience of Bridges and Bridge Networks*. Research Gate.

Katiar, V., Chand, N., & Chauhan, N. (2010). Recent advances and future trends in wireless sensor networks. *Proceedings of International Journal of Applied Engineering Research, Dindigul*, *1*(3).

Kaur, J. (2023). Robotic Process Automation in Healthcare Sector. In *E3S Web of Conferences* (Vol. 391, p. 01008). EDP Sciences.

Kay, R., & Mattern, F. (2004). The Design Space of Wireless Sensor Networks. *IEEE Wireless Communications*, *11*(6), 54–61. doi:10.1109/MWC.2004.1368897

Kellermann, P., Schröter, K., Thieken, A. H., Haubrock, S. N., & Kreibich, H. (2020). The object-specific flood damage database HOWAS21. *Natural Hazards and Earth System Sciences*, *20*(9), 2503–2519. doi:10.5194/nhess-20-2503-2020

Kemker, R., Salvaggio, C., & Kanan, C. (2018). Algorithms for semantic segmentation of multispectral remote sensing imagery using deep learning. *ISPRS Journal of Photogrammetry and Remote Sensing*, *145*, 60–77. doi:10.1016/j.isprsjprs.2018.04.014

Khan, S. & Ashraf, I. (2023). A Systematic Review of Disaster Management Systems: Approaches, Challenges, and Future Directions. *Land*, *12*(8), 1514.

Khan, A., Gupta, S., & Gupta, S. K. (2022). Emerging UAV technology for disaster detection, mitigation, response, and preparedness. *Journal of Field Robotics*, *39*(6), 905–955. doi:10.1002/rob.22075

Khan, R., Shabaz, M., Hussain, S., Ahmad, F., & Mishra, P. (2022). Early flood detection and rescue using bioinformatic devices, internet of things (IOT) and Android application. *World Journal of Engineering*, *19*(2), 204–215. doi:10.1108/WJE-05-2021-0269

Kim Y, Ghorpade A, Zhao F, Pereira FC, Zegras PC, Ben-Akiva M (2018c) Activity recognition for a smartphone and web-based human mobility sensing system. *IEEE Intelligent Systems, 33.*

Kim, M. (2015). Landfast sea ice monitoring using multisensor fusion in the Antarctic. Remote Sens. Research Gate.

Kim, S.S., Shin, D.Y., Lim, E.T., Jung, Y., & Cho, S.B. (2022). Disaster Damage Investigation Using Artificial Intelligence And Drone Mapping. *The International Archives of the Photogrammetry, Remote Sensing and Spatial Information Sciences.*

Kochersberger, K., Kroeger, K., Krawiec, B., Brewer, E., & Weber, T. (2014) Postdisaster remote sensing and sampling via an autonomous helicopter. *Journal of Field Robotics 31.*

Kondaveti, R., & Ganz, A. (2009). Decision support system for resource allocation in disaster management. In: *The Annual International Conference of the IEEE Engineering in Medicine and Biology Society*. IEEE. 10.1109/IEMBS.2009.5332498

Kong, S.G., Jin, D., Li, S., & Kim, H. (2016b). Fast rename detection in surveillance video using logistic regression and temporal smoothing. *Fire Safety Journal, 79.*

Kuang, S., & Davison, B. D. (2017). Learning word embeddings with Chi-Square weights for healthcare tweet classification. *Applied Sciences (Basel, Switzerland)*, *7*(8), 846. doi:10.3390/app7080846

Kuglitsch, M. M., Pelivan, I., Ceola, S., Menon, M., & Xoplaki, E. (2022). Facilitating adoption of AI in natural disaster management through collaboration. *Nature Communications*, *13*(1), 13. doi:10.1038/s41467-022-29285-6 PMID:35332147

Kumar, A., Sah, B., Singh, A. R., Deng, Y., He, X., & Kumar, P. (2017). A review of multi criteria decision making (MCDM) towards sustainable renewable energy development. *Renewable and Sustainable Energy Reviews, 69*. doi:10.1016/j.rser.2016.11.191

Kumar, R., Mittal, H., Sandeep, & Sharma, B. (2022). Earthquake genesis and earthquake early warning systems: Challenges and a way forward. *Surveys in Geophysics, 43*(4), 1143–1168. doi:10.100710712-022-09710-7

Lahiri, S., Snowden, B., Gu, J., Krishnan, N., Yellin, H., & Ndiaye, K. (2021). Multidisciplinary team processes parallel natural disaster preparedness and response: A qualitative case study. *International Journal of Disaster Risk Reduction, 61*, 102369. doi:10.1016/j.ijdrr.2021.102369

Latvakoski, J., Öörni, R., Lusikka, T., & Keränen, J. (2022). Evaluation of emerging technological opportunities for improving risk awareness and resilience of vulnerable people in disasters. *International Journal of Disaster Risk Reduction, 80*, 103173. doi:10.1016/j.ijdrr.2022.103173

Laurenti, L., Tinti, E., Galasso, F., Franco, L., & Marone, C. (2022). Deep learning for laboratory earthquake prediction and autoregressive forecasting of fault zone stress. *Earth and Planetary Science Letters, 598*, 1–14. doi:10.1016/j.epsl.2022.117825

LeCun, Y., Bengio, Y., & Hinton, G. (2015). Deep Learning. *Nature, 521*(7553), 436–444. doi:10.1038/nature14539 PMID:26017442

Lee, S. Im, J., Kim, J., Kim, M., Shin, M., Kim, H.-C., & Quackenbush, L.J. (2016). Arctic Sea Ice Thickness Estimation from CryoSat-2 Satellite Data Using Machine Learning-Based Lead Detection. Remote. Sens. Research Gate.

Leng, P., Yang, Z., Yan, Q.-Y., Shang, G.-F., Zhang, X., Han, X.-J., & Li, Z.-L. (2023). A framework for estimating all-weather fine resolution soil moisture from the integration of physics-based and machine learning-based algorithms. *Computers and Electronics in Agriculture, 206*, 107673. doi:10.1016/j.compag.2023.107673

Li, X. & Wang, D. (2022). Recent advances on early-stage fire-warning systems: mechanism, performance, and perspective. *Nano-micro letters, 14*(1), 197.

Li, Y., Ye, S., & Bartoli, I. (2018). Semisupervised classification of hurricane damage from postevent aerial imagery using deep learning. *Journal of Applied Remote Sensing, 12*(4), p.045008. 10.1117/1.JRS.12.045008

Linardos, V., Drakaki, M., Tzionas, P., & Karnavas, Y. L. (2022). Machine learning in disaster management: recent developments in methods and applications. *Machine Learning and Knowledge Extraction, 4*(2).

Linardos, V., Drakaki, M., Tzionas, P., & Karnavas, Y. L. (2022). Machine Learning in Disaster Management: Recent Developments in Methods and Applications. *Mach. Learn. Knowl. Extr., 4*(2), 446–473. doi:10.3390/make4020020

Ling, Q., Tian, Z., Yin, Y., & Li, Y. (2009). Localized structural health monitoring using energy efficient wireless sensor networks. *IEEE Sensors Journal*, *9*(11), 1596–1604. doi:10.1109/JSEN.2009.2019318

Lingxin, Z., Junkai, S., & Baijie, Z. (2022). A review of the research and application of deep learning-based computer vision in structural damage detection. *Earthquake Engineering and Engineering Vibration*, *21*(1), 1–21. doi:10.100711803-022-2074-7

Lin, T.-H., Huang, J.-T., & Putranto, A. (2022). Integrated smart robot with earthquake early warning system for automated inspection and emergency response. *Natural Hazards*, *110*(1), 765–786. doi:10.100711069-021-04969-2

Liu, T., Yang, L., & Lunga, D. (2021). Change detection using deep learning approach with object-based image analysis. *Remote Sensing of Environment*, *256*, 112308. doi:10.1016/j.rse.2021.112308

Li, Y., Jiang, W., & Zhang, J. (2022). A time series processing chain for geological disasters based on a GPU-assisted sentinel-1 InSAR processor. *Natural Hazards*, *111*(1), 803–815. doi:10.100711069-021-05079-9

Li, Y., Liu, W., Feng, Q., Zhu, M., Yang, L., & Zhang, J. (2022). Effects of land use and land cover change on soil organic carbon storage in the Hexi regions, Northwest China. *Journal of Environmental Management*, *312*, 114911. doi:10.1016/j.jenvman.2022.114911 PMID:35305354

Li, Y., & Xiao, L. (2022). Research on public health crisis early warning system based on context awareness. *Technology and Health Care*, *30*(1), 303–314. doi:10.3233/THC-THC228029 PMID:35124607

Li, Y., Zhang, Z., Wang, W., & Feng, X. (2022, June 2). Rapid Estimation of Earthquake Fatalities in Mainland China Based on Physical Simulation and Empirical Statistics-A Case Study of the 2021 Yangbi Earthquake. *International Journal of Environmental Research and Public Health*, *19*(11), 6820. doi:10.3390/ijerph19116820 PMID:35682403

Llenos, A. L., & Michael, A. J. (2017). Forecasting the (un)productivity of the 2014 M 6.0 South Napa aftershock sequence. *Seismological Research Letters*, *88*(5), 1241–1251. doi:10.1785/0220170050

Llenos, A. L., & Michael, A. J. (2019). Ensembles of ETAS models provide optimal operational earthquake forecasting during swarms: Insights from the 2015 San Ramon, California Swarm. *Bulletin of the Seismological Society of America*, *109*(6), 2145–2158. doi:10.1785/0120190020

Lourens, M., Raman, R., Vanitha, P., Singh, R., Manoharan, G., & Tiwari, M. (2022, December). Agile Technology and Artificial Intelligent Systems in Business Development. In *2022 5th International Conference on Contemporary Computing and Informatics (IC3I)* (pp. 1602-1607). IEEE. 10.1109/IC3I56241.2022.10073410

Lourens, M., Sharma, S., Pulugu, R., Gehlot, A., Manoharan, G., & Kapila, D. (2023, May). Machine learning-based predictive analytics and big data in the automotive sector. In *2023 3rd International Conference on Advance Computing and Innovative Technologies in Engineering (ICACITE)* (pp. 1043-1048). IEEE. 10.1109/ICACITE57410.2023.10182665

Lu, D., Li, G., Valladares, G. S., & Batistella, M. (2004). Mapping soil erosion risk in Rondonia, Brazilian Amazonia: Using RUSLE, remote sensing and GIS. *Land Degradation & Development*, *15*(5), 499–512. doi:10.1002/ldr.634

Lv, L.-Y., Cao, C.-F., Qu, Y.-X., Zhang, G.-D., Zhao, L., Cao, K., Song, P., & Tang, L.-C. (2022). Smart fire-warning materials and sensors: Design principle, performances, and applications. *Materials Science and Engineering R Reports*, *150*, 100690. doi:10.1016/j.mser.2022.100690

Mahesar, R. A., Khalil, H., Shaikh, S., Kalhoro, A., Rajar, A. B., Memon, M. A., & Mamun, M. A. (2023). Exploring suicidality in the aftermath of the 2022 flood in Pakistan: Insights from newspaper reports. *CNS Spectrums*, 1–3. doi:10.1017/S1092852923002419 PMID:37581285

Mahmoudi, S. N., & Chouinard, L. (2016). Seismic fragility assessment of highway bridges using support vector machines. *Bulletin of Earthquake Engineering*, *14*(6), 1571–1587. doi:10.100710518-016-9894-7

Majumder, M. (2015). Multi Criteria Decision Making. In *Impact of Urbanization on Water Shortage in Face of Climatic Aberrations. SpringerBriefs in Water Science and Technology*. Springer. doi:10.1007/978-981-4560-73-3_2

Makkar, S., Bajpai, T., Bhola, M., Mahesh, D., & Manoharan, G. (2022). Blockchain disruption in banking sector. *AIP Conference Proceedings*, *2418*, 020019. doi:10.1063/5.0082288

Mancini, S., Segou, M., Werner, M. J., Parsons, T., Beroza, G., & Chiaraluce, L. (2022). On the use of high-resolution and deep-learning seismic catalogs for short-term earthquake forecasts: Potential benefits and current limitations. *Journal of Geophysical Research: Solid Earth*, *127*(11), e2022JB025202.

Mangalathu, S., Heo, G., & Jeon, J. S. (2018). Artificial neural network based multi-dimensional fragility development of skewed concrete bridge classes. *Engineering Structures*, *162*, 166176. doi:10.1016/j.engstruct.2018.01.053

Manoharan, G. (2022). An evaluation of machine learning techniques and how they affect human resource management and sustainable development. *Manager - The British Journal of Administrative Management*. https://tbjam.org/vol58-special-issue-06/

Manoharan, G., Durai, S., Ashtikar, S. P., & Kumari, N. (2024). Artificial Intelligence in Marketing Applications. In Artificial Intelligence for Business (pp. 40-70). Productivity Press.

Manoharan, G., Durai, S., Rajesh, G. A., Razak, A., Rao, C. B., & Ashtikar, S. P. (2023). A study on the perceptions of officials on their duties and responsibilities at various levels of the organizational structure in order to accomplish artificial intelligence-based smart city implementation. In *Artificial Intelligence and Machine Learning in Smart City Planning* (pp. 1–10). Elsevier. doi:10.1016/B978-0-323-99503-0.00007-7

Mardani, A., Zavadskas, E. K., Govindan, K., Amat Senin, A., & Jusoh, A. (2016). VIKOR Technique: A Systematic Review of the State of the Art Literature on Methodologies and Applications. *Sustainability (Basel), 8*(1), 37. doi:10.3390u8010037

Mardirossian, G., Ranguelov, B., Getsov, P., & Zabunov, S. (2023). Two Innovations for Critical Infrastructure Protection from Natural Disasters. *Dokladi na Bulgarskata Akademiâ na Naukite, 76*(10), 1554–1561. doi:10.7546/CRABS.2023.10.09

McConnon, A. (2018) *AI helps cities predict natural disasters*. WSJ. https://www.wsj.com/articles/ai-helps-cities-predict-natural-disasters-1530065100

McDermid, G. J., Linke, J., Pape, A. D., Laskin, D. N., McLane, A. J., & Franklin, S. E. (2008). Object-based approaches to change analysis and thematic map update: Challenges and limitations. *Canadian Journal of Remote Sensing, 34*(5), 462–466. doi:10.5589/m08-061

Mignan, A., & Broccardo, M. (2020). Neural network applications in earthquake prediction (1994–2019): Meta-analytic and statistical insights on their limitations. *Seismological Research Letters, 91*(4), 2330–2342. doi:10.1785/0220200021

Miller-Hooks, E., & Krauthammer, T. (2007). An intelligent evacuation, rescue and recovery concept. *Fire Technology, 43*(2), 107–122. doi:10.100710694-006-8433-5

Mitsopoulos, I., & Mallinis, G. (2017). A data-driven approach to assess large fire size generation in Greece. *Natural Hazards, 88*(3), 1591–1607. doi:10.100711069-017-2934-z

Mousavi, S. M., Ellsworth, W. L., Zhu, W., Chuang, L. Y., & Beroza, G. C. (2020). Earthquake transformer—An attentive deep-learning model for simultaneous earthquake detection and phase picking. *Nature Communications, 11*(1), 3952. doi:10.103841467-020-17591-w PMID:32770023

Mouzannar, H., Rizk, Y., & Awad, M. (2018). Damage Identification in Social Media Posts using Multimodal Deep Learning. In ISCRAM. Research Gate.

Muhammad, D., Ahmad, I., Khalil, M. I., Khalil, W., & Ahmad, M. O. (2023). A Generalized Deep Learning Approach to Seismic Activity Prediction. *Applied Sciences (Basel, Switzerland), 13*(3), 1598. doi:10.3390/app13031598

Munawar, H. S., Hammad, A. W., & Waller, S. T. (2022). Remote sensing methods for flood prediction: A review. *Sensors (Basel), 22*(3), 960. doi:10.339022030960 PMID:35161706

Munawar, H. S., Hammad, A. W., Waller, S. T., Thaheem, M. J., & Shrestha, A. (2021). An Integrated Approach for Post-Disaster Flood Management Via the Use of Cutting-Edge Technologies and UAVs: A Review. *Sustainability (Basel), 13*(14), 7925. doi:10.3390u13147925

Munawar, H. S., Mojtahedi, M., Hammad, A. W. A., Kouzani, A., & Mahmud, M. A. P. (2022). Disruptive technologies as a solution for disaster risk management: A review. *The Science of the Total Environment*, *806*, 151351. doi:10.1016/j.scitotenv.2021.151351 PMID:34740667

Musa, A., Watanabe, O., Matsuoka, H., Hokari, H., Inoue, T., Murashima, Y., Ohta, Y., Hino, R., Koshimura, S., & Kobayashi, H. (2018). Real-time tsunami inundation forecast system for tsunami disaster prevention and mitigation. *The Journal of Supercomputing*, *74*(7), 3093–3113. doi:10.100711227-018-2363-0

Nabian, M. A., & Meidani, H. (2018b). Deep learning for accelerated seismic reliability analysis of transportation networks. *Computer-Aided Civil and Infrastructure Engineering*, *33*(6), 443–458. doi:10.1111/mice.12359

Neumann, G. B., De Almeida, V. P., & Endler, M. (2018). Smart forests: fire detection service. *Proceedings of the IEEE Symposium on Computers and Communications*, Corfu, Greece.

Nguyen, D. T., Ofli, F., Imran, M., & Mitra, P. (2017). Damage assessment from social media imagery data during disasters. In *Proceedings of the 2017 IEEE/ACM International Conference on Advances in Social Networks Analysis and Mining 2017* (pp. 569-576). IEEE. 10.1145/3110025.3110109

Ofli, F. (2018). All-cause hospital admissions among older adults after a natural disaster. *Annals of Emergency Medicine*, *71*(6), 746–754. doi:10.1016/j.annemergmed.2017.06.042 PMID:28789804

Ogata, Y. (2017). Statistics of earthquake activity: Models and methods for earthquake predictability studies. *Annual Review of Earth and Planetary Sciences*, *45*(1), 497–527. doi:10.1146/annurev-earth-063016-015918

Okyere, M. A., Essel-Gaisey, F., Zuka, F. M., Christian, A. K., & Nunoo, I. K. (2023). Wading out the storm: Exploring the effect of flooding on energy poverty amidst disaster management strategies in Dar es Salaam. *Environmental Science & Policy*, *150*, 103578. doi:10.1016/j.envsci.2023.103578

Oliva, S., & Lazzeretti, L. (2021). Unravelling the Sustainable Resilient Region: Exploring Regional Resilience in Sustainable Transition. In *Rethinking Clusters* (pp. 3–16). Springer. doi:10.1007/978-3-030-61923-7_1

Ou, R., Yan, H., Wu, M., & Zhang, C. (2023). *A Method of Efficient Synthesizing Post-disaster Remote Sensing Image with Diffusion Model and LLM*. 2023 Asia Pacific Signal and Information Processing Association Annual Summit and Conference (APSIPA ASC), Taipei, Taiwan. 10.1109/APSIPAASC58517.2023.10317383

Panakkal, P. (2023). Sensing flooded roads to support roadway mobility during flooding: a web-based tool and insights from needs assessment interviews. *Natural hazards review*, *24*(4), 04023039.

Pang, G., & Pang, G. (2022). Artificial Intelligence for Natural Disaster Management. *IEEE Intelligent Systems*, *37*(6), 3–6. doi:10.1109/MIS.2022.3220061

Pang, Y., Li, Y., Feng, Z., Feng, Z., Zhao, Z., Chen, S., & Zhang, H. (2022). Forest Fire Occurrence Prediction in China Based on Machine Learning Methods. *Remote Sensing (Basel)*, *14*(21), 5546. doi:10.3390/rs14215546

Park, M.-S., & Elsberry, R. L. (2013). Latent Heating and Cooling Rates in Developing and Nondeveloping Tropical Disturbances during TCS-08: TRMM PR versus ELDORA Retrievals*. *Journal of the Atmospheric Sciences*, *70*(1), 15–35. doi:10.1175/JAS-D-12-083.1

Park, M.-S., Kim, M., & Lee, M.-I. (2016). *J.; Park, S. Detection of tropical cyclone genesis via quantitative satellite ocean surface wind pattern and intensity analyses using decision trees.* Remote. Sens. Environ.

Partigöç, N. S. (2022). *The Role of Artificial Intelligence in Disaster Risk Management.* Bilişim Teknolojileri Dergisi.

Pereira, J., Mendes, J., Júnior, J. S., Viegas, C., & Paulo, J. R. (2022). A review of genetic algorithm approaches for wildfire spread prediction calibration. *Mathematics*, *10*(3), 300. doi:10.3390/math10030300

Perwej, Y., Haq, K., Parwej, F., Mumdouh, M., & Hassan, M. (2019). The internet of things (IoT) and its application domains. *International Journal of Computer Applications*, *975*(8887), 182. doi:10.5120/ijca2019918763

Piciullo, L., Capobianco, V., & Heyerdahl, H. (2022). A first step towards a IoT-based local early warning system for an unsaturated slope in Norway. *Natural Hazards*, *114*(3), 3377–3407. doi:10.1007/11069-022-05524-3

Pierleoni, P., Concetti, R., Marzorati, S., Belli, A., & Palma, L. (2023). Internet of Things for Earthquake Early Warning Systems: A Performance Comparison between Communication Protocols. *IEEE Access : Practical Innovations, Open Solutions*, *11*, 43183–43194. doi:10.1109/ACCESS.2023.3271773

Pillai, A. S., Chandraprasad, G. S., Khwaja, A. S., & Anpalagan, A. (2021). A service oriented IoT architecture for disaster preparedness and forecasting system. *Internet of Things : Engineering Cyber Physical Human Systems*, *14*, 100076. doi:10.1016/j.iot.2019.100076

Poslad, S., Middleton, S. E., Chaves, F., Tao, R., Necmioglu, O., & Bügel, U. (2015). A semantic IoT early warning system for natural environment crisis management. *IEEE Transactions on Emerging Topics in Computing*, *3*(2), 246–257. doi:10.1109/TETC.2015.2432742

Pradhan, B. (2009). Flood susceptible mapping and risk area delineation using logistic regression, GIS and remote sensing. *Journal of Spatial Hydrology*, *9*, 1–18.

Prochazka, A., Vysata, O., & Marik, V. (2021). Integrating the role of computational intelligence and digital signal processing in education: Emerging technologies and mathematical tools. *IEEE Signal Processing Magazine*, *38*(3), 154–162. doi:10.1109/MSP.2021.3058634

Prodhan, F. A., Zhang, J., Hasan, S. S., Sharma, T. P. P., & Mohana, H. P. (2022). A review of machine learning methods for drought hazard monitoring and forecasting: Current research trends, challenges, and future research directions. *Environmental Modelling & Software*, *149*, 105327. doi:10.1016/j.envsoft.2022.105327

Purushotham, P., & Caruso, G. D. (2017). The legacy of natural disasters: The intergenerational impact of 100 years of disasters in Latin America. *Journal of Development Economics*, *127*, 209–233. doi:10.1016/j.jdeveco.2017.03.007

Rajendran, L., & Shankaran, R. S. (2021). Bigdata Enabled Realtime Crowd Surveillance Using Artificial Intelligence And Deep Learning. *2021 IEEE International Conference on Big Data and Smart Computing (BigComp)*, (pp. 129-132). IEEE. 10.1109/BigComp51126.2021.00032

Ramchurn, S. D., Huynh, T. D., Wu, F., Ikuno, Y., Flann, J., Moreau, L., Fischer, J. E., Jiang, W., Rodden, T., Simpson, E., Reece, S., Roberts, S., & Jennings, N. R. (2016). A disaster response system based on human-agent collectives. *Journal of Artificial Intelligence Research*, *57*, 661–708. doi:10.1613/jair.5098

Rawat, A. S., & Semwal, M. M. (2022). *Unveiling the Himalayan Nexus: Unraveling Anthropogenic Triggers and Pursuing Sustainable Development in Uttarakhand.*

Razak, A., Nayak, M. P., Manoharan, G., Durai, S., Rajesh, G. A., Rao, C. B., & Ashtikar, S. P. (2023). Reigniting the power of artificial intelligence in education sector for the educators and students competence. In *Artificial Intelligence and Machine Learning in Smart City Planning* (pp. 103–116). Elsevier. doi:10.1016/B978-0-323-99503-0.00009-0

Razali, N., Ismail, S., & Mustapha, A. (2020). Machine learning approach for flood risks prediction. *IAES International Journal of Artificial Intelligence*, *9*(1), 73. doi:10.11591/ijai.v9.i1.pp73-80

Reilly, J., Dashti, S., Ervasti, M., Bray, J. D., Glaser, S. D., & Bayen, A. M. (2013). Mobile phones as seismologic sensors: Automating data extraction for the iShake system. *IEEE Transactions on Automation Science and Engineering*, *10*(2), 242–251. doi:10.1109/TASE.2013.2245121

Richardson, H. J., Hill, D. J., Denesiuk, D. R., & Fraser, L. H. (2017). A comparison of geographic datasets and field measurements to model soil carbon using random forests and stepwise regressions (British Columbia, Canada). *GIScience & Remote Sensing*, *54*(4), 573–591. doi:10.1080/15481603.2017.1302181

Rubí, J. N., de Carvalho, P. H., & Gondim, P. R. (2023). Application of machine learning models in the behavioral study of forest fires in the Brazilian Federal District region. *Engineering Applications of Artificial Intelligence*, *118*, 105649. doi:10.1016/j.engappai.2022.105649

Sachdeva, S., Bhatia, T., & Verma, A. K. (2018). GIS-based evolutionary optimized gradient boosted decision trees for forest fire susceptibility mapping. *Natural Hazards*, *92*(3), 1399–1418. doi:10.100711069-018-3256-5

Saha, S., Bera, B., Shit, P. K., Bhattacharjee, S., & Sengupta, N. (2023). Prediction of forest fire susceptibility applying machine and deep learning algorithms for conservation priorities of forest resources. *Remote Sensing Applications: Society and Environment*, *29*, 100917. doi:10.1016/j.rsase.2022.100917

Saini, K., Kalra, S., & Sood, S. K. (2022). Disaster emergency response framework for smart buildings. *Future Generation Computer Systems*, *131*, 106–120. doi:10.1016/j.future.2022.01.015

Sapena, M. & Taubenböck, H. (2023) Cost estimation for the monitoring instrumentalization of Landslide Early Warning Systems. *Natural Hazards and Earth System Sciences Discussions*, 1-26.

Schofield, M. (2022). An Artificial Intelligence (AI) Approach to Controlling Disaster Scenarios. *Advances in Electronic Government, Digital Divide, and Regional Development*, 28–46. doi:10.4018/978-1-7998-9815-3.ch003

Schumacher, A. B., DeMaria, M., & Knaff, J. A. (2009). Objective Estimation of the 24-h Probability of Tropical Cyclone Formation. *Weather and Forecasting*, *24*(2), 456–471. doi:10.1175/2008WAF2007109.1

Senadheera, H. T., Asai, M., & Morikawa, D. S. (2021). A Feasibility Study for Natural Disaster Simulations Using a Fully Explicit SPH Method in a GPU Environment. In R. Dissanayake, P. Mendis, K. Weerasekera, S. De Silva, & S. Fernando (Eds.), *ICSECM 2019. Lecture Notes in Civil Engineering* (Vol. 94). Springer. doi:10.1007/978-981-15-7222-7_24

Sesnie, S.E., Finegan, B., Gessler, P.E., Thessler, S., Bendana, Z.R., & Smith, A.M.S. (2010). The multispectral separability of Costa Rican rainforest types with support vector machines and Random Forest decision trees. *Int. J. Sens.*

Shaik, M. A., Manoharan, G., Prashanth, B., Akhil, N., Akash, A., & Reddy, T. R. S. (2022). Geetha Manoharan, B. Prashanth, Nune Akhil, Anumandla Akash, and Thudi Raja Shekhar Reddy, "Prediction of crop yield using machine learning". *AIP Conference Proceedings*, *2418*, 020072. doi:10.1063/5.0081726

Shameem, A., Ramachandran, K. K., Sharma, A., Singh, R., Selvaraj, F. J., & Manoharan, G. (2023, May). The rising importance of AI in boosting the efficiency of online advertising in developing countries. In *2023 3rd International Conference on Advance Computing and Innovative Technologies in Engineering (ICACITE)* (pp. 1762-1766). IEEE. 10.1109/ICACITE57410.2023.10182754

Shao, Z., & Cai, J. (2018). Remote sensing image fusion with deep convolutional neural network. *IEEE Journal of Selected Topics in Applied Earth Observations and Remote Sensing*, *11*(5), 1656–1669. doi:10.1109/JSTARS.2018.2805923

Sharma, S. (2020). *Impact of earthquakes based on satellite images using IoT and sensor networks*. Proceedings of the 2020 International Conference on communication Systems and networks, Bangalore, India.

Sha, Y., Li, M., Xu, H., Zhang, S., & Feng, T. (2022). Smart City Public Safety Intelligent Early Warning and Detection. *Scientific Programming*, *2022*, 1–11. doi:10.1155/2022/7552601

Silván-Cárdenas, J. L., & Wang, L. (2014). On quantifying post-classification subpixel landcover changes. *ISPRS Journal of Photogrammetry and Remote Sensing*, *98*, 94–105. doi:10.1016/j.isprsjprs.2014.09.018

Singh, A. (1989). Review article digital change detection techniques using remotely-sensed data. *International Journal of Remote Sensing*, *10*(6), 989–1003. doi:10.1080/01431168908903939

Sit, M. A., Koylu, C., & Demir, I. (2019). Identifying disaster-related tweets and their semantic, spatial and temporal context using deep learning, natural language processing and spatial analysis: A case study of Hurricane Irma. *International Journal of Digital Earth*, *12*(11), 1205–1229. doi:10.1080/17538947.2018.1563219

Sivakumar, P., Sandhya Devi, R. S., Ashwin, M., Rajan Singaravel, M. M., & Buvanesswaran, A. D. 2022. Protocol Design for Earthquake Alert and Evacuation in Smart Buildings. In IoT and WSN based Smart Cities: A Machine Learning Perspective, (pp. 1-14). Springer. doi:10.1007/978-3-030-84182-9_1

Sohraby, K., Minoli, D., & Znati, T. (2007). *Wireless sensor networks: technology,protocols and applications*. John Wiley. doi:10.1002/047011276X

Song, X., Shibasaki, R., Yuan, N. J., Xie, X., Li, T., & Adachi, R. (2017). DeepMob: Learning deep knowledge of human emergency behavior and mobility from big and heterogeneous data. *ACM Transactions on Information Systems*, *35*(4), 1–19. doi:10.1145/3057280

Spalazzi, L., Taccari, G., & Bernardini, A. (2014). *An internet of things ontology for earthquake emergency evaluation and response*. Proceedings of the 2014 International Conference on Collaboration Technologies and sSystems, CTS, Minneapolis, MN, USA. 10.1109/CTS.2014.6867619

Starbird, K., Palen, L., Hughes, A., & Vieweg, S. (2010). Chatter on The Red: What hazards threat reveals about the social life of microblogged information. *Proceedings of the ACM Conference on Computer Supported Cooperative Work*, (pp. 241-250). ACM. 10.1145/1718918.1718965

Subeesh, A., & Mehta, C. R. (2021). Automation and digitization of agriculture using artificial intelligence and internet of things. *Artificial Intelligence in Agriculture*, *5*, 278–291. doi:10.1016/j.aiia.2021.11.004

Sun W, Bocchini P, Davison BD (2020b) Resilience metrics and measurement methods for transportation infrastructure: the state of the art. *Sustainable and Resilient Infrastructure* *5*(3). doi:10.1080/23789689.2018.1448663

Sun, W. (2020). *Applications of artificial intelligence for disaster management*. Springer.

Sung, W.-T., Devi, I. V., & Hsiao, S.-J. (2022). Early warning of impending flash flood based on AIoT. *EURASIP Journal on Wireless Communications and Networking*, *2022*(1), 15. doi:10.118613638-022-02096-5

Sun, J., Qi, W., Huang, Y., Xu, C., & Yang, W. (2023). Facing the Wildfire Spread Risk Challenge: Where Are We Now and Where Are We Going? *Fire (Basel, Switzerland)*, *6*(6), 228. doi:10.3390/fire6060228

Sun, L., Yang, L., Xia, X., Wang, D., & Zhang, T. (2022). Climatological Aspects of Active Fires in Northeastern China and Their Relationship to Land Cover. *Remote Sensing (Basel)*, *14*(10), 2316. doi:10.3390/rs14102316

Sun, W., Bocchini, P., & Davison, B. D. (2020). Applications of artificial intelligence for disaster management. *Natural Hazards*, *103*(3), 2631–2689. doi:10.100711069-020-04124-3

Suriya, M., & Sumithra, M. G. (2019) Enhancing cooperative spectrum sensing in flying cell towers for disaster management using convolutional neural networks. In: *Proceedings of the EAI International Conference on Big Data Innovation for Sustainable Cognitive Computing*, (pp 181–190). IEEE.

Sutton, J., Palen, L., & Shklovski, I. (2008). Backchannels on the Front Lines: Emergent Uses of Social Media in the 2007 Southern California Wildfires. *Proceedings of the 5th International ISCRAM Conference*. IEEE.

Su, Z., Hu, H., Wang, G., Ma, Y., Yang, X., & Guo, F. (2018). Using GIS and Random Forests to identify fire drivers in a forest city, Yichun, China. *Geomatics, Natural Hazards & Risk*, *9*(1), 1207–1229. doi:10.1080/19475705.2018.1505667

Svetnik, V., Liaw, A., Tong, C., Culberson, J. C., Sheridan, R. P., & Feuston, B. P. (2003). Random forest: A classification and regression tool for compound classification and QSAR modeling. *Journal of Chemical Information and Computer Sciences*, *43*(6), 1947–1958. doi:10.1021/ci034160g PMID:14632445

Sweta, K., Goswami, A., Peethambaran, B., Bahuguna, I. M., & Rajawat, A. S. (2022). Landslide susceptibility zonation around Dharamshala, Himachal Pradesh, India: An artificial intelligence model–based assessment. *Bulletin of Engineering Geology and the Environment*, *81*(8), 81. doi:10.100710064-022-02806-9

Takahashi, B. & Carmichael, C. (2015). Communicating on Twitter during a disaster:An analysis of tweets during Typhoon Haiyan in the Philippines. *Computers in Human Behavior, 50.*

Talaat, F. M., & ZainEldin, H. (2023). An improved fire detection approach based on YOLO-v8 for smart cities. *Neural Computing & Applications*, *35*(28), 1–16. doi:10.100700521-023-08809-1 PMID:37362562

Tan, Y. J., Waldhauser, F., Ellsworth, W. L., Zhang, M., Zhu, W., Michele, M., Chiaraluce, L., Beroza, G. C., & Segou, M. (2021). Machine-learning-based high-resolution earthquake catalog reveals how complex fault structures were activated during the 2016–2017 central Italy sequence. *The Seismic Record*, *1*(1), 11–19. doi:10.1785/0320210001

Thavamani, S., Mahesh, D., Sinthuja, U., & Manoharan, G. (2022, May). Crucial attacks in internet of things via artificial intelligence techniques: The security survey. In AIP Conference Proceedings (Vol. 2418, No. 1). AIP Publishing.

Tian, B. (2023). Detecting the unseen: understanding the mechanisms and working principles of earthquake sensors. *Sensors, 23*(11), 5335.

Trinath Basu, M., Karthik, R., Mahitha, J., & Lokesh Reddy, V. (2018). IoT based forest fire detection system. *International Journal of Engineering and Technology (UAE)*, *7*(2), 124–126. doi:10.14419/ijet.v7i2.7.10277

Tripathi, M. A., Tripathi, R., Effendy, F., Manoharan, G., Paul, M. J., & Aarif, M. (2023, January). An In-Depth Analysis of the Role That ML and Big Data Play in Driving Digital Marketing's Paradigm Shift. In *2023 International Conference on Computer Communication and Informatics (ICCCI)* (pp. 1-6). IEEE. 10.1109/ICCCI56745.2023.10128357

Tuladhar, S., Pasakhala, B., Maharjan, A., & Mishra, A. (2021). Unravelling the linkages of cryosphere and mountain livelihood systems: A case study of Langtang, Nepal. *Advances in Climate Change Research*, *12*(1), 119–131. doi:10.1016/j.accre.2020.12.004

UNISDR. (2011a). *Mid-Term Review 2010-2011: Hyogo Framework for Action 2005-2015: Building the Resilience of Nations and Communities to Disasters*. United Nations International Strategy for Disaster Reduction.

Uprety, D., Banarjee, D., Kumar, N., & Dhiman, A. (2023). *Smart Sustainable Farming Using IOT, Cloud Computing and Big Data* (No. 10814). EasyChair

van der Elst, N. J., Hardebeck, J. L., Michael, A. J., McBride, S. K., & Vanacore, E. (2022). Prospective and retrospective evaluation of the U.S. geological survey public aftershock forecast for the 2019–2021 southwest Puerto Rico earthquake and aftershocks. *Seismological Research Letters*, *93*(2A), 620–640. doi:10.1785/0220210222

Varadharajan, M., Balaji, S., Ezhilarasan, V., & Gowthaman, A. (2023). Internet of Things based Natural Disaster Detection and Personalized Notification System. In *2023 Third International Conference on Artificial Intelligence and Smart Energy (ICAIS)*, (pp. 93-97). IEEE. 10.1109/ICAIS56108.2023.10073873

Velev, D., & Zlateva, P. (2023). CHALLENGES OF ARTIFICIAL INTELLIGENCE APPLICATION FOR DISASTER RISK MANAGEMENT. *The International Archives of the Photogrammetry, Remote Sensing and Spatial Information Sciences*.

Vermesan, O., Bahr, R., Ottella, M., Serrano, M., Karlsen, T., Wahlstrøm, T., Sand, H. E., Ashwathnarayan, M., & Gamba, M. T. (2020). Internet of robotic things intelligent connectivity and platforms. *Frontiers in Robotics and AI*, *7*, 104. doi:10.3389/frobt.2020.00104 PMID:33501271

Vermesan, O., Bröring, A., Tragos, E., Serrano, M., Bacciu, D., Chessa, S., & Bahr, R. (2022). Internet of robotic things–converging sensing/actuating, hyper connectivity, artificial intelligence and IoT platforms. In *Cognitive Hyperconnected Digital Transformation* (pp. 97–155). River Publishers. doi:10.1201/9781003337584-4

Vieweg, S., Hughes, A., Starbird, K., & Palen, L. (2010). Microblogging during two natural hazards events: What Twitter may contribute to situational awareness. *Conference on Human Factors in Computing Systems - Proceedings*. ACM. 10.1145/1753326.1753486

Villacrés, D. C., Carrera Villacrés, J. L., Braun, T., Zhao, Z., Gómez, J., & Carabalí, J. Q. (2020). Fog harvesting and IoT based environment monitoring system at the Ilalo volcano in Ecuador. *International Journal on Advanced Science, Engineering and Information Technology*, *10*(1), 407–412. doi:10.18517/ijaseit.10.1.10775

Vinod, A. M., Venkatesh, D., Kundra, D., & Jayapandian, N. (2022). Natural disaster prediction by using image based deep learning and machine learning. In *Second International Conference on Image Processing and Capsule Networks: ICIPCN 2021 2* (pp. 56-66). Springer International Publishing. 10.1007/978-3-030-84760-9_6

Vinod, ANavya, NNatarajan, J. (2019). Big data preprocessing for modern world: opportunities and challenges. In HemanthJ.FernandoX.LafataP.BaigZ. (Eds.), *ICICI 2018. LNDECT* (Vol. 26, pp. 335–343). Springer. doi:10.1007/978-3-030-03146-6_37

Waghmare, G. L., Kumar, S., Udhayakumar, R., Raja Mannar, B., Singh, R., & Rawat, N. (2023). Utilizing Social Media Platforms for Artificial Intelligence-Based Detection and Developing Effective Communications in Disaster-Affected Areas. *2023 3rd International Conference on Advance Computing and Innovative Technologies in Engineering (ICACITE)*, (pp. 501-504). IEEE.

Wang, S., Quan, D., Liang, X., Ning, M., Guo, Y., & Jiao, L. (2018). A deep learning framework for remote sensing image registration. *ISPRS Journal of Photogrammetry and Remote Sensing*, *145*, 148–164. doi:10.1016/j.isprsjprs.2017.12.012

Wang, Z., Zhu, L., Liu, J., Wang, J., & Yan, W. (2022). Gas sensing technology for the detection and early warning of battery thermal runaway: A review. *Energy & Fuels*, *36*(12), 6038–6057. doi:10.1021/acs.energyfuels.2c01121

Weng, Q. (2002). Land use change analysis in the Zhujiang Delta of China using satellite remote sensing, GIS and stochastic modelling. *Journal of Environmental Management*, *64*(3), 273–284. doi:10.1006/jema.2001.0509 PMID:12040960

Wong, Y.K. (2021). *Dealing Disaster Management Using AI*. Research Gate.

Wong, Y. K. (2021). *Applying AI and Big Data for Sensitive Operations and Disaster Management*. Advances in Machine Learning, Data Mining and Computing. doi:10.5121/csit.2021.111429

Wu, X., Zhang, G., Yang, Z., Tan, S., Yang, Y., & Pang, Z. (2023). Machine Learning for Predicting Forest Fire Occurrence in Changsha: An Innovative Investigation into the Introduction of a Forest Fuel Factor. *Remote Sensing (Basel)*, *15*(17), 4208. doi:10.3390/rs15174208

Xiao, Y., Zhong, J., Wang, J., Zhang, L., Qian, X., Liu, W., & Huang, H. (2023). Exploring the Coupling Coordination Relationship of Urban Resilience System in Ecologically Fragile Areas: Case Study of the Loess Plateau in China. *Land (Basel)*, *12*(11), 1997. doi:10.3390/land12111997

Xu, J. Z., Lu, W., Li, Z., Khaitan, P., & Zaytseva, V. (2019). *Building damage detection in satellite imagery using convolutional neural networks*. arXiv preprint arXiv:1910.06444.

Ye, Z., Ye, Y., Zhang, C., Zhang, Z., Li, W., Wang, X., Wang, L., & Wang, L. (2023). A digital twin approach for tunnel construction safety early warning and management. *Computers in Industry*, *144*, 103783. doi:10.1016/j.compind.2022.103783

Yilmaz, I. (2010). Comparison of landslide susceptibility mapping methodologies for Koyulhisar, Turkey: Conditional probability, logistic regression, artificial neural networks, and support vector machine. *Environmental Earth Sciences*, *61*(4), 821–836. doi:10.100712665-009-0394-9

Yuan, F., Sawaya, K. E., Loeffelholz, B. C., & Bauer, M. E. (2005). Land cover classification and change analysis of the Twin Cities (Minnesota) Metropolitan Area by multitemporal Landsat remote sensing. *Remote Sensing of Environment*, *98*(2-3), 317–328. doi:10.1016/j.rse.2005.08.006

Yuliandoko, H. (2023). *Design of Windstorm Disaster Early Warning System based on IoT and Hall Effect Sensor in the Critical Area Location.*

Yu, M., Yang, C., Li, Y., & Zuhairi, A. (2018). Yang, C., Li, Y.: Big data in natural disaster management: a review. *Geosciences*, *8*(5), 165. doi:10.3390/geosciences8050165

Yurtsever & Mustafa. (2022). Emergency management in smart cities. *Artificial Intelligence Perspective for Smart Cities,* 135-153.

Zhang Y. (2009). Planning for housing recovery? lessons learned from Hurricane Andrew. *Journal of the American Planning Association, 76.*

Zhang, Z. (2022). A Dual-Function Sensor for Highly Sensitive Detection of Flame and Humidity. *Small*, *18*(38), 2203334.

Zhang, F., & Yang, X. (2020). Improving land cover classification in an urbanized coastal area by random forests: The role of variable selection. *Remote Sensing of Environment*, *251*, 112105. doi:10.1016/j.rse.2020.112105

Zhang, H., Ning, X., Shao, Z., & Wang, H. (2019). Spatiotemporal Pattern Analysis of China's Cities Based on High-Resolution Imagery from 2000 to 2015. *ISPRS International Journal of Geo-Information*, *8*(5), 241. doi:10.3390/ijgi8050241

Zhang, S., Zhang, J., Li, X., Du, X., Zhao, T., Hou, Q., & Jin, X. (2022a). Estimating the grade of storm surge disaster loss in coastal areas of China via machine learning algorithms. *Ecological Indicators*, *136*, 108533. doi:10.1016/j.ecolind.2022.108533

Zhang, Y., Zou, Q., Zhang, Y., Liu, L., & Pu, C. (2023). Editorial: Advances and applications of artificial intelligence and numerical simulation in risk emergency management and treatment. *Frontiers of Earth Science*.

Zhou, X., Li, H., Wang, J., Zhao, J., Xie, Q., Li, L., Liu, J., & Yu, J. (2022). CloudFAS: Cloud-based building fire alarm system using Building Information Modelling. *Journal of Building Engineering*, *53*, 104571. doi:10.1016/j.jobe.2022.104571

Zhou, X., Wu, D., Li, J., Liang, J., Zhang, D., & Chen, W. (2022). Cultivated land use efficiency and its driving factors in the Yellow River Basin, China. *Ecological Indicators*, *144*, 109411. doi:10.1016/j.ecolind.2022.109411

Zhu, X., Li, N., & Pan, Y. (2019). Optimization Performance Comparison of Three Different Group Intelligence Algorithms on a SVM for Hyperspectral Imagery Classification. *Remote Sensing (Basel)*, *11*(6), 734. doi:10.3390/rs11060734

About the Contributors

Ashwini A., received her B.E. Degree in ECE and M.E. degree in Communication and Networking from Anna University, Chennai. She is university rank holder in UG and PG. She has completed her PhD degree in Anna University Chennai, India. She has published many papers in journal and participated in some International Conferences. Her research interests include Medical Image Processing, Nanotechnology, Image Segmentation, Artificial intelligence, Internet of things.

Kathirvel Ayyaswamy, acquired, B.E.(CSE), M.E. (CSE) from Crescent Engineering College affiliated to University of Madras and Ph. D (CSE.) from Anna University. He is currently working as Professor, Dept of Computer Science and Engineering, Karunya Institute of Technology and Sciences, Coimbatore. He is a studious researcher by himself, completed 18 sponsored research projects worth of Rs 103 lakhs and published more than 110 articles in journals and conferences. 4 research scholars have completed Ph. D and 3 under progress under his guidance. He is working as scientific and editorial board member of many journals. He has reviewed dozens of papers in many journals. He has author of 13 books. His research interests are protocol development for wireless ad hoc networks, security in ad hoc network, data communication and networks, mobile computing, wireless networks, WSN and DTN. He is a Life member of the ISTE (India), IACSIT (Singapore), Life Member IAENG (Hong Kong), Member ICST (Europe), IAES, etc. He has given a number of guest lecturers/expert talks and seminars, workshops and symposiums.

Sunitha Ashtikar is pursuing her Ph.D. programme at SR University.

D. Dhinakaran (M'84) was born in Chennai, Tamilnadu, India, in 1984. He is a distinguished scholar and educator with a passion for advancing the fields of Computer Science and Engineering. Dr. Dhinakaran earned his B.E degree in Computer Science and Engineering from Anna University, Chennai, in 2006, showcasing early dedication to his academic pursuits. Building upon his foundation, he pursued and obtained the M.E degree in the field of Computer Science and Engineering from Anna University,

Trichy, in 2009. Demonstrating a commitment to academic excellence, Dr. Dhinakaran completed his Ph.D. in Computer Science and Engineering from Anna University, Chennai, further solidifying his expertise in the field. Currently serving as an Assistant Professor in the Department of Computer Science and Engineering at Vel Tech Rangarajan Dr. Sagunthala R&D Institute of Science and Technology, Chennai, Dr. Dhinakaran continues to inspire students and colleagues alike. His areas of specialization encompass Privacy-Preserving Data Mining, Artificial Intelligence, Internet of Things (IoT), Mobile Ad Hoc Networks (MANET), Cloud Computing, and Image Processing, reflecting his diverse and extensive contributions to cutting-edge technologies. Dr. Dhinakaran is a prolific researcher, having presented more than 30 papers at various National and International Conferences. His commitment to advancing knowledge is evident through his membership in esteemed professional societies such as IAENG (International Association of Engineers), IFERP (International Foundation for Engineering Research and Publications), and CSTA (Computer Science Teachers Association). Notably, Dr. Dhinakaran has made significant contributions to academic literature, with publications in 50 different international journals and the successful filing of two patents. His work demonstrates a keen interest in addressing contemporary challenges and pushing the boundaries of technological innovation. As an accomplished academic, researcher, and member of professional societies, Dr. Dhinakaran continues to play a pivotal role in shaping the future of Computer Science and Engineering, leaving an indelible mark on both academia and the broader technological landscape.

Geetha Manoharan is currently working in Telangana as an assistant professor at SR University. She is the university-level PhD programme coordinator and has also been given the additional responsibility of In Charge Director of Publications and Patents under the Research Division at SR University. Under her tutelage, students are inspired to reach their full potential in all areas of their education and beyond through experiential learning. It creates an atmosphere conducive to the growth of students into independent thinkers and avid readers. She has more than ten years of experience across the board in the business world, academia, and the academy. She has a keen interest in the study of organisational behaviour and management. More than forty articles and books have been published in scholarly venues such as UGC-refereed, SCOPUS, Web of Science, and Springer. Over the past six-plus years, she has participated in varied research and student exchange programmes at both the national and international levels. A total of five of her collaborative innovations in this area have already been published and patented. Emotional intelligence, self-efficacy, and work-life balance are among her specialties. She organises programmes for academic organisations. She belongs to several professional organisations, including the CMA and the CPC. The TIPSGLOBAL Institute of Coimbatore has recognised her twice (in 2017 and 2018) for her outstanding academic performance.

Lakshmi Haritha Medida is working is as an Associate Professor in the Department of Computer Science and Engineering, R.M.K. Engineering College, Kavaraipettai and received her Ph.D Degree from JNTUA, Ananthapuramu in the year 2022. She has around 2 years of teaching experience and 2 years of industry experience. Her areas of interests include Information Retrieval, Data Mining, Image Processing and Natural Language Processing.

R. Renuga Devi received her Ph.D Degree in the Department of Information and Communication Engineering, Anna University, Chennai in 2022. Her research interest includes wireless sensor network, mobile computing, Machine learning and Internet of Things. She published many papers in International journals and Conferences. Currently, She is working as Associate Professor in R.M.K Engineering College. She has more than 16 years of teaching experience in Engineering College. She is a life member of IAENG and ISTE.

Siva Subramanian R. working in R.M.K College of Engineering and Technology and his research area include Machine Learning, Customer Analysis, Soft Computing and Customer Behaviour Analysis

R. Uma is working as Associate Professor in the Department of Computer Science and Engineering, Sri Sairam Engineering College, Chennai, India. with 23 years of teaching experience for undergraduate and post graduate students in Computer Science Department. She has a Doctorate degree in Computer Science and Engineering from Anna University Chennai, India .She also completed her Master Degree in Computer Science and Engineering from College of Engineering Guindy, Anna University, India and Bachelor Degree from university of Madras. She has published her papers over 14 International Journals. She is a member of CSI,IACSIT and life member of ISTE. Her current research interest includes Information Retrieval, Data Mining, Deep learning and Machine learning .

Col B.S. Rao is the CEO of SRiX.

Abdul Razak works for EDII as Associate Professor.

S. Prince Sahaya Brighty has over 17 years of teaching experience and currently working as an Assistant Professor (Selection Grade) in the Department of Computer Science and Engineering. She completed her B.E(with Distinction) in Computer Science and Engineering from Noorul Islam College of Engineering, Nagercoil (Anna University,Chennai) in 2005. She completed her Masters' (with Distinction) in Computer Science and Engineering from Kumaraguru College of

Technology,Coimbatore(Anna University,Chennai) in the year 2013. Her research area includes AI & Machine Learning, Data Science and Wireless sensor networks,. . She has published 18 papers in reputed International Journals such as Springer, IEEE etc. She has also published papers in 16 International and National conferences. She has received the Best paper award in a Springer and IEEE International Conferences. She has guided around 30 UG projects . She is a lifetime member of CSI, IRACST and IAENG.

S. Gandhimathi Alias Usha is an Associate Professor, with the Department of Electronics and Communication Engineering, Velammal College of Engineering and Technology, Madurai, India. She received her Bachelor's degree in Electronics and Communication Engineering from Madurai Kamaraj University in 2001 and her Master's degree from A.C.College of Engineering and Technology, Karaikudi, Tamilnadu, India in 2009 and received her Ph.D. degree in Image Processing at Anna University, Chennai in 2019. She has published over 45 Technical papers in International Journals and international/ National Conferences. Her current research includes Image Processing and Remote Sensing. She is a Life member of the Indian Society for Technical Education (ISTE) and the Indian Society of Remote Sensing (ISRS).

Index

F

G

I

K

L

M

N

P

R

S

U

V

W

www.ingramcontent.com/pod-product-compliance
Lightning Source LLC
LaVergne TN
LVHW080636011026
849160LV00014B/1234